Forms of faith

I0808578

MANCHESTER
1824
Manchester University Press

Forms of faith

Literary form and religious conflict in early modern England

Edited by Jonathan Baldo and Isabel Karremann

Manchester University Press

Copyright © Manchester University Press 2017

While copyright in the volume as a whole is vested in Manchester University Press, copyright in individual chapters belongs to their respective authors, and no chapter may be reproduced wholly or in part without the express permission in writing of both author and publisher.

Published by Manchester University Press
Altrincham Street, Manchester M1 7JA
www.manchesteruniversitypress.co.uk

British Library Cataloguing-in-Publication Data is available

ISBN 978 0 7190 9681 5 hardback
ISBN 978 1 5261 4354 9 paperback

First published by Manchester University Press in hardback 2017

This edition first published 2020

The publisher has no responsibility for the persistence or accuracy of URLs for any external or third-party internet websites referred to in this book, and does not guarantee that any content on such websites is, or will remain, accurate or appropriate.

Typeset by Out of House Publishing

For Roberta, Nathaniel, David, and all our faithful friends and loved ones
To Eberhard, as always

Contents

Notes on contributors

Jonathan Baldo is Professor of English in the Eastman School of Music, the University of Rochester. His most recent publication, *Memory in Shakespeare's Histories: Stages of Forgetting in Early Modern England* (Routledge, 2012), was nominated for the Renaissance Society of America's 2013 Phyllis Goodhart Gordan Book Prize. His essays on Shakespeare have appeared in a wide range of journals and collections, including *Shakespeare Quarterly*, *Renaissance Drama*, *English Literary Renaissance*, *Borrowers and Lenders*, *Criticism*, and *Modern Language Quarterly*.

Mary A. Blackstone is a freelance dramaturg, cultural historian, and educator. She is Professor Emerita in the Theatre Department at the University of Regina and Director of the SSHRC-funded Saskatchewan Partnership for Arts Research as well as of the Centre for the Study of Script Development. She has published on the role of performers and public performance in the negotiation of shared values and identity in early modern England, and is currently working on a book entitled *The Performance of Commonwealth in Early Modern England*.

Alexandra M. Block is a lecturer at the University of California, Merced, and author of *Sacramental Semiotics: John Donne and the Early Modern Eucharistic Controversy* (BiblioBazaar, 2011).

Brooke Conti is Associate Professor of English at Cleveland State University. She is the author of *Confessions of Faith in Early Modern England* (University of Pennsylvania Press, 2014) and is co-editing a new edition of Thomas Browne's *Religio Medici* as part of Oxford University Press's *Complete Works of Thomas Browne*. She is currently at work on a second monograph, tentatively entitled *Religious Nostalgia from Shakespeare to Milton*.

Joel M. Dodson is Assistant Professor of English at Southern Connecticut State University in New Haven, Connecticut. He has published on Sir Philip Sidney's *Defence of Poesy* and doctrinal harmonies, and is currently at work on a book on confessionalization, ecclesiology, and late Reformation English poetics, from Sidney to Donne.

Phebe Jensen, Professor of English at Utah State University, is the author of *Religion and Revelry in Shakespeare's Festive World* (CambridgeUniversity Press, 2009), and a series of essays on popular religious culture and early modern Catholicism. She is currently completing a reference book, *The Early Modern English Calendar*, and at work on a longer-term book project, *Shakespeare's Clocks and Calendars*.

Isabel Karremann is Professor of English Literature at the University of Würzburg, Germany. Her study *The Drama of Memory in Shakespeare's History Plays* (Cambridge University Press, 2015) was shortlisted for the Shakespeare Globe Book Award 2016. She has co-edited the collections *Forgetting Faith? Negotiating Confessional Conflict in Early Modern Europe* (de Gruyter, 2012) and *Shakespeare in Cold War Europe: Conflict, Commemoration, Celebration* (Palgrave, 2015), and is currently working on a project on conflict and conciliation in the Thirty Years War.

James R. Macdonald teaches in the English Department and the interdisciplinary Humanities program at the University of the South in Sewanee, Tennessee. He is also the author of recent essays on Marlowe's *Doctor Faustus* and Book I of Spenser's *Faerie Queene*.

Thomas J. Moretti is Assistant Professor of English at Iona College, New York and editor of *The Shakespeare Newsletter*. His scholarly interests include religion and gender in early modern English drama and temporality in early modern English theater. His writings on religious mediation, gender performance, and theater have appeared in the journals *Renascence* and *Renaissance Drama*.

Christina Wald is Professor of English Literature at the University of Konstanz, Germany. Her research focuses on contemporary drama, performance, film and TV; early modern drama and prose fiction; and gender and feminist theory. She is the author of *Hysteria, Trauma and Melancholia: Performative Maladies in Contemporary Anglophone Drama* (Palgrave, 2007) and *The Reformation of Romance: The Eucharist, Disguise and Foreign Fashion in Early Modern Prose Fiction* (de Gruyter, 2014) and co-editor of *The Literature of Melancholia: Early Modern to Postmodern* (Palgrave, 2011).

Brian Walsh is the author of *Shakespeare, the Queen's Men, and the Elizabethan Performance of History* (Cambridge University Press, 2009), as well as *Unsettled Toleration: Religious Difference on the Shakespearean Stage* (Oxford University Press, 2016). He has edited a collection of essays on *The*

Revenger's Tragedy for The Arden Critical Guides series, and has authored several articles and essays on early modern drama. He has taught at the University of Illinois, Rutgers University, and Yale University. He currently teaches at Boston University.

Richard Wilson is an internationally acclaimed litarary critic and Shakespeare scholar. Having taught at the University of Lancaster, Cardiff University, and the Sorbonne, he now holds an Anniversary Chair at Kingston University, London. Among his recent books are *Free Will: Art and Power on Shakespeare's Stage* (Manchester University Press, 2013) and *Worldly Shakespeare: The Theatre of Our Good Will* (Edinburgh University Press, 2016).

Jacqueline Wylde is a PhD candidate at the University of Toronto. Her areas of research include early modern drama and popular religious culture in post-Reformation England. Her dissertation, 'Moving Graces: Modes of Religious Persuasion on the Early Modern Stage', explores how persuasive strategies depicted on and deployed by the stage may be read as emerging from a religious, though multi-confessional, culture of persuasion.

Acknowledgments

This collection began as a small but vibrant interdisciplinary conference hosted by Ludwig-Maximilians-Universität München, entitled 'Forgetting Faith? Negotiating Confessional Conflict in Early Modern Europe'. A subsequent request by Jim Siemon to offer a seminar on religion ('Everyone wants to talk about religion', he told us) led to our co-directing a seminar on literary forms as sites for negotiating religious conflict at a meeting of the Shakespeare Association of America. We wish to express our sincere gratitude to Jim, to the Shakespeare Association of America, as well as to the participants in the Munich conference and the SAA seminar, all of whom helped to shape and advance our thinking on the subject of this book.

To our colleagues in the Department of Humanities at the Eastman School of Music of the University of Rochester, as well as in the Institute for Modern Languages and the Centre for Medieval and Early Modern Studies at Würzburg University, we are grateful for helping to create intellectually vibrant and stimulating workplaces and homes for our research. Particular thanks are due to Laura Werthmüller and Kristina Seit for their meticulous copy-editing.

We are grateful to the editors of the University of Chicago Press for permission to reprint Brooke Conti's 'Shylock Celebrates Easter', which originally appeared in *Modern Philology*, vol. 133, no. 2: 178–97. © 2015 by The University of Chicago. All rights reserved.

This collection most likely would never have seen the light of day without the extraordinary support and encouragement of Richard Wilson, who recommended that we realize this project with Manchester University Press and who generously agreed to contribute an afterword to it.

Finally, we wish to thank the editors of Manchester University Press, especially Matthew Frost and Paul Clarke, who made the production of this book so free of conflict and the need for negotiation. Thanks are also due to Sarah Rendell, Alun Clarke and Christopher Feeney for steering the book safely through the production process, as well as to Maureen MacGlashan for compiling the index.

Introduction

A world of difference: religion, literary form, and the negotiation of conflict in early modern England

Jonathan Baldo and Isabel Karremann

Religion's turn

Perhaps no body of knowledge develops in a straight line, least of all that related to the study of literature. Ours is a field in which so many key terms have roots meaning 'a turn' (L. *verso*, Gk. *tropos*) that one might expect its historical progression to bear a sinuous shape, replete with pivots and turns. Inevitably, such turns remind us what questions our most recent critical paradigms might have caused us to neglect. Just as it is impossible to remember without forgetting, so is it inevitable that certain questions be relegated to the margins of scrutiny and debate as others are summoned into the critical spotlight.

In recent years, the most prominent development in literary criticism of early modern Britain is the disputed notion of a 'religious turn', as it has been known for over a decade.[1] It is widely regarded as not a paradigm shift but rather a refocusing within the still dominant paradigm of new historicism. Nevertheless, the astonishing number of new books on religious topics in early modern literary studies attests to a major change in critical attention having occurred over the course of the past two decades. As it was in the early modern period itself, religion has become a hotly debated topic of intense interest among literary scholars. So swiftly and vigorously has religion returned to the center of early modern studies that one might suspect the field of having formerly repeated the gestures of erasure, of willed forgetting or disremembering, of the kind practiced by the Reformation itself. In the middle of *1 Henry IV*, Falstaff briefly accuses himself of having forgotten religion, before projecting the accusatory tone outward, upon others: 'An I have not forgotten what the inside of a church is made of, I am a peppercorn, a brewer's horse. The inside of a church! Company, villainous company, hath been the spoil of me' (Arden

Third Series, 3.3.7–10). Many of us, perhaps, have been unwittingly playing Falstaff, who is well practiced at forgetting, and who is himself a palimpsest, a rewriting (as the name Falstaff was substituted for Oldcastle) of an outrageous rewriting of both the divergent legacies of the Lollard martyr/heretic, Sir John Oldcastle. For a fair stretch of our own history, we have forgotten what the passionate inside of a confessional difference is made of.[2]

For more than a decade, the religious turn in early modern studies has contributed mightily to the ongoing, vigorous investigation of the social processes at work in early modern England, and their cultural effects: from the struggle over religious rites and doctrines, to the persecution of secret adherents, to forbidden practices. So far, the issues of religious pluralization and the divisions between Catholic and Protestant positions, among sectarian movements, or between the Church and the state, have been debated mostly in terms of dissent and escalation. Despite the centrality of confessional conflict, however, it did not always erupt into hostilities over how to symbolize and perform the sacred, nor did it lead to a paralysis of social agency. Rather, people had to arrange themselves somehow with divided loyalties: between the old faith and the new, between religious and secular interests, or between officially sanctioned and privately held beliefs. The order of the day may have been, more often than not, to suspend confessional allegiances rather than enforce religious conflict, suggesting a pragmatic rather than polemical handling of religious plurality, in social practice as well as in textual and dramatic representations. This book sets out to explore such a suggestion. By placing the focus on negotiation instead of escalation, the essays assembled here explore the specific ways available to mediate religious conflict, precisely because faith still mattered more than many other social paradigms emerging at that time, such as nationhood or race.

This collection of new essays explores a range of literary and theatrical forms as means of mediating religious conflict in early modern England. The authors approach the issue from a variety of angles, including the representation of Catholic figures in post-Reformation texts and contexts; the survival and ongoing importance of Catholic ritual as a mode of experience and of representation; and the drama's engagement of the audience in and beyond confessional conflict, especially by exploring religious pluralization and its irenic potential, the possibility that the perception of multiple religious positions may support the practice of mediation rather than exacerbate conflict and reinforce divisions.

Our collection acknowledges the centrality of confessional conflict to early modern English culture, but seeks to go beyond the adversarial stance that marks its more extreme positions. Our focus is not on how confessional conflict was presented in terms of an antagonism but rather how it was mediated in textual and dramatic representations. Can we conceive of these representations as possible sites of de-escalation? Do different discursive, aesthetic, or social contexts inflect or even deflect the demands of religious loyalties? Does literary practice in particular allow for a suspension of faith that may not have been possible in theological discourse? And how do textual or dramatic works both reflect on and perform such an erasure, suspension, or displacement of confessional tensions? What literary forms were available for expressing and, often at the same time, attenuating religious conflict?

In return

To a large extent, every turn in literary studies marks a return, and the so-called 'religious turn' in early modern studies is no exception. The question that preoccupied this newly revitalized area of early modern studies not so long ago – namely, the question whether Shakespeare was a Catholic – dates at least from the mid-nineteenth century: as Thomas Rist has noted, not long after the British Parliament's passage of the Roman Catholic Relief Act of 1829.[3] One of the consequences of the Act was to allow Roman Catholics to occupy seats in Parliament. A generation later, it became possible to ask whether England's ultimate representative on the world stage, the national poet himself, might have been a recusant Catholic, or at least born and raised in recusancy. While risking oversimplified answers, the tantalizing but largely unanswerable question, 'Was Shakespeare Catholic?' prepared the way for more complex approaches to exploring the deep religious divisions and residual presence of the traditional faith in the British Isles during and after the Reformation.

Like Bolingbroke from exile, the question of Shakespeare's religious allegiance and identity returned with spectacular effect, deposing the long-standing image of the national playwright of a sturdily Protestant nation. A secure landing place for the return was prepared by British historians like Christopher Haigh, J. J. Scarisbrick, Eamon Duffy, and John Bossy, whose revisionist work on the English Reformation demonstrated the persistence of Catholic practices and beliefs well into the late sixteenth and seventeenth centuries. Indeed the very idea of 'post-Reformation Britain' has become dubious, as the Reformation has come to be seen as a process that lasted well into the reign of Elizabeth and beyond. Recent scholars have vigorously challenged the earlier orthodoxy, disseminated largely by historian A. G. Dickens in his massively influential *The English Reformation* (1964): namely, the view of the Reformation as a swift movement that had accomplished its ends by the time of the Elizabethan Religious Settlement of 1559. In that watershed year, two Parliamentary Acts, the Acts of Supremacy and of Uniformity, restored both royal supremacy, making Elizabeth head of a Church that was independent from Rome, and Protestantism as England's official faith. Dickens depicted an

England that was only too eager to welcome those Acts of Parliament and to embrace the new, reformed faith.

Concentrating his archival efforts in Tudor Lancashire in the 1970s, Christopher Haigh reached a different conclusion. He discovered an unsettled Elizabethan England in which opposition to Protestantism and support for Catholicism persisted long after the Settlement of 1559. In the work of revisionist historians like Haigh, religious reforms in early modern England came to look as though they were imposed by authorities upon a largely reluctant population. In her important study *Church Papists*, Alexandra Walsham maintains that England's was 'a reformation that generated, at least initially, not rapid conversion but grudging conformity'.[4] According to the revisionist view that has become dominant over the past several decades, the Reformation developed slowly, and in a fitful way, only beginning to accomplish many of its ends in the 1580s, so that, in Peter Marshall's words, 'the later Elizabethan decades can look more like a point of departure than of culmination'.[5] What Patrick Collinson terms a Second English Reformation took place in the 1580s, during which time the cultural effects of reform began to catch up to legislative acts.[6] The more significant cultural shift occurred not between England's last generation of traditional Catholics and first generation of 'Protestant communicators who … were in continuity and communication with the tradition, sharing common cultural ground with their Catholic opponents', but rather 'between the first and second generations of Protestants'.[7] When Shakespeare broke upon the London theatrical scene, many of the more visible and material aspects of reform were indeed of recent memory and coincided roughly with the beginnings of a popular, secular theater in England. By the last years of the sixteenth century, Haigh famously concludes, clergy had created 'a Protestant nation, but not a nation of Protestants'.[8]

The consequences for literary studies of such revisionist historiography have been bracing. In 1999, a landmark conference held at Lancaster University and Hoghton Tower and organized by Richard Wilson, 'Lancastrian Shakespeare: Religion, Region, Patronage and Performance', was hugely influential in calling attention to the extent to which Catholicism formed an important part of the intellectual and cultural landscape of England in the Elizabethan and early Jacobean periods. The Lancashire conference, which probably did more than any other single event in the past two decades to fuel a desire among literary scholars and historians to explore the religious life of early modern England, resulted in two important volumes, *Theatre and Religion* and *Region, Religion and Patronage*, both published by Manchester University Press in 2003 and edited by Richard Dutton, Alison Findlay, and Richard Wilson. Appearing in the same year as the Lancashire conference, Alison Shell's important study *Catholicism, Controversy and the English*

Literary Imagination, 1558–1660 showed the importance of Catholicism to English literary culture: both the ways in which anti-Catholicism stimulated the early modern literary imagination, and rhetorical strategies developed by Catholic writers that enabled them to remain both faithful to their conscience and loyal to their monarch. As Thomas Rist has keenly observed, a profession that has long embraced the value of difference naturally became intrigued by the emerging picture of a highly fragmented and diverse religious landscape.[9] Religion, it became clear by the end of the last century, was fertile ground for pursuing the political and cultural effects of 'difference' in early modern England, responsible for as many fault lines running beneath the landscapes of Elizabethan and Jacobean England as gender, race, and class.[10]

The relation of Shakespeare and his contemporaries to the age that preceded them was complicated, to say the least. Keith Thomas observes that for Elizabethans, there were at least two Middle Ages: 'Early modern England had not one myth of the Middle Ages, but two; and they were sharply opposed to each other. One was supportive of the social order, the other potentially subversive.' Some looked upon the era as 'a dreadful period of brutality and violence'; others viewed it nostalgically as a time of 'feasting praying, chivalry, courtly love and charity'.[11] Perceptions of and attitudes toward the past, however, were not always polarized according to religious affiliation. Eamon Duffy comments, 'Nostalgic idealization of the Catholic past [became] as much the voice of the church papist, and of some backward-looking parish Anglicans, as of conscientiously recusant Catholics.'[12] As Ian Archer writes, 'the intellectual world of Elizabethan England was not rigidly divided between the adherents of a Protestant view of a medieval dark age and a Catholic view of an idealized golden age. Protestants could appreciate the virtue that had existed in former times, and some of [John] Stow's characteristic emphases [in his *Survey of London* (1598)] surface in other more obviously godly writers.'[13] What both views shared was a sense of rupture with the immediate past. For twenty-first-century critics, to return imaginatively to early modern England was no longer to visit the settled world of an 'Elizabethan world picture' envisioned by E. M. W. Tillyard and an older generation: it was to rush once more unto a sometimes terrible breach between past and present.

It is important to bear in mind the early modern period's relation to what preceded it, not in order to construct a seamless, continuous narrative of historical development, but rather to more vividly apprehend discontinuities and to recapture more of the contentious nature of cultural practice and historical memory in the period itself. 'Heaven and Earth! / Must I remember?' one might imagine many so-called church papists asking of the forbidden practices of worship and forms of festivity associated with the old ecclesiastical calendar before its reform. As if in imitation of Hamlet and of the very people whose imaginative lives we study, we early modernists are learning the value of posing the identical question, and of answering in the affirmative.

If memory serves

Our shared interest in the religious turn bears a strong connection to another dynamic and rapidly developing area of early modern studies: memory studies, in which area scholars have been exploring the ways in which the spread of printing, the growth of national identity, and the Protestant Reformation all contributed to a rather volatile and uncertain valuation of ancient forms of commemoration and of remembering and forgetting themselves. Over the past two decades memory studies have seen a growth in interest parallel to that experienced by religion, and it is perhaps no accident that the two areas have developed concurrently. The two approaches to the cultural study of conflict within early modern England are so closely connected that it is not possible to treat the issue of cultural memory in early modern England without taking into account religion, without considering, for example, the widespread cultural disruption that Eamon Duffy describes in *The Stripping of the Altars: Traditional Religion in England, 1400–1580*. Duffy has shown at length how in the pre-Reformation Church, 'the language of memory pervaded the cult of the dead', and it was precisely this language that was disrupted by the Reformation.[14] The Reformation arguably made both time and space a palimpsest for early modern people. The partly effaced landscape of ecclesiastical buildings and structures bore traces, tangible reminders, of the old faith and old religious practices, while Elizabethan and Jacobean reforms of the calendar made time a kind of palimpsest as well, with traditional religious observances overwritten by new celebrations of the Protestant monarchy and Protestant deliverance from popish plots. Queen Elizabeth's accession day, the salvation of Elizabethan England from the Spanish Armada of 1588, and the deliverance of Jacobean England from the Gunpowder Plot all became part of a national political calendar.[15] Early modern England was a place in which both time and space had been overwritten, as it were, but in which traces remained of that which was effaced.

The dominant interest of our collection, namely in how literary studies might serve as platforms for negotiating confessional differences in the early modern period, bears a natural link to memory studies that surfaces from time to time in this collection. Facing unprecedented changes in the related forms of worship and commemoration, early modern British people faced daily challenges in negotiating between remembering and forgetting its recently reformed confessional practices. Some of these involved negotiating generational differences or even differences within a family. For many recusant Catholics, Protestantism threatened to dissolve the bonds of human community, not only between the living and the dead, but also of 'husband and wife, child from parent, dissolving the bonds of memory': a common theme of what Duffy calls the 'conservative voice'.[16] Others seemed content to indulge in the nostalgia that often drifts in the wake behind massive historical change. Alexandra Walsham's work has demonstrated how widespread were the attitudes of so-called cold-statute Protestants, or church papists: those who reluctantly went along with the religious changes imposed upon them, but who also looked upon the past they had left behind with at least some sense of loss.[17]

For those Elizabethans inclined to a more militant use of memory of England's medieval past than Stowe's, the Northern Rising of 1569 proved a focal point for discontent. That rebellion was still a living memory for some members of Shakespeare's audiences in the 1590s. Shakespeare's Percies, of course, are no wholesale historical revisionists driven by religious passion, but some of their Elizabethan descendants more nearly answer to that description. One of their number, Thomas Percy, the seventh Earl of Northumberland, was one of two earls who led the Northern Rising and was executed after its collapse. His replacement, Henry Percy, the eighth Earl, sided with the Queen and helped the royal forces quell the uprising in the interests of gaining his brother's freedom. This eighth Earl was later suspected of involvement in the Ridolfi and Throckmorton plots against Elizabeth, and committed to the Tower. Another descendant, Thomas Percy, cousin to Henry Percy, the ninth Earl of Northumberland, would prove to be one of the chief conspirators in the Gunpowder Plot of 1605. In a play in which the rebel Percies repeatedly sound the theme of memory and enact outright historical insubordination – their account as to how Henry IV came to power differs defiantly from the royal version – it is likely that audiences would have been reminded of one of the most divisive memories for Elizabethan England, the Rising of the Northern Earls, and indeed the whole sequence of subsequent plots against Elizabeth. The unsettled question of Shakespeare's own religious allegiance aside, the history plays' capacity to clandestinely evoke memories of the failed Rising must have confirmed what they have to say about the divisive nature of historical memory and its threat to state power. It allowed Elizabethan audiences to experience, not merely witness, such threats.

Return to form

The ongoing trauma of the Reformation made remembering the past – including the memory of a lost medieval culture of memory with strong ties to the traditional faith – equivocal to people on both sides of the religious divide. To study religion in early modern England is to study the forms and reforms of memory, and to study memory is to study forms of faith. Therefore another re-turn to which this collection contributes is the recent one to questions of aesthetics, genre, and literary form that has been termed 'historical formalism'.[18] As Stephen Cohen points out in his introduction to *Shakespeare and Historical Formalism*, it emerges from a certain discontent with new historicism's insistence on reading all cultural practices and artifacts as texts, a method which effectively elides the specific nature of literary texts. While this denial of the privileged nature of literary discourse emerged out of a discontent with new criticism's problematic insistence on it, one of the founding texts of new historicist criticism itself, Stephen Greenblatt's 'Murdering Peasants: Status, Genre, and the Representation of Rebellion', self-consciously articulated its critical practice as an attempt at historicizing aesthetic form and its ideological investments.[19] Greenblatt's essay focused on what he perceived above all as a representational problem and hence a matter of form: how to represent the victory over rebellious peasants without generating pity for the vanquished or compromising the honor of the noble victors. This, however, did not mean a leveling of differences between literary and non-literary discourses: 'If intention, genre, and historical situation are all equally social and ideological, they by no means constitute a single socio-ideological "language"', Greenblatt insisted.[20] Hence, the difference and specificity of literary language as well as 'the complex relation of the formed artwork with the social reality from which it draws its materials' remain central to a historicizing analysis.[21]

In spite of this insistence on the continuing importance of analyzing genre and form in its exploration of the 'poetics of culture', new historicist readings have in practice tended to treat Renaissance works as 'bundles of historical or cultural content, without much attention to the ways that their meanings are shaped and enabled by the possibilities of form', as Eric Rasmussen claims. Paradoxically, this constitutes a profoundly ahistorical gesture, since early modern writers, readers, and theatergoers were 'very much aware of the distinctive, meaning-producing power of "poesy"'.[22] Moreover, Jean E. Howard reminds us, 'we access history only through its textualizations, which, paradoxically, are at once a response to history and its necessary, otherwise unknowable, instantiation', and hence a denial of (aesthetic) form in favor of (historical) content does not make sense.[23] This does not mean that new formalist readings wish to return to an unexamined assertion of the greatness and autonomy of literary texts, or to a state of innocence regarding the ideological impact of extra-textual historical contexts. On the contrary, Stephen Cohen explains, 'The formal characteristics that distinguish literature from other cultural modes are neither innate nor immutable but rather historically produced and historically productive; consequently, any thoroughly historicist criticism must account for form, even as any rigorous formalism must be historical.' Hence, 'Rather than focusing primarily on the historical content of a text, historical formalism insists on attention to the shape and composition of the text-as-container and the impact they may have on the meaning and functioning of that content.'[24]

This reminder is particularly apt with regard to the content of religion and confessional conflict, since this very content was itself a conflict about form, both ritual and rhetorical. The debate over the status of bread and wine in the Eucharist as either a real presence or as a sign, for example, invigorated an equally intense debate over representation in the literary realm. As Brian Cummings argues in his landmark study *The Literary Culture of the Reformation: Grammar and Grace*, the theological controversies of the Reformation can be fully understood only 'in the context of debates about literary and linguistic meaning in biblical commentary and translation and in theories of language and of literature'.[25] To study the Reformation culturally means to acknowledge it as part of literary culture: the literature of the Reformation tells the story of a literary reformation. This foregrounding of language serves as a salutary correction to a historicist reduction of religion to ideology, raising again the vexed question of the relation of history to language, which Cummings explores through 'an archaeology of grammar' that examines the density and dynamics of religious language as well as through 'the application of literary forms of analysis onto the historical study of the Reformation' that productively complements the historical emergence of literary hermeneutics from religious practice.[26]

The title of our collection, *Forms of Faith*, indicates the necessity for a closer examination of the ways in which religious doctrine was not only a controversial topic but a constitutive element of literary discourse in early modern England. Shifting the focus onto formal matters of genre, aesthetics, and rhetoric does not mean glossing over the urgency of confessional controversies that were articulated in both theological and literary writing but rather acknowledging that literature (in the broadest sense) also offered a cultural mode for negotiation rather than escalation. Neither allowing religious conflict to be sublimated into aesthetics nor reducing it to ideology, the essays collected here aim at exploring the complex interplay between form and faith. Although our contributors inevitably employ historicist and formalist methods to varying degrees, it is the overall partnership between these approaches to reading texts that, we believe, characterizes our collection as a whole.

The essays assembled in this collection can be divided into two modes of engaging with confessional conflict in and through literary form. The first part explores the ways in which specific religious rituals and related cultural practices were taken up by literary texts. The first two chapters present investigations of the devotional differences informing early modern observances of the two most important dates in the Christian calendar, Christmas and Easter. In a compelling rereading of the final act of *The Merchant of Venice*,

Brooke Conti shows how it does not depart from the concerns of Act 4 but rather continues to develop a persistent Easter symbolism. An allusion to the ancient Easter hymn known as the *Exultet* or *Praeconium paschale* is woven throughout the play's final act, suggesting that an attenuated version of the pre-Reformation Holy Saturday service survived either in actual practice or in memory for audience members to hear its reverberations in Shakespeare's play. Presenting an alternative to readings of the play that see it as tilting toward tragedy and expressing a failure of Christian assimilation of the Jew, Conti sees the ending of the play as expressing both the audience's 'desire to look past denominational divides and the difficulty of doing so', since '[t]he Easter Vigil's liminal status and surfeit of possible meanings allows for the coexistence of both a more celebratory and a more skeptical reading of interfaith relations' (cf. p. 23).

Phebe Jensen turns our attention from Easter to Christmas, a holiday that was a source of contention in early modern Britain, outlawed as it was in the mid-sixteenth century by the Scottish Kirk and in the mid-seventeenth century by English Puritans. Reformers regarded festive practices such as dancing, wassailing, gift-giving, play performance, and especially caroling, with its traditionally Marian focus, as popish vestiges, while recusant households striving to maintain a sense of Catholic identity embraced them. But in the vast middle, Jensen shows, the activities associated with this holiday were adopted – often with very little adaptation from their late-medieval forms – in ways that made them appealing to a range of devotional predilections. Jensen richly explores the ways in which Christmas, a potentially divisive holiday reminding worshippers of the gulf between Protestant and Catholic, also provided a confessional bridge uniting different religious constituencies in early modern England and served as a reminder that 'a shared English past could help smooth over devotional differences' (cf. p. 51).

Jacqueline Wylde's 'Singing in the counter: goodnight ballads in *Eastward Ho*' calls our attention to a genre that has seen little critical attention, the goodnight ballad, a variety of the broadside. Purported to have been written by a penitent convict and sung on the scaffold, the goodnight ballad offered a popular stew of moving stories of repentance, salacious details, and religious piety set to a catchy tune. According to Wylde, goodnight ballads were not only commercially successful pieces of public entertainment but also effective forms of predominantly Protestant religious persuasion. Her analysis of Chapman, Jonson, and Marston's 1605 satire *Eastward Ho* demonstrates that such a ballad acts as a catalyst for the many conversions at the end of the play. The play performs a further negotiation of difference, one directed at social class. Mocking popular dramatic and musical tastes, including the taste for the goodnight ballad, the play also directs its satire against the Blackfriars audience, which is ultimately 'transformed into the multitude of Cheapside, curiously eager to see a repentant prodigal offering up his shame for public consumption' (cf. p. 68).

Christina Wald's consideration of Elizabethan romance links this literary form to the sacrament of the Eucharist, one of the most divisive of religious subjects in early modern England. Wald argues that the Eucharist debate, which was at the heart of the confessional conflict in early modern Europe, had an impact on Elizabethan romances, whose negotiation of romantic love as well as of identity formation and transformation was informed by concepts which were at stake in the theological conflict: the differentiation between substance and accidents, the notion of transubstantiation, the idea of mutual physical incorporation, and the concept of multilocation. Rather than employing officially abandoned Catholic rituals and doctrines for promoting a clear-cut religio-political position, however, and instead of fully sidestepping religious issues in escapist romantic plots, authors like Robert Greene, Philip Sidney, and Thomas Lodge redeployed their epistemological and emotional thrills for secular concerns and utilized them for experimenting with the possibilities of the relatively new mode of vernacular prose fiction.

Isabel Karremann's contribution discusses Spenser's complaint poem *The Ruines of Time* in the context of the cultural conflict about the rites of mourning and commemoration permissible in Reformation England. The poem enacts this struggle in its own poetic structure, by evoking the immortality-of-poetry topos only to discard it in favor of a view of poetry that acknowledges the instability of monuments, images, and memories, an instability that is the very legacy of Reformation iconoclasm. Announced by the dedicatory letter as an elegy for the Protestant hero Philip Sidney, *Ruines* raises crucial questions about mourning, remembrance, and the role of poetry. It acknowledges that the memory of the dead cannot and perhaps should not remain fixed, but that it becomes more enduring as well as more endurable if intense grief can be discharged – perhaps even discarded – in poetry. Rejecting the notion of an eternal poetic monument implied by the immortality-of-poetry topos as idolatrous and offering instead 'this broken verse' (p. 93), of which the ruin is a more fitting emblem, *The Ruines of Time* enacts nothing less than a new Protestant poetics of mourning and commemoration.

The second part, 'Negotiating confessional conflict', opens with Brian Walsh's rereading of Samuel Rowley's play about the early Reformation, *When You See Me You Know Me*, which acknowledges the unsettled and ongoing efforts of continuing reform that revisionist historians have attributed to Elizabeth's reign. Written in the first years of King James's reign, the play reflects and responds to the religious uncertainty of those years. While recognizing the anti-Catholic polemics informing the play, Walsh emphasizes the intra-Protestant hostility that it registers 'even as it strives to ameliorate it'. *When You See Me You Know Me* conveys the impression 'that there was no single fount of reformation in England, but any number of canals with varying points of origin and differing paces that were diverted and redirected differently by the whims and temperaments of four Tudor monarchs'. By exposing the 'dialectical processes' that resulted in 'messiness, false starts, and interruptions to reform' in the early years of the English Reformation, Walsh argues, Rowley's play does not seek to discredit religious reform. Rather, it exposes its processes as 'an inevitable and on-going means of mediating the new normality of confessional plurality and what we might term permanent religious "unsettlement"' (cf. pp. 115, 122).

The next two contributions examine the irenic potential of the tragic form. Such potential is often ascribed to stage comedies, romances, and even histories, but not tragedies, which, as Thomas J. Moretti observes in his contribution, 'have worked well for scholarship that notices a religious or cultural rupture represented or exploited on the stage'. By contrast, Moretti's reading of 'Tragic mediation in *The White Devil*' presents Webster's play as a mocking form of religious settlement insofar as it subverts all religious positions and thereby joins its audience in a 'collective sense of troubled faith'. No single religious position or practice receives 'permanent validation or scorn'; 'all are eventually discounted' by the play's skepticism, which has the effect of nudging audiences toward religious pluralism (cf. pp. 127, 129).

In his reading of *Macbeth*, James R. Macdonald calls our attention to the fault line in early modern religious views of witchcraft. Calvinist theology rejected an older Catholic view that stressed the autonomy of the witch's will. Both Middleton's *The Witch* and Shakespeare's *Macbeth* seem aware that 'powerless witches might seem dramatically inert, while powerful witches could become theologically problematic'. By avoiding a consistent model of the witches' causation, both Middleton and Shakespeare choose to have 'the sources and nature of their powers remain opaque enough to avoid heterodox implications' (cf. p. 155). A strategic ambiguity concerning the witches may not repair the ideological fault line inevitably exposed by representations of witchcraft, but it may make it seem to disappear through the lawful magic of stagecraft.

The next three contributions forge thoughtful approaches to and departures from the sermons of John Donne. In her study of '*Henry V* and the interrogative conscience as a space for the performative negotiation of confessional conflict', Mary A. Blackstone argues that the play anticipates later sermons that served to promote 'an interrogative conscience'. In contrast with the majority of 'official and didactic' parish sermons of the day, later sermons of Donne's cultivated a 'questioning conscience'. Blackstone contends that a play like *Henry V* anticipates the turn to questioning in Donne's popular sermons: 'In contrast with the parish church, players and their performances for diverse audiences provided a more engaging and accessible site for the negotiation of confessional conflict.' Answering audiences' own experiences of confessional conflict, Shakespeare and his contemporaries frequently produced 'interrogative performance texts' that encouraged audiences to explore 'for themselves multiple perspectives on some of the most important issues of their day – including religious and political allegiances' (cf. p. 162).

Alexandra M. Block shows how Donne experiments with four different semiotic models of how the sacramental sign is related to its referent. The Donne that emerges in Block's reading is not one who 'was indecisive or omnivorous in his religious beliefs', but rather a writer who deployed various Eucharistic models for the sign in order to reimagine representation itself. Block's Donne, 'in pursuit of writerly goals … seems to have been willing, at times, to decenter religion to some degree, positioning it not as the master a text must serve, but as a resource serving the text' (cf. p. 190).

Joel M. Dodson returns to Donne via Foucault, specifically the later Foucault of *The Care of the Self.* Donne's 'Fishers of Men' sermon delivered in December of 1619 at The Hague offers a 'view of confession as a form of care rather than subjection', anticipating what Foucault terms the 'care of the self'. Donne reimagines confession not as a 'disciplinary subjection to one or another polemical ideal' but rather 'as a form of what Foucault labels a "stylistics of existence"' (cf. p. 197). Could literary forms act as places in which religious tensions and conflicts were tempered in early modern England? Collectively these essays urge a positive if tentative answer, but more important, they serve to encourage subsequent scholarship to explore further the possibility that various sorts of textual and dramatic representations could help to de-escalate religious tensions and mediate conflict.

Finally, we have given the last word to the 'onlie begetter' of this volume, Richard Wilson, a more than generous supporter of this project from inception to completion. Following a seminar on the topic that we had organized and directed, and in which earlier versions of several of this volume's chapters were first presented, Professor Wilson asked if the seminar had been recorded (it had not) and announced in no uncertain terms that 'it must become a book'. His Afterword features its own vigorous engagements with each of the forms of negotiation represented in this volume, and with his fine sense of intellectual division and arbitration, he vividly sets each against the changing backdrop of early modern literary studies.

When first planning this collection, we did not intend to produce a volume that would seem topical in light of escalating religious violence around the globe. Ours is an accidental topicality, or perhaps one that issued from a political unconscious that might have guided us from the beginning. At any rate, we are not interested in exploiting attention to the nearly daily sensational violence in the name of religion, nor do we wish to pretend to offer solutions to such violence. Our contributors have persuaded us that literary forms served as important tools in an earlier age for challenging a hermeneutics of suspicion that underlies the escalation of conflict. If such awareness has any effect on promoting understanding across religious divides, then the accident of our collection appearing at the present moment of widespread religious turmoil and intolerance will be a happy one.

Notes

1 As Ken Jackson and Arthur Marotti observed in their survey of 'The Turn to Religion in Early Modern English Studies' (2004) and as Julia Reinhard Lupton commented in 'The Religious Turn (to Theory) in Shakespeare Studies' (2006), religious contexts and controversies never entirely disappeared from the literary study of the period. According to Lupton, 'Religion has always formed a major tributary of Renaissance literary criticism. … The "religious turn" in Renaissance studies is hardly a turn at all, but rather a reaffirmation of history's hold on what has been, through its constitutive debts to Renaissance humanism itself, a fundamentally historical discipline.' Accordingly, she rejects studies that reside entirely within the established forms of either old or new historicism, restricting 'religious motifs to specific contexts, confessions, or power structures'. Instead she calls for a religious turn that is simultaneously a turn or return to theory, to a willingness to address 'the big questions and systematic frameworks of psychoanalysis, philosophy, theology, and politics from the other side of our immersion in tracts and ephemera'. J. R. Lupton, 'The Religious Turn (to Theory) in Shakespeare Studies', *ELN*, 44 (2006), 145–6, 148. For Jackson and Marotti, although questions of religion did not vanish from critical discourse during the 1980s and 1990s, they tended to be marginalized for the sake of the social, economic, and political subjects favored by new historicists in America and cultural materialists in Britain, particularly those of gender, race, and class. In recent years, this well-established trio has added a new member, religion, and become a quartet. They credit Deborah Shuger with continuing to force 'professionals in the field to take seriously religious beliefs, ideas, and history', even while the field as a whole was largely ignoring such issues. K. Jackson and A. Marotti, 'The Turn to Religion in Early Modern English Studies', *Criticism*, 46 (2004), 167–90.

2 A turn to religion is apparent not only in early modern studies but across the discipline. In 2006, the journal *English Language Notes* marked a 'new beginning' in its publication history with a special issue entitled *Literary History and the Religious Turn: Announcing the New* ELN, covering not only what it called the 'Theo-Political Renaissance' but also much besides, from medieval studies to contemporary Latina fiction and contemporary poetry and a roundtable on Joanna Brooks's *American Lazarus: Religion and the Rise of African-American and Native American Literatures.* See *Literary History and the Religious Turn*, B. Holsinger (ed.), a special issue of *English Language Notes*, 44.1 (Spring, 2006), 1. The turn in early modern studies, however, has been undoubtedly sharper than the soft turn experienced by its immediate neighbor, medieval studies, which never witnessed even a partial disappearance of religion from critical discussion and debate.

3 T. Rist, 'Shakespeare Now and Then: Communities, Religion, Reception', in R. D. Sell and A. W. Johnson (eds), *Writing and Religion in England, 1558–1689: Studies in Community-Making and Cultural Memory* (Farnham: Ashgate, 2009), p. 116.

4 A. Walsham, *Church Papists: Catholicism, Conformity and Confessional Polemic in Early Modern England* (Woodbridge: Boydell Press, 1993), p. 7.

5 P. Marshall (ed.), 'Introduction', in *The Impact of the English Reformation* (London: Arnold, 1977), p. 5.

6 'For the first two or three decades of Elizabeth's reign, much of the old cultural fabric remained intact. … But towards 1580 there was a sea change. Scripture plays and scripture songs became equally obnoxious to many religious people. Christ had not lived and died in order to be a spectacle on stage. There were now fewer godly ballads, and no more plays deriving their matter from scripture.' P. Collinson and E. Murphy, *The Birthpangs of Protestant England* (New York: St. Martin's Press, 1988), pp. 141–2. During this watershed decade, most of the cultural effects of iconophobia – 'the total repudiation of all images', as opposed to the iconoclasm of the first generation of Protestants, a more limited and targeted attack on 'certain unacceptable images' – took place. P. Collinson, 'From Iconoclasm to Iconophobia: The Cultural Impact of the Second English Reformation', in Marshall (ed.), *The Impact of the English Reformation*, pp. 278–307, at p. 282.

7 Collinson, 'From Iconoclasm to Iconophobia', p. 283.

8 C. Haigh, *English Reformations: Religion, Politics, and Society under the Tudors* (Oxford: Oxford University Press, 1993), p. 280.

9 Rist, 'Shakespeare Now and Then', p. 116.

10 There has been a tendency in early modern literary studies to regard the period in light of what follows it. Bold explorations like Franco Moretti's in 'The Great Eclipse: Tragic Form as the Deconsecration of Sovereignty', in S. Fischer, D. Forgacs, and D. Miller (eds), *Signs Taken for Wonders: Essays in the Sociology of Literary Forms*, rev. edn (London: Verso, 1988), pp. 42–82, and David Scott Kastan's in '"Proud Majesty Made a Subject": Representing Authority on the Early Modern Stage', in *Shakespeare After Theory* (New York and London: Routledge, 1999), pp. 109–27, have helped us to see and hear in English Renaissance tragedy the distant stirrings of the English Civil Wars and the eventual beheading of Charles I in the middle of the seventeenth century. The forward-looking tendency has perhaps been reinforced by the recent widespread adoption of the period term 'early modern', since that period, as it is usually conceived, stretches over roughly three centuries, from *c.* 1500 to *c.* 1800. The designation 'early modern' arguably marginalizes the period's relation to the medieval as surely as the earlier term 'Renaissance', which implied that learning and curiosity were reborn following a long period of dormancy and intellectual darkness. The last millennium ended with the strong suspicion that the field of early modern British studies needed to look backward as much as forward. Several recent monographs and collections exploring the relation of the period's most celebrated author, Shakespeare, to the Middle Ages attempt to correct the tendency of early modern studies to largely ignore the study of their authors in relation to a world that had not suddenly disappeared but that lingered on well beyond the Settlement of 1559. See R. Morse, H. Cooper, and

P. Holland (eds), *Medieval Shakespeare: Pasts and Presents* (Cambridge: Cambridge University Press, 2013); M. W. Driver and S. Ray (eds), *Shakespeare and the Middle Ages: Essays on the Performance and Adaptation of the Plays with Medieval Sources or Settings* (London and Jefferson, NC: McFarland Publishers, 2009); and H. Cooper, *Shakespeare and the Medieval World, Arden Critical Companions* (London: Methuen Drama, 2010). Cooper covers the ways in which the medieval was remembered in early modern England (pp. 12–16).

11 K. Thomas, *The Perception of the Past in Early Modern England*, The Creighton Trust Lecture 1983 (London: University of London, n.d.), p. 9.

12 E. Duffy, 'The Conservative Voice in the English Reformation', in S. Ditchfield (ed.), *Christianity and Community in the West: Essays for John Bossy* (Aldershot: Ashgate, 2001), pp. 87–105, at p. 104.

13 I. Archer, 'The Nostalgia of John Stow', in D. L. Smith, R. Strier, and D. Bevington (eds), *The Theatrical City: Culture, Theatre and Politics in London, 1576–1649* (Cambridge: Cambridge University Press, 1995), p. 31.

14 E. Duffy, *The Stripping of the Altars: Traditional Religion in England, 1400–1580* (New Haven: Yale University Press, 1992), p. 338. In an essay on 'The Arts and Acts of Memorialization in Early Modern London', Ian Archer has shown that a 'culture of commemoration' was not entirely swept away by the Protestant Reformation: 'the commemoration of benefactors in the post-Reformation period was often expressed in forms which owed much to the supposedly displaced Catholic forms'; in J. F. Merritt (ed.), *Imagining Early Modern London: Perceptions and Portrayals of the City from Stow to Strype, 1598–1720* (Cambridge: Cambridge University Press, 2001), p. 91.

15 See D. Cressy, *Bonfires and Bells: National Memory and the Protestant Calendar in Elizabethan and Stuart England* (Berkeley: University of California Press, 1989).

16 Duffy, 'The Conservative Voice in the English Reformation'.

17 The example of the antiquarian John Stowe, author of the *Annales, or a Generale Chronicle of England from Brute until the present yeare of Christ* (1580) and *Survey of London* (1598), demonstrates that it was possible to experience nostalgia for England's pre-Reformation past while embracing the Elizabethan settlement. Stowe's antiquarian tastes caused him to be suspected of recusancy and his house to be searched in 1568. Nevertheless, he was able to persuade authorities of his Protestant loyalty and credentials. '[T]he whole drift of Stow's work', according to Duffy, 'was toward a positive reappraisal of the Catholic past, worlds away from the Reformation polemic of a Bale or Lambarde. Nostalgia for the visible remains of Catholicism, and a backward and approving look at the religion which had produced them, were therefore hard to separate.' Duffy, *The Stripping of the Altars*, p. 43.

18 See S. Cohen (ed.), *Shakespeare and Historical Formalism* (Aldershot: Ashgate, 2007) and his earlier essay 'Between Form and Culture: New Historicism and the Promise of a Historical Formalism', in M. D. Rasmussen (ed.), *Renaissance Literature and Its Formal Engagements* (New York: Palgrave, 2002), pp. 17–41. Alternatively, terms like 'new formalism', H. Dubrow, 'Guess Who's Coming to Dinner? Reinterpreting Formalism and the Country House Poem', *Modern*

Language Quarterly, 61:1 (2000), 59–77, and 'new aestheticism', J. Joughin and S. Malpas (eds), *The New Aestheticism* (Manchester: Manchester University Press, 2003), have been put forward; Mark Rasmussen rightly criticizes the first for its claim to innovation (while it is actually a return to a moment when new historicism emerged from struggle with formalism), the latter for eschewing questions of history and power in its focus on the relation between literature and philosophy (Rasmussen, *Renaissance Literature and Its Formal Engagements*, p. 3).

19 Cohen (ed.), *Shakespeare and Historical Formalism*, p. 1.

20 S. Greenblatt, 'Murdering Peasants: Status, Genre, and the Representation of Rebellion [1983]', repr. in A. R. Guneratne (ed.), *Shakespeare and Genre: From Early Modern Inheritances to Postmodern Legacies* (Houndmills, Basingstoke: Palgrave Macmillan, 2011), pp. 39–65, at p. 49.

21 H. Grady, *Shakespeare and Impure Aesthetics* (Cambridge: Cambridge University Press, 2009), p. 232.

22 Rasmussen (ed.), *Renaissance Literature and Its Formal Engagements*, pp. 1, 4.

23 J. Howard, 'Shakespeare, Geography, and the Work of Genre' in Cohen (ed.), *Shakespeare and Historical Formalism*, pp. 49–67, at p. 51.

24 Cohen (ed.), *Shakespeare and Historical Formalism*, p. 2.

25 B. Cummings, *The Literary Culture of the Reformation: Grammar and Grace* (Oxford: Oxford University Press), p. 8.

26 *Ibid.*, p. 13.

Part I

Religious ritual and literary form

1

Shylock celebrates Easter

Brooke Conti

The final act of *The Merchant of Venice* has always struck some readers as superfluous: by the end of Act 4 the pound-of-flesh plot is entirely resolved and even the love plots have few loose ends left to tie up. And yet Shakespeare gives us another whole act, a leisurely, playful return to Belmont and to the very minor problems of a half-dozen generally happy lovers. But if Act 5 feels unnecessary to many readers, it poses a special problem for those who regard Shylock as the play's dramatic and emotional heart. If Shylock is, in whatever sense, the work's hero – and especially if he is intended as a witness to Venetian intolerance and Christian hypocrisy – then how do we account for the insistent festivity of Act 5? For the play does not merely leave Shylock behind; it briskly strips him of both identity and possessions before turning to the moonlit gambols of those responsible for his undoing.

One common response to the seemingly radical tonal shift between Acts 4 and 5 has been to scour the latter for signs of dissension and unease: evidence that all is not as well in Belmont as it appears.[1] But although there are modest hints of possible future marital trouble for one or more of the play's romantic couples, similarly modest hints hover over all the couples in all of Shakespeare's comedies. Even the happiest of Shakespeare's comedic conclusions are shadowed by reminders of the young lovers' rashness, naïveté, or lack of sufficient insight into self or partner, and the fifth act of *Merchant of Venice* is no more ominous in this regard than the fifth acts of *Midsummer Night's Dream*, *Much Ado About Nothing*, or *Twelfth Night*. In *Merchant of Venice*, as in those other plays, the audience is encouraged to suspend their misgivings and give themselves over to the festivities.[2] As the six lovers work out the terms of their relationships with music, moonlight, and practical jokes, the play seems to have discarded Shylock as easily as the Venetians have.

However, while Act 5's light-heartedness may disquiet or even repel modern audiences, it does not represent a radical shift away from the concerns of Act 4. As I shall argue, the two acts are united by a pervasive Easter symbolism that revolves around Shylock's conversion. Act 4's echoes of the passion and crucifixion are well known. But if Act 4 alludes to Good Friday, Act 5 alludes to Holy Saturday and the dawning of Easter Sunday. Beginning with the love duet between Jessica and Lorenzo and continuing through the end of the play, Shakespeare repeatedly evokes the ancient Easter Vigil service, the heart of which involved the reception of new converts into the Church. This extended liturgical allusion suggests the play's continuing preoccupation with Shylock; at the same time, the liturgy's vexed status in Protestant England raises questions about religious change that go beyond the play's Jewish characters.

That this allusion has been ignored by mainstream Shakespeare criticism is not surprising. Although the Easter Vigil dates back to the earliest days of Christianity, it appears to have vanished from English worship at the Reformation.[3] The few scholars who have noticed the allusion have therefore assumed that the service would have been unknown to any but devoted Catholics, and, based on this assumption, adduced the allusion to their case for a 'Catholic Shakespeare'.[4] However, a careful investigation of the liturgy's history shows many longstanding beliefs about its place in post-Reformation Europe to be mistaken. As I will demonstrate, the printed record reveals that the Easter Vigil had a long half-life in the Protestant imagination. Well into the seventeenth century, English writers were still talking about the liturgy and quoting from its most important literary component, the hymn known as the Exultet. There are many reasons that the Easter Vigil remained familiar, but its chief interest for Protestants seems to have been its place in the early Church. Amply described in the writings of the Fathers, the Saturday night service was the first Easter service celebrated by Christians, and for centuries the only Easter service. From its opening hymn to its Scripture readings, the liturgy involves a sustained narration of Christianity's origins in Judaism; it was also, in the ancient Church, the only time of year that converts were baptized.

I will say more about both the service and its place in Protestant thought later, but some of the liturgy's relevance to *Merchant* should already be apparent. The fact that Shakespeare added Shylock's conversion to the material he took from his source narratives suggests its importance to the play,[5] but scholars have long been divided over how to read this conversion – or the conversion of Shylock's daughter Jessica. One line of interpretation, advanced most compellingly by Barbara Lewalski, sees *Merchant* as a largely untroubled articulation of Christian supersessionist theology: a work that celebrates the replacement of the Old Law with the New.[6] Readings in this vein usually do not linger over the conversions of the play's two Jews, regarding them as merely symbolic of the general conversion of the Jews that Christians expected to usher in the apocalypse. But whereas this interpretation suggests that the play sees its Jewish characters primarily as types and abstractions, most readers in the twenty years since James Shapiro's *Shakespeare and the Jews* have been profoundly interested in those characters and the ways they might reflect or occlude the experiences of real European Jews.[7] A great deal of research has helped to illuminate the ways Shakespeare's play engages with early modern understandings of Jewishness as both religion and race; in particular, the fraught nature of Jewish identity and Christian skepticism about whether a Jew truly could 'turn gentle' have led a variety of scholars to see *Merchant* as an unstable work, one that may wish to celebrate the replacement of the letter of law with the law of love but that is unable to do so.[8] Incapable of fully assimilating its Jewish characters or reducing flesh-and-blood Jews to convenient types fulfilled by their Christian anti-types, the play – scholars such as Janet Adelman and Kenneth Gross argue – tilts toward tragedy. In this reading, conversion is where the conflict between the ostensibly happy ending of the play and the problem of the Jews is most evident.

The echoes of the Easter Vigil in Act 5 extend and complicate both of these readings. On the one hand, the liturgy articulates an unambiguously supersessionist vision of the relationship between Jew and Christian, and Act 5's festive setting encourages a celebratory attitude toward both conversions. On the other hand, the liturgy's deep engagement with the Hebrew Bible and its association with the moment when Judaism became Christianity support Adelman's argument that *Merchant* 'persistently troubles the distinction between Christian and Jew'.[9] But while Act 5's allusions to the Easter Vigil foreground some of the same problems of succession and substitution that interest Adelman, they also remind us that Christianity's identity crisis, in the late sixteenth century, is only partly about its debts to Judaism. A service tied to the ancient Church but familiar from the pre-Reformation one, the Easter Vigil mediates between Jew and Christian, Protestant and Catholic. We cannot know precisely what Shakespeare intended in alluding to the liturgy and we cannot know how every one of his audience members would have responded (assuming they recognized the allusions at all). Yet his play's evocation of this service, once thought to have vanished at the Reformation, suggests both a desire to look past denominational divides and the difficulty of doing so. In the end the play's generosity may be limited by the theological presumptions and ethnic prejudices of its age, but the Easter Vigil's liminal status and surfeit of possible meanings allows for the coexistence of both a more celebratory and a more skeptical reading of interfaith relations.

Our Passover feast

Even those who have not noticed the Easter symbolism in Act 5 have often thought that, in opening with Jessica, the play's final scene serves as a commentary on her father's fate. In recent years, critics have tended to focus on the relatively slight evidence for discord between Jessica and Lorenzo – taking it as evidence that Jessica's assimilation as a Venetian Christian will be no smoother than they presume Shylock's could be.[10] However, Act 5's allusions to the Easter Vigil seem to pull in the opposite direction, suggesting the success of Jessica's conversion and quite possibly Shylock's as well. In order to make that case as clearly as possible, for the next several pages I will be taking the play's use of the liturgy relatively straight, by which I mean laying out the allusion's implications for the play as a theologically orthodox late-sixteenth-century Christian might have read them. In the second part of this essay, I will discuss the ways the liturgy's history might have complicated or challenged such a reading.

As the scene begins, Jessica and Lorenzo are inscribing their love story within a larger romantic narrative, seeking precedents in famous lovers past. Much has been written about the Classical precedents they come up with and especially the ominous endings that those lovers meet. But if the local allusions in this duet have been carefully scrutinized, the larger and more structural one has not been. In fact, Jessica and Lorenzo's narrative of repetition and continuity alludes to a far grander one involving the whole of providential history. The lovers' repeated refrain 'in such a night' echoes the formula 'this is the night' [haec nox est] from the Exultet, the hymn that opens the Easter Vigil liturgy. This allusion shows that the play has not left Act 4 or Shylock behind, for the relationship between Jew and Christian remains very much on its mind. Here is the relevant portion of the hymn:

> This is our Passover feast,
> When Christ, the true Lamb is slain,
> Whose blood consecrates the homes of all believers.
>
> This is the night
> When first you saved our fathers:
> You freed the people of Israel from their slavery
> And led them dry-shod through the sea.
> This is the night
> When the pillar of fire destroyed the darkness of sin!
>
> This is the night
> When Christians everywhere,
> Washed clean of sin and freed from all defilement,
> Are restored to grace and grow together in holiness.
>
> This is the night
> When Jesus Christ broke the chains of death
> And rose triumphant from the grave.
>
> What good would life have been to us,
> Had Christ not come as our Redeemer?
> Father, how wonderful your care for us!
> How boundless your merciful love!
> To ransom a slave you gave away your Son.

O happy fault,
O necessary sin of Adam,
Which gained for us so great a Redeemer!

Most blessed of all nights
Chosen by God to see Christ rising from the dead![11]

As one of the earliest articulations of the theological principle of the 'fortunate fall' or 'felix culpa', the Exultet reads Adam and Eve's transgression and all the subsequent events of the Hebrew Bible as necessary preludes to Christ's incarnation and redemption; it therefore gives voice to the supersessionist theology that scholars have long understood Shakespeare's play to be wrestling with.

For the most part, these echoes of the Exultet seem to endorse the liturgy's own understanding of Jewish–Christian succession, though as always in Shakespeare there is room for doubt. Just as Jessica and Lorenzo conflate the story of their love with tales of lovers in times past, so does the Exultet conflate God's deliverance of the Jews with Christ's salvation of Christians. Moreover, the allusion suggests that we might read Jessica's and Shylock's conversion as the latest event in this providential scheme: after all, the conversion of the Jews was regarded by most Christians as a necessary forerunner to the second coming and the end of historical time.[12] Although it is possible that the pessimistic Classical allusions in the love duet override or ironize the more hopeful Christian ones, the tension between the two sets of allusions need not be resolved that way. The fact that Jessica and Lorenzo add their names to a list of lovers whose stories come to bad ends may be simply irrelevant (to the play, if not to them); in the grand scheme of salvation, romantic love is of no consequence. Another possibility is that Jessica and Lorenzo's relationship should be read typologically, as the happy fulfillment of those earlier, equally passionate, but less successful pre-Christian romances. Typology is repetition with a difference.

Shakespeare's interest in the Easter Vigil is not confined to the language of the Exultet but encompasses many of the service's most significant features. As the hymn implies, the Vigil was originally modeled by early Christians on the Passover, and even in its later forms remained peculiarly focused on Israel and its redemption.[13] Traditionally, the service began around midnight and ended at dawn. The congregation assembled in darkness, symbolizing the end of the light of the Old Law. New fire was sparked and blessed, symbolizing the light of Christ, and from this flame the paschal candle was lit. As the deacon recited the Exultet, the other candles in the church were lit, one by one, from the paschal candle, until the entire congregation was illuminated. The liturgy then proceeded to readings from Scripture, all taken from the Hebrew Bible, including some of the same episodes from the patriarchal narratives that Shakespeare recalls elsewhere in the play. However, the center and the highlight of the service in the ancient Church was the reception of converts via baptism followed by holy communion. After the celebration of the Eucharist, the liturgy concluded at first light.[14]

Act 5 of *Merchant* might be said to loosely follow the progress of the liturgy. In addition to opening with the language of the Exultet, the scene moves from darkness to dawn, as the characters repeatedly remind the audience. At the beginning of the act 'the moon shines bright' upon Jessica and Lorenzo (5.1.1), and when Portia and Nerissa arrive it is still dark enough that they can see a candle shining far off in her house; they remark on the power of this single candle, the only source of artificial light mentioned in the scene. In Portia's words, it shines like 'a good deed in a naughty world' (5.1.90). Upon her husband's return, however, Portia notes that the night sky has grown paler, like 'the daylight sick', and at the end of the scene both she and Graziano comment, separately, that it is almost morning (5.1.123–5, 294, 302). These detailed references to the scene's nocturnal setting and its progress toward daylight strengthen the link with the Easter Vigil liturgy, and reading this scene alongside the Exultet provides additional insights into the play's conclusion. According to the Exultet, Easter Eve is a night of miraculous renewal and transformation:

> Of this night scripture says:
> 'The night will be as clear as day:
> it will become my light, my joy.'
>
> The power of this holy night dispels all evil,
> washes guilt away, restores lost innocence,
> brings mourners joy;
> it casts out hatred, brings us peace,
> and humbles earthly pride.
>
> Night truly blessed when heaven is wedded to earth
> and man is reconciled with God!
>
> (lines 56–66)

As several critics have argued, the Belmont of Act 5 seems like something more than the usual Shakespearean green world; it is presented as a heavenly sanctuary of peace and reconciliation where the music of the spheres is apparently audible.[15] If we take Act 5's evocation of the Exultet seriously, however, it is not that Belmont, as a place, is necessarily so very heavenly – but that this specific night has hallowed it, enabling the reunions and reconciliations that conclude the play.

The Exultet's status as a piece of divine music also has consequences for Act 5. The scene offers several examples of music's power to order, reconcile, and harmonize, beginning with the lovers' duet and continuing with Lorenzo's call for Portia's musicians to 'bring [their] music forth into the air' (5.1.52). As he and Jessica wait for the musicians to appear, he points to the stars and explains that the music of the spheres is inaudible while humans are clad in their 'muddy vesture of decay' (5.1.62–3). Presumably, this is why he calls for the musicians – to provide an audible substitute for the inaudible music of the spheres – but Lorenzo's investment in heavenly harmony also has a specific Easter resonance. Each of the stars, Lorenzo claims, sings 'like an angel ... Still choiring to the young-eyed cherubim' (5.1.60–1), words that evoke the opening lines of the Exultet. As the hymn's Latin title suggests, these lines direct the created world, including the denizens of heaven, to jubilation:

> Rejoice, heavenly powers! Sing, choirs of angels!
> Exult, all creation around God's throne!
> ...
> Rejoice, O Mother Church! Exult in glory!
> The risen Savior shines upon you!
> Let this place resound with joy,
> Echoing the mighty song of all God's people!
> (lines 1–12)

There is a continuity, then, between music on earth, music in heaven, and a larger cosmic order.

Despite the many exclamation marks in the Roman missal's English translation of the above passage, the Exultet's plainsong chant is solemn and meditative, more in keeping with Jessica's subsequent remark that she is 'never merry' when she hears 'sweet music' (5.1.68). Some readers have read Jessica's statement as a form of resistance to Lorenzo's musical enthusiasm – a sign that she is refusing to enjoy the music – and then interpreted Lorenzo's lengthy response as a pedantic and disapproving critique that links Jessica's lack of merriment with her father, whose dislike of music and festivity is noted several times in the first four acts of the play.[16] Lorenzo's pedantry is hard to ignore, but his words, for all their tedious excess, are the opposite of a critique. When Jessica says she is never merry when she hears sweet music, he responds that this is because her spirits are 'attentive', or receptive to music, which can stun and gentle even the wildest of animals (5.1.69–78). If Lorenzo is thinking of Shylock when he subsequently declares that '[t]he man who hath no music in himself / ... / Is fit for treasons, stratagems, and spoils' (5.1.82–4), then he is distinguishing Jessica from her father on the basis of her responsiveness to music. Far from criticizing her lack of merriment, Lorenzo reassures Jessica that hers is the appropriate response to sweet music.

As Portia and Nerissa enter, the musicians whom Lorenzo summoned earlier apparently continue playing, for the women remark on their music several lines later (5.1.96–7). But first Portia draws the audience's attention to the candle in her house. Nerissa observes that they could not see it earlier, when the moon shone, and Portia agrees, moralizing thus: 'So … the greater glory dim[s] the less / A substitute shines brightly as a king / Until a king be by, and then his state / Empties itself as doth an inland brook / Into the main of waters' (5.1.92–6). Given the scene's other contextual cues, the mere presence of this single candle may have been enough to remind the audience of the paschal candle in the darkened church at the beginning of the Easter Vigil, but Portia's commentary on its virtues also aligns surprisingly closely with the Exultet's concluding praise of that candle:

> Let [this candle] mingle with the lights of heaven
> And continue bravely burning
> To dispel the darkness of this night!
>
> May the Morning Star which never sets
> Find this flame still burning:
> Christ, that Morning Star,
> Who came back from the dead,
> And shed his peaceful light on all mankind.
> (lines 77–84)

To apply Portia's words to this portion of the hymn, the paschal candle is the 'substitute' that will first 'empt[y] his state' into the greater light of the heavens (including the literal morning star) and then into the even greater light of Christ (the metaphorical morning star). The candle symbolizes but is not as powerful as the lights of heaven, which in turn symbolize but are not as powerful as the light of Christ, who will eventually surpass and subsume those lesser lights. The Christological reading suggested by placing Portia's words alongside the Exultet has larger resonances for a play so preoccupied with issues of succession and substitution. If Antonio in Act 4 is supposed to be read as a sacrificial, Christ-like figure, Portia's words remind us that he is not the thing itself, but a mere prefiguration.[17] Both the hymn and the scene in Belmont also seem to allude to the parable of the wise and foolish virgins trying to keep their lamps going as they wait for the arrival of the bridegroom – traditionally understood as Christ at his second coming (Matt. 25:1–13). The candle in Belmont, of course, burns in anticipation of the return of a literal bridegroom, but he, like Antonio, is only a prefiguration of the real thing. The Easter Eve setting of Act 5 hallows Belmont – it is, in Portia's words, the 'season' that brings the characters' actions '[t]o their right praise and true perfection' (5.1.106–7) – but like all Easter celebrations it both points ahead to the second coming and marks the great distance from here to there.

Although Act 5 contains numerous allusions to the Easter Vigil and the language of the Exultet, even audience members relatively unfamiliar with either the hymn or the service might still have picked up on some of the scene's pervasive Easter symbolism. In addition to the features I have already touched on, Portia and Nerissa are reported to be 'stray[ing] about / By holy crosses' on their way back to Belmont; Lancelot and Stefano make repeated references to the expected return of their 'master'; and Jessica and Lorenzo, like Jesus's disciples (or like the virgins in the parable), intend to stay awake but fall asleep in a garden (5.1.30–1, 34, 46–7, 48–54, 108–9). Lorenzo also makes two allusions to the Eucharist, which is the culmination of the conversion rite at the Easter Vigil but also a commemoration, for all Christians, of the Last Supper. Early in the scene Lorenzo describes the stars as 'patens' – the standard term for Eucharistic dishes – 'of bright gold',[18] and at the end of the scene he tells Nerissa and Portia that they 'drop manna in the way / Of starvèd people' (5.1.57–8, 293–4). Coming as this latter remark does after Nerissa's announcement that 'the rich Jew' has given Jessica and Lorenzo 'a special deed of gift, / After his death, of all he dies possessed of' (5.1.290–1), the reference to manna is hard to hear without an additional valence. Literally, Nerissa is simply saying that Jessica and Lorenzo will inherit Shylock's property. But Lorenzo's claim that this news is like manna in the wilderness – a familiar type of the Eucharist – suggests we might also understand Nerissa's words as a confirmation that Lorenzo and Jessica are heirs not only of Shylock, but also of Jesus, another 'rich Jew' whose death has left them in possession of salvation. The demise of one will answer their material needs, the other, their spiritual. Perhaps this alignment of Shylock with Jesus is only ironic, meant to highlight how worthless the riches of the former are compared with those of the latter. But in a play that has already demonstrated the fungibility of roles such as merchant and Jew, we would do well to take seriously the possibility that in Act 5 it is Shylock – not Antonio, Bassanio, or Portia – who is the Christ figure. After all, like Jesus, Shylock remains irreducibly Jewish even as he is claimed by Christianity, and like Jesus he is absent at Easter. Indeed, as with Jesus' empty tomb, Shylock's absence from Act 5 might be said to be a precondition for belief in his transformation.

Regardless of how one interprets the 'rich Jew', the play's use of the Easter Vigil demonstrates that its attitude toward Shylock's conversion is more complicated than it may initially have seemed. The fact that the announcement of his conversion is swiftly followed by echoes of an early Christian liturgy suggests that Shylock's conversion is symbolic not only of the anticipated conversion of the Jews at the second coming, but also of the earliest Christians, who were simultaneously Jews.[19] In other words, Shylock's conversion might not be a conversion at all, if by that we mean a radical break or reversal. Imagining a Jewish identity that is always already Christian (or vice versa) may be a self-serving Christian fantasy, but it is not the religious triumphalism of many of the play's other characters, who insist, in the words of the Duke of Venice, on 'the difference' between the Christian and Jewish 'spirit' (4.1.363).

Neither Jew nor Greek

While the language and rituals of the Easter Vigil present an uncomplicated narrative of Jewish–Christian succession, the liturgy's complicated history raises implicit questions about that narrative and about the immutability of any religious identity. Given the liturgy's close association with the early Church, Shakespeare's evocation of the service in the context of Jewish conversions could be read as a miraculous reminder of God's faithfulness to his chosen people, drawing an unbroken line from the ancient Israelites to the present hour. On the other hand, as a discarded relic from the past, the liturgy could also have been read as an emblem of rupture and discontinuity. But although the history of the service is a crucial part of its interpretative meaning, much of that history has hitherto been obscure or misunderstood. Whereas some pre-Reformation practices, such as prayers for the dead and the invocation of saints, get discussed and debated for decades, no one seems either to have challenged or applauded the elimination of the Easter Vigil. We know that the liturgy was celebrated during Henry's reign and again during Mary's, but it is absent from even the 1549 Book of Common Prayer. In an effort to explain what might have happened to the liturgy, Eamon Duffy has speculated that the Vigil was simply not a popular feature of late-medieval lay piety, and the few liturgical historians who have considered the question have come to similar conclusions.[20] Duffy is right that by the sixteenth century much of the visual poetry of the service was gone: pushed back to Holy Saturday morning in order to accommodate the many confessions that priests needed to hear before Easter Sunday, the Vigil lost the drama of the single candle in the darkened church and the gradual breaking of Easter dawn. It also lost some of its other associations with its origins: without the early Church's steady supply of converts, baptisms were rarely celebrated. At the time of *Merchant*'s first performance, then, the Easter Vigil would not have been officially celebrated in England for almost forty years, and no living person anywhere in Europe could have celebrated the service in quite the way that it is evoked in the play. This means that Shakespeare's allusions cannot be read as mere detritus from the Catholic past, much less as secret signals to the recusants in his audience. Rather, his use of the Easter Vigil asks us to look harder at the historical record for evidence of what Englishmen and -women might have known about the ceremony and how they might have read it as commenting on Shylock's conversion.

Protestant familiarity with the Vigil appears to have come through multiple channels. First, and most obviously, Protestants might have known of the service from England's pre-Reformation past: at the time of *Merchant*'s first performances, anyone over the age of fifty would have been old enough both to have experienced the service and to remember it, and a certain number of younger people might have either heard about it from their parents or have encountered the liturgy in textual form.[21] Given the play's heavy reliance on the language of the Exultet, it is likely that Shakespeare's own familiarity with the Easter Vigil was at least partly textual – and *Hamlet* gives us another reason to believe that Shakespeare may have had access to either the pre-Reformation Sarum missal or the post-Tridentine Roman missal.[22] Although John Shakespeare's traditionalist leanings are well known, such texts were not exclusively familiar to recusants. After Elizabeth's accession many basically conforming Protestants continued to hold on to articles from their Catholic past, just as many parishes did – whether from nostalgia, inertia, or simply as a hedge against another national change in religion.[23] There are even hints in parish records that the Easter Vigil service may have continued to be celebrated in some form in a handful of places in Elizabethan England and post-Reformation Germany, and not necessarily by those who resisted the new religion.[24] The other obvious vehicle for Protestant encounters with the Easter Vigil is travel to Catholic countries or the narratives of those who had. Anthony Munday's *English Romaine Life* (1582), for example, includes a detailed description of a vigil he witnessed at Rome that even featured the baptism of adult Jewish converts.[25]

But although the liturgy's medieval past and its Catholic present were surely important to its continuing familiarity, surprisingly few works discuss the Easter Vigil in those contexts (or associate the liturgy with popery or superstition).[26] Instead, most of the works I have found discuss the Easter Vigil as celebrated within the early Church. They also indicate widespread familiarity with two of the elements most pertinent to Shakespeare's evocation of the service in *Merchant*: the Exultet and the ancient practice of Eastertide baptisms. Although I cannot find the Exultet printed in full in any work published in the British Isles after Mary's death, lines from the hymn crop up in numerous works. This should not be surprising: the hymn, which dates back to the fourth century, was frequently assigned to the authorship of Augustine, Ambrose, or Gregory the Great, and its theology has an equally venerable pedigree.[27] Perhaps for these reasons, when Protestants quote the Exultet, they seem to expect their readers to know it. Several writers quote lines with no attribution at all,[28] while others identify the source in a minimal way, as 'benedictione cerei' [blessing of candles] or 'Gregory' or 'Ambrose'.[29] Most significantly, two works by prominent churchmen, bishops John Jewel and Joseph Hall, each use the text of the Exultet as evidence against Catholic controversialists, quoting passages from the hymn to prove the antiquity of Protestant doctrines about the Eucharist and salvation, respectively.[30] In other words, both men treat the hymn as an authentically Christian document rather than one tainted by association with Catholicism. But if the Exultet appears to have been a relatively familiar feature of the Easter Vigil, baptism is unquestionably the best-known aspect of the service. References to the early Church's custom of Eastertide baptisms appear in early modern sermons again and again,[31] and the tradition is also mentioned in the Elizabethan Book of Common Prayer, in the header introducing the rite of baptism.[32]

In the popular imagination, then, the Easter Vigil seems to have been far more closely linked to the early Church than to the Catholic Church. This is equally true of Shakespeare's use of the allusion, for *Merchant* goes out of its way to focus on the less controversial aspects of the service. The play omits, for example, any reference to the blessing of new fire or of holy water, rites that Protestants almost universally condemned for their pagan overtones, and even its evocation of the paschal candle transforms that candle into a simple source of illumination far off in Portia's household; it is not blessed, as in Catholic worship, nor does it have any sacramental force. Although Portia moralizes upon the candle using Christological language that echoes the Exultet, in the play the candle is merely a metaphor or a symbol for Christ, rather than a sacred object itself. Some members of Shakespeare's original audience might still have reacted negatively to the allusions as a result of the liturgy's Catholic associations, but the play works to diminish that likelihood by focusing on things that Catholics and Protestants could broadly agree upon.[33]

Shylock's conversion is one of those things. It is not merely that, in the face of Jewish difference, intra-Christian differences look comparatively minor, though that is true, too. Rather, the period evoked by the Easter Vigil is one where the line between Jew and Christian was relatively thin, and the erasure of Jewish difference becomes an erasure of Christian difference. Just as the Exultet's 'this is the night' collapses the Exodus, the crucifixion, and the present liturgy into one single moment, so does Shakespeare's evocation of the Easter Vigil collapse Christian history into a Christian eternity that exists outside of time and denominational division, simultaneously conjuring up the early Church, the medieval Church, and even – through his elimination of the liturgy's more 'popish' elements – a prospectively reunified and purified Christianity. Shylock's and Jessica's conversions, then, become part of the same collapsing of time and religious identity, at once gesturing backward to the moment before Christianity was Christianity and forward to a day when Catholic and Protestant, Jew and gentile are once more the same. The fact that even Shylock is briefly aligned with Christ could be read as the play's most radical denial of religious difference.

Of course, such a denial is not sustainable in the real world of late-sixteenth-century England, and neither is such an ahistorical understanding of a service so closely linked to two discrete moments in Christian history. Indeed, the Easter Vigil's ambiguous status in Protestant England means that the play's use of it potentially undermines the supersessionist argument expressed in the liturgy itself: Christian history is not, as it turns out, a narrative of continuity where the roots of today's faith are easily discernible in the past. Even if the play's evocation of the Easter Vigil conjured up only associations with the early Church and even if Protestants had wholly positive feelings about that part of their past, the allusion could not help but signal the impermanence of religious practice. Centuries earlier the vigil lost its baptisms of converts and its night-time setting; forty years earlier, England lost the service entirely. However unwittingly, the liturgy shows Christian history to be a history of change.

Shakespeare's allusions to the Easter Vigil therefore suggest three different ways of reading the play's attitude toward Shylock's conversion. The first is simply supersessionist. In this interpretation, the allusions I have traced add more evidence to the case that Lewalski and others made decades ago. This is a plausible reading, though one that does not do full justice to the complexities of either the Easter Vigil or Shakespeare's play. A second interpretation, for which I have been arguing in most of this chapter, sees *Merchant*'s use of the liturgy as reflecting a generally supersessionist theology in the service of a broadly inclusive vision. Shakespeare's allusions to a well-known practice from the earliest days of Christianity serve to unite his audience in a common identity based on their shared past as both Christians and Jews. The play is unquestionably more interested in Christian harmony than in Christian–Jewish harmony, but it includes the Jews (at least notionally and rhetorically) in its vision of a world without religious difference. Given the festive energies of Act 5, I read the allusion as an ecumenical celebration of Easter that dissolves Jewish difference and the disruptive forces of Shylock's grief and hatred. This reading does not ask us to ignore the hypocrisy or the selfishness of the play's Christian characters and neither does it deny the humanity and generosity in Shakespeare's depiction of Shylock, but it recognizes the limits of that generosity in Renaissance Europe. An early modern Christian might well have found Antonio's treatment of Shylock abominable, and perhaps even have interpreted Shylock's vengefulness as the result of years of mistreatment and marginalization, but he would still have assumed the non-negotiable truth of Christianity. For an early modern Christian, feeling Shylock's pain is perfectly compatible with rejoicing at his conversion.

That said, I believe it is possible to read the play's use of the Easter Vigil in a third way, one that views the celebration of Shylock's conversion more skeptically and undermines the kind of happy endings set forth in my first two interpretations. The play, in my estimation, does not foreground an ironic reading, but it does not foreclose one, either. In this interpretation, Jewish conversions cannot provide evidence of Christianity's claim to an unbroken chain of succession from Abraham, because the Easter Vigil shows even Christian history to be discontinuous and unstable. Darker readings of the play require ignoring much of the comedy of Act 5 and treating the play's happy ending far more suspiciously than we treat the endings of plays that do not implicate Shakespeare in prejudices from which we would rather exempt him. Nevertheless, there are good reasons not to want to stage a play that presents a forced conversion as a cause for celebration, and familiarity with the liturgy's complicated history permits us to see the play as resisting its own liturgical and theological arguments. But whether we understand *Merchant* as celebrating Shylock's conversion or not, the echoes of the ancient Easter service ensure that he is a palpable presence until play's end.

Notes

1 See, for example, M. J. Metzger, '"Now by My Hood, A Gentle and No Jew": Jessica, *The Merchant of Venice*, and the Discourse of Early Modern English Identity', *PMLA*, 113:1 (1998), 59–60; M. Berley, 'Jessica's Belmont Blues: Music and Merriment in *The Merchant of Venice*', in J. V. Mirollo and P. Herman (eds), *Opening the Borders: Inclusivity in Early Modern Studies* (Newark: Delaware University Press, 1999), pp. 185–205; L. Lampert, *Gender and Jewish Difference from Paul to Shakespeare* (Philadelphia: University of Pennsylvania Press, 2005), pp. 165–7; K. Gross, *Shylock Is Shakespeare* (Chicago: University of Chicago Press, 2006), pp. 30–1; J. Adelman, *Blood Relations: Christian and Jew in 'The Merchant of Venice'* (Chicago: University of Chicago Press, 2008), pp. 76–7; A. Kitch, 'Shylock's Sacred Nation', *Shakespeare Quarterly*, 59:2 (2008), 154–5. Of course, there is a long tradition of reading Act 5 as a wholly harmonious conclusion to the play, but such readings generally draw no meaningful connection between the satisfying closure of the play's love and friendship plots and Shylock's conversion in the previous act; in such readings Shylock is no more or less important to the play in which he appears than Malvolio is to his. See, e.g., C. L. Barber, *Shakespeare's Festive Comedy* (Princeton: Princeton University Press, 1959), p. 187; L. Danson, *The Harmonies of 'The Merchant of Venice'* (New Haven: Yale University Press, 1978), pp. 170–95.

2 The conclusion of *A Midsummer Night's Dream* seems an especially relevant analogue. The bed-blessing functions, in itself, as a satisfying and celebratory conclusion. But as the fairies bless the future issue of Theseus and Hippolyta's bed, those audience members who catch the allusion will realize that, as happy as the couple may now be, a much darker future lies ahead. Perhaps not coincidentally, the bed-blessing is also (like the allusions to the Easter Vigil that I will expand upon) a pre-Reformation practice.

3 For the early history of the Easter Vigil service, see T. M. Finn, 'It Happened One Saturday Night: Ritual and Conversion in Augustine's North Africa', *Journal of the American Academy of Religion*, 58:4 (1990), 589–616; T. F. Kelly, *The Exultet in Southern Italy* (Oxford: Oxford University Press, 1996), pp. 31–43; J. W. Tyrer, *Historical Survey of Holy Week: Its Services and Ceremonials* (Oxford: Oxford University Press, 1932), pp. 147–74. The medieval history of the liturgy is summarized by F. C. Senn in *The People's Work: A Social History of the Liturgy* (Minneapolis: Fortress, 2006), pp. 162–5. A movement to restore the Easter Vigil to Churches in the Anglican Communion began in the nineteenth century, but the liturgy was not actually added to the Book of Common Prayer until the 1970s.

4 Thirty-five years ago, M. L. Gnerro noted the presence of this allusion in a short essay, 'Easter Liturgy and the Love Duet in *MV* 5.1', *American Notes & Queries* (October 1979), 19–21. However, Gnerro does not pursue the full extent of this allusion, and the few scholars who have either cited him or noted the allusion on their own tend to be using it in the service of more or less tendentious arguments about Shakespeare's alleged Catholic sympathies. See M. Wynn-Davies, 'Rubbing at Whitewash: Intolerance in *The Merchant of Venice*', in Richard Dutton and Jean E. Howard (eds), *A Companion to Shakespeare's Works: The Comedies* (Oxford: Blackwell, 2005), p. 366; C. Asquith, *Shadowplay: The Hidden Beliefs and Coded Politics of William Shakespeare* (New York: Public Affairs, 2005), pp. 119–21; D. Teti, 'The Unbloody Sacrifice: The Catholic Theology of Shakespeare's *Merchant of Venice*', *Interpretation: A Journal of Political Philosophy*, 33:1 (2006), 45–91.

5 In *Il Pecorone*, as in other similar pound-of-flesh stories, the Shylock figure merely tears up the bond and departs in a fury. Shakespeare also reduces the usual financial cost of conversion, allowing Shylock to keep half his goods; throughout Europe, even willing Jewish converts were expected to forfeit all their goods.

6 B. K. Lewalski, 'Biblical Allusion and Allegory in *The Merchant of Venice*', *Shakespeare Quarterly*, 13:3 (1962), 327–43. See also J. S. Coolidge, 'Love and Law in *The Merchant of Venice*', *Shakespeare Quarterly*, 27:3 (1976), 243–63; and Danson, *Harmonies*, pp. 55–81.

7 J. Shapiro, *Shakespeare and the Jews* (New York: Columbia University Press, 1996).

8 A partial list of the works that consider *Merchant* in terms of early modern conceptions of Jewish identity includes Adelman, *Blood Relations*; Lampert, *Gender and Jewish Difference*; Metzger, '"Now by My Hood"'; Kitch, 'Sacred Nation'; and M. L. Kaplan, 'Jessica's Mother: Medieval Constructions of Jewish Race and Gender in *The Merchant of Venice*', *Shakespeare Quarterly*, 58:1 (2007), 1–30.

9 Adelman, *Blood Relations*, p. 4.

10 See, e.g., *ibid.*, pp. 66–98; Lampert, *Gender and Jewish Difference*, pp. 160–7; Shapiro, *Shakespeare and the Jews*, pp. 131–65; Metzger, '"Now by My Hood"', 52–63. M. L. Kaplan is among those who see a smoother path to assimilation for Jessica than for her father – based on her gender and her marriage into the nobility. See Kaplan, 'Jessica's Mother'.

11 English translation taken from the 1970 Roman missal, lines 30–55. For the full Latin text of the Easter Vigil in something close to the form that Shakespeare most likely knew, see *The Sarum Missal: Edited from Three Early Manuscripts*, ed. J. W. Legg (Oxford: Clarendon Press, 1916), pp. 115–34.

12 For more on the apocalyptic significance of Jessica and Shylock's conversions, see Lewalski, 'Allusion and Allegory', 334, 341; Shapiro, *Shakespeare and the Jews*, pp. 133–4.

13 See especially T. J. Talley, *The Origins of the Liturgical Year* (New York: Pueblo Publishing Company, 1991), pp. 5–7, 49–50.

14 See Tyrer, *Historical Survey*, pp. 147–69.

15 See, e.g., Lewalski, 'Allusion and Allegory', 343; Coolidge, 'Love and Law', 261–3.

16 For this reading, see especially Berley, 'Belmont Blues', pp. 185–204.

17 In fact, Antonio seems less like a typical Christ figure than like Isaac bound for sacrifice on Mount Moriah – an event linked in both Judaism and Christianity to the Passover. Late Second Temple and Rabbinic Judaism traditionally read Isaac not as a helpless child, but as a young man who willingly submitted himself to God's demand for sacrifice. The earliest Christians inherited this reading and assimilated it to their understanding of Jesus' sacrifice. Isaac is therefore a type of Christ. See Talley, *Origins of the Liturgical Year*, pp. 49–50; Jon D. Levenson, *The Death and Resurrection of the Beloved Son: The Transformation of Child Sacrifice in Judaism and Christianity* (New Haven: Yale University Press, 1995), pp. 111–12, 125–42.

18 The term 'patens' is more strongly associated with the Catholic Church than the English, but it is used in the Book of Common Prayer in both its 1549 and 1662 editions.

19 For a somewhat different take on the way Shylock aligns with early Jewish–Christian converts, see ch. 3 of J. R. Lupton, *Citizen-Saints: Shakespeare and Political Theology* (Chicago: University of Chicago Press, 2005).

20 E. Duffy, *The Stripping of the Altars: Traditional Religion in England 1400–1580*, 2nd edn (New Haven: Yale University Press, 2005), pp. 29–31; Senn, *People's Work*, pp. 162–5.

21 Apart from England's return to Catholicism under Mary, evidence that the Easter Vigil service was restored and being observed even up to the eve of Elizabeth's accession comes from sources that describe the centrality of the paschal candle to London parish life. See *Articles to be enquired of in the generall visitation of Edmonde Bisshoppe of London* (London, 1554), sig. Cii 1r and the March 21, 1558 entry from *A London Provisioner's Chronicle, 1550–1563, by H. Machyn: Manuscript, Transcription, and Modernization*, at http://quod.lib.umich.edu/m/machyn/, accessed November 18, 2016.

22 The Sarum rite was the most widespread Christian rite in pre-Reformation and Marian England. However, the post-Tridentine Roman rite soon became the standard for most of the Catholic Church. Stephen Greenblatt has noted that Hamlet's 'hic et ubique?' (1.5.158) is likely an echo of the Sarum liturgy for the dead (in fact this portion of the liturgy is the same in both the Sarum and the Roman rites): *Hamlet in Purgatory* (Princeton: Princeton University Press, 2001), pp. 16, 234–5.

23 Upon Mary's succession, most churches had found themselves suddenly needing to reacquire, often at great expense, items that had been sold, destroyed, or given away only a few years earlier. See, for example, A. Walsham, *Church Papists: Catholicism, Conformity, and Confessional Polemic in Early Modern England* (Woodbridge: Boydell Press, 1993), pp. 14–21; Duffy, *The Stripping of the Altars*, pp. 570–93; Patrick Collinson, 'William Shakespeare's Religious Inheritance and Environment', in *Elizabethans* (Cambridge: Cambridge University Press, 2003), pp. 222–7, 231–2.

24 Research undertaken by the Oxford Movement into the ceremonies of the post-Reformation Church quotes an entry from the account books for St. Mary's parish in Shrewsbury which shows payments for wax for the paschal candle during

Elizabeth's reign (no specific year is noted). Since there is no rite involving a paschal candle in the sixteenth-century Book of Common Prayer – all ceremonial candles were seen as 'popish' – this strongly suggests the continuing celebration of the Easter Vigil service at least at this one parish, and at least for a short while into Elizabeth's reign. See *Hierurgia Anglicana or Documents and Extracts Illustrative of the Ritual of the Church of England after the Reformation* (London, 1848), p. 346. R. Bagnall, a Lutheran liturgist, has also found evidence that Lutherans in Dessau in the 1540s continued to celebrate a form of the Easter Vigil liturgy that involved the singing of the Exultet. See 'Liturgia Augustana: The Paschal Vigil', *Lutheran Forum*, 24:1 (1990), 25–6.

25 Munday's description of the conversion of Jews during the Easter Vigil service takes place in Rome, rather than Venice, but it highlights many of the same features as the allusion in Shakespeare's play, including the paschal candle. Despite Shakespeare's known associations with Munday, to my knowledge no one has noted the similarities between *Merchant* and this passage from Munday. See *English Romaine Life* (London, 1582), pp. 32–3.

26 I have found one wholly negative account by a Marian exile, who translates the Easter Vigil service into English with the stated purpose of showing the English exactly how offensive they should find their participation in it; three other works single out for negative attention certain rites within the Vigil, specifically the blessing of fire, the paschal candle, and holy water. See N. Dorcastor, *The Doctrine of the Masse Booke* (Wyttonburg [London?], 1554), sigs. Biiii 4^{v}–7^{r}, Ciii–Ciiii 3^{r}; T. Naogeorg's *The Popish Kingdom*, trans. B. Googe (London, 1570), p. 52; P. van Marnix van St. Aldegonde, *Bee Hive of the Romish Church*, trans. G. Gylpen (London, 1579), sigs. 128^{v} and 223^{r}; T. Becon, *Reliques of Rome* (London, 1563), sigs. 166^{r}–167^{r}. Despite his dislike of the rites of hallowing, Becon still expends several sentences on the debate over the authorship of the Exultet and elsewhere speaks approvingly of the primitive Church's custom of limiting baptisms to Easter and Pentecost (sigs. 166^{r}, 95).

27 The ascription of the Exultet to Augustine rests partly on Augustine's own claim to have written a hymn in praise of candles and partly on the great antiquity of an Easter Vigil liturgy involving the blessing of the paschal candle. A number of different blessings with similar tropes and forms once existed, and the Exultet itself appears to be a composite text, with parts dating from the fourth century and parts as late as 600 CE. See Kelly, *Exultet in Southern Italy*, pp. 31–53.

28 One interesting example comes from a contestant in the 'querelle des femmes' who takes the four lines that describe the 'necessary fault of Adam' and claims that it is actually Eve whose actions the verse redeems. D. T. [Daniel Tuvell], *Asylum Veneris, or a sanctuary for ladies* (London, 1616), p. 9. For other texts that quote the Exultet without attribution, see G. Goodman, *The Fall of Man* (London, 1616), p. 435, and C. Hampton, *Threefold State of Man upon Earth* (Dublin, 1620), p. 61.

29 J. Jewel, *Replie Unto M. Hardings Answeare* (London, 1565), p. 337; J. Hall, *The Olde Religion* (London, 1628), p. 46, marginal note; G. Downame, *A Treatise of Justification* (London, 1633), p. 551. All three identify their quotations as being from the Easter Vigil service, though only Jewel gives a detailed citation ('they

were wonte to singe at the blissinge of the P. Taper, *Haec sunt festa Paschalia, in quibus verè Agnus occiditur. This is the Paschal Feaste, wherein verily, and indeede the Lambe is slaine'*). Both Hall and Downame cite their source as 'benedictione cerei'.

30 Jewel quotes the 'this is our paschal feast' portion of the Exultet (see previous note) to argue that 'verily' does not mean Christ's body and blood are literally present in the Eucharist (Jewel, *Replie*, p. 337), while Hall argues that the Catholic Church misunderstands the way the ancients used the word 'merit', and uses the 'O felix culpa' portion of the Exultet as proof that redemption is not something human beings earned (Hall, *Olde Religion*, p. 46).

31 For a few of the many references to Eastertide baptisms, see D. Chytraeus, *A postil or orderly disposing of certeine epistles usually red in the Church of God*, trans. A. Golding (London, 1570), pp. 98–9; H. Clapham, *Theological Axioms* (London, 1597), esp. sig Biii 1^{v}; L. Andrewes, 'A Sermon Preached before the King's Majestie at White-Hall, on the V. of Aprill, A. D. MDCXVIII, being Easter Day', in *XCVI Sermons* (London: 1629), pp. 529–30; J. Donne, *Complete Sermons*, 10 vols, ed. G. R. Potter and E. Simpson (Berkeley: University of California Press, 1953–62), vol. 5: pp. 162, 222.

32 See the 1559 Book of Common Prayer, at http://justus.anglican.org/resources/bcp/1559/Baptism_1559.htm, accessed November 18, 2016.

33 In *Shakespeare's Tribe: Church, Nation, and Theatre in Renaissance England*, J. Knapp argues persuasively for just this kind of broad-based, inclusive Christianity on the part of both Shakespeare and the Renaissance stage more generally (Chicago: University of Chicago Press, 2002).

2

Protestant faith and Catholic charity: negotiating confessional difference in early modern Christmas celebrations

Phebe Jensen

At the end of John Taylor's pamphlet *The Complaint of Christmas* (1631), the narrator (Christmas), coming to the end of his travels through Catholic and Protestant Europe, sums up the lessons of his trip:

> The Roman Catholics boast they have Charity living with them (which they reverence as much as they do their Saints) by which, with the help of good works they hope to merit [salvation]. Alas, alas, they are deceived, their Charity will do them little good, except they have the help of her elder sister, Faith. Therefore I think it not amiss, if the Romanists would borrow some of our Faith for some of their Charity and good deeds, for we want one, as much as they do the other.[1]

This passage is predictably anti-Romanist in claiming that Catholics lack faith, but the final sentence strikingly admits that Protestants would do well to adopt Catholic forms of charity – thereby voicing the common Catholic complaint that the reformed faith had banished charity when it rejected a theology of works.[2]

Published in 1631 and so predating the better-known controversy over Christmas in the 1640s, Taylor's pamphlet epitomizes the role the holiday came to occupy in late Tudor and early Stuart English religious culture, when Christmas celebrations provided a place for recusant Catholics, church papists, and conservative and mainstream Protestants to meet, literally and figuratively, and share plum puddings, games of cards and dice, doctrinally innocuous carols, and a Christian story whose edges had been softened to blur divisive doctrinal differences. This Christmas *détente* was possible partly because of the holiday's traditional association with benign communal good-will, though it was in fact during this period that this idea (so important to the later, Victorian reconfiguration of Christmas) was solidified.[3] In addition to the obvious liturgical changes in the religious celebration of Christmas at the Reformation, subtle adjustments to popular devotional customs, including the English carol, made Christmas less devotionally inflected, therefore allowing it to be shared by English Christians with different doctrinal orientations. At the same time, the secular elements of the holiday's celebration became more central to its cultural meaning, as the peaceful celebration of Christmas became increasingly defined as an ancestral inheritance that set the English apart from their more contentious neighbors on the Continent.[4] Taylor's pamphlet, in the context of other late Tudor and early Stuart representations of Christmas in carols, ballads, and Thomas Nashe's *Summers Last Will and Testament*, illustrates the way that at Christmas sectarian differences were negotiated and at times put aside in favor of communal harmony.

The unity offered by Christmas did not, however, include those religious believers who most threatened English harmony in this period: hotter Protestants who denounced the holiday absolutely, and at the other end of the spectrum, Catholic recusants who in isolated communities seized on Christmas as a way to define their opposition to mainstream religious culture.[5] But the presence in English society of such extremists only served to bring everyone in the vast middle of the religious spectrum together. For everyone but these fringe groups, the twelve days of Christmas became an important space for compromise, as Christmas was rebranded as an English holiday that transcended the country's religious divides.

Although at the Reformation the liturgical celebration of Christmas was transformed, most of the traditional secular pastimes associated with the Twelve Days in late-medieval England continued with relatively minor changes, as Ronald Hutton has shown.[6] The purpose of Protestant calendrical reform was to banish non-biblical saints from popular worship and to refocus devotion on events recorded in the New Testament, specifically in the life of Christ and his family: the only saints commemorated with holy days in Thomas Cranmer's Book of Common Prayer (1549) were the twelve disciples, four evangelists, and St. Stephen, whose martyrdom (described in Acts) has biblical sanction. Given these criteria, it happened that the twelve days of Christmas needed little in the way of reforming. The Twelve Days began with the Nativity on December 25, followed by St. Stephen's day on December 26, St. John the Evangelist's day on December 27, and on the 28th, the Feast of the Holy Innocents. With the neat excision from December 29 of St. Thomas à Becket, the holiday continued with the celebration of the Feast of the Circumcision on New Year's Day, and Epiphany, January 5 (Twelfth Night), commemorating the visit of the Three Kings to Bethlehem.

The English Protestant monarchy took the lead in exemplifying the continued importance of Christmas to post-Reformation England. Christmas celebrations at the court of King Edward VI were elaborate, and Queen Elizabeth and King James I continued and indeed augmented the practice of holding a series of feasts with entertainment throughout the Twelve Days. Mostly these celebrations, which by the early seventeenth century had consolidated into a list of customary foods, activities, and entertainments, carried little or no potentially objectionable devotional content. The central ideal for the season was open-handed generosity, signified primarily by the copious amounts of food showered on guests. 'My master and my dame are well provided', says a servant in a seventeenth-century English carol; 'the poor as well as rich / May come, they will not grudge, / They'll think no cost too much / For time of Christmas'.[7] The principle was that rich men would turn no one away in the Christmas season; as Felicity Heal has shown, this highly impractical 'myth of hospitality' was honored more in the breach than the observance. But some gentry and aristocratic families lived up to it, and it was quite common, as Heal's analysis of household records has shown, for the wealthy to entertain their social peers as well as tenants, servants, and local social inferiors, and to make arrangements for alms of food to the poor (locals or strangers) who appeared at their gates. After the Reformation, Christmas remained the 'prime occasion in the year for the provision of general entertainment'.[8]

Traditional foods consumed during the holiday included roast meats, mince pies, and plum puddings – not the modern sweet pudding but a noxious-sounding stew of preserved meat, suet, raisins, and vinegar – washed down with wine, strong beer, and the 'strong brown ale' in the wassail cup.[9] Traditional activities included singing carols, dancing, and story-telling, preferably by the fire; George Puttenham's *Art of English Poesy* describes 'old Romances or historical rhymes, made purposely for the recreation of the common people at Christmas dinners & brideales, and in taverns & alehouses and such other places of resort'.[10] Mumming or guising – not Mummers' Plays, which developed later, but the potentially disruptive practice of calling in disguise at houses and demanding food and drink – seemed to have continued despite numerous proclamations outlawing it.[11] The games most identified with Christmas were cards and dice, the last legal only at Christmas for tradesmen, laborers, apprentices, farmers, servants, and fishermen, and only then within the master's 'house or presence'.[12] Hosting or performing plays became more common in the late sixteenth and early seventeenth century, especially at court and in the law schools and universities, though as Peter Greenfield has shown, the early modern tradition in the provinces was to host local amateurs (not professional actors) at this time of year, an aspect of holiday hosting that further reveals the importance of neighborliness to the season.[13]

Most of these customary Christmas activities are doctrinally neutral, though plays and stories could in certain situations carry a sectarian punch. But one of them was too doctrinally inflected to survive the Reformation unchanged: the traditional English Christmas carol. As Robert L. Greene notes, 'in spite of continual loose references to "old carols" in Elizabethan and Jacobean England it is no common thing to find a carol of established early date in any modern source, oral, written, or printed.'[14] In 1591 Will Summers in Thomas Nashe's pageant *Summers Last Will and Testament* registers this decline at the entrance of the character Christmas:

> Christmas, how chance thou com'st not as the rest,
> Accompanied with some music, or some song?
> A merry Carol would have graced thee well;
> Thy ancestors have us'd it heretofore.[15]

Why the English stopped singing the carols that flourished in late-medieval culture is clear from even a cursory examination of surviving fifteenth- and sixteenth-century collections, including the manuscripts of John Audelay's poems, Richard Hill's commonplace book, and the last extant sixteenth-century printed book of carols, *Kele's Carols Newly Imprinted*, compiled by Edward Kele in 1545.[16] All of these works clearly demonstrate the centrality of the veneration of Mary to popular devotion at Christmas in late-medieval England. In Kele, for example, out of fourteen extant carols, Mary appears in ten, often as the speaker or central figure. 'O my heart is woe', for example, is Mary's first-person account of the crucifixion, while in 'Our lady and her son', Mary's voice is overheard by a narrator as she laments Christ's death. In the Kele as in the Audelay and Hill collections, carols for St. John's Day invariably stress John's role as Mary's comforter; for example, in 'Mary mother, come and see: / Thy Son is nailed on a tree', Christ from the cross entrusts John with the care of his mother: 'Mother, to Johan I thee betake; / Johan, keep this woman for my sake'.[17] Elsewhere in the Kele collection an annunciation carol recounts the Archangel Gabriel's salutation, 'hail Mary full of grace', the English translation of the Latin rosary prayer. Another song begins with the Latin Marian antiphon, *Salve regina mater misericordie; / Vita, dulcedo, et spes nostra, salve*, which the carol translates into the vernacular, stressing Mary's role as an intercessor as the narrator prays: 'We sinners, lady, to thee we cry'; 'To thee we call ever at our need'; 'Thy eye of pity from us not hide / While we here in this world abide; / Thou govern us and be our guide'.[18]

Obviously, a genre so intensely focused on Mary as intercessor and object of veneration, and so saturated with the Latin phrases of Catholic devotional culture, could not survive the Reformation. When new carols appear in the seventeenth century in Catholic contexts, they tend to replicate the late-medieval focus on Mary, but that is not true, unsurprisingly, of the handful of Protestant carols that date from the sixteenth and early seventeenth centuries.[19] Of these, the longest-surviving series appears in a book of popular religious songs, John Rhodes' *The Country Man's Comfort, or Religious Recreations Fit for All Well Disposed Persons*, published in 1637 but written 'in the year of our Lord 1588, when the Devil, Pope, and Spaniard did rage against our late Q. *Elizabeth*', a polemical context that identifies these carols as distinctly

Protestant. (Rhodes's anti-papist credentials were buttressed in 1602, with *An Answer to a Romish Rime Lately Printed*, and in 1606, with a verse re-telling of the Gunpowder Plot, designed to help the ignorant so 'that they be not seduced any longer by papists'.)[20] Rhodes wrote *A Country Man's Comfort* for simple country folk, 'the Scholars of petty Schools', who ask, 'what shall we do in the long winter nights: how shall we pass away the time on Sundays, what would you have us do in the Christmas Holydays'?[21]

The answer appears in a series of Christmas carols that, as with the older carols, follows the festivals during the Twelve Days: two carols for Christmas Day, then one each for St. Stephen's Day, St. John's Day, Holy Innocents, New Year's Day, and Epiphany. The dominant characteristic of these carols, especially compared to the Kele carols, is how quickly they dispense with references to the Holy Family and avoid the emotionalism (and focus on Mary's suffering) evident in late-medieval carols. Instead, these carols put the nativity into its larger theological and salvational context. So, for example, the first 'Carrol for Christmas Day' recounts the Creation and the Fall of Man, recalls the promise that 'the womans seed / should break the Serpents head', recaps Old Testament prophecies, including the one that a 'Virgin pure' would bear the savior, and describes the life of John the Baptist. Exactly halfway through the poem 'God sent his Son, / in shape of sinful flesh', but at the nativity scene near the end of the carol the rest of the Holy Family is nowhere to be seen – only Angels, Shepherds, and the Magi are present, beholding the Christ child as he 'meekly lay swaddled in hay'.[22] The second carol, 'Remember O Thou Man' (set to music by Thomas Ravenscroft in 1611) is 'made as if it were spoken by Christ to Adam and his posterity', and avoids all mention of Mary or Joseph.[23] Even more striking is the absence of any mention of Mary in 'A Carroll for Saint Johns Day', given how closely linked Mary was with St. John in late-medieval carols.[24] The carol on the circumcision, unlike late-medieval carols that used the circumcision as the prefigurement of the passion, linking Mary's sympathetic tears at the crying of her baby to her sorrow at his death, focuses instead in good Protestant fashion on 'the true circumcision of the heart'.[25]

Such changes in the English Christmas carol at the Reformation clearly reflect the theological shift from Catholicism to Protestantism. However, a more interesting point for understanding the early modern ecumenicalism of the holiday is that the actual end product – the carols produced by militantly Protestant writers such as Rhodes – did not necessarily carry clear devotional markers. Most carols that were written in the Elizabethan and Jacobean period – including Rhodes's – are doctrinally neutral, and there is evidence they were shared by Catholics and Protestants. For example, one of the Catholic Edmund Bolton's contributions to *England's Helicon* (1600) is 'The Shepherd's Song: A Carol or Hymn for Christmas', a poem that retells the nativity from the point of view of the shepherds, fittingly for the pastoral orientation of the overall collection; the carol is utterly innocuous doctrinally, bearing no obvious Catholic or Protestant inflections.[26] The travels of another carol, 'From virgins wombe this day did spring', a carol 'For Christmas Day' that first appeared in *The Paradise of Daintie Devises* (1585), more dramatically represent the boundary-crossing abilities of Christmas carols. On its initial publication the carol was ascribed to Francis Kindlemarsh (a friend of George Gascoigne); it also focuses generally, like Rhodes's carols, on the salvational context for the nativity, the topic to which it moves almost immediately from the 'virgins womb' of the first line.[27] The carol was copied at some point by the end of the sixteenth century into a Catholic Elizabethan commonplace book with a number of recusant ballads, including 'A songe of four priests that suffered death at Lancaster to the tune of Dainty come thou to me'.[28] Either before or after that transcription the text was used by William Byrd, who set it to music in *Songs of Sundrie Natures*, and whose biography expresses the compromise and negotiation typical of many Catholics in Protestant English culture: himself a recusant, he was assimilated in Protestant culture through his role as a royal musician at the court of Elizabeth, though he spent the last thirty years of his life in semi-retirement in Essex among fellow Catholics, writing music for the Latin mass.[29] Finally, 'From Virgins Womb' appeared in a Catholic book published in Rouen in 1604, *Epitaphs, the First, upon the Death of… Marie, Late Queene of Scots*, where it is one of two Christmas carols that appear in the midst of Southwell and Walpole poems and admiring memorials of Mary, Queen of Scots and the executed Elizabethan Catholic priests Nicholas Garlick, Robert Ludlam, and Richard Simpson.[30]

The peregrination of 'From Virgins Womb' provides an object lesson in how Christmas celebrations could – with the kind of repackaging and doctrinal tweaking seen in the excision of St. Thomas à Becket from the Christmas season and the demotion of Mary's role at the nativity – appeal to English Christians within the range of the confessional spectrum that reached from Catholic recusants on the one end, to mainstream Protestants on the other. However, though such relatively subtle shifts in emphasis were sufficient to allow Christmas celebrations to continue in England throughout the post-Reformation period, the holiday was simultaneously under attack by radical reformers, especially in Scotland, the Netherlands, and reportedly in Calvin's Geneva. The primary reasons for opposition to the celebration of Christmas by the godly were first, that there was no biblical precedent for the celebration of Christ's birth on December 25; second, that the holiday had unabashed pagan roots; and third, that Christmas mirth was profane and encouraged lewd behavior. This attack on Christmas was enacted into law in Scotland when Christmas and the Feasts of the Circumcision and Epiphany were outlawed by the Scottish Kirk in 1561; Christmas was similarly suppressed in

William Bradford's Plymouth, and later in the century, the Massachusetts Bay Colony passed a law declaring that 'whosever shall be found observing any such day as Christmas or the like, either by forbearing labour, feasting, or any other way upon any such account as aforesaid, every such person so offending shall pay five shillings as a fine to the county'.[31] The controversy in England over Christmas did not come to a head until 1642–43, when at the start of the Civil War the English Parliament chose to sit on Christmas Day, thereby enacting into law the views that aligned the nascent English Commonwealth with London shopkeepers who kept their businesses open – like Taylor's 'prick-ear'd Puritan' – on December 25, and provoking a pamphlet war on the subject that revealed a deep English attachment to Christmas; the holiday was restored at the Restoration in 1660. But rumors that Christmas was banished in Amsterdam and in Calvin's Geneva were widely disseminated, for example in Richard Bancroft's *A survey of the pretended holy discipline*, which asserted (erroneously) that 'Geneva hath abolished … Christmas-day, Easter-day, Ascension-day, [and] Whitsontide'.[32]

But throughout the late-Tudor and early-Stuart period there were also English objections to the holiday, of varying intensities and degrees. 'Hath Jesus Christ comen into the flesh', asks Robert Travers, in *A Learned and a Very Profitable Exposition Made upon the CXI Psalme*. '[H]ath he obtained by his coming twelve days of God the Father for carding, dicing, and looting, for masking and mumming, for mocking & mowing, for crying and laughing, for the practicing of every vain device that commeth to our heads all the year?'[33] It is not perhaps surprising to find Philip Stubbes in 1583 attacking 'cards, dice tables, masking, mumming, bowling, & such like fooleries' as part of 'wicked games used in Christmas time'.[34] But this anti-Christmas polemic also attacked the practice of neighborly hospitality. 'We keep good houses at Christmas', says a speaker in *A Dialogue between a Virtuous Gentleman and a Popish Priest* (1581), 'we are merry & have our friends about us, and many a poor body at our gates do fill their bellies with that which we leave when our bellies are full.' This statement encapsulates the central values of generosity, good fellowship, honest mirth, and charity towards the poor that were central to the season. But that speech is put into the mouth of the 'popish Priest'; to it the 'virtuous gentleman' responds that 'This is an oration, that if it had been made before the devil, it would have pleased him very well.'[35] This argument is replicated in Thomas Lovell's *A Dialogue between Custom and Verity Concerning the Use and Abuse of Dancing and Minstrelsy* (1581), dedicated to two godly Church of England vicars, Thomas Brasbridge and Robert Crowley. Custom's opinion is that 'Christmas is a merry time, good mirth therefore to make: / Young men and maids together may their legs in dances shake'; Verity responds that 'filthy dancing is no mirth', and attacks 'men of countenance and wealth' who host 'Cards and Dice', and encourage 'wantons, drunkards, gluttons, and in lusts, Idolatry'.[36] Christmas celebrations were excuses for greed and gluttony, and the mingling of the profane with the sacred so anathema to Protestant reformers (as it was also to the post-Tridentine Catholic Church). The argument was not against charity, but as the 'virtuous gentleman' puts it, 'prefer[ing] one time before another, as your Christmas': Christians should practice hospitality at all times, and not make 'a difference of days, months, & times'.[37]

Against this backdrop of overt opposition to Christmas, the holiday in Elizabethan and Jacobean England begins to come into focus as a time during which feasting and reveling, especially with neighbors of different devotional orientations, could be a self-conscious show of English unity in the face of religious sectarianism. A striking aspect of the Christmas hosting in this period is the breadth of participation from families throughout the devotional spectrum. Unlike the godly in Amsterdam or Scotland, hotter Protestants in England seemed to have defied their brethren's more radical attacks on the holiday, and hosted their neighbors and dependants extensively, presumably inspired not by the salvific function of good works but by a Reformed understanding of the Christian injunction to neighborliness and charity. Though dicing, dancing, and other especially objectionable elements of the holidays may have been absent from such occasions, some more godly Protestants were known as good Christmas hosts, including Richard Stonley of Essex, John Bruen of Cheshire, and the Suffolk gentleman Sir Edward Lewkenor.[38] On the other end of the spectrum Catholics were famous for Christmas hospitality, extending Christmas largesse across confessional boundaries. This was especially true of the Petre family of Essex (neighbors to William Byrd in the early seventeenth century); as Heal notes, at their extensive Christmas feasts 'there must have been a substantial core of Catholics among the guests', yet Church of England clergymen were also invited, and 'there was no attempt to exclude non-Catholics'.[39]

Aside from Catholic families, the social group most known for Christmas hospitality was the English clergy. Archbishop Whitgift (according to his first biographer in 1612) 'always [kept] a great and bountiful house .... And at Christmas, especially, his gates were always open, and his Hall set twice or thrice over with strangers'.[40] Lancelot Andrewes was similarly famous for hospitality, 'his Table being ever bountifully and neatly furnished with provisions ... that his guests would often profess ... that his Lordship kept *Christmas* all the year'.[41] Tobie Matthew, the Archbishop of York, hosted an extraordinary series of Christmas feasts throughout the Twelve Days at Bishopthorpe in 1624, feasting in succession tenants, local gentry, local Church officials, and at least one group of artisans (the apothecaries); in the heavily Catholic North of England, these neighbors would have naturally included a large Catholic contingent.

Especially in light of the sectarian divisions that were plaguing much of Europe in the late sixteenth and early seventeenth century, the ability of the English to unite in the celebration of Christ's nativity begins to be noted in the popular literature as a mark of national and cultural exceptionalism. This idea is crudely expressed in Thomas Churchyard's patriotic ballad, 'The Misery of Flanders, Calamity of France, Misfortune of Portugal, Unquietness of Ireland, Troubles of Scotlande: And the Blessed State of England'. One sign of England's peacefulness included the unity of Christmas celebrations:

> Here mercy rules, and mildness reigns,
> and peace great plenty brings:
> And solace in his sweetest voice,
> The Christmas carol sings.
> Here friends may feast, and triumph too,
> in surety void of ill:
> And one the other welcome make,
> with mirth and warm good will.[42]

The 'Pleasant country … ditty: merrily showing how to drive the cold winter away' also emphasizes the importance of Christmas in smoothing over neighborly divisions, and though these are not explicitly devotional the emphasis on unity rather than division could also have extended to sectarian tensions, as neighbors gather, 'Forgetting old wrongs, / With Carols and Songs' as 'Old grudges forgot / are put in the Pot' and 'kind neighbours together meet'.[43]

This patriotic dimension of Christmas Christian unity is also evident in laments for the decline of Christmas that increased in number and intensity around the turn of the century.[44] Christmas laments, which nostalgically located the true English Christmas spirit in the past, were one segment of larger satirical attacks on the wealthy in the face of social and economic crises, including the concentration of wealth in London, the crisis in poor relief, the continuing ill effects of enclosure, and food supply emergencies resulting from bad harvests.[45] But there was a sectarian dimension to these satires, one that joined social conservatives of different devotional allegiances. That alliance is quite strikingly suggested by a 'Song bewailing the time of Christmas' that appears, like 'From Virgins Womb', in both Catholic and Protestant contexts: printed as a ballad in 1635, it also survives in a slightly different version in a manuscript book compiled by the Catholic Shanne family between 1611 and 1632. The ballad claims gentry and nobility have 'flown, to London-ward / Where they in pomp and pleasure do waste, / That which Christmas was wonted to feast', illustrating this outrage with conventional motifs: an abandoned country home with cold chimneys, dead livestock, and plowmen and farmers ruined by the drastically jacked-up rents that support fine clothes, money 'in misers bags', coaches and other luxuries. The two versions of the ballad diverge only in the fourth stanza, in which the Catholic manuscript version puts the blame for the end of Christmas solely at the feet of Protestants:

Go to the *Protestant*, he'll protest, he'll protest, he'll protest,
He will protest and boldly boast;
And to the *Puritan*, he is so hot, he is so hot, he is so hot
He is so hot he will burn the Roast;
The *Catholic* good deeds will not scorn,
Nor will not see poor Christmas forlorn
Wellay day!
Since Holiness no good deeds will do,
Protestants had best turn Papists, too.[46]

Alternatively, in the printed version of this stanza the Protestant is replaced by a 'Country man', who protests at the thought of sacrificing his 'Bull Beef' for Christmas feasting; the hot Puritan becomes a hot Citizen; and finally, the hero of the song is not the Catholic, but the Courtier:

The Courtier he good deeds will not scorne,
Nor will he see poor Christmas forlorne,
Welladay.
Since none of these good deeds will do,
Christmas had best turn Courtier too.[47]

On the one hand these two versions reflect a division between Catholic and Protestant understandings of the decline of Christmas; the difference here shows how the substitution of a few words could give a standard satirical attack a sectarian dimension. But at the same time, the broadly moralistic content of the rest of the ballad indicates larger areas of unity on this subject between Catholics and socially conservative Protestants, who were united in their interest in defending Christmas from Puritans and misers.

The sectarian tensions that simmered under early modern English debates over Christmas can also be seen in a brief passage from Nashe's *Summers Last Will and Testament*, a pageant written and performed for a religiously centrist patron: that celebrated holiday host, Archbishop Whitgift. Nashe must have been still close enough to Whitgift, who three years earlier had probably hired him to respond to the Marprelate pamphlets, to compose *Summers Will* on short notice, when the Archbishop's household was detained at Croydon past the end of summer due to the plague.[48] Indeed, the satire of Christmas in *Summers Last Will* can perhaps be understood as a reprisal of attacks on the godly also undertaken in the Marprelate controversy. Nashe makes the character of Christmas a villain in the story: a miser (the word used is 'snudge') who is too cheap to feed his servants properly, let alone host at Christmas. When Summer admonishes him that 'Christmas is god of hospitality', Christmas responds that 'there is many an old god that is now grown out of fashion. So is the god of hospitality'.[49] These lines recall radical reformer attacks on Christmas celebrations as popish and idolatrous – a sentiment directly attributed to the Martinists by John Lyly in another of the Marprelate tracts, *Pappe with a Hatchet*.[50] Indeed, Christmas sometimes speaks the language of extreme reformers, with phrases such as 'antiquity was the mother of ignorance', 'Gluttony is a sin', 'Feasts are but puffing up of the flesh', and the claim that feasting originated with Roman emperors who were 'tyrants, whoremasters, unthrifts'.[51] The association of godly language with economic motives replicates typical polemical rhetoric that exposed Puritan hypocrisy, so that religious language was revealed as a mask for craven appetites, as in the grotesque figure of the stage Puritan.[52] In response, Will Summers delivers the authorial position that reiterates the Elizabethan *via media* on festivity, reflecting Whitgift's own reputation as a generous and tolerant host, and identifying Christmas hosting as an English ancestral heritage:

It is the honor of Nobility
To keep high days and solemn festivals,
Then, to set their magnificence to view,
To frolic open with their favorites,
And use their neighbours with all courtesy.
(*Summers Last Will*, lines 1722–9)

The tensions over Christmas evident in Nashe's pageant and Elizabethan sectarian controversy become more overtly political when, beginning in 1615, King James issued a series of proclamations, buttressed by a 1616 Star Chamber speech, that ordered the gentry and aristocracy to return to the country and 'keep House and Hospitality'.[53] The campaign did not only concern Christmas, and it needs to be seen as part of the King's response to larger social and economic problems.[54] But the proclamations did single out Christmas hospitality as an 'ancient and laudable custom of this Realm' that set England apart from 'the manner in foreign countries', therefore putting into political terms the cultural association of Christmas with English national identity.[55] James I's initiative on Christmas is clearly reflected in Taylor's *Complaint of Christmas*, the pamphlet that ends with the strikingly ecumenical suggestion that Protestant faith could use a little bolstering with Catholic charity, and vice versa, and a work that sums up the prevailing ideas about Christmas in the period before the Civil War.[56]

As Bernard Capp has shown, John Taylor was a social conservative who 'saw the decay of traditional values epitomized in the decline of Christmas'.[57] In *The Complaint*, Taylor's social conservatism clearly trumps religious sectarianism.

In the pamphlet's plot (such as it is) Christmas literally goes between Catholics and Protestants as he travels to Russia, Muscovy, Poland, Sweden, Hungary, Austria, Bohemia, Germany, Spain, Italy, France, the Netherlands, and of course, England.[58] Christmas's picaresque journey becomes the predictable comic occasion for the satirical representation of broad cultural stereotypes, such as the brined and pickled Northerners, 'so well seasoned, that the men doe naturally sweat salt, and the women doe weep brine', and the sartorially ridiculous French, whose clothes were 'cut and slash'd and carbonadoed into Rashers, Collops, Steaks, and Spitchcocks; that it was no more but cast a handful of salt upon a Gentleman, and he was ready for the broiling'.[59] Beneath this comedy, though, is a serious point, for the overall structure of the pamphlet links the 'Christian world', underscoring the common ground that Christmas potentially creates in devotionally distinct groups.[60] As critics have shown, Taylor across his writing career was equally hostile to both Catholics and Puritans, but in *The Complaint* his essential social conservatism leads to a temporary religious plurality.[61] The pamphlet includes some predictable anti-Catholic satire (including a hilarious account of Christmas with the fish-eating Carthusian friars), but Christmas has many positive things to say about his entertainment by Catholics – even in Rome, where he 'was mightily feasted, for they thought nothing too hot, too heavy, or too dear for me: I met with no sects of dull or cynical *Diogenes*, there was no parsimonious banquets, or Philosophical kind of feasting'.[62] Here Taylor takes a swipe at hot Protestant reformers who endlessly harped on the importance of the spiritual over the gustatory gifts of the season, as in (for example) Thomas Becon's *A Christmas Banquet Garnished with Many Pleasant and Dainty Dishes*, a treatise filled with moral tidbits instead of roasted meats and mince pies.

While joining Christians from across Europe at Christmas, Taylor's pamphlet also identifies a special English attachment to the holiday. As soon as he disembarks onto English soil Christmas 'cut a caper for joy, assuring my self that I was now in my ancient Harbor or heaven of happiness', elevating his rhetoric as he apostrophizes: 'thou (o *England)* hast ever given old Christmas … good entertainment, with such cheer, hospitality, and welcome, as the Christian world never hath done the like'.[63] But in England Christmas actually finds (at first) the lack of hospitality emphasized in the lament literature. The images are again highly conventional: at a nobleman's mansion Christmas finds the gates shut, and an old serving-man complaining that the 'house that from the Conquest hath been famous for Hospitality, is now buried in her own ruins' by the profligacy of the 'young Master, who instead of making his Chimneys smoke in the Country, makes his nose smoke in a Tobacco-shop in the City'.[64] Christmas does not find that special English welcome in this shut-up aristocratic manor, nor in the empty house of a gentleman who is away in London, explicitly violating 'the Proclamation that summons all Country-Gentlemen to return into the country'.[65] But Taylor's pamphlet restores the true English Christmas by pushing its celebration down the social ladder, to the house of 'a plain Country man', a yeoman farmer who is hosting 'maid-servants' as well as plowmen and the poor.[66] This celebration includes all of the conventional Christmas food and entertainment: roasted meats, 'brave plum broth in bowl-dishes of a quart', bread, beer, cheese, cake, mince pies, the spiced ale of the Wassail bowl, 'Winter-tales', cards, carols, dancing, and 'Gambols'.[67]

The good country farmer is the rough social equivalent of the hard-working urban tradesmen (and women) who were Taylor's primary audience, and indeed, as in Taylor's work more generally, *The Complaint* forges an imaginative solidarity between the farmer who hosts Christmas in the countryside and the tradesmen and citizens at his next stop, London, where 'whole Parishes of people came to invite [me] to dinner'.[68] Finally, Christmas receives 'the most royalist, noblest, and worthiliest' entertainment of all 'at Court, Inns of Court, and Temples, where I was resident until Candlemas, and then left this Land'.[69] But the end of the pamphlet continues the lament for the failure of true Christmas hospitality with an attack on the institutionalization of poor relief – the fact that the Londoners, despite their care for Christmas, leave the poor 'to the parish', instead of welcoming them to the communal Christmas table. 'How can you make me truly welcome', Christmas laments, 'except the poor feed with me?'[70]

Christmas's critique of the Tudor and Stuart innovations in poor relief that made charity less a personal than an institutional matter is in keeping with the social conservatism John Taylor demonstrated across his career. This perceived deficiency in true Christmas Christian charity is what prompts Christmas's claim that Protestants would do well to exchange some of their 'faith' for some of the 'Charity and good deeds' practiced by Catholics. This moment of religious pluralization is prompted, then, by socially conservative views, and also by the fact that celebrating the nativity of their shared savior was one thing that Protestants and Catholics could agree on. The 'Old grudges forgot, and put in the pot' with the plum pudding each year seem to have included religious differences, making Christmas a holiday that could move a Protestant like Taylor to admit some good in Catholicism. The cultural meanings attached to Christmas in late-Tudor and early-Stuart popular literature show how once a year, the higher values of neighborliness and a shared English past could help smooth over devotional differences. These were, it seems, more easily dissipated in the presence of good food and drink, and in the spirit of communal revelry that continued to characterize the English Christmas after the Reformation.

Notes

1 J. Taylor, *The Complaint of Christmas, and the Tears of Twelfetide* (London, 1631), p. 25.
2 F. Heal, *Hospitality in Early Modern England* (Oxford: Clarendon Press, 1990), pp. 124–5.
3 On Victorian Christmas, see M. Connelly, *Christmas: A History* (London: I. B. Tauris & Co., 2012).
4 This process is akin to the shift from religious to national holidays described by D. Cressy, in *Bonfires and Bells: National Memory and the Calendar in Elizabethan and Stuart England* (Stroud: Sutton Publishing, 1980).
5 On Protestant opposition to Christmas, see C. Durston, 'Lords of Misrule: The Puritan War on Christmas, 1642–60', *History Today*, 35 (1985), 7–14; R. Hutton, *The Rise and Fall of Merry England: The Ritual Year 1400–1700* (Oxford: Oxford University Press, 1994), pp. 203–17; and R. Hutton, *The Stations of the Sun: A History of the Ritual Year in Britain* (Oxford: Oxford University Press, 1996), pp. 25–33. On the special Catholic attachment to Christmas, see J. Bossy, *The English Catholic Community, 1570–1850* (London: Darton, Longman & Todd, 1975), pp. 110–21; F. McKay, 'Survival of the Carol in the 17th Century', *Anglia*, 100 (1982), 36–48, esp. 36–7; and P. Jensen, '"Honest Mirth & Merriment": Christmas and Catholicism in Early Modern England', in L. Gallagher (ed.), *Redrawing the Map of Early Modern Catholicism* (Toronto: University of Toronto Press, 2012), pp. 213–34.
6 Hutton, *Stations*, pp. 16–18.
7 Bod. MS Eng. poet. b.5, p. 56.
8 Heal, *Hospitality*, p. 113, and on Christmas hosting, pp. 71–7.
9 Anonymous, *A Pleasant New Country Ditty, Merrily Showing How to Drive the Cold Winter Away* (London, 1625), n.p.
10 G. Puttenham, *The Art of English Poesy* (London: 1589), p. 69.
11 M. Twycross and S. Carpenter, *Masks and Masking in Medieval and Early Tudor England* (Aldershot: Ashgate, 2002), pp. 82–110; Hutton, *Stations*, pp. 11–12, 21–2, and on the multiplication of scholarly error that led to a belief in the ancientness of the Mummers' Play, pp. 70–80.
12 W. Lambarde, *Eirenarcha: Or of the Office of the Justices of Peace* (London, 1581), vol. 2: p. 376.
13 P. Greenfield, 'Festive Drama at Christmas in Aristocratic Households', in M. Twycross (ed.), *Festive Drama* (Cambridge: D. S. Brewer, 1996), pp. 34–40.
14 R. L. Greene, 'The Traditional Survival of two Medieval Carols', *English Literary History*, 7 (1940), 223–38, esp. 224. On the late-fifteenth- and early-sixteenth-century carol, see E. B. Reed (ed.), *Christmas Carols Printed in the Sixteenth Century* (Cambridge, MA: Harvard University Press, 1932); and Greene, *The Early English Carols* (Oxford: Clarendon Press, 1977); on its decline, see McKay, 'Survival', 36, and Jensen, '"Honest Mirth"', pp. 217–19.
15 T. Nashe, *Summers Last Will and Testament*, in R. B. McKerrow (ed.), *The Works of Thomas Nashe* (Oxford: Basil Blackwell, 1958), vol. 3: pp. 227–95, lines 1622–6.

16 E. Keats Whiting (ed.), *The Poems of John Audelay* (London: Early English Text Society, 1931). Hill's carols are printed in R. Dyboski (ed.), *Songs, Carols, and Other Miscellaneous Poems from the Balliol Ms. 354* (London: Early English Text Society, 1907); R. Kele, *Christmas Carols Newly Imprinted* (London, 1545). On the complex bibliography of the Kele collections see Reed, *Christmas Carols Printed in the Sixteenth Century*, pp. xxxvii–lvi.
17 Greene, *The Early English Carols*, p. 105. (Since Kele's *Christmas Carols* is unpaginated, quotations are taken from Greene's modern edition.)
18 Greene, *The Early English Carols*, pp. 162, 138.
19 Jensen, '"Honest Mirth"', p. 218.
20 J. Rhodes, *The Country Man's Comfort, or Religious Recreations Fit for All Well Disposed Persons* (London, 1637), sig. A2^{r}; *A Brief Sum of the Treason Intended Against the King and State* (London, 1606); *An Answer to a Romish Rhyme Lately Printed* (London, 1602), title-page.
21 Rhodes, *The Country Man's Comfort*, sigs. A2^{r}–A2^{v}.
22 *Ibid.*, sig. D7^{r}.
23 *Ibid.*, sigs. E^{r-v}.
24 *Ibid.*, sig. E2^{v}.
25 Ibid., sig. E5^{r}.
26 E. Bolton, 'The Shepherd's Song: A Carol or Hymn for Christmas', in H. MacDonald (ed.), *England's Helicon* (Cambridge, MA: Harvard University Press, 1962), pp. 135–6.
27 F. Kindlemarsh, 'Rejoyce, rejoyce, with hart and voice', in R. Edwards, *The Paradise of Daintie Devises* (London, 1585), sigs. B2^{v}–B3^{r}.
28 British Library MS Additional 15225; the carol is transcribed in H. Rollins (ed.), *Old English Ballads, 1553–1625, Chiefly from Manuscripts* (Cambridge: Cambridge University Press, 1920), pp. 238–9.
29 C. Monson, 'Byrd, William (1539x43–1623)', in *Oxford Dictionary of National Biography* (Oxford: Oxford University Press, 2004); online edition, January 2008, accessed November 18, 2016.
30 A. F. Allison and D. M. Rogers (eds), *The Contemporary Printed Literature of the English Counter-Reformation between 1558 and 1640* (Cambridge: Scholar Press, 1994), vol. 2: pp. 186–7.
31 Quoted in Cressy, *Bonfires and Bells*, p. 200.
32 R. Bancroft, *A Survey of the Pretended Holy Discipline* (London, 1593), p. 341.
33 R. Travers, *A Learned and a Very Profitable Exposition Made upon the CXI Psalme* (London, 1579), p. 45.
34 P. Stubbes, *The Anatomy of Abuses Containing a Discovery* (London, 1583), sig. 07^{v}.
35 I. B., *A Dialogue Between a Virtuous Gentleman and a Popish Priest* (London, 1581), sig. Diiii^{r}.
36 T. Lovell, *A Dialogue Between Custom and Verity Concerning the Use and Abuse of Dancing and Minstrelsy* (London, 1581), sig. C2^{v}.
37 I. B., *A Dialogue*, sigs. D4^{v}–D5^{r}.
38 Heal, *Hospitality*, pp. 174–7.
39 *Ibid.*, pp. 172–3.

40 Sir P. George, *The Life of the Most Reverend and Religious Prelate John Whitgift, Lord Archbishop of Canterbury* (London 1612), p. 77; Heal, *Hospitality*, pp. 280–2.
41 H. Isaacson, *The Life of the Reverend Father in God Lancelot Andrews* (London, 1650), sig. **2^{V} [*sic*]; B. Capp, *The World of John Taylor the Water Poet* (Oxford: Clarendon Press, 1994), p. 47.
42 T. Churchyard, *The Misery of Flanders, Calamity of France, Misfortune of Portugal, Unquietness of Ireland, Troubles of Scotlande: And the Blessed State of England* (London, 1579), sig. Eii^{r}.
43 Anon., *A Pleasant Country New Ditty*, n.p., *c.* 1601.
44 Heal, *Hospitality*, pp. 93–4; Hutton, *Stations*, p. 19.
45 Heal, *Hospitality*, p. 113.
46 From the manuscript version of the ballad (from British Library Additional MS 38599), printed in Rollins, *Old Ballads*, pp. 372–5, esp. pp. 372, 373–4.
47 Anon., *Christmas Lamentation for the Loss of his Acquaintance* (London, 1635), n.p.
48 On the dating (1591 or 1592) and the original performance of the pageant, see M. Axton, 'Summer's Last Will and Testament: Revel's End', in C. L. Barber and M. Axton (eds), *Thomas Nashe* (Burlington, VT: Ashgate, 2011), pp. 291–306; C. L. Barber, 'Prototypes of Festive Comedy in a Pageant Entertainment: *Summer's Last Will and Testament*', in Barber and Axton (eds), *Thomas Nashe*, pp. 261–89; and E. Cook, '"Death proves them all but toyes": Nashe's Un-idealising Show', in D. Lindley (ed.), *The Court Masque* (Manchester: Manchester University Press, 1984), pp. 17–32.
49 Nashe, *Summers Last Will*, lines 1722–9.
50 J. Lyly, *Pappe with a Hatchet* ([London?], 1589), sig. D2^{r}.
51 Nashe, *Summers Last Will*, lines 1626, 1639, 1661, 1685.
52 On the stage Puritan, see K. Poole, *Radical Religion from Shakespeare to Milton* (Cambridge: Cambridge University Press, 2000), pp. 16–44; and P. Collinson, 'Ecclesiastical Vitriol: Religious Satire in the 1590s and the Invention of Puritanism', in J. Guy (ed.), *The Reign of Elizabeth I: Court and Culture in the Last Decade* (Cambridge: Cambridge University Press, 1995), pp. 150–70.
53 James I, 'A Proclamation Commanding the Repair of Noblemen and Gentlemen into Their Several Countries', October 24, 1614, in J. F. Larkin and P. L. Hughes (eds), *Stuart Royal Proclamations* (Oxford: Clarendon Press, 1973), vol. 1: p. 324.
54 Heal, *Hospitality*, pp. 117–20, esp. p. 118. This encouragement to Christmas hospitality might also be seen in the terms proposed by Leah Marcus, who has argued that the Stuart kings encouraged regional festivity as part of a conscious project to deploy royal power through the countryside; *The Politics of Mirth* (Chicago: University of Chicago Press, 1986), pp. 1–23.
55 James I, 'His Majesties Proclamation, Requiring the Residency of Noblemen, Gentlemen, Lieutenants, and Justices of Peace, upon their chief Mansions in the Country', December 9, 1615, in Larkin and Hughes (eds), *Stuart Royal Proclamations*, vol. 1: p. 356.
56 Ben Jonson's *Christmas His Masque* of 1615–16 also reflects the prevailing cultural view of Christmas against hot Protestant attacks when the title character claims that he is 'no dangerous person … and though I come out of *Popes-head-alley*, as

good a Protestant, as any i' my Parish'; in C. H. Herford Percy and E. Simpson (eds), *Ben Jonson* (Oxford: Clarendon Press, 1941), vol. 7: p. 437. For a reading of this work as an ironic commentary on London citizen's failure to keep proper Christmas, see L. Marcus, '"Present Occasions" and the Shaping of Ben Jonson's Masques', *English Literary History*, 45 (1978), 201–25.

57 Capp, *The World of John Taylor*, pp. 100–1.

58 For parallels between *The Complaint of Christmas* and Taylor's creation of 'a distinctly English authorial persona predicted upon notions of English civility and hospitable reception' in Taylor's other travel writing, see J. Fischer, 'Fashioning Familiar Space in the Domestic Travel Writing of John Taylor the Water-Poet', *Explorations in Renaissance Culture*, 35:2 (2009), 194–219, esp. 195; see also W. W. Wooden, 'The Peculiar Peregrinations of John Taylor the Water-Poet: A Study in Seventeenth-Century British Travel Literature', *Prose Studies*, 6:1 (1983), 3–20.

59 Taylor, *The Complaint*, p. 4.

60 *Ibid.*, p. 1.

61 J. Mardock, 'The Spirit and the Muse: The Anxiety of Religious Positioning in John Taylor's Prewar Polemics', *Seventeenth Century*, 14 (1999), 1–14, esp. 3; Capp, *The World of John Taylor*, pp. 122–30.

62 Taylor, *The Complaint*, p. 2.

63 *Ibid.*, p. 8.

64 *Ibid.*, p. 10.

65 *Ibid.*, p. 19.

66 *Ibid.*, p. 21.

67 *Ibid.*, pp. 22–3.

68 *Ibid.*, p. 23; and cf. Capp, *The World of John Taylor*, pp. 66–71.

69 Taylor, *The Complaint*, p. 25.

70 *Ibid.*, p. 24.

3

Singing in the counter: goodnight ballads in *Eastward Ho*

Jacqueline Wylde

At the end of *Eastward Ho*, a play written by Chapman, Jonson, and Marston and performed at the Blackfriars, Quicksilver the prodigal tells the musical story of his downfall – from his drunkenness and womanizing, to his disgraceful release from his goldsmith apprenticeship, to his offshore financial scheme – in his ballad entitled 'Repentance'. It is, as he says, 'all the testimony I shall leave behind me to the world, and my master, who I have so offended'.[1] The song is the climax of the play, sung to convince Quicksilver's prison audience of the sincerity of his contrition, the truth of his transformation from rogue to penitent, and to articulate the religious character of his conversion. Given that the play is a sharp satire aimed at the prodigal plays popular in public theatres, it is hard to take such a song at face value; Quicksilver's conversion seems both theatrical and convenient, and the musical form that he uses to perform his conversion is hardly known to be a refined and reputable genre. Quicksilver himself acknowledges that his song is 'in imitation' of the ballad made famous by the unsavory character of Mannington, 'he that was hang'd at Cambridge, that cut off the horse's head at one blow' (5.5.37–8). But while Quicksilver sings to prove his sincerity, many critics consider his musical performance evidence of the insincerity of his conversion from spendthrift social-climber to thankful, hard-working Protestant. Brian Gibbons claims that Quicksilver's public singing implies hypocrisy 'simply by the fact that he expresses [his repentance] in Puritan jargon'. C. G. Petter, editor of the New Mermaids edition of *Eastward Ho*, states, 'Quicksilver's repentance is more expedient than sincere', while Linda Phyllis Austern agrees that the performance is 'magnificently insincere'.[2] The play is too universally satirical for the ending to be played straight and Quicksilver's piety is too overdrawn and subscribes too closely to the conventions of the conversion narrative to be genuine. He must therefore be 'converting' in order to dupe his mentor Touchstone and others into releasing him from prison.

Other interpretations have glossed over the satire of the play when it comes to the final prison conversions. David Nicol, in his review of the 2002 Royal

Shakespeare Company's performance of *Eastward Ho*, reports that the production 'took the ending at face value, and Quicksilver's repentance song was not represented comically ... the absurdities [of the lyrics] were obscured in favour of focusing on the beauty of the music, so as to emphasize sentiment over satire'. Nicol's comment underscores the centrality of the ballad to the satire of the entire play.[3] While the latter interpretation is obviously problematic for a satire, the former approach creates a mean-spirited interpretation if the flawed but generally goodhearted Touchstone is gullibly converted by the prodigal's false act of contrition. As much as *Eastward Ho* has fun at the expense of the taste of the attendees of public theatres, such a reading impoverishes its more broadly aimed satire. Paul Stevens nicely articulates the slippery duality at the heart of *Eastward Ho* by calling Quicksilver's embrace of Touchstone's ethos of thrift 'difficult to take ... at face value' given the audience makeup and the 'self-reflexive and anti-mimetic style' typical of the Blackfriars theatre in 1605. Quicksilver's scripted, rehearsed, and reproduced musical repentance, he claims, calls the sincerity of the repentance into question as the whole performance may be mere artifice, and yet 'the reality of the need for grace is not in doubt'.[4]

The ballad is at the center of the debate regarding Quicksilver's sincerity; the final act's conversions, reconciliations, and recognitions hinge on its persuasive success. Quicksilver himself identifies the ballad's indebtedness to George Mannington's popular and well-known ballad 'I wail in woe, I plunge in pain' (1576), one of many well-known goodnight ballads that circulated throughout the country.[5] A variety of broadside ballad, goodnight ballads (also known as 'neck verses' or 'the last goodnight') were sung from the perspective of the condemned before their executions.[6] They purported to be composed by the prisoners themselves, but appear to have been penned by mostly anonymous ballad writers.[7] The resulting songs could combine familiar music, catchy rhymes, and the drama of the scaffold to make persuasive moral, religious, or even confessional cases – but in such a way that eschewed divisive polemic in favor of inculcating basic religious values.

Inasmuch as artifice can simulate sincerity, it can also facilitate, communicate, and even help to create it. Quicksilver's specifically Protestant conversion is identified by his ardent psalm-singing and reference to Protestant devotional texts, but his personal religious conviction and transformation is, in a way, impossible to discern because the screens of conventional actions become more important than the emotions that should drive them; but while this issue may be worthy of satire, the capacity for conventions to give shape and meaning to, and even to create such honest emotions should not be discounted. This chapter will examine how the conventions of the goodnight ballad contribute to or even constitute both how and what the songs communicate. In *Eastward Ho*, an understanding of the public use and persuasive power of the goodnight ballads clarifies the satirical and coercive intent of the final song. Instead of dwelling on the sincerity and agenda of a single character, such a reading finds the play satirical about drama yet serious about grace, providing a commentary on how style, form, and convention can simultaneously and uneasily both facilitate and subsume sincerity and honesty.

Like other ballads, the goodnight ballads were popular forms of public entertainment, heard in myriad public places and seen on broadsides in peddlers' packs or tacked up on walls for inexpensive home decor. Ballads are strophic solo songs with narrative text and, according to Christopher Marsh, they could be heard and found everywhere in early modern England; it has been estimated that up to 4 million ballad sheets may have been printed by 1600.[8] The subjects of the ballads were many and varied, and catered to a popular audience by mixing issues of politics and religion with tales of loves won and lost, thieves executed, and babies born with three heads.

Our access to such ballads may be through print, but Bruce Smith rightly reminds us that simply reading the text of a ballad will not provide sufficient interpretation. He contends that the ballad is more than a genre and more than a medium – it is to be considered 'a complete system of communication'.[9] Ballads, Smith asserts, have implications and meanings that are physiological and physical through the act of singing; they are social in the way that they figure in the exchange of news and create certain kinds of communities through singing, participating, and listening; they are political in their statements about the object of the ballad and in their performance of different and widely varied subject positions (ballads tend to be written in the first person although not exclusively); they are psychological in their investigation of the subjecthood of another, or in the opportunity to become another person by assuming their voice.

Goodnight ballads fit well into Smith's balladic assessment as they are psychological, social, and emotional as well as both political and religious; they create communities though participation and inclusion as well as through delineation and exclusion. To my mind, the goodnight ballads are themselves something of a hybrid of the godly ballad (some of which focus on repentance or the moments before death) and the popular news ballad (wherein current and particularly criminal events were declaimed, disseminated, and interpreted via memorable musical medium, usually in the third person). They were a popular variety of ballad and would have been among the selection hawked by a ballad monger.[10]

While every goodnight ballad deviates somewhat from the conventions, most follow a highly recognizable script. The subject often begins by introducing themselves with some interesting or distinguishable personal detail and proceeds to describe a kind of chain of sin (the descent from innocence to anti-social behavior, to petty crime, to increasingly desperate actions that culminate in something terrible like murder). For example, in the ballad 'John Spenser a Chesshire gallant', Spenser's shooting ability, skill at drumming, and agility on the dance floor are depicted as amiable qualities in moderation but they seemed to have gone to the man's head. The song describes him beginning to dress in silk and satin, leaving his wife in penury while he spends their money on women and fashion, and generally 'Ryoting' until he mistakenly kills a friend in a drunken quarrel.[11] Ballads then usually proceed to briefly describe the crime. In 'A Warning for All Desperate Women' (1628), for example, the singer anticipates the crime for several stanzas, but the act itself is described bluntly and quickly: 'And then I tooke a little knife / and stab'd him in the heart. Whose Soule from Body instantly, / my bloody hand did part.'[12] In the case of the trio of ballads that concern the murder of a Master Page of Plymouth by his wife and her lover, the murder is only obliquely referred to in one of the three ballads; instead, all three ballads focus on explaining motives and expressing repentance.

By glossing over the gory details, ballads are free to emphasize the psychological process of conversion and repentance; the tension in the songs typically peaks at the lengthy description of the moment of repentance and spontaneous change of heart. There is then usually an apology to the convict's own family or community for disappointing them and bringing shame. Such an apology is an opportunity to tug on heartstrings, as when a son apologizes to his 'mother milde, and dame so deer'.[13] Following this glimpse into the personal life and emotional attachments of the convict's life, there almost always follows a warning for God-fearing folks not to follow in the footsteps of sin. Most ballads end with a plea to God for forgiveness.

Such narrative conventions are quite similar to those found in crime ballads, but the goodnight ballads distinguish themselves from their news-reporting counterparts by their formal conventions, and it is my contention that the formal conventions are what grant the songs their persuasive power. The goodnight ballads are most prominently defined by the use of the first-person perspective, a narrative technique that invites listeners to imaginatively participate in the inner life of the speaker.[14] The singer *becomes* the ballad's protagonist. In *Bartholomew Fair*, Nightingale claims that his new ballad 'A Caveat against Cutpurses' is 'made as t'were in mine own person'.[15] Bruce Smith insists 'the "I" of a song invites imaginative complicity even more insistently than a play with its diversity of characters and points of view'.[16] In the ballad, the only point of view available becomes the singer's own. The excitement derived from participation in news is amplified in a goodnight ballad, where the singer has a chance to role play at the extremes of human emotion – to become the Earl of Essex, Sir Walter Raleigh, a common cutpurse, or a murderous wife.[17] The audience response to such an intimate identification with the convict could be varied and layered: one could feel a sense of superiority and edification, experience the vicarious thrill of law-breaking, fear the consequences of sin, or be reassured by the grace of God.

One of the other distinguishing features is that the speaker almost always switches addressees at some point in the ballad. The songs begin by speaking to the crowd, but by the end the ballad is addressed more specifically. In many cases, the speaker apologizes to his or her family for the pain that they have caused; but in nearly all goodnight ballads there is a passage wherein the convict speaks to God or Christ. So while the narrative conventions may create a sense of insincerity born of the repetitive adherence to certain accepted scripts, the formal conventions convey the personal, individual humanity of the convict by allowing him or her to speak (in the first person) directly to God immediately before death. These direct addresses to God vary widely in their emotional impact, but are generally the most moving moments of the ballad.[18] In 'The Complaint of Mrs. Page for causing her Husband to be Murthered, for the love of George Strangwidge, who were executed together', the convict (who had colluded in the murder of the husband her parents had forced her to marry) addresses God directly in three distinct stanzas, and the ballad peaks in the final stanza: 'And now O Christ to thee I yield my breath, / Strengthen my faith in bitter pangs of Death: / Pardon my faults and follies I thee pray, / And with my blood wash thou my sins away.'[19] The turn to Christ at the end of the ballad is not an afterthought – it is personal, forceful, and anguished. The ballad may foist the blame from the perpetrators to the parents for ignoring true love in favor of wealth, but it also models a relationship between the dying self and God with an acceptance of death, acknowledgment of sin, and hope for redemption.

Just as the first-person perspective demands a degree of empathy and psychological identification, the music of the ballads is likewise designed to encourage audience participation. Instead of being printed on the top of the page in musical notation, the tunes were named in the title of the ballad: 'Murder upon Murder, Committed by Thomas Sherwood, alias, Countrey Tom: I Elizabeth Evans, alias, Cambrye Bess … To the tune of Bragandary downe' (1635).[20] Naming instead of notating the tune reduces the need for musical literacy, increasing the likelihood that laypeople and ballad mongers of limited musicianship would be able to easily reproduce the tune from memory. The ballads were often sung to a small selection of tunes ('Fortune my Foe' was famously connected to the genre) and the tunes conveyed a sense of mourning and sentimentality by association.[21]

But if, as I am arguing, the goodnight ballads are a persuasive form of communication, what is their persuasive aim? Goodnight ballads have a history of being considered politically coercive, as their representation of spectacular execution scenes could reinforce conformity to the ideology and values of the state.[22] But critics have also questioned the Foucauldian account of the stage of execution in early modern England, disputing the notion that religious belief in general and the expression of repentance before death in particular is always and easily manipulated by authorities.[23] When the goodnight ballads re-enact the relationship between the repentant sinner and God in the moment before death, they appear surprisingly religious and particularly Protestant in their emphasis on the dramatic, unearned descent of God's grace. While the religious and political aims of the persuasive medium are deeply entangled and at times contradictory, the political, moral, and social aims of the songs are achieved through a formal and narrative framework that is a product and producer of religious and more specifically Protestant ideas, approaches, and assumptions.[24]

This said, the goodnight ballads are not generally – as a body of work – written and conceived with overt and coherent confessional aims; they instead articulate a more generic approach to repentance and salvation. When the intimate, participatory, and affective 'I' subject turns his or her attention and voice to address God directly, asking for forgiveness and displaying repentance in deeply personal language as is conventional in almost all goodnight ballads, the ballad enacts a kind of basic Protestant relationship between the self and God – direct, personal, and unmediated. The singers who participate directly in the ballad and inhabit the subject position of the convict then re-enact this relationship, practicing it for themselves and repeatedly displaying it for listeners. The participatory drive of the first-person perspective makes the ballads that much more persuasive; the ballads do more than model a Protestant spiritual relationship, they provide an opportunity to repeatedly rehearse one.

There is also a notable absence of any intermediaries referred to in the ballads – God or Christ is the only confessor mentioned – even when we know that ministers were integral to the conversion and repentance of the convict.[25] The role of an intercessor and the importance of a ministering third party in the penitential process is erased in the ballads, thereby magnifying the sense of the individual and unobstructed relationship with God. The ballads often depict the moment of conversion from evil murderer to repentant sinner as an immediate and dramatic change of heart that occurs upon the commission of the crime or apprehension and incarceration, thereby following the Augustinian/Calvinist model of divine grace bestowed on the sinning soul. In 'The Unnatural Wife', Alice Davis stabs her husband in the heart and then immediately runs out of the house 'quite undon', whereupon she confesses to her neighbors. She repents immediately, even before the constables could take her away: 'Life faine I would haue fetcht againe, / but now it was too late, / I did repent I him had slaine, / in this my heavie state.'[26]

None of these ideas are necessarily un-Catholic or anti-Catholic, neither are they uniquely Protestant; instead, the Protestantism seems to be located in the emphasis placed on spiritual interiority and of participation in the soul's unmediated relationship with God. Rather than anti-Catholic rants or didactic sermons, these ballads appear to spread basic and generally Protestant ideas that are largely inoffensive. They would not have alienated Catholic or Catholic-leaning listeners – such alienation would not have been good for business. However, the ballads do inculcate a basic Protestant understanding of repentance and salvation that may, after repeated listening, have laid the groundwork for a possible conversion or revitalization of lukewarm faith. With constant repetition, such ideas begin to become part of received wisdom, whether doctrinally precise or not.

Even though they are not purposively and didactically evangelical, the goodnight ballads remain effective modes of religious persuasion; but what and how they communicate is essentially different from sermons, pamphlets, private conversations, or other musical forms like metrical psalms. As a body of work, they are not self-conscious, purposeful vehicles of Protestant doctrine aimed at converting the masses. Instead, the ballads build the experience of conversion or of finding and communicating with God into the form of the song so that singers and listeners can vicariously experience the turn to God, reminding them of their own faith and reinforcing their own beliefs, arguably more potently and more repetitively than any sermon could. Unlike more theologically exact forms of persuasion, the ballads do not introduce, clarify, explain, or refine any particular point of Protestant doctrine. Instead, the form entrenches basically Protestant concepts that are already available and then repeats and reinforces them, reinvigorating them with various stories and various tunes. Such an imprecise method of persuasion would be effective in creating generations of people with ingrained assumptions about spiritual interiority, grace, and repentance, cultivating a receptivity to more precisely Protestant ideas.

But the particular confessional bent of the goodnight ballads is peripheral to the point that I am making here. My argument is interested in how they function as a form of persuasion, how their very formal structure is integral to what and how they persuade, and how such methods translate onto *Eastward Ho*'s very secular, satirical stage. In *Eastward Ho*, Quicksilver's life depends on the persuasive success of the ballad. While goodnight ballads are effective persuaders, as discussed earlier, they are not generally catalysts of spiritual epiphanies and sudden conversions. Instead, they fortify and strengthen ideas, making them part of received wisdom and infiltrating the way people think. Quicksilver's ballad works in a similar way. In order to be affected, his listeners need an introduction to the ideas presented in the song.

The first hint of the prodigal's change of heart comes from Wolf (the keeper of the prison), who visits Golding and Touchstone with letters of supplication from his prisoners. Wolf claims that he was persuaded to bring the letters because he was 'never so mortified with any men's discourse or behaviour in prison; yet I have had all sorts of men i'the kingdom under my keys, and almost of all religions i'the land, as Papist, Protestant, Puritan, Brownist, Anabaptist, Millenary, Family o'Love, Jew, Turk, Infidel Atheist, Good Fellow etc.' (5.2.31–7). He describes Quicksilver as the most self-denying penitent ever hosted, citing the prisoner's absolute refusal of alms and comfort for himself, his all-night psalm-singing that edifies 'the whole prison', and his recitation of all of the stories from the *Book of Martyrs* and the *Sick Man's Salve* from memory (5.2.51–2). While such examples of piety may soften Touchstone's heart, Quicksilver's newfound religion keeps the entire prison awake and the keeper may well be supporting Quicksilver's story of conversion because he wants the annoyingly enthusiastic convert pardoned and out of the prison as soon as possible. And while the humorous extremity of Quicksilver's religion is not in itself cause to doubt his sincerity, there is something performative in all of the evidence cited by Wolf. Quicksilver indulges in classic outward displays of piety and conversion, performed with such gusto and then reported so breathlessly that it is hard to take him seriously, especially when acts such as psalm-singing were usually linked to hypocritical stage Puritans in the seventeenth century.

Wolf's reports prime listeners to be prepared for a changed Quicksilver, but it is the ballad itself that does much of the work of conversion. His repentance is performed less through his words and more through the performer–audience dynamic and the expectations of repentance that inhere in the conventions of the form. Quicksilver is meticulous in his observation of all of the conventions of the goodnight ballad in his attempt to perform and prove his conversion. To begin with, he conforms to performance expectations: his stage audience, comprising fellow prisoners (which unbeknownst to him includes his Master, Touchstone), gather around him as listeners might in a public square and there is a sense of social engagement and interaction between performer and audience as Quicksilver seeks to 'sell' his story.[27] His song proceeds to tell us where he lives and what he does for a living; he valorizes Touchstone (his 'master good and kind'), who warned him of the consequences of bad behavior (5.5.54). He details his descent to increasingly reckless behavior, beginning with his penchant for dressing and acting above his station in 'silks and satins gay' paired with 'false manners'; and his sins become more serious as he begins scorning his master, drinking, whoring, and investing in a plan that would have seen him leave England and his debts forever on an ill-fated ship (5.5.66–7).[28]

Quicksilver's recounted moment of epiphany is likewise entirely conventional, but he rewrites his own narrative to better fit ballad expectations. Ballad conventions dictate that conversion be a sudden change of heart, but Quicksilver's conversion is more of a process. It begins during a speech in which he acknowledges the justness of the scuttling of his 'wicked' nautical hopes

(4.1.73) after he washes up on shore at the ominous location of Wapping (a well-known execution spot for pirates). Despite his growing sense of unease, he makes a final stab at criminality through counterfeiting. His eventual transformation from scheming rogue to (perhaps) penitent Protestant likely occurs after he has been hauled off to prison and has some time for further contemplation. In the song, however, there is little sense of this gradual loss of self-confidence; he describes his moment of conversion as being suitably sudden, occurring after the wake-up call of ill luck and incarceration:

> Still 'Eastward Ho' was all my word;
> But westward I had no regard,
> Nor never thought what would come after,
> As did, alas his youngest daughter.
> At last the black ox trod o' my foot,
> And I saw then what longed unto't;
> Now cry I, 'Touchstone, touch me still,
> And make me current by thy skill.'
> (5.5.81–8)

R. W. Van Fossen notes that the 'black ox' trotting over one's foot is proverbial, indicating adversity, so in Quicksilver's retelling, ill luck quickly opened his eyes to repentance.[29] Quicksilver's clarifying moment of truth in the prison seems conveniently drawn up for the ballad and it makes for better, more convincingly repentant material than a description of his waffling, unsure state. The performance of the repentance eclipses the repentance itself as Quicksilver contorts his story to fit the expected narrative.[30]

Quicksilver is also careful to change addressees in the middle of his song. These stanzas should be the most persuasive aspects of Quicksilver's ballad, as the audience overhears his more private thoughts and conversations, but they are also the most uncomfortable and comical sections of the song. In the first instance, he turns not to God to ask for forgiveness as would be expected, but to Touchstone. This makes sense as it is Touchstone who has the power to drop the charges, but Quicksilver goes too far: 'Touchstone, touch me still, / And make me current by thy skill' (5.5.87–8). Quicksilver intimates that Touchstone has the alchemical power granted by his goldsmithing to reconvert the penitent back to his pure state, portraying the goldsmith as a God- or Christ-like figure able to bestow forgiveness and life upon his subjects. The comparison of Touchstone to Christ makes both Quicksilver and Touchstone the more laughable – the former for getting caught up in his own rhetoric and the latter for being flattered by it. Quicksilver's conflation of Christ and Touchstone may be incompetent in that the poetry is terrible and he makes a mess of the tradition of addressing God with humility, but it remains a winning persuasion tactic. Here 'Repentance' achieves its goal of successfully persuading Touchstone, who is unrefined enough to be moved by excessive and inappropriate flattery, to free the imprisoned balladeer.

The subsequent stanza changes addressees again; but rather than being addressed to God the stanza addresses Mannington, the famous murderer and 'author' of the repentance ballad:

> O Mannington, thy stories show,
> Thou cutt'st a horse-head off at a blow.
> But I confess I have not the force
> For to cut off the head of a horse;
> Yet I desire this grace to win,
> That I may cut off the horse-head of Sin,
> And leave his body in the dust
> Of sin's highway and bogs of lust,
> Whereby I may take Virtue's purse,
> And live with her for better, for worse.
> (5.5.99–108)

Quicksilver takes an intimate climax that is typically the most moving, most persuasive moment of the song and instead belabors an extended, awkward metaphor about Virtue and the 'horse-head of Sin' that contradicts the very notion of repentance. Mannington's many transgressions apparently included equine decapitation; by claiming to cut off the horse-head of Sin, Quicksilver offers to excise sin by committing sin. Likewise, his assertion that he will 'take Virtue's purse' proposes that his path to virtue includes theft and even rape. The appropriated lines from the marriage service hardly convey his lifelong commitment to virtue, but instead suggest that Virtue has been stolen and forced into a marriage where the emphasis is on the worse rather than the better. His metaphors raise doubts as to the authenticity of his conversion or at least paint him as a hilariously and enthusiastically incompetent penitent and poet. If the connection between Christ and Touchstone is awkward but practically effective, allying God and a convicted murderer goes beyond inadequate to potentially blasphemous. But this incompetence is precisely what is so funny. The scene mocks Quicksilver for creating and performing such drivel, mocks Touchstone and the prison audience for being in the thrall of such an overblown performance, mocks ballads themselves for their glorification of murderers like Mannington and for their emotional and artistic simplicity, and even mocks the kind of drama that imitates the process of repentance and grace.

The inappropriate metaphors bolster the reading of Quicksilver as an insincere manipulator. His desire to obtain virtue by theft certainly raises doubts as to the authenticity or depth of his conversion, and while the prison audience may be deceived by his appeals to Mannington, the song is easily read as a self-conscious joke on the gullible Touchstone. Quicksilver is so precise and personal in the catalogue of his transgressions that the song appears to relish the details. Moreover, the conventions of the goodnight ballad are so closely followed but coupled with such inappropriate content that the ballad becomes a hypocritical outward display of piety that has little connection to an internal state of grace.

But such a reading is at odds with the rest of the play. If Quicksilver is insincere in his conversion then the satire is directed at Touchstone and disregards the sins of the social-climbing, law-breaking miscreants. Throughout the production, Quicksilver is an exemplary prodigal – he embraces sin while rejecting honest labor, fulfilling every convention of a young man on a downward spiral. Despite his many moral failings, his enthusiasm and energy make him an appealing and sympathetic character. His conversion is likewise hilariously overblown – from the loud and unceasing psalm-singing, to the displays of self-sacrifice – but for him to transform into a sober, contemplative, quiet penitent would betray his personality. The play already has such a pious and worthy character in Golding (who, for all his goodness, is still subject to gentle mockery for being thrifty to the point of joylessness when he and his betrothed insist that leftovers are all that is necessary for their wedding 'feast'). Quicksilver is an archetypal, over-the-top rake who converts into an archetypal, over-the-top penitent. His conventionality makes his conversion more authentic and sincere, not less so.

In this reading, Quicksilver honestly believes that singing a goodnight ballad is the most effective and convincing way of conveying the sincerity of his repentance – and in the world of the play, he is right. The language and narrative of his ballad matter less than the fact that he is singing one at all: listeners gloss over the ridiculous content because they expect to be convinced by the inherently persuasive form. As is the case with the goodnight ballads, Quicksilver's song does not transform his listeners from skeptical unbelievers into enthusiastic converts. Instead, his song cements, displays, and reflects his conversion, which in turn convinces his listeners of his sincerity by reinforcing that which they were already predisposed towards believing. Even in the case of Touchstone, for whom the sounds of 'Repentance' prompt a profound change of heart, the ballad is more of a reminder of his basic optimism and belief in conversion narratives rather than a rational argument that sways his mind. Touchstone perceives himself as being susceptible to persuasion and having perhaps too much faith in the goodness of others. He does not want to receive the prisoners' letters from Wolf because 'I find mine own easy nature, and I know not what a well-penn'd, subtle letter may work upon it' (5.2.4–6), and after Wolf's tales of Quicksilver's penal piety, Touchstone laments: 'No more; I am coming already. If I should give any farther ear, I were taken. Adieu, good Master Wolf. – Son, I do feel mine own weaknesses; do not importune me. Pity is a rheum that I am subject to; but I will resist it' (5.2.73–7). Touchstone converts because of his personality, his personal investment in his former apprentice and perhaps most of all because he believes himself to be a kind-hearted and important individual; he wants to fulfill his role as forgiver in the conversion narrative that Quicksilver has artfully delivered. The ballad sequence has meaning to Touchstone, and his familiarity with the conventions precipitate his conversion, rather than any argument or demonstration in the ballad itself. My argument is somewhat similar to Stevens's claim that in *Eastward Ho*, 'artifice effects grace'. Stevens points to the artifice of the scene which Golding manages and directs, in order to encourage Touchstone to witness Quicksilver's repentant song and subsequently forgive him. The whole charade may be a parody, but artifice, convention, and even parody itself can lead to real change and indeed, grace.[31]

While artifice may effect grace, Touchstone's uncritical acceptance of Quicksilver's ridiculous goodnight ballad nevertheless remains problematic. Instead of only taking satirical aim at particular characters and types, *Eastward Ho* directs some of its sharpest satirical sting at those who are seduced by forms, conventions, and style, all but ignoring content (a sin of which all of its characters are somewhat guilty). Alexander Leggatt makes this point when he notes that 'the parody of the prodigal story becomes simply the vehicle for a deeper satire on those who see life in terms of theatrical conventions'.[32] He cites Gertrude, who wants her life to proceed as a rags-to-riches fairy tale, and Touchstone, who wants his workshop to emulate the plays that he has seen, casting Golding as the theatrical citizen-hero and Quicksilver as the fictional Prodigal. This satire culminates in the ballad and Touchstone's swooning reaction in which he pronounces himself 'ravished' for artistic rather than moral reasons. The ballad is a moment of the deepest satire, when content matters less than form. Quicksilver has taken the persuasiveness of the structure of the goodnight ballad too far: the performance of the convention itself has done the persuading, rather than the honesty and sincerity that should fill the conventional form with compelling and authentic content. This does not make Quicksilver self-consciously deceitful or insincere, just enthralled, like everyone else, in the production of repentance. And while being under the spell of a conventional production is part of the problem, it is also part of the solution – such a ridiculous performance can lead to sincere change, even if sincerity did not motivate the performance in the first place.

While the satire makes a mockery of the dramatic and musical tastes of the citizenry, it compliments the Blackfriars audience on their preference for well-written content over the slavish adherence to unsophisticated dramatic narratives. Such a compliment aims to seduce the audience into continuing their monetary support, and it persuades much like the goodnight ballads – by fortifying and reiterating beliefs already firmly held by the spectators. The mockery of the prodigal conventions continues to the play's final moments, with an epilogue that emphasizes commercial values over moral ones, and directly appeals to the audience to return to ensure a long run.

But in this slippery play the satire is on constantly shifting ground; at the same time as the ending fortifies the audience's feelings of comfort and self-satisfaction, it also challenges them. Quicksilver insists on retaining his prison garb as he walks through the streets after obtaining his freedom 'as a spectacle, or rather an example, to the children of Cheapside' (5.5.216–17). In the epilogue, Quicksilver looks directly out at the audience:

> I perceive the multitude are gather'd together to view our coming out at the Counter. See, if the streets and the fronts of the houses be not stuck with people, and the windows fill'd with ladies, as on the solemn day of the Pageant! (Epilogue, 1–5)

The Blackfriars audience has been transformed into the multitude of Cheapside, curiously eager to see a repentant prodigal offering up his shame for public consumption. This move seems to undermine the class-based satire of the play, implying that the tastes of the 'sophisticated' coterie audience and the more coarse inhabitants of east London are not so different. While the audience may laugh at the predictability and conventionality of forms like those of prodigal plays and goodnight ballads, narratives of sin and repentance are undeniably universal and moving, as is the more prurient interest in the spectacle of shame. At the same time, however, it is entirely in keeping with the satire of the play in that everyone is lampooned, everyone is the target of good-humored mockery – including the audience. So while the play ridicules pedestrian citizen tastes and reinforces popular assumptions, it also gently suggests that the spectators perform a little self-examination. In the very final moments, *Eastward Ho* continues to perform its persuasion of the audience.

Notes

1 George Chapman, Ben Jonson, and John Marston, *Eastward Ho*, ed. R. W. Van Fossen (Manchester: Manchester University Press, 1979), 5.5.32–3. All subsequent citations for the play will be found in textually embedded parentheses.

2 Brian Gibbons, *Jacobean City Comedy: A Study of Satiric Plays by Jonson, Marston and Middleton* (London: Rupert Hart-Davis, 1968), p. 11; Ben Jonson, George Chapman, and John Marston *Eastward Ho*, ed. C. G. Petter (Kent: Ernest Benn Limited, 1973), p. xxxvi; L. Phyllis Austern, 'Musical Parody in the Jacobean City Comedy', *Music and Letters*, 66:4 (1985), 355–65, 363.

3 Nicol's point also emphasizes the importance of music to the interpretation of the ballads. D. Nicol, 'Review of *Eastward Ho!* Performed by the Royal Shakespeare Company at the Swan Theatre', *Early Modern Literary Studies*, 8:2 (2002), at http://extra.shu.ac.uk/emls/08-2/eastrev.html, accessed October 22, 2014.

4 P. Stevens, 'The New Presentism and Its Discontents: Listening to *Eastward Ho* and Shakespeare's *Tempest* in Dialogue', in Ann Baynes Coiro and Thomas Fulton (eds), *Rethinking Historicism from Shakespeare to Milton* (Cambridge: Cambridge University Press, 2012), pp. 133–58, 155, 156.

5 'A sorrowfull sonnet, made by M. George Mannington, at Cambridge Castle. To the tune of Labandala Shot', in *A Handful of Pleasant Delights* (1584), by Clement Robinson and divers others, ed. H. E. Rollins (Cambridge, MA: Harvard University Press, 1924), pp. 65–8.

6 The term 'goodnight ballad' is now used quite uniformly to describe the particular kind of ballad described here by current scholars such as P. Marby Harrison and C. Marsh. Pioneering scholars in the field of sixteenth- and seventeenth-century balladry, such as H. E. Rollins, likewise identify this type of ballad as a '"good-night" or last farewell'. This term comes from sixteenth-century descriptions of and terms for ballads of repentance sung on the scaffold; there is, for example, a ballad composed on the death of the Earl of Essex entitled: 'Essex's last Goodnight: A Lamentable new Ballad upon the Earle of Essex his Death', *Roxburghe Ballads*, vol. 1: p. 571.

7 Later in the seventeenth century some ballad writers such as Martin Parker eschewed anonymity.

8 C. Marsh, *Music and Society in Early Modern England* (Cambridge: Cambridge University Press, 2010), p. 226.

9 B. R. Smith, *The Acoustic World of Early Modern England: Attending to the O-Factor* (Chicago: University of Chicago Press, 1999), pp. 172–3.

10 Many goodnight ballads could be found in the collections of compilers such as Pepys. For more on ballad collecting, the limits of our ballad knowledge, and the problem of dating ballads, see A. McShane, 'Ballads and Broadsides', in Joad Raymond (ed.), *The Oxford History of Popular Print Culture*, vol. 1, *Cheap Print in Britain and Ireland to 1660* (Oxford: Oxford University Press, 2011), pp. 339–62.

11 Thomas Dickerson (?), 'John Spenser a Chesshire Gallant, his life and repentance, who for killing of one Randall Gam: was lately executed at Burford a mile from Nantwich. To the tune of *In Slumbering Sleep*', in *A Pepysian Garland: Black-Letter Broadside Ballads of the Years 1595–1639. Chiefly from the Collection of Samual Pepys*, ed. Hyder E. Rollins (Cambridge: Cambridge University Press, 1922), pp. 256–62.

12 'A Warning for All Desperate Women', in *A Pepysian Garland*, pp. 288–92, p. 290.

13 'Mannington', line 1961.

14 Some ballads, such as 'John Spenser, a Cheshire Gallant' noted above, are in two parts: the first part is a third-person descriptive crime ballad, while the second part is written in the first-person perspective of the prisoner.

15 Ben Jonson, *Bartholomew Fair*, in *The Alchemist and Other Plays*, ed. Gordon Campbell (Oxford: Oxford University Press, 1998), pp. 327–433 (3.5.38–9).

16 B. R. Smith, 'Reading Lists of Plays: Early Modern, Modernist, Post-Modern', *Shakespeare Quarterly*, 42 (1991), 129–44, 141.

17 See 'Sir Walter Rauleigh his lamentation: Who was beheaded in the old Pallace at West-minster the 29 of October. 1618. To the tune of *Welladay*', in *A Pepysian Garland*, pp. 89–95; 'A Lamentable Ditty composed upon the Death of Robert

Lord Devereux, late Earle of Essex, who was beheaded in the Tower of London, on Ashwenesday in the morning, 1600', in *The Roxburghe Ballads*, vol. 1: p. 564.

18 In the ballad of Ned Smith there is little indication of what his sins may have been and almost half of the ballad addresses Jesus directly, repenting and requesting grace and comfort. By contrast, in 'Anne Wallen's Lamentation', only one line directly addresses God in the very last line of the ballad: 'In burning flames of fire I should fry, / Receive my soul sweet Jesus now I die.' 'The wofull lamentation of Edward Smith, a poore penitent prisoner in the Iayle of Bedford, which he wrote a short time before his death' (London: C. W. Pepys, 1624), *English Broadside Ballad Archive* (*EBBA*), http://ebba.english.ucsb.edu/ballad/20038/xml, accessed August 4, 2014; 'Anne Wallens Lamentation, For the Murthering of her husband Iohn Wallen a turner in Cow-lane neere Smithfield; done by his owne wife, on satterday the 22 of June. 1616. Who was burnt in Smithfield the first of July following', in *A Pepysian Garland*, pp. 84–9.

19 'The sorrowful complaint of Mistris Page for causing her husband to be murthered for love of George Strangwidg, who were executed both together', in *The Shirburn Ballads 1585–1616*, ed. Andrew Clark (Oxford: Clarendon Press, 1907), pp. 111–13.

20 'Murder upon Murder, Committed by *Thomas Sherwood*, alias, *Countrey Tom: I Elizabeth Evans*, alias, *Cambrye Bess … To the tune of Bragandary downe*', repr. in *Blood and Knavery: A Collection of English Renaissance Pamphlets and Ballads of Crime and Sin*, ed. Joseph H. Marshburn and Alan R. Velie (Rutherford, NJ: Fairleigh Dickenson University Press, 1973), p. 67.

21 For more on ballad tunes, see C. Simpson, *The British Broadside Ballad and its Music* (New Brunswick, NJ: Rutgers University Press, 1966).

22 Michel Foucault, *Discipline and Punish: The Birth of the Prison*, trans. A. Sheridan (Harmondsworth: Penguin Books, 1979). J. A. Sharpe, '"Last Dying Speeches": Religion, Ideology, and Public Execution in Seventeenth-Century England', *Past and Present*, 107 (1985), 144–67.

23 See amongst others, P. Lake and M. Questier, 'Prisons, Priest and People', in N. Tyacke (ed.), *England's Long Reformation 1500–1800* (London: Routledge, 1997); P. Marby Harrison, 'Religious Rhetoric as Resistance in Early Modern Goodnight Ballads', in Sally McKee (ed.), *Crossing Boundaries: Issues of Cultural and Individual Identity in the Middle Ages and the Renaissance* (Turnhout: Brepols, 1999), pp. 107–25; L. Hutson, *The Invention of Suspicion: Law and Mimesis in Shakespeare and Renaissance Drama* (Oxford: Oxford University Press, 1997).

24 The goodnight ballads seem to emerge out of the godly ballad tradition. Tessa Watt chronicles the rise and fall of religious balladry and notes that ballads were initially deployed to spread aspects of Protestant doctrine in the early years after the Reformation. They fell out of favor with evangelical reformers after the first generation, but they continued to be reprinted well into the seventeenth century. See T. Watt, *Cheap Print and Popular Piety 1550–1640* (Cambridge: Cambridge University Press, 1991), pp. 39–73. Overtly confessional goodnight ballads were often ballads of martyrdom. In 'The Ballad of Anne Askew', the subject warns against popish ceremonies, masses, chantries, idols, and the seductive wiles of the

persuasive Bishop Gardiner. A Catholic example of a goodnight ballad in manuscript can be found in 'True Christian hearts, cease to lament', which purports to be the final words of John Thewlis, a priest executed at Lancaster in 1616. 'Anne Askew, Intituled, I am a Woman Poor and Blind', *EBBA*, http://ebba.english.ucsb.edu/ballad/31664/album, accessed August 5, 2014; 'True Christian hearts, cease to lament', in *Old English Ballads 1553–1625: Chiefly from Manuscripts*, ed. Hyder E. Rollins (Cambridge: Cambridge University Press, 1920), pp. 79–86.

25 Anne Saunders, for example, was famously spiritually tended to by several ministers (including one who fell in love with her). Her ballad makes no mention of any assistance.

26 'The unnaturall Wife: Or, The lamentable Murther, of one goodman Davis, Lock-Smith in Tutle-streete, who was stabbed to death by his Wife, on the 29 of June, 1628. For which fact, She was Arraigned, Condemned, and Adiudged, to be Burnt to Death in Smithfield, the 12 of July 1628', in *A Pepysian Garland*, pp. 284–7.

27 Throughout his song, prisoners are constantly commenting and interrupting the song, and we overhear conversations between listeners about the ballad.

28 For a chronicle of a similar descent into sin, see, for example, 'The Sorrowful Complaint of Susan Higges' (London: H. G., 1630?), *EBBA*, http://ebba.english.ucsb.edu/ballad/20002, accessed August 4, 2014.

29 Some ballads depict repentance occurring upon incarceration, as the title indicates in 'John Spenser his Repentance in Prison, Written with his owne hands as he lay in Chester Castle'.

30 Quicksilver also makes sure to include a typical warning, wherein he cautions Cheapside and his 'dear fellow prentices' to learn from his fall to: 'Shun usurers, bawds, and dice, and drab / Avoid them as you would French scabs. / Seek not to go beyond your tether, / But cut your thongs unto your leather' (5.5.124–7).

31 Stevens, 'The New Presentism', p. 159.

32 A. Leggatt, *Citizen Comedy in the Age of Shakespeare* (Toronto: University of Toronto Press, 1973), p. 52.

4

Romancing the Eucharist: confessional conflict and Elizabethan romances

Christina Wald

In one of the most erotically charged scenes of Philip Sidney's *Arcadia*, a young princess called Philoclea finds herself in a perplexing situation. When she talks to her dear friend, the Amazon Cleophila, in a lonely pastoral setting, she is unexpectedly invited to witness 'a miserable miracle of affection': Cleophila asks Philoclea to '[b]ehold here before your eyes Pyrocles, prince of Macedon'.[1] Alas, the only person whom Philoclea can discern is Cleophila; the legendary male prince does not appear. Or does he? Does his hidden, but real presence exist beneath the Amazon's external appearance, as she claims? And can the young princess penetrate the misleading looks, Pyrocles' 'unused metamorphosis', to see this alleged substance beneath?[2] In Sidney's romance, Philoclea is ready to believe in Cleophila's hidden male core. She is even immensely relieved by Cleophila's assertion since she felt an unspeakable and indeed unthinkable desire for her female friend all along. When the narrator describes Philoclea's feelings, he resorts to Ovid's *Metamorphoses*, comparing her excitement with '[t]he joy which wrought into Pygmalion's mind while he found his beloved image wax little and little both softer and warmer in his folded arms'.[3] The narrator here offers his readers a literary paradigm of supernatural shape-shifting to understand Philoclea's overwhelming emotions, even though Cleophila does not alter her shape in any visible or palpable manner. Instead, it is the faith and imagination of Philoclea which transforms the Amazon into a valiant prince, at least from her perspective.

The erotic excitement evoked in scenes like this was severely criticized in a number of Elizabethan treatises. In one of the most influential condemnations of the new vogue of prose narratives, Roger Ascham presents a transformation scenario which likewise draws on Ovid's tales. Ascham describes the transformative effect which reading fiction might have on readers as a metamorphosis of men into beasts. He fears that 'some Circe' might convert Englishmen into lascivious Italians with 'at once in one body the belly of a swine, the head of an ass, the brain of a fox, the womb of a wolf'.[4] This monstrous transmutation is, however, a metaphorical vision of the inner change since the readers of romance 'remain men in shape and fashion', as Ascham emphasizes.[5]

Thus, both the *Arcadia*, the most influential Elizabethan romance, and *The Schoolmaster*, the most influential Elizabethan humanist treatise warning against romances, invoke processes of internal, concealed transformation that are not registered in the outward appearance. Nonetheless, they refer to 'metamorphosis' to describe this invisible change and to illustrate its profundity. The importance and fertility of the notion of metamorphosis have long been acknowledged in the study of early modern English literature and culture as going far beyond its etymological meaning of shape-shifting. In Ovid's *Metamorphoses* and their manifold adaptations in early modern narratives, plays, poems, rhetorical handbooks, paintings, and pamphlets, the manifest outward change often has a complex relationship with the psyche of the transformed figure. For example, the metamorphosis sometimes completes the pre-existing inner change of the transformed figure, or it preserves his or her human consciousness despite the external transmutation into an animal or a plant. Still, invoking Ovidian shape-shifting to come to terms with a purely internal transformation, as Sidney and Ascham do, stretches the meaning of metamorphosis to its limit. Early modern authors apparently employed the popular notion of metamorphosis for lack of a more suitable concept.

And yet, an alternative concept of invisible, internal identity transformation had existed for a long time in England and was deeply embedded in the Elizabethan cultural imaginary, but it was politically highly charged: transubstantiation. The term transubstantiation precisely describes a transformation of essence which is not visible from the outside, neither in 'shape' nor 'fashion', as Ascham puts it. When early modern Catholic believers were celebrating the Eucharist, they were asked for a leap of faith that is similar to the experience of Princess Philoclea: during consecration, the priest elevated bread and wine and announced that they were the body and blood of Christ – to 'behold' Christ's body 'here before your eyes', communicants had to see beyond deceptive outer appearances, just like Philoclea.

The belief or disbelief in transubstantiation was at the heart of the heated Eucharist debate during the Reformation and became a touchstone of religious allegiance for centuries to come. According to the Catholic doctrine of transubstantiation, the celebration of the Eucharist is a repetition of Christ's original sacrifice. 'Hoc est corpus meum', Christ's (translated) words which are spoken by the priest, mean that the bread is indeed transformed into Christ's body. Liturgy here counters sensual experience since the outward appearance of the elements of bread and wine remain unchanged by the priest's words. Catholic theology has hence developed an elaborate theory which maintains that the 'accidents' (the outward appearance of bread and wine) remain unaltered, while their 'substance' changes. Invisible to the eye but discernible to true believers, bread and wine transubstantiate. Believers consuming the Eucharist incorporate Christ's body into their own body; the communion entails the intermingling of identities which Christ envisioned according to John: 'Iesus said … For my flesh is meat in dede, & my blood is drink in dede. He that eateth my flesh, and drinketh my blood, dwelleth in me, and I in him.'[6] Protestant thinkers attacked the Catholic dogma as being a too literal reading of 'this is my body'. They did so to different degrees. Martin Luther held a comparatively moderate position by arguing that a process of consubstantiation takes place, in which the substances of wine and bread coexist with the real presence of Christ's body and blood 'in, with and under' bread and wine.[7] Luther's position on the Eucharist was challenged by the Swiss Reformer Huldrych Zwingli, who refuted the Catholic doctrine far more fiercely. Zwingli argued that the Eucharist remembers the Last Supper and Christ's crucifixion, but does not repeat them: bread and wine are figurative signs which represent Christ's absent body. For Zwingli, Christ's words read, 'hoc significat corpus meum'. No material change takes place; it is the task of the believers to commemorate Christ's death. Bridging the gap between Luther and Zwingli, Protestant theology developed a fourth interpretation of 'this is my body', which was promoted by John Calvin: Christ's presence in the elements of bread and wine is 'true' rather than 'real'; it is spiritual rather than physical. What all three Protestant positions share is a focus on the believers who perceive and consume the elements of bread and wine: it is through their faith that bread and wine come to entail Christ's real (Luther), true (Calvin), or figurative presence (Zwingli) – an emancipation of the believer which was reinforced by having the mass read aloud in the vernacular rather than in (often mumbled) Latin as in the Roman Catholic Sarum mass and by administering bread and wine to the laity, too.

The Roman Catholic liturgy and doctrine of transubstantiation were maintained during the early years of Reformation under Henry VIII. When Henry's young son Edward ascended the throne, the English Reformation gained momentum. Thomas Cranmer, Archbishop of Canterbury and the leading theologian during the reigns of Henry VIII and Edward VI, gradually adopted Zwingli's figurative understanding of the sacraments as the official Anglican position, and reformed the liturgy accordingly. After Edward's early death, Mary I retracted the reformation of the liturgy and re-established the Latin Sarum mass. Hence, the official English position on the Eucharist returned to the Catholic doctrine of transubstantiation after a brief time of Zwinglian dominance during Edward's reign. Eventually, when Elizabeth I ascended the throne, a version of Calvin's intermediate stance came to define the Anglican position on the Eucharist.

In the fraught historical context, authors of prose fiction could not have used Eucharist vocabulary, least of all the provoking term 'transubstantiation', without taking sides in the political and religious struggles of the day. Employing transubstantiation purely for its conceptual implications as a model of thought that allows readers to reflect on internal identity change was virtually impossible – depending on the current official religious position, this would have risked the dangers either of blasphemy or of heterodoxy. As a consequence, the term appears in prose fiction only in contexts which are clearly marked as satire of Catholicism (and only in texts that are published under Protestant governments), for instance in William Baldwin's *Beware the Cat*, written in 1553, during the last days of the reign of Edward VI, and published in 1561, once Elizabeth I had ascended the throne. Elizabethan romances are far from straightforward contributions to religious questions; and yet, as I shall argue, the cultural and poetic fertility of the Eucharist (and in particular of transubstantiation) continues to inform the concern with identity change in romantic narratives. This chapter will focus on crucial moments in Sidney's romance narrative *Arcadia* that are informed, as I shall argue, by Eucharistic thinking, rituals, and emotional experience.

As a remnant of the officially abandoned faith, the Catholic Eucharist remained an active force in Elizabethan culture for a wealth of reasons: not only did a considerable group of Englishmen and women cling to the old faith, but the potential official return to Catholicism also remained an issue in the sixteenth and seventeenth centuries. An ongoing concern with the Catholic Eucharist in Anglican England also seems plausible in view of its entrenched social and psychological functions. Scholars have shown that during the late Middle Ages and the pre-Reformation sixteenth century the Eucharist 'organize[d] people's utmost feelings, thoughts, and actions' and that Eucharistic concepts and rituals shaped 'the way ordinary men and women conceived of political power, interpreted their social world, and established the relation between the sacred and society'.[8] If this is true, then it is hard to imagine that the Catholic Eucharist could have been so quickly and fully given up that it disappeared without a trace in England once the Anglican Church was established. Quite on the contrary, the traumatic processes of reform and counter-reform in England even reinforced the Eucharist's central importance. The intense theological and political struggles, including the public questioning and burning of martyrs on both sides, made each individual's stance towards the Last Supper quite literally a matter of life and death. I shall argue that, in this historical context, early modern prose narratives engage with the Eucharist, in particular with the spectres of transubstantiation in Elizabethan culture. Their adaptations of Eucharistic concepts and structures of feeling creatively transform the heritage; they at once forget and remember the officially abandoned ritual.

Assuming that during the long process of Reformation, officially abandoned theological doctrines and liturgical rituals migrated from theology to prose fiction, this chapter follows the argument of earlier studies, for instance Elizabeth Mazzola's *The Pathology of the English Renaissance*, which has shown that 'abandoned [Catholic] symbols or practices do not simply disappear from the mental landscape', but can attain a new cultural meaning in secular contexts and in particular in poetry.[9] According to Mazzola, 'Renaissance literature might therefore be approached in terms of a sacred history of lost ideas, and read in terms of sacred signs which were downplayed or even disowned.'[10] Such arguments are based on a concept of cultural memory that includes repressed and censored cultural practices. If we understand culture as a palimpsest of memory layers, cultural memory consists of 'an inextricable tangle of old and new, of obstructed and buried material, of detritus that has been reused or rejected. In this way tensions arise, rejections, antagonisms, between what has been censored and uncensored, the canonical and the apocryphal, the orthodox and the heretical, the central and the marginal, all of which makes for a cultural dynamism', as Jan Assmann points out.[11] The Eucharist is a particularly pertinent example of such processes of cultural memory, as frequently changing 'old' and 'new', 'censored' and 'uncensored', 'heretical' and 'orthodox' versions circulated in the long course of the English Reformation and overwrote each other in the palimpsest of cultural memory. In the cultural dynamism stemming from the religious and political upheavals, prose fiction drew on some aspects of the new Anglican celebration of the Eucharist, but also adopted the 'obstructed and buried material' of the Catholic liturgy for its own cultural and aesthetic concerns. The very fact that concepts like transubstantiation and multilocation were, at least officially, cultural 'waste', that they were no longer sacrosanct doctrines but discarded, superstitious beliefs that could be taken up by pamphlets and literary texts in a satirical manner facilitated the unorthodox adoption of Eucharistic concerns in prose fiction. As Aleida Assmann has argued with reference to the waste of cultural memory, it can witness 'unexpected renaissances and resurrections', because it 'exists materially or intellectually in a state of latency from which it may be rediscovered, reinterpreted, and imaginatively revived'.[12] The actual status of the Catholic Eucharist in Elizabethan England was, of course, more complicated than the official denouncement as cultural 'waste'; this tension was poetically productive and led to unexpected appropriations of Eucharistic patterns in prose fiction.

The particular appeal of the Eucharist for Elizabethan romances is that it offers ways to explore questions of identity formation and transformation. Thus, the notion of transubstantiation also kept preoccupying Elizabethans because it captured a widespread concern with change. In pre-Reformation England, as Paul Strohm has emphasized, '[a]t the heart of sacramentality lay a concept of transformation; the sacrament is ministered in a ritual or ceremony which possesses the power to alter status or identity, even in the absence of apparent or outward change'.[13] This power to alter status or identity caused ambivalent responses in the sixteenth and seventeenth centuries, when the dynamics of social change that had begun in the high and late Middle Ages accelerated and unsettled the traditional notion of inborn and fixed identity. In a culture which was used to thinking in the Aristotelian categories of substance and accidents, and whose socio-political and economic reality made identity categories increasingly fluid, the idea that a person might transubstantiate triggered anxieties in some, and wishful fantasies in others.

That aspects of the 'repressed' old faith resurface in vernacular romance seems apt for a mode of writing which Helgerson called the 'subconscious of Renaissance story telling' since it tends to cater to the emotional and sensual needs of its readers and was therefore denigrated by moralists, the 'superego' of Elizabethan consciousness.[14] Moreover, during their century-old history, romantic formulae changed only slowly; as Helen Cooper has argued in her expansive study *The English Romance in Time*, 'any disruption of memetic replication takes place only over a long time-scale. Elizabethan England was only a generation, or the width of the Channel, away from a fully Catholic culture, and those ways of thinking, its imagery, and its books did not disappear with the Act of Settlement.'[15] In a similar vein, Northrop Frye has construed romance as a kind of 'secular scripture' because it protects and reinvigorates cultural discards,[16] and Nandini Das has argued that Renaissance romance 'operates as a memorial link handed down across generations'.[17] Early moderns like Ascham were well aware of this: in his criticism of fictional prose written in the vernacular, Ascham associates medieval English chivalric romances with the Catholic past of England, 'when papistry as a standing pool covered and overflowed all England'.[18] Nevertheless, Ascham famously presents medieval English romances as less harmful than the new Italianate books (that is, narratives that are translated or written in the style of Italian models): 'And yet ten *Morte Darthurs* do not the tenth part so much harm as one of these books made in Italy and translated in England'; 'More papists be made by your merry books of Italy than by your earnest books [i.e. Catholic theological pamphlets] of Louvain.'[19] Elizabethan romances, which drew on English medieval romance as well as on early modern Italian fiction (and many more sources), demonstrate how literary imagery and generic plot patterns function as media of cultural memory, which preserve, transmit, but also reform inherited models of thought – including discarded Eucharistic concepts.

However, Elizabethan romances do not employ officially abandoned Catholic rituals and doctrines for promoting a clear-cut religio-political position in favor of or against the Catholic, Lutheran, Calvinist, or Zwinglian interpretation of the Last Supper. Neither do they fully sidestep religious issues in their escapist romantic plots. Instead, authors like Robert Greene, Philip Sidney, and Thomas Lodge redeploy the epistemological and emotional thrills of the Eucharist for secular concerns and utilize them for experimenting with the possibilities of the relatively new mode of vernacular prose fiction. The narratives therefore offer instances of a pragmatic rather than polemical handling of religious plurality, as Isabel Karremann and Jonathan Baldo so aptly put it in their introduction to this volume – a pragmatically poetic handling, as it were.

The existing versions of Sidney's *Arcadia* present a number of scenarios that can be read from the vantage point of the Eucharist. In particular, moments of disguise raise questions about the essence beneath the camouflage, or, in theological terms, the substance beneath accidents. Can this invisible substance change? Must the substance change once the accidents have altered? A large amount of the *Arcadia*'s suspense and entertainment stems from a case of cross-gender disguise, which raises the question of whether the masquerade involves a more permanent change of gender identity. After falling in love with a picture of Philoclea, the young Macedonian prince Pyrocles disguises himself as the Amazon Cleophila. Regarding the relationship between substance and accidents, and between identity and outward appearance, Pyrocles introduces his clothing as an ambiguous sign. On the one hand, it certainly is a disguise, and one taken on for strategic reasons: as a woman, he can come closer to Philoclea than any man. On the other hand, Pyrocles claims that his clothes are not a mask but rather the apt expression for his altered inner state, which seeks utmost unity with his beloved, even in terms of gender identity. His new, anagrammatic name is meant to symbolize this desire for identification: 'As for my name, it shall be Cleophila, turning Philoclea to myself, as my mind is wholly turned and transformed into her.'[20] Pyrocles is, as he later comments in a sonnet, 'Transformed in show, but more transformed in mind / … What marvel, then, I take a woman's hue, / Since what I see, think, know, is all but you [i.e. Philoclea]?'[21]

Here Pyrocles imagines his quasi-magical transformation by love, to which he has to surrender helplessly. Indeed, his elder cousin Musidorus initially believes that the disguise not only expresses, but also reinforces Pyrocles' transformation. Musidorus loathes the vision since he sees heterosexual passion as the intrusion of uncontrollable magic into their lives:

> [I]ndeed, the true love hath that excellent nature in it, that it doth *transform the very essence* of the lover into the thing loved, uniting and, as it were, *incorporating* it *with a secret and inward working* …. And this effeminate love of a woman doth so womanize a man that, if you yield to it, it will not only make you a famous Amazon, but a launder, a distaff-spinner.[22]

In this passage, Musidorus envisions the dangerous potential of love as a scenario of supernatural transubstantiation – the Catholic version of the Eucharist likewise employs a 'secret and inward working' to 'transform the very essence' of bread and wine which are thought to 'incorporate' Christ's body.

Pyrocles' female clothes, Musidorus fears, will not only make visible, but also further promote this transubstantiation of Pyrocles' gender identity: 'see how extremely every way you endanger your mind; for to take this woman's habit, without you frame your behaviour accordingly, is wholly vain';[23] 'habit' as dress and as behavior ought to and will eventually be reconciled, Musidorus emphasizes. In the heated argument with his love-struck cousin, he outlines a vicious circle in which passionate love causes effeminacy, which triggers a disguise as a woman, which in turn further reinforces the femininity of Pyrocles.[24] By evoking a scenario of Eucharistic transformation and by insisting on the importance of the appropriate appearance in order to sustain the changeable male identity, Musidorus shows an insistence on the inseparability of accidents and substance comparable to that of Cranmer, who confronted his Catholic opponent Gardiner in the Eucharist debate as follows: 'take away the accidents, and I pray you what difference is between the bodily substance of the sun and the moon, of man and beast, of fish and flesh, ... between a man and a woman?'[25]

Pyrocles not only sees love as a more positive power (and women as less contemptible) than Musidorus, but he also comes to deny the gender-transformative power of clothing. Subsequent to striking the rhetorical pose of the helplessly transformed lover, he explains to his anxious cousin that female clothes will not transubstantiate his manliness, but will, on the contrary, reinforce it: 'Neither doubt you, because I wear a woman's apparel, I will be the more womanish; since, I assure you, for all my apparel, there is nothing I desire more than fully to prove myself a man in this enterprise.'[26] Indeed, the disguised Pyrocles will prove his masculine 'substance' in terms of heterosexual courtship and chivalric feats, both made possible by his witty control of signifiers, or, as Helen Hackett puts it, his 'strategic use of voluntary effeminisation in the cause of virility'.[27] Pyrocles' comment on his identity change, '[t]ransformed in show, but more transformed in mind', can in this context also be understood as a comment on how, through his manipulation of visual signs ('transformed in show'), he is 'transformed in the mind' of others.[28] Thus, as it turns out, Pyrocles' claim of a gender transformation by love is, above all, a rhetorical strategy which justifies his disguise. Likewise, the ensuing action elucidates that Pyrocles' declared longing to incorporate the beloved, as expressed in his anagrammatic name change, aims not only at a psychic identification with Philoclea, but also at a physical, sexual union (to which the narrator, as we will see, concedes only ironically the spiritual idealization which Pyrocles repeatedly invokes).[29]

Among the implications of the Eucharistic ritual for romance, it is in particular the experience of attaining physical union with Christ which lends itself to eroticization. Calvin describes the experience as mutual engrafting: 'Christ to have been so engrafted in us as we, in turn, have been engrafted in him',[30] and the Communion liturgy in the Elizabethan Prayer Book likewise explains it as a reciprocal incorporation and, in consequence, a unification of identities: when 'we receive that holy sacrament … then we spiritually eate the fleshe of Christ, and drincke his bloode, then we dwell in Christe and Christe in us, we be one wyth Christ, and Christe with us'.[31] In the mutually influencing genres of medieval romance and the autobiographic accounts and hagiographies of medieval mystics, communion is frequently eroticized as a sacrament of love in both religious and secular contexts.[32] For example, in a Eucharistic vision from the thirteenth century, a communicant described how Christ approached her from the altar 'in the form and clothing of a Man … wonderful, and beautiful, and with glorious face' and gave himself to her in his other form, the Eucharistic bread. Afterwards, the incorporation by consumption is followed by a more sexual attempt to merge physically: 'he came himself to me, took me entirely in his arms, and pressed me to him; and all my members felt his in full felicity, in accordance with the desire of my heart and my humanity. So I was outwardly satisfied and fully transported.'[33] After this erotic encounter, the vision disappears, but her sense of physical and spiritual unification is enhanced:

> I lost that manly beauty outwardly in the sight of his form. I saw him completely come to naught and so fade and all at once dissolve that I could no longer recognize or perceive him outside me, and I could no longer distinguish him within me. Then it was to me as if we were one without difference …. I wholly melted away in him and nothing any longer remained to me of myself.[34]

I propose that the *Arcadia* revitalizes this literary and religious heritage and puts it to ambiguous uses. On the one hand, the notion of incorporation is employed in an idealized, spiritual manner in the typical early modern amalgamation of Platonist, Christian, and Petrarchan discourses. However, the *Arcadia* intertwines the spiritual desire for unification with physical desire, rather than treating them as irreconcilably dual. Therefore, on the other hand, the Eucharistic scenario is also adapted for erotic fantasies and sexual encounters which not only undermine the spiritualization of love, but also oppose the morality of Sidney's day which sanctioned premarital sexual intercourse. Just like the protagonist's double code of preaching a spiritual identity transformation but simultaneously practicing a deception strategy for erotic ends, the *Arcadia* as a whole rhetorically invokes a theology of love, but contrasts it with a different course of action that at least challenges its rhetoric and sometimes fully strips the amorous of the transcendental.

References to the spiritual or mental union of the lovers, or, put in Eucharistic terms, the notion that communion entails mutual incorporation, recur throughout both *Arcadia* versions. Modeled on Pyrocles' telling name change to Cleophila as an expression for his love for Philoclea, Musidorus and Pamela carve their names into tree trunks as 'Pamedorus and Musimela'.[35]

In the finale of the romance, they name their daughter 'Melidora', while the son of Pyrocles and Philoclea is called 'Pyrophilus'.[36] In a similar vein, both Musidorus and Pyrocles envision in the *New Arcadia* that they enclose the beloved in their minds or that their own minds are engulfed in the beloved.[37]

Towards the more physical pole of the spectrum of Eucharistic allusions, the first moment in the revised *Arcadia* when Pyrocles sees his beloved is cast in blatantly sexualized terms. Pyrocles recounts to Musidorus how his aroused senses, during a (first, rather than Last) supper with the royal family, mistook wine for Philoclea's body:

> my eyes ... when the table was stayed and we began to feed, drank much more eagerly of her beauty than my mouth did of any other liquor .... And so was my common sense deceived, being chiefly bent to her, that as I drank the wine and withal stale a look on her, meseemed I tasted her deliciousness. But alas, the one thirst was much more inflamed than the other quenched.[38]

Sidney here offers, I propose, a scenario of communion between lovers (albeit as yet unidirectional) which is modeled on the Eucharistic ritual. He goes further than earlier narratives, for example in an analogous synaesthetic feeding experience in George Pettie's *Petite Palace*: 'After this amarousin counter [*sic*], he caused the company to sit downe to the banquet, and so disposed the matter, that *Gamma* sat right ouer at the table against him, wherby hée fréely fed his eyes on that meat which conuerted rather to nourishment of sicknesse.'[39] While Pettie's tale draws on the notion of lovesickness, Sidney's description also has Eucharistic overtones. Just as Pyrocles 'drank the wine ... withal stale a look on her', believers who consume (or just see) wine and bread as Christ's body and blood often gazed at depictions of the crucified Christ behind the altar.[40] Moreover, Pyrocles' consumption of the wine values its sensuous qualities, as the Anglican ritual encouraged believers to do. Thus, Cranmer argued in his 'Defence' that Christ indeed is 'put into all ... senses' of the communicants: 'To the intent that as surely as we see the bread and wine with our eyes, smell them with our noses, touch them with our hands, and taste them with our mouths; so assuredly ought we to believe, that Christ is our spiritual life and sustenance, like as the said bread and wine is the food and substance of our bodies.'[41] However, by turning the sensuous into the sensual, Pyrocles' erotic imagination grows so intense that it transcends not only the metonymic association of wine and bodily liquid in the Anglican rite, but also their literal equation by Catholic doctrine: in Pyrocles' profane Eucharist, the wine is not only transubstantiated into Philoclea's 'deliciousness' in a brief moment of erotic ecstasy, but also its accidents have changed (at least pertaining to its taste) to provide an experience of physical fusion for the enamored prince. In line with Protestant criticism of the Catholic ritual, Pyrocles experiences 'an elusion of [his] senses'.[42] His 'Eucharistic miracle' resembles the above-quoted vision from the thirteenth century, which the woman concludes with a comparison that equates consumption and seeing, religion and romance: 'It was thus: outwardly, to see, taste, and feel in the reception of the outward Sacrament. So can the Beloved, with the loved one, each wholly receive the other in all full satisfaction of the sight, the hearing, and the passing away of the one in the other.'[43]

Nonetheless, immediately after his pseudo-Eucharistic erotic vision, Pyrocles recovers his 'common sense' and with it, his longing for an actual physical fusion; as described, his 'thirst' for Philoclea is 'much more inflamed'. To ultimately 'taste' Philoclea's 'deliciousness', Pyrocles realizes, he will have to rely on his disguise and his cunning manipulation of signifiers, rather than aim at supernatural transformation. Pyrocles' subsequent attempts to come closer to Philoclea (as well as Musidorus' attempts to come closer to Pamela) adapt the desire for the corporeal experience of 'real presence' as an erotic pattern and as narrative structure: the sexual encounters with the princesses are constantly deferred, but the yearning is fueled by the increasing intimacy between the princesses and the disguised princes. The supper scene of a quasi-Eucharistic communion is original to the revised *Arcadia*, but the earlier version contains a similar scenario in the first eclogues, in which the lovers reflect on their desires. Here, Pyrocles in Petrarchan manner blends amorous and religious imagery to express his alteration by love and his desire to reveal himself to Philoclea. In a metaphoric scenario of sacrificing pieces of his wounded heart, that is, his flesh and blood, Pyrocles uses the term 'oblation', which was central to the Eucharist debate: 'And for a sure sacrifice I do daily oblation offer / Of my own heart, where thoughts be the temple, sight is an altar.'[44]

Spenser's *Faerie Queene*, published in the same year as Sidney's *Arcadia*, likewise associates wine, flirtation, and the Eucharist in its famous 'sacrament prophane in mistery of wine'.[45] Paridell and Hellenore, modeled on Paris and Helen of Ovid's *Heroides*, secretly communicate their desire for each other during supper, supervised by Hellenore's jealous husband. At first, they exchange flirtatious gazes, which, in keeping with the topos of love at first sight, have the effects of a 'fyrie dart' that penetrates the heart (III.ix.28.8, 29.2), but soon they devise an additional means of communication:

> Thenceforth to her he sought to intimate
> His inward griefe [that is, his desire for her], by meanes to him well knowne,
> Now Bacchus fruit out of the siluer plate
> He on the table dasht, as ouerthrowne,
> Or of the fruitfull liquor ouerflowne.
> And by the dauncing bubbles did diuine,
> Or therein write to let his loue be showne;
> Which well she red out of the learned line,
> A sacrament prophane in mistery of wine.

And when so of his hand the pledge she raught,
The guilty cup she fained to mistake,
And in her lap did shed her idle draught,
Shewing desire her inward flame to slake:
By such close signes they secret way did make
Vnto their wils, and one eies watch escape.
(III.ix.30.1–31.6)

As Mihoko Suzuki has shown, Paridell's line is 'learned' and his 'meanes … well knowne' since it draws on Ovid's *Heroides*, where Paris writes *amo* in spilt wine – a gesture which was discussed as a potential strategy of courtly love in Castiglione's *Il Cortegiano.*[46] In the politically and religiously charged climate of England in the 1580s and 1590s – possibly even more so for writers like Sidney and Spenser who were involved in the English imperialist project to subdue the Catholic Irish – the pagan association of wine and secular sexuality has Eucharistic overtones, as Spenser's explicit reference to 'sacrament prophane in mistery of wine' shows. Scholars agree that Spenser's invocation of the Eucharist for the depiction of blatantly sexual, adulterous love play is meant to reinforce criticism of the lovers for their 'shocking blasphemy',[47] their 'blasphemous perversion of Holy Communion'.[48] By contrast, the *Arcadia*'s secular Eucharist scenarios do not demonize the lovers as unequivocally, which might be one of the reasons why its Eucharistic imagery is more implicit. Instead, they are in line with the narrator's ironic but affectionate view of the imperfect, often too passionate, and at times culpable protagonists.[49]

Carol V. Kaske's *Spenser and Biblical Poetics* investigates the *Faerie Queene*'s 'farcical sexual travesty of the true Eucharist' in comparison with other moments in which cups of wine are presented in the romance, differentiating between *in bono* and *in malo* uses of the Eucharistic reference.[50] The adaptation of the Eucharistic ritual by the adulterous lovers is, for Kaske, clearly an example of *in malo* use, but she identifies more forthright criticism of the Catholic Eucharist in Spenser's depiction of the whore Duessa's cup that is 'replete with magick artes' and contains 'secret poison' (I.viii.14):

Which [the contents of Duessa's cup] after charmes and some
enchauntments said,
She lightly sprinkled on his [Timias'] weaker parts;
Therewith his sturdie courage soone was quayd,
And all his senses were with suddeine dread dismayd.
So downe he fell before the cruell beast,
…
No power he had to stirre, nor will to rize.
(I.viii.14–15)

This scene offers a demonic version, as Kaske observes, of not only the Roman Catholic mass in general, but of transubstantiation in particular:

Duessa's 'enchantments said' resemble the priest's performative 'hoc est corpus meum', and the enthrallment of Timias' senses after (albeit unwillingly) consuming the wine, as well as his kneeling, are further markers of (the Protestant critique of) the Catholic ritual.[51] The general function of Spenser's shifting use of the image of the cup is that of an 'exercise in readerly discrimination' according to Kaske: to make readers aware of the importance of exactly how Eucharistic rituals and symbols are used and to join Spenser in 'fine-tuning' their 'definition of a good Eucharist'.[52] Kaske concludes that by means of this complex eliciting of careful perception and subsequent judgment, which sidesteps 'the either/or thinking of the iconoclast', the 'social purpose' of Spenser's *Faerie Queene* ultimately is the promotion of 'religious toleration'.[53]

In a similar vein, critics have tried to find evidence for Sidney's precise religious position in his fictional writings, with very differing results: Sidney has been associated with Ancient Theology, moderate Protestantism, more radical Calvinism and fierce anti-Catholicism, and Philippism; however, critics have also detected surprisingly pro-Catholic strands in his narrative.[54] In contrast to these studies, I do not suggest reading Sidney's *Arcadia* as a comment on topical religious debates or as a manifestation of Sidney's affiliation with a particular religious or political group in the increasingly pluralized Elizabethan society. Instead, it appears more fruitful to explore how Sidney adopts figures of thought from the Eucharist for aesthetic (and hence never fully determinate) ends. The Eucharist provided Sidney with a conceptual pattern to think about the invisible change of a person's substance and its impact on the imagination – and vice versa, the impact of imagination on unseen identity change. By adapting Eucharistic theorems, the romance can explore phenomena that accompany the experience of love, such as psychic alterations, the transformation of the lover's perception, and the (trans-)formation of the beloved in the lover's perception. Further, the Eucharist's preoccupation with 'real presence' and mutual incorporation is employed to depict the yearning for not only spiritual and psychic, but also bodily unification of the lovers.

Thus, just like other Elizabethan narratives inspired by the mode of romance, the *Arcadia* 'romances' the Eucharist. It creatively adapts hotly contested theological and liturgical issues for its thematic concerns and its aesthetic experiment in the form of prose fiction rather than making a religio-political case for one particular form of faith.[55]

Notes

1 Philip Sidney, *The Countess of Pembroke's Arcadia: The Old Arcadia*, ed. Katherine Duncan-Jones (Oxford: Oxford University Press, 1994), p. 105.

2 *Ibid.*

3 *Ibid.*, p. 106, and Philip Sidney, *The Countess of Pembroke's Arcadia: The New Arcadia*, ed. Victor Skretkowicz (Oxford: Oxford University Press, 1987), p. 231.

4 Roger Ascham, *The Schoolmaster*, ed. Lawrence V. Ryan (Ithaca, NY: Cornell University Press, 1967), pp. 62, 66.
5 *Ibid.*, p. 66.
6 John 6:53–56, in *The Geneva Bible: A Facsimile of the 1560 Edition*, ed. Lloyd E. Berry and William Whittingham (Peabody, MA: Hendrickson, 2007).
7 'Consubstantiation' is not Luther's term, but was applied in retrospect to characterize his position.
8 M. Rubin, *Corpus Christi: The Eucharist in Late Medieval Culture* (Cambridge: Cambridge University Press, 1991), p. 361; C. Elwood, *The Body Broken: The Calvinist Doctrine of the Eucharist and the Symbolization of Power in Sixteenth-Century France* (Oxford: Oxford University Press, 1999), p. 4.
9 Elizabeth Mazzola. *The Pathology of the English Renaissance: Sacred Remains and Holy Ghosts* (Leiden: Brill, 1998), p. 1.
10 *Ibid.*, p. 9.
11 J. Assmann, *Religion and Cultural Memory: Ten Studies*, trans. R. Livingstone (Stanford: Stanford University Press, 2006), p. 25.
12 A. Assmann, *Cultural Memory and Western Civilization: Functions, Media, Archives* (Cambridge: Cambridge University Press, 2011), p. 398.
13 P. Strohm, 'The Croxton Play of the Sacrament: Commemoration and Repetition in Late Medieval Culture', in T. Döring and S. Rupp (eds), *Performances of the Sacred in Late Medieval and Early Modern England* (Amsterdam: Rodopi, 2005), p. 33.
14 R. Helgerson, *The Elizabethan Prodigals* (Berkeley: University of California Press, 1976), p. 91. Helgerson sees 'humanism and romance as opposed members of a single consciousness, as superego and id of Elizabethan literature, competitors in a struggle to control and define the self. Humanism represented paternal expectation, and romance, rebellious desire' (*ibid.*, p. 41).
15 H. Cooper, *The English Romance in Time: Transforming Motifs from Geoffrey of Monmouth to the Death of Shakespeare* (Oxford: Oxford University Press, 2004), p. 250.
16 N. Frye, *The Secular Scripture: A Study of the Structure of Romance* (Cambridge, MA: Harvard University Press, 1976).
17 N. Das, *Renaissance Romance: The Transformation of English Prose Fiction, 1570–1620* (Aldershot: Ashgate, 2011), p. 5.
18 Ascham, *The Schoolmaster*, p. 68.
19 *Ibid.*, pp. 69, 68.
20 Sidney, *The Old Arcadia*, p. 17.
21 *Ibid.*, p. 26. For an alternative reading of the scene in the light of the Neoplatonic concept of divine versus human love, see W. Davis, 'A Map of Arcadia: Sidney's Romance in Its Tradition', in W. R. Davis and R. A. Lanham (eds), *Sidney's Arcadia* (New Haven: Yale University Press, 1965), pp. 1–79, at pp. 69–71. V. Olejniczak Lobsien and E. Lobsien likewise relate the scene to the Neoplatonic ideal of courtly behavior as phrased by Castiglione (*Die unsichtbare Imagination: Literarisches Denken im 16. Jahrhundert* [Munich: Fink, 2003], pp. 203–30). See also Olejniczak Lobsien's examination of Pyrocles' cross-dressing as an 'allegory of his courtly self' in her essay '"Transformed in show, but more transformed in mind": Sidney's *Old Arcadia* and the Performance of Perfection', in Döring and Rupp (eds), *Performances of the Sacred*, p. 113.

22 Sidney, *The Old Arcadia*, p. 18, and *The New Arcadia*, pp. 71–2, my emphasis.

23 Sidney, *The Old Arcadia*, p. 18.

24 Some critics have followed Musidorus in his assumption of a complete inner and outer transformation of his cousin. For example, reading the *Arcadia* versions as stories of 'quasi-Ovidian change', E. Dipple argues for a 'total physical change which is urged by a new interior experience and performed with idealistic ignorance' and which makes Pyrocles 'launch … completely into a new persona' in the *Old Arcadia*; 'Metamorphosis in Sidney's *Arcadia*', in A. F. Kinney (ed.), *Essential Articles for the Study of Sir Philip Sidney* (Hamden, CT: Archon Books, 1986), pp. 328, 338. I will argue that this vision of interconnected transubstantiation and metamorphosis is most of all a rhetorical strategy, as other critics have observed (e.g. Olejniczak Lobsien and Lobsien, *Die unsichtbare Imagination*, p. 211).

25 T. Cranmer, 'An Answer to a Crafty and Sophisticated Cavillation Devised by Stephen Gardiner', in J. E. Cox (ed.), *Writings and Disputations of Thomas Cranmer Relative to the Sacrament of the Lord's Supper* (Cambridge: Cambridge University Press, 1844 [1551]), p. 260. As J. H. Anderson points out in her detailed analysis of the debate between Cranmer and Gardiner, 'Cranmer's objection operates within Gardiner's terms, insisting only that accidents must inhere in their proper substance and not questioning the basic division of objects into substance and accident', as other Protestant treatises did ('Language and History in the Reformation: Cranmer, Gardiner, and the Words of Institution', *Renaissance Quarterly*, 54:1 [2001], 34–5).

26 Sidney, *The Old Arcadia*, p. 21.

27 H. Hackett, *Women and Romance Fiction in the English Renaissance* (Cambridge: Cambridge University Press, 2000), p. 113.

28 Sidney, *The Old Arcadia*, p. 131.

29 Olejniczak Lobsien and Lobsien (*Die unsichtbare Imagination*, pp. 210–11) explore the ambiguity of the disguise as a conflict between personal agency and the extra-personal power of love as personified by Eros, which the *Old Arcadia* invokes but does not fully endorse. Cf. C. R. Kinney 'The Masks of Love: Desire and Metamorphosis in Sidney's *New Arcadia*', *Criticism: A Quarterly for Literature and the Arts*, 33:4 (1991), 461–90 for a discussion of the complex role of Cupid in the *New Arcadia*.

30 Jean Calvin, *Institutes of the Christian Religion: 1536 Edition*, trans. and annotated by F. Lewis Battles, rev. edn (Grand Rapids, MI: Eerdmans, 1986), p. 102, IV.C.24.

31 B. Cummings (ed.), *The Book of Common Prayer: The Texts of 1549, 1559, and 1662* (Oxford: Oxford University Press, 2011), p. 132.

32 B. Newman, 'Exchanging Hearts', presentation at Harvard's Medieval Colloquium, October 1, 2009. See also the second chapter of W. W. E. Slights's *The Heart in the Age of Shakespeare* (Cambridge: Cambridge University Press, 2008), which traces literary and visual examples of the 'interchange of hearts' motif from medieval to early modern times. Slights explores how '[t]he amorously inflamed heart of the lover from innumerable medieval romances finds a shocking new context for

display in the hands of devout nuns offering themselves to Christ and receiving Him into themselves' (p. 50).

33 Hadewijch, *The Complete Works*, ed. Columba Hart (New York: Paulist Press, 1980), p. 281.

34 *Ibid.*, pp. 281–2. For a discussion, see C. Walker Bynum, 'Women Mystics and Eucharistic Devotion in the Thirteenth Century', *Women's Studies: An Interdisciplinary Journal*, 11:1–2 (1984), 179–80.

35 Sidney, *The Old Arcadia*, pp. 174.

36 *Ibid.*, p. 361.

37 Sidney, *The New Arcadia*, pp. 309–10.

38 *Ibid.*, p. 86. In the Elizabethan Book of Common Prayer, the sacrament of Communion is also compared to a secular banquet; a 'riche feaste' 'with al kynde of provision' (Cummings, *Book of Common Prayer*, p. 130).

39 G. Pettie, *A Petite Pallace of Pettie His Pleasure: Contaynyng Many Pretie Hystories by Him Set Foorth in Comely Colours, and Most Delightfully Discoursed* (printed at London: By R. W[atkins], 1576 [EEBO]), p. 4, image 7.

40 See J. L. Koerner's study *The Reformation of the Image* (Chicago: University of Chicago Press, 2004), which shows how altarpieces usually focused on Christ's Passion and Crucifixion and only with the Reformation and its new focus on Communion and remembrance began to concentrate on the Last Supper (pp. 340–61).

41 T. Cranmer, 'Defence of the True and Catholic Doctrine of the Sacrament', in G. E. Duffield (ed.), *The Work of Thomas Cranmer* (Philadelphia: Fortress Press, 1965), p. 71.

42 *Ibid.*, pp. 87–8. Cranmer goes on: 'And so we make much for their purposes that said that Christ was a crafty juggler, that made things to appear to men's sight that indeed were no such things, but forms only, figures and appearances' (p. 88).

43 Hadewijch, *The Complete Works*, pp. 281–2.

44 Sidney, *The Old Arcadia*, p. 78. Cf. Cummings, *Book of Common Prayer*, pp. 701 and 731. In an advanced stage of the narrative in the *New Arcadia*, when Musidorus has already revealed his true identity to Pamela, the drinking of wine is again erotically charged. Here, Musidorus attempts to kiss Pamela, '[b]ut she, as if she had been ready to drink a wine of excellent taste and colour which suddenly she perceived had poison in it, so did she put him away from her' (p. 309). That wine and sexuality are associated in an ambivalent manner is characteristic of the *Arcadia*'s overall ambiguous attitude towards premarital sexuality. It is also due to the gender ideals of the age, whose 'aristocratic "double standard" tolerated strong sexuality in young noblemen if not young women'; D. Norbrook, *Poetry and Politics in the English Renaissance*, rev. edn (Oxford: Oxford University Press, 2002), p. 90. Wine-as-sexual-encounter provides a wishful fantasy of physical union for Pyrocles – though critics disagree about the extent to which this desire and its later premarital fulfillment in the *Old Arcadia* compromise Pyrocles' status as an ideal gentleman – but sexual-encounter-as-wine appears as a poisonous danger to Pamela, who attempts to protect her chastity, and hence shows her adherence to the ideal of the gentlewoman.

45 Edmund Spenser, *The Faerie Qveene*, ed. A. C. Hamilton, Hiroshi Yamashita, and Toshiyuki Suzuki, rev. edn (Harlow: Pearson, 2007 [1596]), III. 9.30.9.
46 M. Suzuki, *Metamorphoses of Helen: Authority, Difference, and the Epic* (Ithaca, NY: Cornell University Press, 1989), p. 164.
47 R. Tuve, *Elizabethan and Metaphysical Imagery: Renaissance Poetic and Twentieth-Century Critic* (Chicago: University of Chicago Press, 1947), p. 221.
48 Suzuki, *Metamorphosis of Helen*, p. 164.
49 This attitude comes particularly to the fore in the *Old Arcadia*, in which the narrator is more overt and borders on becoming homodiegetic. Here, he explicitly declares his 'compassion' with Pyrocles (p. 25). The narrator's affectionate view of the protagonists is particularly noteworthy given Pyrocles' consensual premarital sexuality and Musidorus' intention to violate Pamela while she is asleep. By contrast, the revised version delegates the darker sides of sexuality to the new character Amphialus.
50 C. V. Kaske, *Spenser and Biblical Poetics* (Ithaca, NY: Cornell University Press, 1999), p. 51.
51 *Ibid.*, pp. 42 and 44. Cf. also D. D. Waters, *Duessa as Theological Satire* (Columbia: University of Missouri Press, 1970), pp. 104–6.
52 Kaske, *Spenser and Biblical Poetics*, pp. 48, 49.
53 *Ibid.*, p. 97.
54 D. P. Walker traces Sidney's inclination towards Ancient Theology in *The Ancient Theology: Studies in Christian Platonism from the Fifteenth to the Eighteenth Century* (Ithaca, NY: Cornell University Press, 1972), p. 163. A. Sinfield contradicts Walker, arguing instead that Sidney would have shared the Protestant view that '[s]alvation is granted only through true religion'; 'Sidney, De Plessis-Mornay and the Pagans', *Philological Quarterly*, 58 (1979), 29. More recently, B. Worden's study of the *Arcadia* versions as political allegories has read the *Old Arcadia* in the light of the political crisis caused by Queen Elizabeth's apparent intention to marry the Duke of Anjou and the *New Arcadia* as concerned with the threat presented by Mary, Queen of Scots (*The Sound of Virtue: Philip Sidney's Arcadia and Elizabethan Politics* [New Haven: Yale University Press, 1996]). B. Brumbaugh's reading of the *New Arcadia* follows Worden and proposes to regard Cecropia as a demonic personification of the Church of Rome; 'Cecropia and the Church of Antichrist in Sir Philip Sidney's *New Arcadia*', *Studies in English Literature, 1500–1900*, 38:1 (1998), 19–43. By contrast, K. Duncan-Jones highlights Sidney's Catholic sympathies in 'Sir Philip Sidney's Debt to Edmund Campion', in T. M. McCoog (ed.), *The Reckoned Expense: Edmund Campion and the Early English Jesuits: Essays in Celebration of the First Centenary of Campion Hall, Oxford (1896–1996)*, 2nd, rev. edn with additional material (Rome: Institutum Historicum Societatis Iesu, 2007), pp. 85–118, and J. Kingsley-Smith likewise discovers astonishingly positive attitudes towards Catholicism in Sidney's *Arcadia*, while arguing that Sidney's Protestant beliefs developed from a Calvinist to a Lutheran bias: 'Cupid, Idolatry, and Iconoclasm in Sidney's *Arcadia*', *Studies in English Literature, 1500–1900*, 48:1 (2008), 66.

Most convincing to me seems R. E. Stillman's account, which proposes to overcome 'the failed paradigm of Calvinist piety for interpreting Sidneian poetics' in favor of Philippism, which reconciled Protestant and Catholic attitudes, also with regard to the Eucharist; see 'Deadly Stinging Adders: Sidney's Piety, Philippism, and the Defence of Poesy', *Spenser Studies: A Renaissance Poetry Annual*, 16 (2002), 236.

55 This chapter draws on my study *The Reformation of Romance: The Eucharist, Disguise, and Foreign Fashion in Early Modern Prose Fiction*. Anglia Book Series 44 (Berlin: de Gruyter, 2014).

5

Edmund Spenser's *The Ruines of Time* as a Protestant poetics of mourning and commemoration

Isabel Karremann

> I have completed a memorial more lasting than bronze and higher than the royal grave of the pyramids.
>
> Horace, *Odes*, Book 3, Ode 30

According to Horace, the poem is a memorial surpassing the commemorative function of funeral monuments like the pyramids. This claim to the superior mnemonic power of poetry derives from the immateriality and consequently, the argument goes, the immortality of the poem as well as the person commemorated by it. The immortality-of-poetry topos is thus informed by a structural opposition between the material monument on the one hand, which is subject to decay, destruction, and erasure, and the immaterial monument that lasts forever. Highlighting the decay, past and future, of material monuments, the ruin is a conceptual feature of this topos. In spite of being a constant figurative element, however, the significance of ruins changes according to different temporal and cultural contexts. Thus in the wake of Reformation iconoclasm, ruin poems took on a specific function in England. This choice of ruins as a topic in themselves is perhaps not surprising since the dissolution of the monasteries 'left a landscape virtually littered with ruins', as Philip Schwyzer has pointed out; hence 'the link between the creation of so many new English ruins and the subsequent burgeoning of the ruin theme in English poetry seems self-evident'.[1] But the vogue for ruin poems in Elizabethan England was more than a simple coincidence, let alone self-evident: ruin-poetry, I will argue, fulfilled important social, mnemonic and poetic functions after the Reformation. This essay seeks to reconstruct these functions and to show how they informed one particularly instructive text, Edmund Spenser's *The Ruines of Time* (1590).

Previous critics have tried to specify the cultural function of ruins in early modern England. Anne Janowitz, for example, has argued that 'the ruin of the monasteries' after the dissolution amounted to 'a constitutive moment of English absolutism', a visible sign of England's break with Rome and thus of its claim to political and religious autonomy. Ruins became a point of identification for a Protestant English nation, an identity that was imagined and made immortal especially in poetry. Hence, Janowitz argues, in Renaissance England 'the immortality-of-poetry topos was most unproblematically a fixture of poetic practice and served as well to build the sense of nationhood by offering the poem as the permanent image of the nation'. Rephrasing the ancient topos in an imperial register, she claims more generally that 'ruin imagery cannot help asserting the visible evidence of historical and imperial impermanence'. This 'ephemerality of empire' is counterbalanced by the 'assertion of the permanence of art', and in particular of poetry, which is immaterial and hence not subject to decay. It is precisely because of this immateriality as an indicator of immortality that poetry had been enlisted to 'preserve the founding of the nation in a permanent image', a collaboration which became most obvious in the genre of epic.[2] While I agree with Janowitz that ruin-poetry was an important imaginative site of nation-building in early modern England, it seems rather unlikely that this function was being fulfilled 'most unproblematically' at the time. I would argue to the contrary that the topos as well as the imaginative uses of ruins were in fact highly problematic and far from stable in post-Reformation literature.[3]

The historically specific instability of the topos emerges when we look at texts about monastic ruins in particular. Far from affording a clear, stable focus for an emergent Protestant Englishness, they vary considerably in their confessional and political attitudes toward Reformation iconoclasm. Examples would include passages from Samuel Daniel's *Complaint of Rosamond* (1592) and *Musophilus* (1599), where Daniel tries to make monastic ruins emblematic only of the power of time and in so doing evacuates contemporary confessional conflicts of their political and moral explosiveness, thus effectively answering one act of erasure with another; different and differently valorized scenes of iconoclasm from Spenser's *Faerie Queene*, such as the destruction of the sinful Bower of Bliss, or the Blatant Beast's devastation of a monastery, which oscillate between enthusiastic Protestant applause on the one hand and implicit Catholic grief on the other; the anonymous 'Lament for Our Lady's Shrine at Walsingham' that articulates intense sorrow for the fall of the famous Catholic abbey, but does so, curiously, through the tropes and vocabulary of Protestant reform; the conspicuously anachronistic scene from Shakespeare's *Titus Andronicus* when the invading Goths stumble upon the ruin of a Christian monastery on the margins of pre-Christian Rome; and the beautifully ambivalent image of the 'bare ruined choirs' in Shakespeare's Sonnet 73.[4] Indeed, the spectacle of monastic ruins apparently was able to render confessional loyalties irrelevant altogether, as one non-literary example suggests: Michael Sherbrook was a priest of the reformed Church of England, yet in his *Fall of Religious Houses* (*c.* 1591) he idealized monastic life and regretted the dissolution. Confronted with the wreck of the monasteries, distinct confessional identities, views, and conflicts dissolve and become meaningless. This may in fact have been one of the particular pleasures ruins provided in late-sixteenth-century England, Philipp Schwyzer concludes: 'There seem to have been some Elizabethans who valued the ruins in their midst for precisely this reason – gazing on a shattered abbey, they might leave behind or suspend the allegiances which structured and straitened all social and private life.'[5] In this sense, Elizabethan ruins functioned not only as national *lieux de mémoire*, as Janowitz suggested, but also as places of forgetting the religious conflicts of the time.

Ruin poetry did not simply offer an escape from the trauma of destruction and instability, however. In keeping with the Reformation's valorization of the word over the image, the immortality-of-poetry topos promised that poetic language could provide a haven of stability, truth, and permanence. But while the word clearly won the struggle over the image,[6] it did not escape unscathed, as the dire fate of the dissolved monastery libraries shows. As Jennifer Summit has argued, the Reformer's destruction of monastic libraries in 1535 had a destabilizing impact on the material and epistemological status of the written word. According to her reading, Spenser's *The Faerie Queene* offers a poetic reflection on this instability in the library of Eumenestes in Book II. The two texts that are mentioned explicitly in Spenser's description of that library – *Briton moniments* and *Antiquitie of Faerie lond* – signal a preoccupation with the endangered status of books and the memory they contain: 'monument' and 'antiquity' became charged terms in the project of rescuing and preserving medieval books. Moreover, both books are highlighted as unfinished, textual ruins: 'there abruptly it did end', we learn about the *Antiquitie*, which breaks off with the story of Arthur's father, Uther Pendragon.[7] This gap in the record, Jennifer Summit argues, reflects the instability of the written record.[8] Precisely because 'the dissolution had been a textual as well as an architectural disaster', Schwyzer concurs, ruins (and especially monastic ruins) could not 'be easily subsumed under the Horatian topos of the endurance of language any more'.[9] The doubt thus cast on the stability of language generally also has implications for poetic language, and in particular for those poetic monuments whose task it traditionally had been to convey immortality and enduring memory: laments and elegies.

A striking case in point is *The Ruines of Time*, the opening poem of Spenser's volume of *Complaints*, which functions as a programmatic poetological statement as well as being an elegy for the Protestant hero Philip Sidney. The poem falls roughly into two parts. The first, comprising about two-thirds of the text, is a lament by the mythical figure of Verlame, who bewails her own oblivion by the world and takes this as an occasion to call for a proper commemoration of that 'mightie Prince' of poetry, Sidney.[10] The second, shorter part, consisting of two sets of dream visions, answers to this call by offering a poetic monument to Sidney's memory. Yet what the poem does is much more complicated than this brief summary suggests: it explores the cultural conflict about the modes of mourning and commemoration permissible in post-Reformation England, and it performatively enacts this struggle in its own poetic form. It does so by evoking the immortality-of-poetry topos, yet only to evacuate and discard it in favor of a view of poetry that acknowledges the instability of monuments, images, and memories. This semiotic instability, in Schwyzer's view, is a legacy of Reformation iconoclasm.[11] In this sense, I will argue, the poem's treatment of the topos serves to develop a poetics of mourning and commemoration suited to a post-Reformation sensibility.

The prefatory matter to *The Ruines of Time* already draws attention to the instability of both poems and memories. The dedicatory epistle from 'The Printer to the Gentle Reader' presents the volume of *Complaints* as a (re-) collection of poems that 'were disperst abroad in sundrie hands .... Of the which, I haue by good meanes gathered togeather these fewe parcles present.'[12] The printer-editor thus highlights the fragmentary status of the entire collection and foreshadows the final acknowledgment that *Ruines* is itself a piece of 'broken verse' (line 678). The following dedication to Sidney's sister Mary, Countess of Pembroke, confesses Spenser's admiration for his patron Philip Sidney, 'that most brave Knight your noble brother deceased'. It confesses likewise his failure to have adequately expressed this admiration and his sorrow about Sidney's death until now. Spenser explicitly regrets 'that I haue not shewed anie thankefull remembrance towards him or any of them [the other members of the family]; but suffer their names to sleep in silence and forgetfulnesse'. By way of compensation and atonement, *The Ruines of Time* is explicitly 'intended to the renowning of that noble race, from which you and he sprong, and to the eternizing of some of the chiefe of them late deceased'.[13]

The dedicatory letter thus evokes the conventional topos of the immortality of poetry written to defy 'silence and forgetfulnesse'. The poem that follows, however, does not so much seek to redress this neglect as to address the vexed question of how what looks like forgetful silence can in fact be a more proper way of commemoration in keeping with a Protestant theology. For the proper 'eternizing' of the Protestant hero Sidney does not lie in any of the highly conventionalized utterances of grief that constitute the greatest part of the poem, as C. J. Rasmussen points out, but 'in the dramatic unfolding of the sequence and in particular of the remarkable visions that conclude it'.[14] The poem deconstructs the desire for eternal memorialization as a worldly, specifically Roman Catholic, vanity and presents instead a different, distinctly Protestant practice of commemoration as a perpetual task. While the first mode of mourning places memory and oblivion in opposition, thus affirming the immortality-of-poetry topos and wishing to erect the poem as an eternal monument, the latter integrates forgetting and remembering into a re-creative circle of destruction and reconstruction. It is more wary of any claims to eternity on earth that the first, and rather treats poetry as a mode of perpetual becoming whose permanence lies in changeability.

The co-presence of both these modes in the poem has given rise to two radically divergent critical readings of *Ruines of Time*. The one stresses the validity of the immortality-of-poetry topos and sees Spenser's *Ruines* as an embodiment of it; the other acknowledges the poem's wariness about the very possibility of achieving such durability in this world. While both readings locate Spenser's poem in the context of and as a reaction to Reformation iconoclasm, they do so within a significantly different interpretive framework. The first reading adopts what may be called a 'compensation model' in that it subscribes to the view – familiar since antiquity – that the durability of poetry functions as a substitute for the transience of the material monument: the poem compensates in effect for the oblivion that results from the tomb's eventual ephemerality. In spite of acknowledging the historically specific situation after the iconoclastic surges of the Reformation, this reading therefore tends to emphasize a transhistorical permanence of poetry, mimicking the very topos it seeks to describes.[15] The second reading is more skeptical and more radically historicizing, answering to what I call a 'model of complementarity'. Eschewing the binary oppositions of mortality versus immortality, monument versus poem, oblivion versus memory, which structure the first reading, such a view recognizes instead that these are complementary forces at work everywhere in early modern culture and its artifacts, be they material or verbal.[16] In so doing, it seems to me, such a complementary stance toward commemoration is able to capture more comprehensively the memory crisis triggered by Reformation iconoclasm and the contemporary responses to it, among which the desire to compensate for what is lost was only one of many.

Spenser's poem signals its preoccupation with a new post-Reformation anxiety about the instability of monuments, memory, and mourning already at the very outset. The narrator, ambling 'one day beside the shore / Of siluer streaming Thamesis' (lines 1–2), comes across the site of the ancient city of Verulamium. He does not, however, see the ruins of a city, a view that might give him pause to contemplate the vanity of all worldly things and might lead him, by comparison and contrast, to a praise of the immortality of poetry. In fact, there are no ruins to see at all. Verulamium is truly gone, 'Of which there now remaines no memorie, / Nor anie little moniment to see' (lines 4–5). The poem thus sets in with the absence of memory, or to be more precise, with the evocation of a historically false *lieux de mémoire*: Verulamium in fact never was located on the shores of the Thames, an original absence that is marked by the conspicuous absence of any material ruins. They exist only in the lament of Verlame, 'th' auncient *Genius* of that Citie'.[17] Verlame's lament for the city makes up the greatest part of the text, and in this sense the poem might indeed seem to step in for the absent memorial. It thus appears quite in keeping with the immortality-of-poetry topos and the compensations it promises. The effect of this opening is not, however, a neat replacement of a poetic for a material monument, as Rebecca Helfer cautions, but rather a 'confusion of material and memorial ruin' that points to 'the poem's central paradox: poetic monuments, like material ones, fall to ruin'. Instead of repairing the ruins through his immortal verse, 'Spenser locates immortality in ruin itself – in poetry's ruins – and in the process of recollection.'[18] Throughout, the poem presents itself not as a durable, unchanging memorial, but as a dynamic, perpetual process of recollection that integrates acts of remembering as well as of forgetting. From this perspective, poetry does not appear as a stable mnemonic artifact that must compensate for the oblivion materialized in ruins. On the contrary, ruins emerge as a figure of thought for the ongoing process of recollection which poetry itself enacts.

At first sight, this seems to be a counterintuitive claim. After all, Verlame's lament insistently articulates an oppositional pattern of presence and absence correlating with the dichotomous relation between poem and monument, memory and oblivion that makes the former function as compensation for the latter. Verlame enumerates her former glories, 'the beawtie of my buildings fayre, / Adorned with purest golde, and precious stone' (lines 85–6), the

> High towers, faire temples, goodly theaters,
> Strong walls, rich porches, princelie pallaces,
> Large streetes, braue houses, sacred sepulchers,
> Sure gates, sweete gardens, stately galleries,
> Wrought with faire pollours, and fine imageries.
> (lines 92–6)

These stanzas close with a gesture of loss and erasure – 'All those (O pitie) now are turned to dust, / And ouergrowed with blacke obliuions rust' (lines 97–8) – that points out the contrast between then and now in terms not only of former glories defaced but specifically in terms of the decay of memory. The contrast between what is remembered and what is now forgotten becomes the pattern, repeated in an accelerating rhythm, of the next couple of stanzas. This movement of recall and erasure is rendered in a series of opposing deictic references oscillating between 'where was' and 'there now' (stanzas 19–23), which might easily slide into a nostalgic valorization of the lost past, offering it as a stable reference point from which to judge the defective present.

Yet the quantitative prominence of Verlame's lines (covering exactly two-thirds of the poem) is undercut by her being presented as a highly unreliable narrator. This is achieved through various intertextual and contextual references that frame her ironically and distance the reader from what emerges increasingly as an embodiment of traditional Roman Catholic modes of mourning and commemoration. Already the very conspicuousness of Verlame's grief sets her apart from a Protestant sensibility that, as C. J. Rasmussen has shown, rejected excessive mourning for the dead, as they were in God's keeping now.[19] Another ironic frame is provided by the poem's intertextual references to the Geneva Bible, that foundational textual monument of the Protestant Reformation. Verlame's lament recalls, at times verbatim, biblical precursors such as the ruin of Babylon in the Book of Revelation that, for Protestants, prefigured the deserved downfall of Rome and the Roman Church.[20] Verlame's language echoes in particular the complaints of the ungodly, whose desire for worldly fame culminates too late in the insight that 'Our name also shalbe forgotten in time, an no man shal haue our workes in remembrance' (Wisd. of Sol. 2:1–15). Moreover, Verlame explicitly presents herself as a dutiful daughter of Rome. She nostalgically sympathizes with the fallen empires of Assyria, Persia, Greece (stanza 10) and with Rome itself: 'O Rome thy ruine I lament and rue, / and in thy fall my overthrowe' (lines 78–9); 'And of the whole world as thou wast the Empresse, / So I of this small Northerne world was Princesse' (lines 83–4). This genealogy of heathen and Catholic empires would have served to forestall a similar empathy in the contemporary Protestant reader, Rasmussen claims: 'England had severed its ties with papal Rome, and English Protestants were not inclined to admire the papacy's imperial predecessor, either. They would have held with St. Augustine in the City of God that the fall of Rome was divine retribution for godlessness and unbridled lust for dominion.'[21] The poem's ironic framing of Verlame's voice thus indicates a skeptical perspective that would be at odds with a genuine lament for the downfall of a daughter of Rome, making it possible to read Verlame's lament as a parody of a Catholic complaint about the effects of the Reformation. Given this persistent ironic distancing, Deborah Cartmell argues, the poem should be read as 'a celebration of the Elizabethan break with Rome' rather than a lament for the fallen Rome.[22]

If these intertextual echoes cast a negative light on Verlame, inviting the implied Protestant readers to distance themselves from her lament, then this raises difficult questions about the poem's central issues of mourning and memory, announced in the dedicatory epistle as the 'renowning' and 'eternizing' of Sir Philip Sidney and his family.[23] It is, after all, the unreliable, recognizably Catholic figure of Verlame that calls for and performs a passionate elegy for the Protestant hero-poet. What are we to make of this discrepancy? I would argue that this paradox serves to highlight two central and related concerns of the poem: what might be a proper way, after the Reformation, of mourning and commemoration? And what kind of poetry might be able to perform it? How does one, in other words, commemorate a Protestant poet? This poetological preoccupation with a development from traditional

Catholic modes of commemoration to Protestant ones is in keeping with the entire volume's status as a developing 'poetics in practice', as R. D. Brown has claimed. Despite their seemingly disparate topics, all poems are connected by their emerging, practical concern with metapoetic issues: '*Complaints* is a self-conscious collection of poems linked formally by their evocation (and eventual transformation) of traditional literary forms, and thematically by their concern with poetry and the role of the poet.'[24] Taken together, the poems enact a shift from moralistic forms of complaint and traditional notions of poetry to a more transitional, self-consciously unstable complaint and an innovative poetics. Katherine Craik makes a similar point when she reads the *Complaints*, published between the first and second part of the *Faerie Queene* (1590 and 1596), neither as mere 'training ground [n]or as a kind of nostalgia for epic achievement' but rather draws attention to the poetic possibilities which emerge from the supposedly 'minor voice' of the plaintive mode.[25] The complaint mode lends itself particularly well to this self-reflexivity since it is 'a metagenre: a genre about genre', in Patrick Cheney's formulation.[26] Spenser uses traditional complaint to explore problems in poetics, and by so doing he 'transforms complaint, creating a new, self-conscious form of poetry'. This transformation can be observed in particular in *The Ruines of Time*, which begins quite conventionally 'as a lament for the Dudley-Sidney family and hence as a meditation on the evanescence of mortal endeavour, yet becomes a theological debate about poetry'.[27]

In order to become available as a literary form for problematizing poetic commemoration, complaint had to become problematic as a form of ritual remembrance. Rather than articulating a clear and irreversible break with pre-Reformation modes of mourning and commemoration, however, *Ruines* seems to test their theological and poetological use value in a Protestant world. Carl Rasmussen has shown that there are in fact two such traditional modes at work in the poem, the *consolatio* and the lament: 'I suggest that the *consolatio* tradition – which was still of considerable importance in Spenser's time – underlies *The Ruines of Time* as a set of expectations that generates an ironic tension. In despair over earthly transience, Verlame['s lament] will seek to eternize fleeting glory in poetry. The *consolatio* tradition, however, teaches us to accept mortality: it eternizes nothing.'[28] The *consolatio* tradition, in other words, provides yet another ironic frame that serves to discredit Verlame's lament as a model for Spenser's Protestant poetics of mourning and commemoration. Nevertheless, the very fact that both complaint and consolation are employed in *The Ruines* performatively constitutes an act of poetic commemoration, since both modes also appear in Philip Sidney's own discussion of the functions of elegy in his *Defence of Poesy*, where he distinguishes between an affirmative 'compassionate accompanying just causes of lamentation' and a skeptical 'painting out how weak be the passions of woefulness'.[29] Verlame's lament would correspond to a compassionate indulgence in one's grief, whereas Spenser's poem, following the verdict of Sidney, develops towards a purging of that grief by 'painting out how weak be the passions of woefulness'. In the terms of our discussion, the tragedy of Verlame results from her stubborn insistence to monumentalize and eternize her sorrow in poetry, in misrecognition of the fact that neither monuments nor poetry last. Spenser, on the other hand, acknowledges that the memory of the dead cannot and perhaps should not remain fixed, but that it becomes more enduring as well as more endurable if intense grief can be discharged, perhaps even discarded, through poetry.

Even though both modes coexisted in post-Reformation England, as Sidney's *Defence* shows, the lament was viewed with considerable suspicion because of its proximity to Roman Catholic practices of mourning, while the *consolatio*, despite its long philosophical and literary tradition, had apparently not yet been satisfyingly adapted to Protestant uses. This lacuna in Protestant poetics of mourning might explain why Verlame claims, rather surprisingly, that Sidney had not been commemorated at all after his death: 'and all his glorie gone, / And all his greatnes vapoured to nought / … His name is worne alreadie out of thought, / Ne anie Poet seekes him to reuiue' (lines 218–23). Given the fact that a veritable flood of some 200 elegies was written in memory of Sidney immediately after his death, this claim needs some qualification. The *Spenser Encyclopedia* explains it as Spenser's rather unconvincing attempt to cover up his own tardiness in commemorating Sidney: the *Complaints* was published in 1591, a full five years after Sidney's death in 1586.[30] Verlame's claim can, however, also be understood as a quite justified criticism that the initial upsurge of occasional commemorative poetry was not followed by any sustained efforts at recollecting and 'reuiu[ing]' Sidney. Moreover, Spenser's own tardiness might be attributed to a sense that there was no adequate poetic model available for mourning this Protestant hero. At least one other, even more belated elegy for Sidney, written by his former schoolmate, the physician Thomas Moffet, suggest such religious misgivings. Moffet defends his own 'silence and forgetfulnesse' (as Spenser's dedication puts it) explicitly in terms of a lack of Protestant modes of poetic mourning. He explains his long hesitance in writing his *Nobilis, or a View of the Life and Death of a Sidney* (1593) with the impropriety of bewailing 'one who passed so splendidly and auspiciously'.[31] Because of his magnificence and his heroic death in defense of the Protestant cause, he claims, Sidney cannot be adequately mourned; by contrast, Verlame's excessive lament must appear as a highly inappropriate form of commemoration such as, in Moffet's words, only 'childish women' and 'hired female mourners' would practice.[32] In this view, the traditional practices and forms of mourning are associated with the wrong gender and the wrong confession. But if such misgivings were valid, why is Verlame's lament not rejected outright by the poem's narrator? Why is she allowed to voice her grief and anxiety at all, and to do so in the devalued terms of complaint?

One possible answer has been that her lament permits the reader to empathize with her grief, giving voice to deep feelings of mourning in ways that, after the Reformation, were not acceptable anymore. In Rasmussen's words:

> Through her expressions of grief, the reader is able to cathartically experience his own grief – even while the fiction surrounding the lament reminds the reader that such grief is inappropriate. This poignant tension … arises from a deep human response measured against an equally deep religious expectation … that trusts to the divine ends served by the world's progress. Such an expectation, though perhaps harsh seeming, is at the heart of the Protestant sensibility.[33]

In keeping with this cathartic reading, Verlame is first allowed to indulge her (and her like-minded readers') womanish, Catholic desire for eternizing memory. But even she is made to voice eventually what would appear as a more manly, Protestant poetics of grief that culminates in a recognition that his memory actually resides 'both here and there'. This double spatiality is important because it opens up the possibility that Sidney's poetry, rather than functioning as an eternal monument that removes his memory from earthly decay into transcendence, instead keeps inspiring emulation of his 'excellent desart' on earth (lines 342–3). For two brief stanzas, Verlame therefore 'seems to recognize that poetry exists only in time, that it can only be *perpetual*, not eternal. Because it exists only in time, poetry has as its function the inspiration of mortals with intimations of true immortality. Consequently, poetry about Sidney should neither mourn nor eternize him but communicate his eternalness to those still living in time.'[34] Moreover, this notion of poetic immortality as perpetual recollection and re-enactment (rather than an eternal monument set up for idolatrous adoration) is entirely in keeping with Sidney's own poetics as expounded in his *Defence*. According to Sidney, poetry functions like the art of memory in that both employ the technique of image-making as memory-making; and both aim to provide a medium for improving human behavior.[35] Sidney makes this connection explicit when he argues that poetry employs the same methods and has the same 'effect perfectly' as the art of memory; in fact, versification *is* a superior form of memory-making, since in verse 'every word having its natural seat, which seat must needs make the words remembered'.[36] Sidney's definition of poetry as an art of memory is performatively enacted by Spenser's poem, as will be shown in greater detail below.

There is also a more implicit connection with Sidney's poetics that allows us to understand poetry as an art of memory founded on the image of the ruin. In a complex relay of poetological allusions which Rebecca Helfer has recently unearthed, Sidney's *Defence* in turn 'recalls *The Shepheardes Calender* and its apology for poetry through a witty parody of Spenser's first literary critic, E.K.'.[37] E.K. had written a dedicatory epistle for *Shepheardes Calender* in which he criticized Spenser's archaic style in terms that equate such philological remembrance with the ruin of language, warning that 'nether everywhere must old words be stuffed in, nor the common Dialecte and maner of speaking so corrupted therby, that as in old buildings it seme disorderly and ruinous'. While E.K.'s introductory letter to the *Calender* acknowledged Spenser's 'choyse of old and unwonted words' as a feat of memory that revives 'such good and natural English words as have been long time out of use', it also articulated an anxiety that the house of English literature, uninhabited for so long, might crumble into ruin even while a new generation of poets seeks to renovate it.[38] Sidney's *Defence* takes up E.K.'s imagery when Sidney complains that poetry in England is indeed in decline – with the notable exception of Spenser. Moreover, it is not his archaic versification that can be held accountable for this dismal state of things. While they live in a time of peace and prosperity that 'should seem to strew the house for poets', the house of English poesy is not strewed with fresh rushes or flowers but on the contrary decked 'with fewer laurels than it was accustomed'.[39] It is through this neglect that English culture appears as an abandoned, derelict building.

The image of poetry as a house in ruins was neither E.K.'s nor Sidney's invention but, as Rebecca Helfer demonstrates, refers us back to Cicero's *De oratore*. It occurs in the context of his discussion of the art of memory, at the outset of which, famously, lies a disorderly and ruined building. The poet Simonides of Ceos, Cicero reports, attended a banquet cut short by an earthquake that destroyed the building and killed all the guests. Only Simonides escaped and was able to identify the bodies, mutilated beyond recognition, by remembering the exact order in which they had been seated in the now ruined banqueting hall. This mnemonic feat is usually read as enabling two distinct cultural practices of remembering, the rhetorical *ars memorativa* and the ritual commemoration of the dead.[40] It also bears pointing out, I think, that the mythical founder of these mnemonic practices born out of ruins was a poet. Poetry is thus intimately linked with memory and mourning, but also with the figure of the ruin and the catastrophic forgetting it stands for. This latter link is borne out by Cicero's *De oratore* itself, Helfer argues: his account of the origins of the *ars memorativa*, which ends in a ruin, concludes Book II, and Book III begins with a description of a Rome in ruins, in terms that link it to the tale of Simonides. Cicero recounts this story as part of the history of rhetoric to his brother at a time when the art of rhetoric, just like the Roman republic, lay in ruins. Not having been present at this dialogue on oratory but recollecting it at second hand, Cicero's relating it in *De oratore* becomes itself a textual feat of memory in the face of cultural ruins. Yet at the same time his confession that he can only 'shadow forth' the dialogue from 'the topics and heads of the discussion' also indicates the limits of his art, be it rhetoric, mnemonic, or poetic.

It cannot truly revive the dead nor rebuild the past, making the orator feel like 'a spectator to the ruins of my country': rhetoric and, by extension, poetry cannot compensate for an enduring monument, but always only represent 'an edifice in ruins, a locus for future recollection'.[41] It is thus not so much the idea of a poetry in ruins, or of poetry as opposed to them, but a poetry out of ruins that thus underpins both Sidney's and Spenser's poetics.

Spenser's *Shepheardes Calender* provides a good example of this. It is itself a fragment, a poetic ruin, because the final emblem is missing. Each month's eclogue ends with an emblem consisting of a motto and poem, yet the final eclogue dedicated to December (and with it, the text of the *Calender*) breaks off after the colon that announces 'Colin's emblem: …'. Despite or because of this rather conspicuous authorial omission, E.K. decided to 'repair' the textual ruin by filling in the blank space where the emblem should be with an assertion of the immortality-of-poetry topos: 'The meaning whereof is that all things perish and come to theyr last end, but workes of learned wits and monuments of Poetry abide forever',[42] he writes in the face of an incomplete poetic monument – not getting the joke, Helfer points out, that Spenser locates the immortality of poetry not in the verses themselves but in the ongoing dialogue of interpretation between text and reader: 'Spenser's poetry as ruins provides a place for recollection for readers who, inevitably, will change the Calendar through their interpretations.'[43] By providing that final gloss, E.K. unwittingly responded to the invitation issued by the poem-as-ruin, mistaking with involuntary irony the very point his gloss proves.

Sidney, by contrast, does get the joke and places the paradox that ruins provide the location for poetic immortality at the very center of his *Defence*. Despite their common functions, poetry and the art of memory differ in one important aspect. While the art of memory, born of a desire to repair material and mnemonic ruins, is a key technique of poetry, poetry itself goes beyond the desire to repair and repeat. Sidney's simile to describe this imaginative surplus is telling: whereas the art of memory is like 'a gorgeous palace, the architecture, with declaring the full beauties, might well make the hearer able to repeat, as it were by rote, all he had heard, yet should never satisfy his inward conceits with being witness to itself of a true lively knowledge', poetry by contrast produces 'lively knowledge' in the sense that it provides a memory that comes to life in virtuous action.[44] This is the true defense of poetry: the images of the past must be translated into the present, and this translation occurs through poetry:

> But if anything be already said in the defence of sweet poetry, al occureth to the maintaining the heroical, which is not only a kind, but the best a most accomplished kind of poetry. For as the image of each action stirreth and instructeth the mind, so the lofty image of such worthies most inflameth the mind with desire to be worthy, and informs with counsel how to be worthy.[45]

Sidney's prime example for a poetic image of the heroic past capable of inciting virtuous action in the present is Virgil's *Aeneid*: 'Only let Aeneas be worn in the tablet of your memory', Sidney advises, 'how he governeth himself in the ruin of his country; in the preserving of his old father, and carrying away his religious ceremonies …'.[46] In the course of this translation from memory to life, the poem itself is translated from mere edifice into edification. The ruin rather than the 'gorgeous palace' is a more fitting emblem for this kind of living poetry since it invites the reader not to mechanical repetition and embellishment but to imaginative recollection and interpretive emulation.

Spenser's *Ruines of Time* enacts this ideal reader response in the space between Verlame's lament, constituting the long first part, and the dream visions that conclude the poem. These are spoken by the unnamed speaker who at the beginning encountered her, complaining and mourning, on the banks of the Thames. The speaker's reaction to such grief is speechless astonishment and compassionate sorrow, followed by an attempt at imaginative recollection: 'Renewing her [Verlame's] complaint with passion strong' (line 479). Instead of rationally extracting the meaning of what seems to him 'her doubtfull speech' (line 484), he gives himself over to two dream visions. The first set of these 'tragicke pageants' (line 490) seem only to repeat the message of Verlame's lament that all tends to ruin, including altars, towers, gardens, and bridges, which 'all serve as visual emblems, speaking pictures, of the ruins of time'.[47] Yet in an act of interpretive emulation, this knowledge of the frailty and consequently of the futility of every human construction now extends even to poetry: the garden of Belphoebe, for example, another name for Spenser's epic poem *The Faerie Queene*, also appears subject to decay.[48] Again the speaker reacts with emotional and cognitive confusion, though this time 'a voyce' spells out the message that 'all is vanitie and griefe of minde' (line 583). This differs significantly from Verlame's grief for the world's transience since the disembodied voice at the same time affirms the existence of divine providence and promises both transcendence and revelation through poetry.[49] This promise is enacted in the second set of visions representing the death and resurrection of Sir Philip Sidney. Each vision shows the metamorphosis of one poetical symbol associated with Sidney into a heavenly constellation, thus playing upon his literary persona Astrophil: the swan, the harp, or the treasure-box become stars that commemorate both poetry and the poet Sidney.[50] The tenor of these stanzas is that Sidney, having 'become an heauenly signe' and been 'Enclosde therein for endles memorie', is given 'a second life, / To liue in heauen, where happines is rife' (lines 601, 662, 669–79). Each vision of the second set ends on the narrator's dejection and sense of loss, contrasting with Sidney's joy: 'There now his joy is his, here sorrow mine' (line 602).

These lines seem to assert the legitimacy of grieving for the deceased, which a strictly Protestant theology would deny. The following 'Envoy' however asks the potential new patroness, the Countess of Pembroke, to overcome her grief and shed only 'some few siluer dropping teares' (line 683) on her brother's hearse. She should aspire to heaven instead and 'loath this drosse of sinful worlds desire' (line 687), to shun an excessive desire for the world, the weak and disordered passions that in their attachment to the world generate woefulness.[51] The final stanza of the poem thus articulates a thoroughly reformed notion of mourning and commemoration: it is transformed into an elating knowledge of the beloved person's transcendent immortality. The medium through which this transformation is achieved is poetry. What is more, the very notion of commemorative poetry has been transformed. While the 'Envoy' presents *The Ruines of Time* as 'this moniment of his last praise' (line 682), it is emphatically not a monument built for eternity. Indeed, in the very moment the poem is completed, it already begins to decay and to become a ruin itself, turning into 'this broken verse' (line 678). Significantly, this is not seen as a reason for lament in itself, but rather as the natural condition of poetry as a thing *of* this world and existing only *in* this world. When the narrator says that his poetic monument is 'broken with sighs' (line 679) this foreshadows Shakespeare's sonnets, which also acknowledge the material and hence transient nature of poetry and memory. Sonnet 18 ends, having preached the ephemerality of life and beauty, with a praise of the immortality of poetry: 'So long as men can breathe or eyes can see, / So long lives this, and this gives life to thee.'[52] It would be a mistake to read this as a conventional articulation of the immortality-of-poetry topos, however. For in the context of a reformed Protestant poetics, 'so long' spells not simply a promise of durability but rather the condition of its permanence: poetic commemoration lives as long as one human being breathes and reads and, reading aloud, gives new life to the memory embodied in verses which, unread, would be a dead monument.

The figure of the ruin in the post-Reformation poetic imagination thus is emphatically not a figure of destruction and absence against which poetry defines itself, but a site of recollection and a central trope for a new poetry. This poetry is not timeless or universal, liberated from the material conditions of the world. It is on the contrary very much a product of its time, the confessional conflicts of the Reformation; its material signature is that of destruction and recreation, dispersal and recollection, embodied in the figure of the ruin. This is the conceptual jest condensed in the title of Spenser's poem: *The Ruines of Time* does not present poetry as an antidote to the ruins produced by time; poetry, rather, resides within them as well as within time. If poetry conveys immortality, this is not because it erects 'a monument that never falls to ruin, but because poetry's ruins create a place for a process of recollection'.[53]

This transforms the mnemonic and poetic dimensions of the traditional topos profoundly, adapting it to the post-Reformation English sensibility.

Just how directly Spenser's poetics of mourning and memory spoke to the Protestant sensibility of his time can be seen from an epigram that lamented his death early in 1599. Here, the figure of poetic ruins becomes the very topos through which Spenser is commemorated. John Weever, who about thirty years later would write a truly Verulamian lament for the funeral monuments ruined by Reformation iconoclasm, praises Spenser's poetic achievement explicitly in terms of ruins:

> Colin's gone home, the glorie of his clime,
> The Muses Mirrour, and the Shepheards Saint;
> Spencer is ruined, of our latter time,
> The fairest ruine, Faeries foulest want:
> Then his Time-ruines did our ruine show,
> Which by his ruine we untimely know:
> Spencer therefore thy Ruines were cal'd in,
> Too soone to sorrow least we should begin.[54]

Spenser is remembered by his greatest poetic achievements, among which, remarkably from our latter-day perspective, is *The Ruines of Time*. Not only that, the very terms in which Spenser is commemorated and mourned are derived from this poem. The key word of the epigram is 'ruine', both as a noun and a verb. Indeed, it is used so often that in the space of a few lines it acquires a variety of meanings, from 'deceased' and 'death' (lines 3, 6) over 'poet' or 'poetic monument' (line 4), 'loss' or 'desolate state' (line 5) to an altogether enigmatic 'Ruines' (line 7) oscillating between possible meanings. It is the only instance of a capitalized spelling apart from the titles of his works, which would suggest that it refers also to a work, *The Ruines of Time*. The fact that the *Complaints* volume, of which *Ruines* is the first, programmatic poem, indeed was 'cal'd in' by the authorities seems to affirm this as the dominant meaning. The allusion however falls somewhat flat since the text that specifically motivated the censorship – the denigration of the Queen's chief minister, Lord Burghley, in *Mother Hubberds Tale* – is not mentioned at all, Richard McCabe cautions.[55] Weever's epigram focuses on *The Ruines of Time* instead, and this intertextual reference as well as the immediate semantic context of this line allow us to construe it as referring also to Spenser's soul, or, in keeping with the plural form and supported by the dispersal of Sidney-Astrophel across the night sky in *Ruines*'s final visions, to his poetic powers that are now 'cal'd in' or 'gone home'.

This plurality of meanings shows a keen understanding of the ambivalent semiotics of ruins in post-Reformation England. Moreover, the different referents arguably re-enact the development of ruins from a figure of material deformation to a topos of reformed poetry itself that Spenser's poem performs: 'ruines' does not only denote death, loss, and grief, but also the poetic monument (or individual work) and the poet's power, perhaps even his immortal soul. The epigram acknowledges that *all* are subject to decay, even poetry; but it also holds out the promise of the soul's redemption and transcendent immortality. It is therefore no surprise that the epigram ends on an ambiguous note of despair and relief: Spencer was 'cal'd in' both 'untimely' and just in time, 'least we should begin … [t]oo soone to sorrow' (line 8). Given the speaker's obvious admiration and pain, this can hardly indicate a relief that Spenser died before his fame did. The line becomes fully intelligible, I think, only in the context of post-Reformation anxieties about the proper mode and the proper time to mourn the dead. The epigram acknowledges *The Ruines of Time* as the prototype for a suitable mode of experiencing and expressing loss. It is 'his *Time-ruines*' which show to Spenser's admirers 'our ruine' and makes them truly know their sorrow; at the same time, it provides them with the words and images to articulate this grief. Weever's epigram thus in turn offers us the image of poetry out of ruins as a memorable emblem of Spenser's Protestant poetics of commemoration and mourning.

Notes

1 P. Schwyzer, *Archaeologies of English Renaissance Literature* (Oxford: Oxford University Press, 2007), pp. 73–4.

2 A. Janowitz, *England's Ruins: Poetic Purpose and the National Landscape* (Oxford: Basil Blackwell, 1990), pp. 1–19, at pp. 4, 5, 8–9.

3 Janowitz concedes that ruins do become imaginative sites of personal and national fragmentation in Romantic and even more so in Modernist literature; indeed this claim informs the deep structure of her argument. It is thus not blindness to the potential instability of the immortality-of-poetry topos itself but rather to the historical instabilities in the wake of the Reformation that leads her to this superficial conclusion.

4 For a detailed discussion of these and other examples, see Schwyzer, *Archaeologies*, pp. 81–91.

5 *Ibid.*, p. 92.

6 For an excellent essay that reconstructs the struggle between image and word in the realms of Renaissance art and literature, see L. Barkan, 'Ruins and Visions: Spenser, Pictures, Rome', in J. K. Morrison and M. Greenfield (eds), *Edmund Spenser: Essays on Culture and Allegory* (Aldershot: Ashgate, 2000), pp. 9–36.

7 Edmund Spenser, *The Faerie Queene*, ed. A. C. Hamilton and Hiroshi Yamashita (London and New York: Routledge, 2013), II.10.68.

8 J. Summit, 'Reading Reformed: Spenser and the Problem of the English Library', in C. Ivic and G. Williams (eds), *Forgetting in Early Modern English Literature and Culture: Lethe's Legacies* (London and New York: Routledge, 2004), pp. 165–78.

9 P. Schwyzer, 'Dissolving Images: Monastic Ruins in Elizabethan Poetry', in *Archaeologies*, pp. 72–98, at p. 80.

10 Edmund Spenser, *The Ruines of Time*, in *The Works of Edmund Spenser: A Variorum Edition*, 2 vols, ed. Edwin Greenlaw, Charles Osgood, and Frederick Morgan Padelford (Baltimore: The Johns Hopkins Press, 1947), vol. 2: pp. 37–65, at line 218. All further references to the poem will be given parenthetically in the text.

11 Schwyzer, *Archaeologies*, pp. 75–7.

12 Spenser, *Works*, vol. 2: p. 33.

13 *Ibid.*, pp. 35–6.

14 C. J. Rasmussen, '"How Weak Be the Passions of Woefulness": Spenser's *Ruines of Time*', *Spenser Studies*, 2 (1981), 159–81, at 160.

15 For instance Janowitz, *England's Ruins*; B. van Es, *Spenser's Forms of History* (Oxford: Oxford University Press, 2002), pp. 21–48; H. Melehy, 'Antiquities of Britain: Spenser's *Ruines of Time*', *Studies in Philology*, 102:2 (2005), 159–83.

16 See Rasmussen, '"How Weak"'; R. Helfer, 'Remembering Sidney, Remembering Spenser: The Art of Memory and *The Ruines of Time*', *Spenser Studies*, 22 (2007), 127–51; and R. D. Brown, 'A "Goodlie Bridge" between the Old and the New: The Transformation of Complaint in Spenser's *The Ruines of Time*', *Renaissance Forum* 2:1 (1997), n.p., at www.hull.ac.uk/renforum/v2no1/brown.htm, accessed 2 November 2016, repr. in R. D. Brown, *'The New Poet': Novelty and Tradition in Spenser's Complaints* (Liverpool: Liverpool University Press, 1999), pp. 99–132.

17 William Camden, *Britain* (1586; Engl. 1610), p. 19. Camden's work, which is explicitly referenced in Spenser's poem as the only extant memorial to Verulamium (*Ruines*, lines 168–75), points out that the ancient city was situated by a 'brook' or 'a standing poole' (*Britain*, pp. 408–9), giving rise to the durable if false legend that Verulamium had once been located by the river Thames.

18 Helfer, 'Remembering Sidney', 128.

19 In an earlier article, Rasmussen showed how this Protestant view of excessive mourning as 'sinful dispair' developed in Jan Van der Noot's collection *A Theatre for Worldlings* (1567; Engl. 1569), a series of emblematic visionary sonnets to whose English version a youthful Spenser contributed a translation of Joachim du Bellay's *Songe* and *Antiquitez du Rome*; C. J. Rasmussen, '"Quietnesse of the Minde": A Theatre for Worldlings as Protestant Poetics', *Spenser Studies*, 1 (1980), 3–27. Spenser's transformation, imitation, and reworking of du Bellay's Roman model there is discussed in detail by Barkan, 'Ruins and Visions', and, with focus on the later *Complaints* volume, by Melehy, 'Antiquities of Britain'; while the latter acknowledges the complementarity of destruction/recreation and the ruinous state of poetry, it still clings (somewhat inconsistently) to the validity of the immortality-of-poetry topos that opposes the two notions.

20 Rasmussen, '"How Weak"', 162–3.

21 *Ibid.*, 162.

22 D. Cartmell, '"Beside the shore of siluer streaming *Thamesis*": Spenser's *Ruines of Time*', *Spenser Studies*, 6 (1986), 77–82, at 79. Likewise, the historical Verlame as Rome's minion would have been the enemy of great British heroes. And indeed, in recounting her own history in stanza 16, she boasts of having outshone

Troynovant (the foundation of London), thus establishing an alternative history to the Trojan genealogy the British were so proud of; of having fought Uther Pendragon, the father of mythical King Arthur from whom the Tudors traced their family descent; and of having waged war successfully against Bonduca, the warlike queen who had held out against the Romans and was venerated as a prefiguration of Queen Elizabeth. Spenser was well aware of these political myths and their relevance for Elizabethan England, having commemorated and celebrated them in *The Faerie Queene* (see Rasmussen, '"How Weak"', 162). In *Ruines*, they arguably serve to distance the patriotic reader from the figure of Verlame.

23 De Neef separates the entangled strands of the family line connected with Spenser through patronage, beginning with Robert Dudley, the first Earl of Leicester, and progressing through succeeding generations to Philip Sidney and his sister Mary; A. Leigh de Neef, '"The Ruines of Time": Spenser's Apology for Poetry', *Studies in Philology*, 76 (1979), 262–70. This section of the poem (stanzas 27–67) also includes a negative image of patronage that, however, is not meant to reflect on the Sidneys but rather on Spenser's altogether unsatisfactory relation with Lord Burghley, who apparently had a poor estimation of poetry. Brown notes that Verlame's praise of poetry as an antidote against oblivion in stanzas 50–2 can be construed as an implicit critique of merely monetary patronage: since only few can afford to be a patron of poets (and even fewer have a true regard for poetry), eternal commemoration would after all be only for the rich and the great. This commodification of memory has theological implications as well: the notion that immortality could be achieved through commemoration in poetic works is profoundly at odds with the Lutheran tenet that justification can only come through faith and cannot be purchased through good works – the key to salvation is faith, not fame (Brown, '"Goodlie Bridge"', §§50–2). Readings of the *Complaints* volume as concerned with the poetics and politics of patronage (rather than mourning and memory) have become the dominant paradigm of the last decade; for an overview and bibliography, see R. McCabe, 'Shorter Verse Published 1590–1595', in Bart van Es (ed.), *A Critical Companion to Spenser Studies* (Houndmills, Basingstoke: Palgrave Macmillan, 2006), pp. 166–73.

24 Brown, *New Poet*, pp. 7–8.

25 K. Craik, 'Spenser's *Complaints* and the New Poet', *Huntington Library Quarterly*, 64:1/2 (2001), 63–79, at 63.

26 P. Cheyne, *Spenser's Famous Flight: A Renaissance Idea of a Literary Career* (Toronto: University of Toronto Press, 1993), pp. 3–4.

27 Brown, *New Poet*, pp. 30–1.

28 Rasmussen, '"How Weak"', 164. While Verlame's excessive verbalization of grief would seem to distance her lament from the consolation tradition, it shares with Boethius' *De consolatione philosophiae* the themes of ubi sunt, human vanity, and the vicissitudes of time and fortune, just as the framework of dream visions links the two texts formally.

29 Philip Sidney, *The Major Works*, ed. Katherine Duncan-Jones (Oxford: Oxford University Press, 2002), p. 229.

30 See the entry 'Philip Sidney', in A. C. Hamilton (ed.), *The Spenser Encyclopaedia* (Toronto: University of Toronto Press, 1990), p. 656.
31 Thomas Moffet, *Nobilis, or A View of the Life and Death of Sidney and Lessus Lugubrius* [1593], ed. Virgil B. Heltzel and Hoyt H. Hudson (San Marino: The Huntington Library, 1940), pp. 35, 70.
32 *Ibid.*, p. 69.
33 Rasmussen, '"How Weak"', 166.
34 *Ibid.*, 168.
35 Mary Carruthers has demonstrated how the medieval practice of memorized reading functioned as a source of ethical action and of a pre-modern kind of subjectivity; her prime example is Heloise, whose moral decision to take the veil is introduced, authorized, and even performed through a memorized quotation from Lucan's poem about Pompey's virtuous, self-sacrificial wife Cornelia: 'Heloise's moment of moral decision is articulated as a rhetorical action'. Mary Carruthers, *The Book of Memory: A Study of Memory in Medieval Culture* (Cambridge: Cambridge University Press, 1990), pp. 179–80.
36 Sidney, *Major Works*, p. 234.
37 Helfer, 'Remembering Sidney', 135.
38 Spenser, *Works*, vol. 1: p. 8; Helfer, 'Remembering Sidney', 135.
39 Sidney, *Major Works*, p. 214. K. Duncan-Jones glosses 'strew' as: 'Prepare a welcome by spreading fresh rushes and flowers' (*Major Works*, p. 385). The OED gives the meanings 'displayed' (1.d) and 'to be spread' (3.a) as specifically Spenserian uses of the word. Helfer's reading (p. 135) suggests that she takes 'strewed' as an abbreviation or corruption of 'destroyed', which would fit her argument well but is not substantiated by the OED.
40 See, respectively, F. Yates, *The Art of Memory* (London: Routledge & Kegan Paul, 1996) and S. Goldmann, 'Statt Totenklage Gedächtnis: Zur Erfindung der Mnemotechnik durch Simonides von Keos', *Poetica*, 21 (1989), 43–66.
41 Helfer, 'Remembering Sidney', 139.
42 Spenser, *Works*, vol. 1: pp. 15–120, at p. 119.
43 Helfer, 'Remembering Sidney', 141.
44 Sidney, *Major Works*, p. 222.
45 *Ibid.*, p. 231.
46 *Ibid.*
47 De Neef, 'Apology', 271.
48 *Ruines*, stanzas 75–6. As Brown comments in detail, the third vision describing the destruction of 'a pleasant Paradize' (line 519) implies a connection between this garden and Spenser's own poetry by recalling figures from an episode of *The Faerie Queene*: Merlin, Belphoebe, and the 'gentle squire' Timias (lines 521–5). The garden is 'Made' through artifice or 'Magicke', and thus as transitory as all 'vaine labours of terrestrial wit' (line 510). 'The implication is that the dissolution of this poetic garden undercuts Verlame's confidence in the power of poetry to transcend death' (Brown, '"Goodlie Bridge"', §55).
49 Rasmussen, '"How Weak"', 175.

50 W. L. Renwick (ed.), *Complaints* (London: The Scholar's Press, 1928), decodes the symbolism of the second set of dream visions as specific icons of Sidney's life and death: the swan singing before death is a fitting symbol for the poet who died untimely; the harp of Orpheus and the constellation Lyra are images for Sidney as a poet; the 'black coffer' refers to the *Black Pinnace*, the ship in which Sidney's body was brought back to England; Pegasus is again an obvious poetic symbol; and Mercury is the guide of souls from this life to the next (pp. 202–3).

51 Rasmussen, '"How Weak"', 177.

52 William Shakespeare, *The Sonnets*, ed. Katherine Duncan-Jones. The Arden Shakespeare Third Series (Walton-on-Thames: Thomas Nelson, 1997), p. 147.

53 Helfer, 'Remembering Sidney', 145.

54 Repr. in H. S. V. Jones, *A Spenser Handbook* (New York: Appleton Century Crofts, 1930), p. 74.

55 MacCabe, 'Shorter Verse', pp. 166–8.

Part II

Negotiating confessional conflict

6

Letters to a young prince: confessional conflict and the origins of English Protestantism in Samuel Rowley's *When You See Me You Know Me* (1605)

Brian Walsh

In a recent assessment of the state of Reformation historiography, Peter Marshall notes that scholars have moved past both the traditional narrative of a 'swift Protestant victory' as well as the view of the 'long-drawn-out and remarkably successful Catholic rearguard action portrayed by 1980s revisionism'. According to Marshall, we have begun to acknowledge instead that 'the Reformation in England was a thorny and protracted process and by no means straightforwardly unidirectional'; in other words, we recognize 'the utility of a notion of plural reformations'.[1] The notion of 'plural reformations' complicates the attempt to craft a linear history of the Reformation in England from a modern perspective, as well as it did from the perspective of Elizabethan and Jacobean authors who were, naturally, better placed to recognize this plurality. For those authors, religious legitimacy itself was at stake in the discussion of the origins of the Protestant English Church. Catholic polemicists derisively posed the question 'Where was your Church before Luther' again and again as part of their claim that the Roman Church, centered on the papacy, represented continuity from Peter until the present day. The standard Protestant answer usually involved some argument that they had not invented a new Church but merely resurfaced, revived, or reconnected to a primitive one that the papacy had corrupted.[2] Archbishop Cranmer even fixed a date 600 CE as the moment when Roman influence cut the English Church off from apostolic purity, and John Jewell amplified this claim by challenging Catholic writers to prove that various Roman doctrines pre-dated that year.[3] Cranmer himself could become the focus of such a contested historical genealogy: Queen Mary's Archbishop of Canterbury, Reginald Poole, imagined, as Eamon Duffy has put it, a 'ladder of witness' among English divines dating back from himself to the Apostolic Church and ultimately Peter and Christ, with only one false rung, Cranmer, whom Poole called in a bluntly effective figure, a 'broken steppe'.[4]

Thus, throughout the mid and later sixteenth century, figures like John Foxe and Matthew Parker sought, through various publishing channels, to discredit medieval Catholicism while Catholics, largely in exile, fired back with their claims about continuity between the primitive and the contemporary Catholic Church. In the early 1600s, in the waning years of Elizabeth's reign and into the early years of James's, playwrights began to investigate the course of the Reformation on the popular stages. There was a mini vogue for plays about the reigns of Henry VIII and his children as the history play genre, which in the 1590s had most often focused on contests for the medieval English kingship, turned to the more recent past and to the pressing question of the origins of the current religious landscape. In addition to two now-lost plays on Cardinal Wolsey, the stages between 1601 and 1605 featured works about the Tudor monarchs that were each to different degrees influenced by John Foxe's *Acts and Monuments*: *Thomas Lord Cromwell*, *Sir Thomas Wyatt*, parts *1* and *2* of *If You Know Not Me, You Know Nobody* (plays about the life and reign of Queen Elizabeth), as well as *When You See Me You Know Me*, a play that featured King Henry VIII, Prince Edward, and other key early Reformation figures.[5] And this is not to mention *Sir John Oldcastle*, *Sir Thomas More*, *The Whore of Babylon*, or *Henry VIII*, which are each relevant to this trend, although outliers for various reasons.[6] There is considerable overlap among these plays, but each possesses its own complexity and nuance regarding formative moments in the development of the Reformation. To see any of them as only Protestant propaganda, despite their indebtedness to Foxe and a common strain of anti-Catholicism, is reductive.[7] Each in its own way demonstrates Annabel Patterson's claim that the Reformation, because of the 'divisive forces [it] unleashed', made impossible the production of a unifying or monologic historiography of the years covering and following Henry's reign.[8]

In this essay, I will concentrate on *When You See Me You Know Me* (*c.* 1605). Written by Samuel Rowley and performed by Prince Henry's Men, perhaps at court as well as on the popular stage, this play delves deeper than the others into the historiographical dynamics and contemporary resonances of early Tudor confessional conflicts.[9] It deserves closer examination than it has hitherto received for the provocative way that it historicizes the origins of English Protestantism, and the canniness with which it makes this story present to Jacobean audiences. Post-Reformation England struggled with what it meant to live in a world fragmented by religious change. Rosamund Oates has claimed that in the sixteenth and seventeenth centuries, Church 'histories were powerful tools in confessional debates because they were central to evolving confessional identities'.[10] *When You See Me You Know Me* reveals the lack of a stable origin story for English Protestantism itself. This does not lend ammunition to Catholic polemic about the new-fangledness of Protestantism, though. Rowley's Protestant sympathies are clear, and the play is bitterly satirical about Catholic abuses. But the play does anatomize Protestantism alongside its broad anti-papal jokes and critiques. One scholar has noted that, alongside 'emphasizing the power of anti-Catholicism', increasingly Reformation 'historians have highlighted the mutual hostility between different sorts of Protestants'.[11] I argue that *When You See Me You Know Me* registers aspects of such hostility even as it strives to ameliorate it. I will consider 'Lutheran' as a key term through which Rowley explores issues of Reformation historiography and Jacobean intra-Protestant confessional conflict. I will then consider a central scene in *When You See Me You Know Me*'s presentation of the history of the Reformation in England in which the young Prince Edward reads dueling letters from his sisters, Mary and Elizabeth. Here, Rowley opens to scrutiny the turbulence of England's history since Henry VIII. The play subtly triggers awareness in audiences of the messiness, false starts, and interruptions to reform the nation had witnessed. Rowley does not seek to resolve or gloss over this, but rather suggests something more practical: that these dialectical processes, whatever the uses to which they might be put by anti-Protestant polemicists, are not necessarily a discredit to reform but an inevitable and ongoing means of mediating the new normality of confessional plurality and what we might term permanent religious 'unsettlement'.

I have said that the plays on Tudor history should not be consigned to a narrow category of Protestant propaganda. But it is true that in the first part of Thomas Heywood's *If You Know Not Me, You Know Nobody* (*c.* 1605), a play set in the reign of Queen Mary, English Catholics are presented in one scene in particular as cartoonish villains. In this sequence, a dumb show, a friar attempts to murder the sleeping Princess Elizabeth, who is shown imprisoned at the behest of her elder sister. The friar is prevented by an angel, who rescues her and, importantly, places in her hand an English-language Bible. Stephen Gardiner, the Bishop of Winchester and the designated Catholic villain in a number of these early-seventeenth-century plays, later can only admit in frustration that Elizabeth's 'life is garded by the hand of heauen, / And we in vaine pursue it.'[12] In this moment, the contours and inevitable outcome of Catholic–Protestant conflict are rendered in the easily grasped terms of an apocalyptic battle between the Reformed Church (vernacular Bible literally in hand) and the papist forces of Antichrist. What this scene allegorizes plays out through the historical events depicted: Mary dies, and Elizabeth succeeds her, and the second part of *If You Know Not Me* concludes with the defeat of the Spanish Armada. The plays dramatize an arc from the rescue of the true Church, imperiled under Mary, to the triumph of the English Protestant project under Elizabeth.

In Rowley's *When You See Me You Know Me*, written around the same time, the emphasis shifts from an account of the Reformation defined by the Catholic–Protestant binary of Mary vs. Elizabeth to include also consideration of a diffuse Protestantism.[13] The play certainly contains numerous harsh jokes and digs about Catholic belief and practice, and is staunchly anti-papal; but it also concludes with a friendly visit to England by the Holy Roman Emperor Charles, and so, probably influenced by the recently concluded peace with Spain (and displaying, then, a different ideological agenda than *If You Know Not Me*), offers a less clearly militant vision of Protestant triumph. But *When You See Me* complicates its historical project more radically by enlarging its scope to cover material relating to King Henry and Edward, the Prince of Wales and future king of England, in addition to Mary and Elizabeth, thus, as we will see, forcing audiences to consider the Reformation as a longer and more divergent process than *If You Know Not Me* renders it. The notion of the Reformation's origins with King Henry is scrutinized skeptically. Following the cue of Foxe and others, Rowley presents an unvarnished portrait of Henry, who, despite one episode in which he is a swashbuckling and charismatic figure stalking the streets of London to right wrongs, is for most of the play a gouty, easily duped blowhard who remains in awe of Rome and the Pope's authority.[14] This is despite the fact that Rowley starts the play long after the crisis surrounding Henry's divorce; indeed, long after the death of Ann Boleyn. Henry's allegiance to the Pope at this stage is more than just a bumbling anachronism on Rowley's part, but seems rather a strategic anachronism that comments on Henry's weak commitment to reformed ideals.[15] His stance stands in contrast to his wife, the good Queen Katherine Parr, who is described throughout the play as a vigorous Protestant. More specific and noteworthy is the fact that Rowley attaches to her the label 'Lutheran' insistently. The motif of direct references to Martin Luther and his followers, usually in reference to Katherine, is one of the most striking features of the play's verbal texture, with over twenty iterations of his name or of the term 'Lutheran' occurring. This is extremely unusual on the early modern stage, where, to my knowledge, there are just a few other instances.[16] For instance, when Will Sommers, Henry's fool, informs Cardinal Wolsey of the King's intentions to marry her, Wolsey is aghast:

> Holy Saint Peter sheeld his Maiestie,
> She is the hope of Luthers heresie:
> If she be Queene, the Protestants will swell,
> And Cranmer, Tutor to the Prince of Wales,
> Will boldly speake gainst Romes Religion.
> (lines 1489–93)

When the Queen at one point agrees with an anti-papal quip by Will the jester, who happens also to be the play's most outspoken anti-Catholic,

Henry says: 'Take heed what yee say Kate, what a Lutheran?' (line 1611). A bit later, as Gardiner and Bishop Edmund Bonner complain about the growing Protestant threat, Gardiner asserts that 'Queene *Katherns* a strong *Lutheran*' (line 2125, italics in original). When the King, at Gardiner's prompting, begins to suspect his wife's loyalty, he declares that she is 'the greatest Lutherin' (line 2354).

Katherine's risky religious ideas and, indeed, her identity are thus specifically characterized as Lutheran. This confessional categorizing is entirely absent in the section about Henry VIII's reign in *Acts and Monuments* that Rowley used as source material for Katherine's story.[17] Rowley's innovative choice to inject the name of Luther and its adjectival form into his depiction of Queen Katherine calls attention to itself, and raises the question of how the words may have signified in 1604. On the one hand, this was simply shrewd dramatic construction. For the Jacobean theater audience, endowed with a post-Reformation historical consciousness, to hear a reformer from the 1540s like Katherine described as a follower of Martin Luther, or as a 'Lutheran' is historically fitting. It would have emphasized historical change for, as one historian has noted, English Protestants eventually 'passed beyond that initial Lutheran phase to come under the influence of the Swiss Reformation'.[18] On the other hand, 'Lutheran' may not have been contained neatly by this historicizing function. While it was a historical term in the context of English Protestantism, there were obviously still Lutherans abroad, so that to invoke them resonated in contemporary debates with and about continental Churches. And, according to historian Anthony Milton, 'by the 1590s the Lutherans were the bugbear of much reformed thinking'.[19] The Puritan lecturer William Bradshaw in 1606 took a shot against those in the established Church of England he perceived as straying from Calvinist beliefs when he warned of the danger of teachings 'which have been accounted and are in truth, popish or Lutheran errors'.[20] Gradually, then, 'Lutheran' had accrued ambivalent or explicitly negative connotations in England and so was deployed as an abusive term in polemics between English Protestants. By highlighting 'Lutheran' as a controversial term, Rowley brings to the forefront a history of change within English Protestantism, from Lutheran beginnings to a Swiss model. Further, there may have been an ecumenical agenda at work. Through the positive depiction of Katherine, he calls attention to Lutheranism – for which Katherine stands in the play – as embodying a fortress of values that would still appeal to English Protestants *c.* 1604, such as an insistence on the vernacular Bible, the rejection of papal authority, the strong condemnation of the belief in purgatory and the financial manipulations that surround it, as well as other Catholic institutions such as pilgrimages.[21] The course of the English Reformation, we are reminded, has not been unidirectional, but, Rowley also seems to insist, the things that still bind distinct sects of Protestants together are more important than the things that divide them in the kinds of nasty polemical debates in which Bradshaw was participating.

It is Prince Edward who must save King Henry from following his instincts to believe blindly in his Catholic bishops and have Katherine put to death. Bishop Gardiner has convinced Henry that Katherine's religious leanings are blasphemous and subversive, and he in turn grants the Bishop the power to execute her. But the Prince manages to step in and help Katherine plead for her life. Rowley adds another wrinkle here, though, by complicating Katherine's status as the play's most important voice of reform. She had seemed poised to emerge as the play's true Protestant hero, but this is undercut a bit when, once Edward convinces his father to give her a fair hearing, she retreats from her strident proselytizing in order to pacify Henry's raging ego.

> What I did speake, was as my womans wit,
> To hold out Argument could compasse it,
> My puny schollership is helde too weake
> To maintaine proofes about religion,
> Alas I did it but to wast the time,
> Knowing as then your grace was weake and sickly,
> So to expel parte of your paine and griefe.
>
> (lines 2666–72)

Katherine now claims that her attacks on the papacy and on doctrinal errors were in fact idle words to distract her husband from his aching leg. The importance of young Prince Edward in saving Katherine, then, sets her submission in a larger historical narrative in which Edward takes the torch of reform forward. Rowley also presents Edward being tutored by Cranmer to reject purgatory as the boy matures into a stalwart Protestant activist. Cranmer is given his due, but he is a scant presence in the play, ultimately, and his own near-death from Catholic conspiracy and eventual rescue are handled offstage and without much attention. It would seem, then, that in the choice to use Edward as Katherine's savior (which was not in Rowley's source material) the play locates in Edward the real beginnings of English Protestantism, implying a kind of supersession narrative: his youthful determination will carry forward the reformed energy she more or less abandons when she capitulates to Henry. At one point Henry even says of his son, in a striking moment of insight, that 'he [Prince Edward] is all our hopes, / That what our age shall leave unfinished, / In his faire raigne shall be accomplished' (lines 1557–9), a comment I shall return to.

For a key scene in charting Edward's development, Rowley cleverly adapts the morality play trope of dueling influences competing for a protagonist's soul, in this case the Prince's. Edward receives two letters simultaneously, one from his sister Mary, the other from his sister Elizabeth, each offering the boy advice on his spiritual progress. Edward reads portions of both aloud, starting with Mary's. She opens her letter '*The blessed mother of thy redeemer with all the Angels & holy Saints Be intermissers*' and encourages her brother to '*invocate the Saintes for helpe*' (lines 2399–401). Edward is disgusted by this: 'Ile read no farther: to him will *Edward* pray / For preseruation, that can himself presereue me, / Without the helpe of Saint or cerimonie' (lines 2405–7). From Elizabeth he reads advice to '*let thy prayers / Be dedicate to God onely, for tis he alone / Can strengthen thee*', and '*to shun Idolatrie*' (lines 2411–12, 2416). Edward responds happily to this letter, promising his absent sister that 'thy lines shalbe my contemplations cures / And in thy vertues will I meditate, / to Christ Ile onely pray for me and thee' (lines 2421–3).

Mary and Elizabeth are not represented on stage, but through the synecdotal letters we see in this scene a familial and confessional triptych, as well as a series of planes of historical futurity – or, a sense of the future ascribed to the past – opening up. That is, to invoke dynastic historical labels, we see the Edwardian, Marian, and Elizabethan futures adumbrated within the Henrician time frame of the play, all from the longer historical perspective of the Jacobean present of its performance. An interesting contrast to this triptych and the messy past it presents can be found in a play that was partially inspired by, and takes many verbal cues from, *When You See Me*: Shakespeare and Fletcher's *Henry VIII*. At the end of that play, Cranmer gives his famous prophecy about the future he envisions for the infant Elizabeth. After Cranmer expounds his vision of Elizabethan bliss, Henry responds by noting the comfort the words give him, and by making the rather surprising claim that 'Never before / This happy child did I get anything' (5.4.63–4). The statement stands out because of the obvious elision of Henry's eldest child. The King refers to her by name earlier in the play when he speaks of 'our daughter Mary' (2.4.172), and Shakespeare and Fletcher make the audience conscious of the Princess when Katherine, although not calling her by name, does express her hope that Henry will treat their daughter well, and characterizes her as of a 'noble and modest nature' (4.2.131). That Henry would erase her now is, on one level, perfectly sensible. It is in keeping with the King's logic of divorce from Katherine: if the marriage was incestuous then Mary is illegitimate and not to be counted among the benefits Henry has bequeathed his people. Elizabeth can thus emerge as a new beginning for the King and the nation. But the technical sense in which Henry might claim that only now does he have a true and worthy child cannot hide the fact that Mary did ascend to the throne. If Henry is represented here as viewing her as a legal or political non-entity who, from his perspective, would not participate in the nation's future, Jacobean audiences know this is an exercise in wishful thinking, even denial. The exclusion of Mary and her place in the history of England at this moment is so blatant it calls attention to itself as an attempt at rhetorical erasure more than it operates as a deft – much less efficacious – bit of genealogical whitewashing.[22]

The prophecy states that under Elizabeth, the land will prosper and that 'every man … will sing the merry songs of peace to all his neighbours' (5.4.34–5). Most pointedly for a play that represents the origins of the Reformation, we learn also that in Elizabeth's time, 'God shall be truly known' (5.4.36). Cranmer does not posit Elizabeth as the one who restores religion after the Marian interruption of the break with Rome. And he does not acknowledge the reign of Edward and its development of Henry's more modest Church reforms at all, thus obscuring the reality of England's shuttling between religious postures after Henry's death and before Elizabeth's ascension. Given the massive cultural importance of Foxe's *Acts and Monuments* alone, it is difficult to imagine that this speech could erase knowledge of the religious tribulations of England after Henry's death. Perhaps repressing memory, as Jonathan Baldo has argued about the play, is the particular political work of the prophecy, which serves as a solicitation to the audience to reflect on the turbulent early years of the Reformation as a cleaner and smoother process than it was, an offer of a kind of contract to accept Cranmer's prophecy as their history, and thus wilfully repress the emergence of Edwardian Protestantism as antidote to his father's weak version, the Marian interruption and the violence it occasioned, as well as the continued sectarian divisions in English culture that continued up to the moment of the play's performance.[23]

Rowley, meanwhile, represents the growth of Edward's spiritual sensibility in relation to his sister's epistolary advice and to the variously inflected beliefs of his father, his step-mother Katherine, his tutor Cranmer, and the reactionary Bishop Gardiner. There is also the almost ghostly presence of Martin Luther himself, who, as noted earlier, is referenced in this play multiple times. Gardiner's ally Bonner at one point notes that 'Luther hath sowne well, and Englands ground / Is fatte and fertile to increase his seed' (lines 2113–14), whereby the play suggests that Luther is really the origin point for the English Church. But the fact that, by the end of the sixteenth century, Foxe had to include in *Acts and Monuments* an extended apology for Luther in the wake of the English adoption of a more Swiss-style reformation indicates that for a Jacobean audience, Luther may be a starting point, but Lutheranism from this vantage point is *passé*, if not a kind of backsliding, as we have seen it could be in Elizabethan and Jacobean polemic. Elizabeth is honored through the letter she sends to Edward. The emphasis is on her as an incubator of Edward's faith as well as its eventual torchbearer, for audiences know she is also his successor. The letter scene may give a clear sense that Edward chooses the right path, but audiences are also aware of how that path will be interrupted by Mary's infamous reign. It is Elizabeth, rather than Edward, then, who really carries Protestantism forward to the early seventeenth century after the reversion to Catholicism under Mary. And yet even this common-sense notion of Elizabeth as the nation's most important spiritual benefactor, which will later be trumpeted in Cranmer's speech in *Henry VIII*, could have been subject to re-evaluation by the time that *When You See Me* is performed. As the Hampton Court Conference, which took place shortly before the play was probably written, made clear, Elizabeth's reign and pragmatic compromises possibly prevented civil war, but still provoked enough dissatisfaction with the state of reform among highly vocal elements of the populace that the new king felt pressure to hold this gathering and to more or less reaffirm, to the more ardent reformers' continued dissatisfaction, Elizabethan Protestantism.

Such a drawn-out sense of history lends itself to the tragico-comic perspective of Foxe: the true faith is always under attack, will always face trial, triumphs will always be shadowed by backsliding and apostasy. While Rowley, unlike Shakespeare and Fletcher, acknowledges Edward and Mary explicitly, Rowley's emphasis on the dynamism of the Prince of Wales itself elides the fact of Edward's sickly life and stunted reign, showing how fragile reform was from the start and the necessary role of Elizabeth in re-setting the Protestant track in controversial ways. Given the Jacobean historical perspective, then, Henry's line that Edward is 'all our hopes, / That what our age shall leave unfinished, / In his faire raigne shall be accomplished' (lines 1557–9) feels strained as a historicizing move, for the death of a king at age sixteen, prompting the succession of a Queen bent on reversing her predecessor's work, makes the notion of 'all our hopes ... accomplished' seem naïve, like just another thing Henry gets wrong. If Luther represents an origin point for the English Reformation without continuity to the present, then the same can be said for Edward; and while even if most subjects still nominally admired her, Elizabeth cannot be held up as a unifying spiritual leader given the reality of contentious religious difference under her that continued into James's reign.

Scholars have noted that *When You See Me* was performed by the newly minted acting troupe that was nominally patronized by the contemporary Prince of Wales, James's eldest son Henry. The emphasis on Edward could be, then, a friendly gesture to Prince Henry, who might be understood as the real object of King Henry's claim that the king's son is the hope of the nation's future.[24] Of course, such a compliment to Prince Henry as the nation's hope is fraught. It works as a fawning tribute to him at the same time as it could be an edgy remark at the expense of his father through the obvious implication that James, like Henry VIII, is not fervent enough in his dedication to the true Church. This raises the stakes of the line and the larger representation of Henry and Edward here, and it raises also the degree of difficulty of Rowley's project to tell a story about religious change and its relevance for the present that is not offensive to monarchs past or present. Edward's religious purity is not in doubt. But given the fact that his evangelical Protestantism was generally known to be more ardent than Elizabeth's, not to mention the fact that his physical weakness and swift demise brought Mary to the throne, what he represents in terms of understanding the history, or even the future, of Protestantism for playgoers in the early seventeenth century is unclear. Perhaps he represents the foreclosed possibility of a more far-reaching English Reformation, one that later, moderate Protestants might shudder at while their more zealous contemporaries might regard it as a tragically lost opportunity. I think that ultimately the perspective that emerges from *When You See Me* is that, when it comes to religious reform, whether we are in the Henrician moment represented, the Edwardian, Marian, and Elizabethan moments envisioned, or the Jacobean moment of performance, the present is never pure enough. The notion of an 'accomplished' Reformation is something that will always be in the future.

Jacobean theater audiences were well aware of the religious divisions of their time, of the broad spectrum of belief that could mark everyday life with discord. The Venetian ambassador claimed during James's reign that there were some twelve different religious parties in England – including three kinds of Catholics, two kinds of Puritans, and most ambiguously 'four of the religion of his Majesty [James]'.[25] Whether or not the number or nature of the groups he posited was accurate, his perception of multiplicity and lack of consensus on spiritual matters even within ostensibly homogenous groups certainly was, and Rowley's play helps to account for this by suggesting there was no single fount of reformation in England, but any number of canals with varying points of origin and differing paces that were diverted and redirected differently by the whims and temperaments of four Tudor monarchs. This ascension of a new king from a different line and even different country could only provoke more uncertainty for audiences *c.* 1604/5.

One historian has recently commented that 'incompatible readings of the Church's origins and development underpinned the confessional identities which emerged in sixteenth century England, and the variety of histories which persisted through Elizabeth's reign evince some of the deep-rooted tensions at the heart of the Reformation process'; while another states that 'Early seventeenth-century Protestant writers did not generally view the Reformation as a past historical event. Instead, the phrase "the reformation of the church" was usually employed to designate a work in progress'; it was a 'process, not an event'.[26] In *When You See Me You Know Me* it is possible to see that Henry was an attenuated reformer, that Edward's work would be reversed by Mary, and that his legacy would be revived, but also in a sense revised, by Elizabeth; and that, if we take King Henry's line about Edward as a nod outward to the playing company's patron, Prince Henry, after Elizabeth's passing a new Prince of Wales apparently will still have work to do in the wake of her, and the current king's, reigns. In Rowley's sober evaluation, England's Reformation was a convoluted story that was still unfolding, and the fate of its fractured religious culture was still to be determined.

Notes

1 P. Marshall, '(Re)defining the English Reformation', *Journal of British Studies*, 48:3 (2009), 564–86, here at 565, 567.

2 See A. Milton, *Catholic and Reformed: The Roman and Protestant Churches in English Protestant Thought, 1600–1640* (Cambridge: Cambridge University Press, 1995), pp. 270ff.

3 R. Oates, '"For the lacke of true history": Polemic, Conversion and Church History in Elizabethan England', in N. Lewycky and A. Morton (eds), *Getting Along? Religious Identities and Confessional Relations in Early Modern England – Essays in Honour of Professor W. J. Sheils* (Aldershot: Ashgate, 2012), pp. 133–52, here at p. 137.

4 E. Duffy, *Fires of Faith: Catholic England under Mary Tudor* (New Haven: Yale University Press, 2009), p. 55.

5 For evidence of the lost Cardinal Wolsey plays, see Philip Henslowe, *Henslowe's Diary*, ed. R. A. Foakes (Cambridge: Cambridge University Press, 2002), pp. 171, 180 and *passim*.

6 *Oldcastle*'s story of religious dissent and martyrdom is obviously relevant to English Protestant historiography, but its central figure is a Lollard in the time of Henry V, and so not technically part of a trend on the Reformation under the Tudors. There is still uncertainty about when exactly *Sir Thomas More* was first written, and later revised; as well as about whether it was ever performed. *Henry VIII* is clearly related to these early-seventeenth-century Tudor histories, but comes along several years later, *c.* 1613. *The Whore of Babylon* is chronologically closer, *c.* 1606, and covers similar ground in its depiction of sixteenth-century religious politics, but remains something of an anomaly due to its heavy-handed allegorical form.

7 J. Doolin Spikes's landmark essay on this and other 'Foxean' history plays, 'The Jacobean History Play and the Myth of the Elect Nation', *Renaissance Drama*, 8 (1977), 117–49, helped to bring attention to these works as worthy of deeper consideration. Some subsequent critics have worked to bring out the finer gradations in these works' political commitments and representations of religious controversies: G. K. Hunter, 'Religious Nationalism in Later History Plays', in V. Newey and A. Thompson (eds), *Literature and Nationalism* (Savage, MD: Barnes and Noble Books, 1991), pp. 88–97, usefully takes up and complicates Spikes's premise. Other work that has more specifically attended to *When You See Me*'s considerable interest and complexity includes M. S. Robinson, *Writing the Reformation: 'Actes and Monuments' and the Jacobean History Play* (Aldershot: Ashgate, 2002); T. Grant, 'History in the Making: The Case of Samuel Rowley's *When You See Me You Know Me* (1604/5)', in T. Grant and B. Ravelhofer (eds), *English Historical Drama, 1500–1660: Forms Outside the Canon* (New York: Palgrave, 2008), pp. 125–57; and M. Gurnis-Farrell, 'Martyr Acts: Playing with Foxe's Martyrs on the Public Stage', in J. Hwang Degenhardt and E. Williamson (eds), *Religion and Drama in Early Modern England: The Performance of Religion on the Public Stage* (Burlington, VT: Ashgate, 2011), pp. 175–93, esp. pp. 177–8. The most significant recent intervention about religious issues in the early modern history play, and about Rowley's work in particular, comes in D. Womersley's *Divinity and State* (Oxford: Oxford University Press, 2010), esp. pp. 148–67.

8 That holds true except in the case of the most baldly partisan accounts that attempt to impose coherence onto the past, and even those sometimes show internal ideological inconsistency. A. Patterson, '"All is True": Negotiating the Past in *Henry VIII*', in R. B. Parker and S. P. Zitner (eds), *Elizabethan Theater: Essays in Honor of S. Schoenbaum* (Cranbury, NJ: Associated University Presses, 1996), p. 156.

9 *When You See Me* was performed by the playing company formerly known as the Admiral's Men, and who, upon the ascension of James, came under the patronage of James's eldest son, Prince Henry. E. K. Chambers, *The Elizabethan Stage* (Oxford: Clarendon Press, 1923), vol. 2: p. 186. The title-page of the 1605 quarto makes this affiliation clear, indicating, after the long title for the play, that the text presents it 'As it was playd by the high and mightie *Prince of Wales his seruants.* / By Samuel Rowley, seruant to the Prince'. The quarto does not, however, identify a venue for the performance, so we must speculate over whether it was played only at the group's nominal home, the Fortune Theater, or at court before the royal family as well. The Prince's Men did play at court several times when *When You See Me* was fresh in their repertoire. Not all play titles from the records of payment for those appearances are preserved, but given the timing it is highly likely that they did present the play before the royal family sometime between 1604 and 1605. On court performances, see Chambers, *The Elizabethan Stage*, vol. 2: p. 189.

10 Oates, '"For the lacke of true history"', p. 136.

11 J. Coffey, *Persecution and Toleration in Protestant England, 1558–1689* (New York: Longman, 2000), p. 3.

12 Thomas Heywood, *If You Know Not Me, You Know Nobody, Part 1*, Malone Society Reprint, ed. Madeleine Doran (Oxford: Oxford University Press, 1935), lines 1049–53; 1150–1.

13 S. Rowley's *When You See Me You Know Me* will be quoted from the Malone Society Reprint, ed. F. P. Wilson (Oxford: Oxford University Press, 1952), cited by through line number in the text.

14 On jaundiced representations of Henry, see, for instance, William Shakespeare, *Henry VIII*, ed. G. McMullan (London: Cengage, 2000), pp. 76–7. All quotations in this chapter from *Henry VIII* are taken from this edition.

15 See Womersley, *Divinity and State*, pp. 158–9.

16 'Lutherans' are twice mentioned in Marlowe's *Massacre at Paris*, and there is one reference to them in Shakespeare's *Henry VIII* in a moment that is almost certainly a direct imitation of Rowley's play. In *Three Lords and Three Ladies of London* there are two references by a Spanish character to '*Lutheranos Angleses*'. See *An Edition of Robert Wilson's 'Three Ladies of London' and 'Three Lords and Three Ladies of London'*, ed. H. S. D. Mithal (New York: Garland, 1988), p. 91. For *Massacre at Paris* references, see F. Romany and R. Lindsey (eds), *Christopher Marlowe: The Complete Plays* (New York: Penguin Books, 2003), Scene 5, lines 11–39. For the reference in *Henry VIII*, see 3.2.98, along with the editor's gloss on its probable relation to Rowley.

17 See the 1583 edition of John Foxe's *Acts and Monuments* (London, 1583). The Parr episode appears there on pp. 1242–4.

18 D. D. Wallace, *Puritans and Predestination: Grace in English Protestant Theology, 1525–1695* (Chapel Hill: University of North Carolina Press, 1982), p. 5. On Lutheranism and the development of the English Church, see also W. Brown Patterson, 'The Anglican Reaction', in L. W. Spitz and W. Lohff (eds), *Discord, Dialogue, and Concord: Studies in the Lutheran Reformation's Formula of Concord* (Philadelphia: Fortress Press, 1977), pp. 150–65; B. Hall, 'The Early Rise and Gradual Decline of Lutheranism in England (1520–1600)', in D. Baker (ed.), *Reform and Reformation: England and the Continent ca. 1500–1750* (Oxford: Basil Blackwell, 1979), pp. 103–31; R. H. Fritze, 'Root or Link? Luther's Position in the Historical Debate over the Legitimacy of the English Church, 1558–1625', *Journal of Ecclesiastical History*, 37:2 (1986), 288–302; Milton, *Catholic and Reformed*, pp. 384–95; and A. Ryrie, 'The Strange Death of Lutheran England', *Journal of Ecclesiastical History*, 53:1 (2002), 64–92. Ryrie notes that 'Edward VI's religious settlement, largely resurrected by his half-sister Elizabeth, was, for all its idiosyncrasies, firmly within the emerging Reformed tradition' (65).

19 Milton, *Catholic and Reformed*, p. 386.

20 Quoted in N. Tyacke, 'Archbishop Laud', in K. Fincham (ed.), *The Early Stuart Church, 1603–1642* (London: Macmillan, 1993), p. 55.

21 See Katherine's speech at lines 2253–60.

22 See I. Kamps, *Historiography and Ideology in Stuart Drama* (Cambridge: Cambridge University Press, 1997), p. 134 and p. 136 for more on Mary's pointed absence in a speech by Cranmer, a man she put to death during her reign.

23 See J. Baldo, 'Necromancing the Past in *Henry VIII*', *English Literary Renaissance*, 34 (2004), 359–86, for a reading of the play that highlights its emphasis on forgetting, as well as Baldo's 'Forgetting Elizabeth in *Henry VIII*', in E. H. Hageman and K. Conway (eds), *Resurrecting Elizabeth I in Seventeenth-Century England* (Madison, NJ: Fairleigh Dickinson University Press, 2007), pp. 132–48, esp. p. 144 on Mary and p. 142, where he refers to the play as a 'grand pageant of oblivion'. On Cranmer's attempts to massage dynastic elisions, see D. L. Keegan, 'Performing Prophecy: More Life on the Shakespearean Scene', *Shakespeare Quarterly*, 62:3 (2011), 420–43, esp. 440.

24 See, for instance, G. Bullough, *Narrative and Dramatic Sources of Shakespeare* (New York: Columbia University Press, 1966), vol. 4: pp. 438–40; F. M. Nostbakken, 'Rowley's *When You See Me You Know Me:* Political Drama in Transition', *Cahiers Elisabéthains*, 47 (1995), 71–8; Grant, 'Rowley's *When You See Me You Know Me*', p. 132; and M. Rankin, '*Henry VIII*, Shakespeare, and the Jacobean Royal Court', *Studies in English Literature*, 51 (2011), 349–66.

25 Quoted in Milton, *Catholic and Reformed*, p. 7.

26 Oates, '"For the lacke of true history"', p. 152; Marshall '(Re)defining the English Reformation', 570.

7

Tragic mediation in *The White Devil*

Thomas J. Moretti

> Observe, that no society hath the privilege to be free from a Judas.
>
> Thomas Adams, 'The White Devil' (1613)[1]

For decades, John Webster's *The White Devil* has been pushed and pulled between the poles 'early' and 'modern': on one end is the claim that the play in fact offers a complexly moralist, even providentialist worldview; on the other end is the reading of *The White Devil* as a cynical, even radical tragedy, one which bears witness to a culture facing nihilistic anxieties and which represents the many subversive tendencies of early modern English tragedies more generally.[2] Either the lust, duplicity, and treachery prefigure the justice meant to purge vices from the stage, or they expose the injustices of any and all ideologies or belief-systems as the play's plot swirls and twists toward its cynical resolutions. Likewise, either Christianity coincides with an otherwise classical moral framework that leads to the villains' demise, or Christian institutions, epistemologies, practices, and soteriologies are uprooted and cast aside (like mandrakes) during the unfolding treachery and resulting bloodshed.

I suspect that *The White Devil*, with its many religious references and performances, offers less than moralism, more than cynicism. Since performance is exposed as inauthentic during the play – since the villain Flamineo mocks dramatic conventions even as he participates in them – it is hard to take anything in the play at face value, let alone accept the possibility of moralist outcomes. Rather, the play offers nothing to reassure troubled theatergoers or to reconstitute the systems that the play undermines. As in Thomas Adams's sermon, there is a Judas everywhere in Webster's *The White Devil*. Every religious and theatrical position and practice represented on stage and beheld from the auditorium is mocked and inauthenticated. So, what religious function could Webster's play serve? Adams cajoles his auditors to be more vigilant; what does Webster's play do, if not warn them of the hypocrisies and failings of all Christian positions?

Perhaps cynical representations of various Christian professions and practices could offer an ironic service to religion, one neither moral nor denominational but nonetheless inclusive, irenical, or ecumenical. I pose this possibility – that the play offers less moralism than some might hope, but that its cynicism mediates religious tension – as the focus of this essay, one that participates in the 'religious turn' in early modern scholarship. Since at least Debora Shuger's *Habits of Thought*,[3] scholars have sought to uncover the ways in which religion was necessarily imbricated in culture, not merely as a top-down ideology or as an 'instrument of state power – a façade of sanctity indispensable to its operation' – but rather as a cause and function of the complex, sometimes conflicted habits of thought and behaviors in early modern England.[4] Following this longstanding evaluation of religion in early modern English studies, my chapter re-examines the purpose of religious performance, cynicism, and meta-theatricality in *The White Devil*.

In a bleak Jacobean tragedy that sensationalizes, or simply exposes, the potential for villainy and sinfulness in every single religious and theatrical position available in early modern England, Webster pushes for religious mediation. The ensuing panic and confusion over the failures of Christianity on the stage result in a collective sense of troubled faith in Christianity. Webster ironically, if only intermittently, mediates the religious differences among its audience members through shared affect. The religious losses in *The White Devil* would have temporarily elided differences among Red Bull attendants in 1612 who could tolerate the February cold and dark.[5] By exposing the inadequacies, if not villanies, of each religious position in the play, Webster somehow comes close to Christian inclusivity and religious cohesion among unsettled theatergoers.

Webster's play defies the very correlation between tragedy, English reform, and religious crisis that it and other early modern English tragedies have typically been seen to confirm. This essay therefore continues an effort to shift course against what had been a prevailing trend in the religious turn of early modern English studies – to link particular religious categories to particular dramatic genres and theatrical conventions. At least since Huston Diehl's 1997 book on the relationship between reformed epistemology and early modern theatricality, scholarly works that address the function of religion on the early modern English stage have tended to restrict their scope to genre.[6] Romances, comedies, and even histories are typically given as evidence of a theater that can mitigate religious tensions, or even achieve religious inclusivity.[7] Comedies especially invite scholars to consider how traditional religious sentiments still resonated in the early modern English theater.[8] Tragedies complement this trend, since they have worked well for scholarship that notices a religious or cultural rupture represented or exploited on the stage.[9]

Either they promote Protestant suspicions over visual and theatrical representations, or they resort to and anticipate (post)modern opportunism, if not cynicism. Diehl had argued the former: 'dramatists seek to reform the stage, developing rhetorical strategies that disrupt older modes of sight and producing plays that conform to Protestant theories of art and representation'.[10] It is worth emphasizing that she relied only on tragedies to support her claim.[11] For Robert Watson, tragedies offer nothing less than the Pyrrhonic anxieties that he contends pervaded the period's literary culture.[12] The genre brings spectators to behold the existential abyss: if death is annihilation and not a precursor to the parousia, it is best to watch how plays like *The Spanish Tragedy* regulate and exploit the subsequent despair.

Diehl and Watson more recently have hinted that generic conventions might actually impose fewer restrictions on religious representation and categorization than their previous scholarship presumed. For Diehl, *The Winter's Tale*, despite its iconic ending, apparently defends the theater as a place for preaching – a defense in Protestant, even Puritan terms, against antitheatricalists who used idioms of reform to excoriate the theater.[13] For Watson, existential angst and morbidity propel *As You Like It*.[14] With the failure of likeness to unify man and nature, Shakespeare's comedy anticipates *King Lear*, for it 'echoes the characteristic cries of a culture in the agony of a major epistemological transformation'.[15] Because there is something ultimately lacking in our ability to 'know things only as we liken them, never in or as themselves', a play with similes for a title cannot help but map out the fault lines between identity formation and human isolation and alienation.[16] Watson treats fragmentation and loss as conditions that can traverse genre, just as Diehl no longer binds Protestant epistemologies to the conventions of tragedy.

Genre, therefore, does not necessarily steer playwrights, players, and audience members toward one particular religious perspective or epistemology. Playwrights as deft and apt as Shakespeare and Webster can blur or cement religious categories with any dramatic form. Their artistry allowed for the possibility of religious mediations in early modern London theaters, where communities strained by various, conflicting attempts at religious settlement during the reigns of Elizabeth and James went for entertainment.[17] Not that true mediation was ever likely, but the desire for it must have had especial presence at Clerkenwell and nearby London parishes, where, as Mark Bayer has demonstrated, Jesuit safehouses stood in the same neighborhoods as Protestant print-houses.[18] With tendencies toward religious pluralism, a play as skeptical as *The White Devil* is responsive to the relative heterogeneity of Christian belief-systems, practices, and predilections in Jacobean communities surrounding the Red Bull (and in Jacobean London more generally).[19]

The White Devil is especially attuned to religious mediation as a process of inter-subjectivity. Because religious mediation relies upon the relationalities among subjects situated along a wide religious spectrum, the play serves up a variety of religious positions to trouble theatergoers no matter their preferred modes of Christian belief and practice.[20] The play's representations of religion are as exaggerated and ridiculous as Isabella's sensuous and idolatrous devotion to her husband Brachiano's portrait, as horrific and vindictive as Lodovico and Gasparo's parodically sacramental visitation to the poisoned and dying Brachiano, and as futile as Vittoria's preaching and Flamineo's private musings. In other words, while certain actions, spectacles, and speeches might recall various doctrinal, ecclesiological, and devotional positions along England's religious spectrum, not one religious act or habit is straightforwardly affecting, though all are eventually discounted.[21] Nor does any receive permanent validation or scorn. Along its macabre, circular plots, this play upends every major religious position available to and extant among its early modern audience, but the play does not split audience members from their most basic religious sensibilities.[22] And since early modern London audience members could retain their commitments to Christianity even during a performance of *The White Devil*, it is hard to presume that early modern English plays could evacuate the theater of religious meaning.[23]

The play begins its work with the stereotypical villainies and practices of early modern non-Christians during Brachiano and Vittoria's wooing scene. Webster codifies the villainy as Jewish and Muslim from the onset.[24] In 1.2, when Flamineo plays the pander for his sister Vittoria and her lover Brachiano, and after he convinces Vittoria's husband Camillo to be jailed in his chambers, he has Zanche the Moor lay a carpet and two cushions for the lovers. With Zanche, the Muslim act of worship is perverted into a precursor for adultery and fornication, and audience members tread a familiar path that leads to grotesque figurations of the other. Even her name and ethnicity, pronounced 'Zank the Moor', is close enough phonetically to Christopher Marlowe's Ithamore in *The Jew of Malta* to recall a theatrical tradition of the sinister Muslim.

This same theatrical tradition redeploys typological associations between the Muslim and the Jew.[25] If Zanche the Moor sets the stage for debauchery, Vittoria and Brachiano flirt with multi-layered puns and rhymes that enmesh sex, sin, and Jewishness. First, the lovers quip with 'Jewel', Vittoria's 'ornament / Of a weake fortune' (1.2.207–8). Brachiano will 'change' his for hers and entice her to wear her 'Jewel' 'lower' (1.2.211). Vittoria then abruptly shifts from this lewd talk to retell her dream of a 'Eu' tree (215). Camillo and Isabella, Brachiano's wife, plan to uproot the tree to make room for a 'blacke-thorne', under which they 'vow'd' to bury Vittoria alive. A whirlwind breaks a 'massy arme' from the 'Eu', and strikes both dead (216–38).

The tale pressures Brachiano to plot a double-murder even as it makes the lovers' treacheries sound 'Jewish'. That is at least how Cornelia, Flamineo and Vittoria's mother, sees it: 'Bee thy act *Judas*-like', she harangues her daughter, 'betray in kissing' (282). 'Jewel … Eu … Judas': Webster deploys puns on 'Jew' as villains sit on a blanket spread by a Moor to transpose a scene of lust into a non-Christian register. Webster's concern here is not the extent of the pun's logic (or lack thereof), but rather the subtle, phonetic resemblances between Jewishness and the unfolding villainy. If in post-Reformation England there persisted an 'anxiety that Jewishness was on the verge of reasserting itself from within', if in England, 'Jewish crime – like Jewishness itself – was invariably hidden and insidious, a secret waiting to be unearthed', then Webster begins his play by marking the spot of Jewish treachery (and Islamic hedonism) on a stage devoid of Christianity.[26] Isabella and Camillo's plot in Vittoria's dream is to exchange a 'Eu' for a 'black-thorne', as if Isabella and Camillo are similarly conspiring offstage, as if the only option for the audience is Jews or Moors, one adulterous relationship or another. The audience is not given much of an alternative. By the end of 1.2, the only professed Christian is Vittoria's husband, Camillo, a cuckold locked out of the lovers' scene.

Webster heightens desire for a specifically Christian resolution to the non-Christian malevolence that begins the play. Because a Moor's blanket is the spot for 'Jewish' villainy, audience members are led to hope or desire that the play will retrieve some Christian tradition or performance to offset anathema. The rest of the play's key moments test one Christian mode after another in a deliberate search for alternatives that, taken one at a time and in isolation, might alienate some in the audience, but together and as a response to the play's unending collusions and perfidies, join audience members in a shocking realization that Christianity, in all its expressions, ultimately fails to prevent tragedy. At each turn, Webster toys with the dramatic potency of Christian prayer and preaching, but he refuses to grant them soteriological finality. In a sign of the importance of religion to this play, the theatricality of religion is at its peak during the most gruesome, shocking, or affecting of episodes – at Isabella's death, Vittoria's trial, Brachiano's deathbed scene, Flamineo's fratricide of Marcello, Flamineo's vision of Brachiano's ghost, and Flamineo's death scene. If I shift between scenes, it is because of the play's unique, layered form, which would have audience members recall one scene – Isabella's dumb show kiss of a poisoned portrait of Brachiano, for instance (2.2.23.1–12) – when they behold another – such as Brachiano's dying refusal to be kissed, 'for I shall poyson thee' (5.3.26).

Once Vittoria and Brachiano apostatize with their kisses and pervert the sacrament of matrimony in the process, Isabella's appearance as Brachiano's devoted wife acts as a potential, yet irritating corrective. Her devotion to her husband during her twice-performed divorce with Brachiano in 2.1 reaffirms the one sacrament which perhaps held the most consistent, shared value for the majority of audience members. Only the most radical hot Protestant would take firm, declarative issue with a ritual that bonded woman to man according to the cultural traditions that Thomas Cranmer smoothly ritualized in the Book of Common Prayer, which cues the husband to proclaim, 'With this ring I thee wed: with my body I thee worship, and with all my worldly goods I thee endow.'[27] In 2.1, this seems not the vow of Brachiano, but rather Isabella, first, when she accepts Brachiano's wilful and private commitment to divorce, and second, when in public she plays the hysterical wife who feigns a desire to divorce her husband. Both Brachiano and Isabella's disavowals center on the wedding-ring as a sacramental object that they re-service to concretize the divorce. To commit to a vow by disenchanting the token of wedlock not only parodies a marriage ceremony; it also disturbs audience members, no matter their placement along the Jacobean religious spectrum, whose attitudes toward the wedding-ring were likely more compatible than attitudes toward other ceremonial objects.[28]

Brachiano's cruel dismissal of his marriage vow reasserts the value of that vow, just as the desacralized wedding-ring reaffirms its value to audience members; his abhorrent curse against 'the Priest / That sang the wedding Masse, and even my Issue' (2.1.190) positions audience members with Isabella and with the vows and values which she upholds. Yet, those same auditors are increasingly burdened when this devoted wife takes too far her vow to 'be subject to [her] own husband' and scorns her husband and marriage in public.[29] To sacrifice her reputation for his, she troubles the very spousal obeisance to which she subjects herself. Together with her husband, she shocks audience members into shared affect – a guttural reaction against a matrimonial sacrilege that is spectacularized for theatrical pleasure. Even if any Red Bull attendants were radical enough to eschew wedding-rings and other trappings of marriage rituals, watching a marriage doubly fray and experiencing the virtue of a wife by means of her false, white-devilish performance – 'And thinke with what a piteous and rent heart, / I shall performe this sad insuing part' (2.1.223–4) – audience members share the loss of and concomitant desire for a firmly upheld and valued marriage. This rehearsed, then play-acted divorce reinforces the religious value of matrimony in the auditorium by devaluing it on the stage.

However, when Isabella idolizes her estranged husband's portrait after their divorce, she pervertedly takes upon herself the wifely vow that she feigned to break. It is still early in the play when she idolizes a painting of Brachiano in a dumb show. She 'doe's three reverences to it, and kisses it thrice', then dies from poison-laced canvas (2.2.23.7–12). A conjurer has brought the scene in real time to Brachiano's chambers, and explains

> 'twas her custome nightly
> Before shee went to bed, to go and visite
> Your picture, and to feed her eyes and lippes
> On the dead shadow.
>
> (2.2.25–8)

Her kissing, an obvious parody of Catholic ritual, is to blame as much as Brachiano's cruelty. And her fall was to be expected upon her first stage entrance.

> *Brachiano* So I wondered much,
> What amorous whirlewind hurryed you to *Rome*.
> *Isabella* Devotion, my Lord.
>
> (2.1.149b–51a)

Because it has been two months since she last saw her husband, she hopes that her *devotio in absentia* can '[m]erit one kisse': like the caricature of a good Catholic, she believes that good deeds deserve reward, that her works should elicit her 'Lord's' love (156a). When he kisses her hand and vows never to lie with her again, he gives the lie to her worldview. Even when she laments that 'the Saints in heaven / Will knit their browes' (198a–9a), audience members can only question how possible that is when none intercede on her behalf. Her devotion is her good Catholic deed, so her death seems as much a result of her superstition as it is a product of murderous collusion. After a divorce that draws on audience sympathy for the jilted wife, Webster would have us believe that Isabella got what was coming to her. Sudden shifts in allegiances and affiliations are conventions of early modern tragedies. Worth noting here is how such shifts lead to shared affect among attentive theatergoers who might otherwise separate along religious lines. All regret the divorce, all blame Isabella's misplaced worship and Brachiano's treachery for her death.

Iconoclasm stands as a poor alternative to idolatry when Marcello dies at the hands of Flamineo, a brother whose villainy first surfaced when he was an infant.

> *Marcello* Was not this crucifix my father's?
> *Cornelia* Yes.
> *Marcello* I have heard you say, giving my brother suck,
> He took the crucifix between his hands
> *Enter Flamineo*
> And broke a limb off.

Cornelia Yes, but 'tis mended. ...
Flamineo runs Marcello through
...
Marcello Oh, mother, now remember what I told
Of breaking off the crucifix. Farewell!
(5.2.8–19)

Perhaps Flamineo's desecration of this family heirloom signals his social 'rise / By all dishonest meanes' (21–2).[30] Nevertheless, the religious impact of this broken crucifix is immediate. Webster ties Flamineo's wrath, vengeance, and villainy to an infant iconoclast's impulse that portends malice. No one should praise Flamineo's iconoclastic past, since it is only meant to predict his murderous future. Certainly the crucifix could not be as obscene a worshipped image as Brachiano's portrait, but it nonetheless forces attentive audience members to reconsider any aversion toward sensory devotion. Isabella's earlier, feigned words to Brachiano – 'Let not my former dotage / make thee an unbelever' – gain meta-theatrical value here. Even theatergoers dismissive of or repulsed by traditional religious icons outside the theater are meant to connect sadism and its attendant affects to iconoclastic fervor (2.1.259–60).

Preaching and prophesying, no matter how vitriolic, are just as vexing as iconoclasm and iconic worship in this play. During Vittoria's trial for Camillo's murder, they effect nothing. If she thinks she can persuade the judges on stage and in the auditorium, she ends up doubting her curse-laden rhetoric: 'Dye with those pils in your most cursed mawe', 'while you sit a'th Bench, / Let your own spittle choake you', and 'That the last day of judgement may so find you, / And leave you the same devill you were before' (3.2.275–80). Although '[s]he's turn'd fury' (278), Vittoria's words offer little recourse: 'O womans poore revenge / Which dwels but in the tongue' (284). As she suspects, her oratory performance does not lessen her sentence – confinement in 'a house of convertites', of 'penitent whoores' (264, 267). When she later returns to doomsday prophesies, she again falls flat:

Vittoria I prithee, yet remember,
Millions are now in graves which at last day
Like mandrakes shall rise shrieking.
Flamineo Leave your prating,
For these are but grammatical laments,
Feminine arguments, and they move me
As some in pulpits move their auditory
More with their exclamation than sense
Of reason or sound doctrine.
(5.6.67–74)

No matter that sermons in early modern England were meant to affect attendants 'with their exclamation'.[31] Here, Flamineo's attitude toward his sister's prophetic voice leaves his audience wondering what they should do when, at St. Paul's, a minister like Francis Rollenson proclaims that in hell 'shall *Dogges* endure *paines* most *bitter* and *eternall*; namely, *a fire unquenchable, and a worme that shall never cease gnawing*'.[32]

The actions at Brachiano's deathbed grant more theatrical power to preaching, but only by tainting it with cruelty (5.3.150–72). Dressed as Capuchin friars and praying in Latin, Lodowico and Gasparo seem like confessors and administers of Roman Catholic last rites, but they lead Brachiano to despair: 'thou shalt die like a poore rogue', 'stink like a dead flie-blowne dog', and 'be forgotten before thy funerall sermon' (5.3.162–4). These devilish friars then torture and strangle the poisoned Brachiano, another 'cursed devil' (5.3.165). Earlier, Flamineo saw no power in his sister's short, poetic warning, but Vittoria now sees 'hell' at Brachiano's bedside (176), and attentive audience members are similarly affected. Brachiano's dying leads to 'extreame unction' (5.3.39), a Roman Catholic anointing of the sick that is susceptible to scorn. Despite the religious affiliation of that ritual, Brachiano's need for physical and spiritual relief before death could affect hope for the 'Christian charity' that Gasparo and Lodovico pretend to offer (5.3.170). The ceremonial trappings of the scene – the Latin prayers, the elevated crucifix, the hallowed candle – may parody or exaggerate Catholic ritual, but the essential purpose of those trappings – to bless a man who soon will die – becomes something desired, even as audience members might feel a contradictory excitement over the death of the corrupt aristocrat and repulsion over the superstitious trimmings of the murder plot. Lodowico and Gasparo's prophesies at Brachiano's bedside, like Vittoria's later preaching to Flamineo, might lack 'sound doctrine' (5.6.74), but they should horrify audience members.

So far, I have read scenes that test the theatrical potency of a variety of religious practices and performances. The destruction of a crucifix may not absolve idolaters, but it may have audience members reconsider the importance of iconic worship. The act of preaching might prove unsuccessfully transparent at a rigged trial and before a cynical brother, but its hold over spectators during a ghastly death bears witness to its continued draw. Perhaps it was possible for early modern English 'audiences to engage synchronically in … belief *and* metadramatic awareness'.[33] Since theater can be obvious artifice here, and riveting, absorbing performance there – since imagery and affective worship can be discredited, only to figure into the terrors of this play – then it is possible for Christian performances to approximate a unifying experience for audience members who are all left in doubt, no matter their religious commitments outside the theater.

In the play's final scenes, Flamineo brings the play's twisted path toward religious mediation to a head. Equal parts upstart courtier, alleged atheist, cynical villain, and meta-theatrical parodist, he exposes the very performativity at which he excels. It is not just that he mocks religion whenever he confronts its expressions: that he sees Giovanni's call for him to repent as a sign of Giovanni's villainy (5.4.24); that he mocks Vittoria's preaching; that he exposes Vittoria's feigned study of books and vaguely Christian piety when he goads her into shooting an empty pistol at him (5.6.1–149).[34] In brief moments, he validates the very religious sentiments to which he plays the cynic. Consider his confrontation with Brachiano's ghost as it enters in silence, wearing 'leather cassock and breeches, boots, a cowl, [and carrying] a pot of lilyflowers with a skull in it':

> *Flamineo* Ha! I can stand thee. Nearer, nearer yet.
> What a mockery hath death made of thee! Thou look'st sad.
> In what place art thou? In yon starry gallery,
> Or in the curséd dungeon? No? Not speak?
> Pray, sir, resolve me, what religion's best
> For a man to die in? Or is it in your knowledge
> To answer me how long I have to live?
> That's the most necessary question.
>
> (5.4.125–32)

From that 'Ha!' onward, Flamineo mocks the theatrical entrance meant to grant him star power. Brachiano's 'death' is nothing more than the loss of a character in a play, a 'sad' or shameful demotion for an actor who must now play what was a cliché by 1612 – a ghost seeking retribution.[35] As if to set the stage to mock another version of Hamlet's ghost, Flamineo lampoons Hamlet: 'I have a strange thing in me, to th' which / I cannot give a name, without it bee / Compassion' (5.4.107–9). What begins as a potentially riveting moment of spectacular theater – a monologue interrupted by a ghost who throws a skull and dirt at his former confidante – ends in a charade. And a poignant question for spectators – what is the best religion – has become a line wedged within satire.

Flamineo's irreverence toward religious practices and their theatrical representations frustrates any drive to seek in the theater a path toward justice, equity, hope, or redemption, since the theater is always and already a place of inauthenticity. Consider his double-death. First, he is shot with his own unloaded pistols by Vittoria and Zanche. He then rises, but his return to life is shortened when Lodovico and Gasparo barge in, tie him up to a post, and stab him, his sister, and Zanche. He ridicules their assault – after all, their knives, like his pistols, are harmless props – but then he speaks as if in despair and dies.

But who is to say that this second death and his last words are to be accepted when just a few moments earlier his death was feigned? If religious practice has been enervated at each turn in this play, then we would be remiss to accept at face value Flamineo's nihilism, expressed as it is with the very tools of the trade that the play has already utilized and cast aside – the 'pratings' of Vittoria, the prophesies of Lodovico and Gasparo at Brachiano's deathbed, and Flamineo's own morbid musings before and during his encounter with Brachiano's ghost. At the same time, when Flamineo is stabbed, his dying on stage retrieves a certain meta-dramatic force and lets audiences struggle between disbelief and belief. Flamineo no longer channels Hamlet, but rather revises the role; the rest is not silence, but rather 'rest breeds rest, where all seeke paine by paine' (5.6.268), an adage that he levels at audience members who seek leisure, recreation, entertainment in the pain, suffering, and dying performed on stage. This desire for theatergoers who find entertainment in tragedy, who 'seeke' the anxiety, pain, shock, and skepticism that result from the evils presented on stage, is analogous to the goal of the Christian, a goal sought when the worshipper, churchgoer, or devotee finds relief in remembering the pain that another endured for the sake of those who beheld, imagined, or devoted themselves to the outcome of his suffering, bound, stabbed body. Flamineo is no Christ, but during and after the villain's death, theatergoers are brought together with a shared sense of epistemological loss during Flamineo's second death.

This play, more even than other tragedies, bears witness to an anxiety over unredeemed death or over an immoral world. And yet, its resulting effect is community rather than isolation and cynicism. By play's end, theatergoers are left with only a vague, inclusive sense of their Christianity, one that they can reinscribe or reconstitute with various, distinctive, and polarizing denominational practices and thoughts after they leave the Red Bull, but which here has nothing to delimit it. Ironically, then, this cynical play could somehow still manage to bring together audience members of varying Christian persuasions. Perhaps some audience member could find meaning or could rest assured in Flamineo's last request to 'Let no harsh flattering Bels resound my knell, / Strike thunder, and strike lowde to my farewell' (269–70). Whether bells are vestiges of a corrupt English Catholic past or an accepted or tolerated *adiaphora*, they are not for the nihilistic, vicious Flamineo. No matter what a theatergoer might think about church bells, each sees Flamineo as a villain or, worse, a player wrapped in a cynic's hide. Thunder from backstage would serve him best.

Watching the suffering during Flamineo's final moments, theatergoers may have a shared, vexing sense of relief and satisfaction, discomfort and anxiety, the kind of complicated affect sought at St. Paul's, in many a church, and every ritual, festival, or religious meeting in England, from Presbyterian meeting house to Jesuit safehouse. Far from a conscious, wilful decision to accept a generalized Christianity, auditors share affectively, emotively, somatically in ways unavailable whenever religion turns into discourse, susceptible as that is to analysis, categorization, and polemic. Webster does not give theatergoers a roadmap for the 'best religion', but he shows them what they most certainly are not – Italian villains, 'Jews', 'Moors', or atheists who pervert religion into self-serving performance. Christianity remains an identity that each audience member can claim, despite (or even because of) the play's tragic impulses, and despite the many differences and animosities shared among them in Jacobean Clerkenwell (and London more generally). Outside the theater – in church, in the street, at the pulpit, in the court – Londoners could not escape the crises of confessional identity that certainly existed in 1612. But in the Red Bull, Webster mediated confessional differences for those able to hear, to see, to stay warm and awake by undermining every Christian performance available in early modern England.

Notes

1 Thomas Adams, *The Works of Thomas Adams*, ed. Joseph Angus (Edinburgh: James Nichol, 1862), vol. 2: p. 224. For the linkages between Adams's sermon and Webster's play, see E. Rhatigan, 'Reading *The White Devil*', in A. Streete (ed.), *Early Modern Drama and the Bible: Contexts and Readings, 1570–1625* (New York: Palgrave Macmillan, 2012), pp. 176–94.

2 For the play as ultimately providentialist, see John Webster, *The White Devil. The Works of John Webster*, ed. David Gunby, David Carnegie, and Arthur Hammond (Cambridge: Cambridge University Press, 1995, 2004), vol. 1: pp. 27, 60 and *passim*. C. Luckyj does not go so far when she discovers a complex morality in the innovative form of the drama (*A Winter's Snake: Dramatic Form in the Tragedies of John Webster* (Athens, GA: University of Georgia Press, 1989), pp. 151–4. J. Dollimore considers the play as a subversive response to the very institutions and power structures responsible for justice and equity in *Radical Tragedy: Religion, Ideology and Power in the Drama of Shakespeare and His Contemporaries* (Chicago: University of Chicago Press, 1984), pp. 231–46. R. Watson, albeit briefly (because Webster is 'an obvious example' of nihilism in early modern English tragedies [p. 47]), considers *The White Devil* as a product of a culture anxious over 'unredeemed death'; *Back to Nature: The Green and the Real in the Late Renaissance* (Philadelphia: University of Pennsylvania Press, 2006), pp. 47, 347, n. 29.

3 D. Shuger, *Habits of Thought in the English Renaissance: Religion, Politics and the Dominant Culture* (Toronto: University of Toronto Press, 1990).

4 Dollimore, *Radical Tragedy*, p. 231. The list of scholars who have played key roles during the 'turn to religion' in early modern English studies is extensive. It includes D. Shuger, P. Whitfield White, J. Knapp, S. Monta, A. Walsham, J. Waldron, E. Williamson, J. Hwang Degenhardt, H. Diehl, P. Jensen, and J. Reinhardt Lupton.

For a more comprehensive, yet by now dated list, see K. Jackson and A. F. Marotti, 'The Turn to Religion in Early Modern English Studies', *Criticism*, 46 (Winter 2004), 167–90. For a more updated canvas, see the contributions to Jackson and Marotti's most recent collection of essays, *Shakespeare and Religion: Early Modern and Postmodern Perspectives* (South Bend, IN: Notre Dame University Press, 2011), which collectively celebrate the historicist and postmodern approaches to early modern religion.

5 In his 'To the Reader', Webster blamed the poorly received first performance of *The White Devil* on poor lighting and a cold winter, as well as 'ignorant asses' in the audience (Webster, *The White Devil*, p. 140).

6 H. Diehl, *Staging Reform, Reforming the Stage: Protestantism and Popular Theatre in Early Modern England* (Ithaca, NY: Cornell University Press, 1997).

7 J. Knapp looks to these genres to imagine a communal theatre, one that promoted and instilled religious inclusivity. See *Shakespeare's Tribe: Church, Nation, and Theatre in Renaissance England* (Chicago: University of Chicago Press, 2002).

8 P. Jensen argues, for instance, that *As You Like It* offers a Catholic aesthetic in *Religion and Revelry in Shakespeare's Festive World* (Cambridge: Cambridge University Press, 2008), pp. 194–233. Such studies countervail both Diehl's and O'Connell's premise that the theater expanded and developed along the same, ultimately linear track as the Reformation. Even though they call attention to the residue of traditional religion, Diehl's and O'Connell's accounts do not do enough to acknowledge the switchback nature of the Reformation, nor do they consider the albeit overly optimistic and contentious push toward religious consensus in Jacobean Church and court. See M. O'Connell, *Religion and Revelry in Shakespeare's Festive World* (Cambridge: Cambridge University Press, 2008). For recent correctives, see J. Waldron, *Reformation of the Body* (New York: Palgrave Macmillan, 2013), pp. 12–14 and p. 59; A. Walsham, 'Migrations of the Holy: Explaining Religious Change in Medieval and Early Modern Europe', *Journal of Medieval and Early Modern Studies*, 44:2 (2014), 241–80.

9 S. Greenblatt's *Hamlet in Purgatory* (Princeton: Princeton University Press, 2001) is an example: his reading of *Hamlet* suggests that 'the power of Shakespeare's theatre is frequently linked to its appropriation of weakened or damaged institutional structures [like the Catholic Church]' (pp. 253–4).

10 Diehl, *Staging Reform*, pp. 66.

11 For this critique, see K. Cartwright, 'Book Review: Staging Reform, Reforming the Stage: Protestantism and Popular Theater in Early Modern England', in J. Pitcher (ed.), *Medieval and Renaissance Drama in England* (Rutherford, NJ: Fairleigh Dickinson University Press, 2001), pp. 264–70.

12 See R. Watson, *The Rest Is Silence: Death as Annihilation in the English Renaissance* (Berkeley: University of California Press, 1994).

13 See H. Diehl, '"Does not the stone rebuke me?": The Pauline Rebuke and Paulina's Lawful Magic in *The Winter's Tale*', in P. Yachnin and P. Badir (eds), *Shakespeare and the Cultures of Performance* (New York: Ashgate, 2007), pp. 69–2. Diehl's reading of *The Winter's Tale* extends an argument that she has made about reform and comedies like Jonson's *Bartholomew Fair*: 'Rather than simply repudiating puritan

culture, the comedies of early modern England … imaginatively engage its assumptions, cleverly appropriate and transform its genres, and creatively respond to its challenges to the stage' ('Disciplining Puritans and Players: Early Modern English Comedy and the Culture of Reform', *Religion and Literature*, 32:2 [2000], 88).

14 Watson, *Back to Nature*, pp. 77–107.

15 *Ibid.*, p. 78.

16 *Ibid.*, p. 77.

17 Historiography on the religious situations in early modern England is rich and ongoing. For the problems of mediation – that is, for 'moderation' as coercive, even violent attempts to control the populace, and for the shifts between tolerance and persecution in early modern England – see E. Shagan, *The Rule of Moderation: Violence, Religion and the Politics of Restraint in Early Modern England* (Cambridge: Cambridge University Press, 2011) and A. Walsham, *Charitable Hatred: Tolerance and Intolerance in England 1500–1700* (Manchester and New York: Manchester University Press, 2006).

18 M. Bayer, *Theater, Community, and Civic Engagement in Jacobean London* (Iowa City: University of Iowa Press, 2011), pp. 117–24 and *passim*. Despite the diverse religious culture which Bayer correctly recounts, his study insists that the Red Bull served a mainly Protestant agenda. His understanding of religious heterogeneity in early modern London, and in the parish of St. James Clerkenwell more specifically, contradicts his depiction of Red Bull theatergoers as fairly uniform in their religious proclivities. For a fuller response to his general description of Red Bull audiences and residents of Clerkenwell, see my article '*Via Media* Theatricality and Religious Fantasy in Thomas Dekker and Philip Massinger's *The Virgin Martyr* (1622)' in *Renaissance Drama*, 42:2 (Fall 2014), 243–70.

19 Lake and Questier have examined how a religiously hybrid, as opposed to polarized, populace in early Stuart England demanded that dramatists, clergy, and printers take a more tolerant and tolerable approach from the pulpit, in the theater, and in the London marketplace more generally: P. Lake with M. Questier, *The Antichrist's Lewd Hat: Protestants, Papists and Players in Post-Reformation England* (New Haven: Yale University Press, 2002), pp. xxxi, 713, and *passim*. Also see T. Watt's *Cheap Print and Popular Piety, 1550–1640* (Cambridge: Cambridge University Press, 1993) for evidence in print and other cultural artifacts that suggests a less bifurcated, more heterogeneous religious situation in early Stuart England. For instance, she insists that reform did not totally do away with visual representation in popular culture: the 'inward-looking' iconoclasm of 'hardline Protestants' should not lead to 'wider claims for the notion of "iconophobia"' across 'the nation as a whole'. Rather, Watt contends, there were 'some ways in which visual communication continued to play a role in mainstream Protestant culture; and, conversely … post-Reformation religion continued to have a place in the mainstream visual culture' (p. 136). Watt points to *A schole-house for the needle* (London, 1624) as an example of continued iconography in Jacobean England. Ladies who used the guidebook 'embroidered not only unicorns, peacocks, flowers and abstract designs, but scenes of Adam and Eve, the pelican in her piety, and even the crucifixion' (p. 137; *A schole-house*, sigs. A2–A4).

20 The religious 'spectrum' of Jacobean England is P. White's coinage in 'The *via media* in the Early Stuart Church', in K. Fincham (ed.), *The Early Stuart Church, 1603–1642* (Stanford: Stanford University Press, 1993), pp. 211–12.

21 Lake and Questier similarly discover that 'the same people might react positively to what were, in formal terms, radically different, indeed, on occasion, mutually incompatible [religious] messages' (*The Anti-Christ's Lewd Hat*, p. 713).

22 See Luckyj, *A Winter's Snake*, for the rich complexities of Webster's experimental, circular, tragic form in *The Duchess of Malfi* and *The White Devil*.

23 For theater as secular or secularizing, an institution devoid of religious meaning, see S. Greenblatt, *Shakespearean Negotiations: The Circulation of Social Energy in Renaissance England* (Berkeley: University of California Press, 1988); L. Montrose, *The Purpose of Playing: Shakespeare and the Cultural Politics of the Elizabethan Theatre* (Chicago: University of Chicago Press, 1996). S. Beckwith refutes Greenblatt's revised, more nuanced claim on the theater's evacuation of religion in *Hamlet in Purgatory* in 'Stephen Greenblatt's *Hamlet* and the Forms of Oblivion', *Journal of Medieval and Early Modern Studies*, 33:2 (2003), 203. Indeed, many scholars have effectively countered Greenblatt's characterization of the theater, including A. Dawson, who nonetheless insists on theater as a 'secularizing' institution that could affect something like religious feeling, but nothing like full-fledged religious experience or identification; 'Shakespeare and Secular Performance', in Yachnin and Badir (eds), *Shakespeare and the Cultures of Performance*, pp. 83–97.

24 See L. Bovilsky, 'Black Beauties, White Devils: The English Italian in Milton and Webster', *English Literary History*, 70:3 (2003), 638, for the expected criminality and blasphemy of Italians on the English stage.

25 For more on these associations between Jew and Turk or Moor on and off the stage, see J. Shapiro, *Shakespeare and the Jews* (New York: Columbia University Press, 1996), D. Vitkus, *Turning Turk: English Theater and the Multicultural Mediterranean, 1570–1630* (New York: Palgrave Macmillan, 2003), J. Burton, *Traffic and Turning: Islam and English Drama, 1579–1624* (Newark, DE: University of Delaware Press, 2005), esp. pp. 196–232, J. Reinhard Lupton, 'The Wizards of Uz: Shakespeare and the Book of Job', in Jackson and Marotti (eds), *Shakespeare and Religion*, pp. 171–4, D. Britton, 'Muslim Conversion and Circumcision as Theater', in Hwang Degenhardt and Williamson (eds), *Religion and Drama in Early Modern England*, pp. 71–86 and Sr. J. R. Andreas, 'The Curse of Cush: Othello's Judaic Ancestry', in P. C. Kolin (ed.), *Othello: New Critical Essays* (New York: Routledge, 2002), pp. 169–87. The play makes this link between Jew and Muslim later as well (5.4.256).

26 Quotations from Shapiro, *Shakespeare and the Jews*, pp. 8–9.

27 Thomas Cranmer, *The Book of Common Prayer, 1559: The Elizabethan Prayer Book*, ed. John E. Booty (Charlottesville: University of Virginia Press, 1976, 2005), p. 293. As D. Cressy observes, the ring's 'transfer during the marriage service was, except for sedulous puritans, as crucial as the crown in coronation' in early modern England (*Birth, Marriage, and Death: Ritual, Religion, and the Life-Cycle in Tudor and Stuart England* [Oxford: Oxford University Press, 1997], p. 343). It is worth noting, then, that King James endorsed the use of the ring in marriage during the Hampton Court Conference of 1604 (*ibid.*, p. 345).

28 Cressy provides a thorough examination of the ring in early modern English marriages (*Birth, Marriage, and Death*, pp. 342–7). He reminds us that only one ring was exchanged during the ceremony – from husband to wife. Performing Isabella and Brachiano's divorce scene, then, should involve only one ring, not two. Contrary to editions of the play (like the Cambridge edition referenced in this essay) which direct both characters to return rings to each other, it is possible that Brachiano removes the ring from Isabella's finger. Isabella might then retake it secretly while kissing him in public, then give it back to him as she calls for a divorce.

29 Cranmer, *Book of Common Prayer*, p. 298.

30 For the crucifix as a family heirloom rather than a religious symbol that determines the owner's religious stance, see E. Williamson, 'The Domestication of Religious Objects in *The White Devil*', *Studies in English Literature*, 47:2 (2007), 473–90.

31 Like B. Crockett (*Play of Paradox: Stage and Sermon in Renaissance England* [Philadelphia: University of Pennsylvania Press, 1995], p. 8), Diehl contends that the 'Protestant preacher … used theatrical playing to achieve disciplinary ends, arousing emotions understood to be conducive to spiritual conversion, including guilt, shame, awe, and fear, and seeking to elicit behaviors believed to be central to the godly life, such as self-scrutiny, compassion, and repentance' (Diehl, 'Disciplining Puritans and Players', 85).

32 F. Rollenson, *Sermons Preached Before His Majestie* (London: 1611), sig. L1^{v}.

33 S. Brietz Monta, '"It is requir'd you do awake your faith": Belief in Shakespeare's Theater', in Hwang Degenhardt and Williamson (eds), *Religion and Drama in Early Modern England*, p. 116.

34 He mocks religion elsewhere. After Flamineo has murdered his brother Marcello, Flamineo calls his mother Cornelia's mourning 'superstitious howling' (5.4.59). Flamineo also scorns the practice of exorcism and religious oaths (5.6.16–20 and 93–9).

35 For the many ways that the play examines death on the stage as a performance, see R. Barker, '"Another Voyage": Death as Social Performance in the Major Tragedies of John Webster', *Early Theater*, 8:2 (2005), 35–56, esp. 47–8.

8

'A deed without a name': evading theology in *Macbeth*

James R. Macdonald

In the *Life of Samuel Johnson*, James Boswell records a conversation on April 8, 1779 among the guests at Allan Ramsey's house whose subject apparently turned to *Macbeth*. Dr. Johnson opined that Shakespeare's witches 'are beings of his own creation; they are a compound of malignity and meanness, without any abilities: and are quite different from the Italian magician. King James says in his *Daemonology*, "Magicians command the devils: witches are their servants." The Italian magicians are elegant beings.'[1] With typical acuity, Johnson raises a question of agency that turns out to be crucial for understanding the nature of the play's tragedy. What power, if any, are the Weird Sisters shown to possess? Do they provoke Macbeth with empty words or manipulate him using genuine magic? Where is the moral boundary between their solicitation and Macbeth's actions?[2] But while Johnson makes clear that the Weird Sisters are not magicians in the sense that James defines the term, he also never quite affirms that they conform to the King's view of witches as the devil's minions.[3] If Shakespeare's Weird Sisters are indeed 'beings of his own creation', how do they relate to different conceptions of witchcraft circulating through Jacobean culture? And why is the play, more perhaps than any other Stuart witchcraft drama, so reticent about defining the source, nature, and scope of occult power?

Within the context of these questions, this essay has two goals. Its first section will explore different layers of theological uncertainty with which *Macbeth* confronts its spectators. Stephen Greenblatt observes that Shakespeare never offers the audience a clear understanding of the Sisters, instead 'staging the epistemological and ontological dilemmas that in the deeply contradictory ideological situation of his time haunted virtually all attempts to determine the status of witchcraft beliefs and practices'.[4] I would suggest that the play presents two distinct but interlocking epistemological struggles, one that centers on classification (as Macbeth and Banquo attempt to determine what kind of beings the Sisters are) and subsequently one of definition (as the characters and spectators alike try to understand the scope of their powers). Strikingly, the dramatic irony created by the audience's exposure to the Sisters' private colloquies is turned back on them; rather than a hidden key to the drama, the idea of witchcraft becomes increasingly vexatious. The second section examines the reasons behind the play's remarkable reserve by connecting epistemological uncertainty to textual instability. Since the belated publication of Thomas Middleton's *The Witch* in 1778, scholars have recognized its strong textual connection with *Macbeth*.[5] More recently, Gary Taylor's 'genetic text' of *Macbeth* in the Oxford Middleton has claimed a wider role for that dramatist in the preparation of the First Folio version, attributing to him portions of 1.1, 1.3, 3.5, 4.1, 4.2, and 5.10, and detecting passages of mixed authorship elsewhere.[6] Middleton's putative changes certainly heighten the ambiguity of the Sisters' nature through contradiction and obfuscation, but the presence within *The Witch* of direct textual borrowings from contemporary writings on witchcraft militates against the idea that Middleton unintentionally or clumsily scrambled the dynamics of supernatural agency. *The Witch*'s apparent failure instead suggests a plausible rationale for Middleton's pattern of adaptation within *Macbeth*: the deliberate evasion of theology, in which the play strives to present the excitement of occult effects within the theatre while frustrating any effort to draw out religious implications from the witches' existence, or even to infer a consistent model of their magical powers.

The fundamental indeterminacy of the Weird Sisters is neither Shakespeare's nor Middleton's invention, but a key facet of *Macbeth*'s source material. In the *Chronicles of England, Scotland and Ireland*, Raphael Holinshed variously describes the beings Macbeth and Banquo encounter on the heath as 'three women in strange and wild apparel, resembling creatures of elder world … either the Weird Sisters, that is (as ye would say) the goddesses of destiny, or else some nymphs or fairies endued with knowledge of prophecy by their necromantical science'.[7] For Holinshed, the term 'Weird Sisters' seems to apply exclusively to the fates themselves, and if *Macbeth* were to follow him in using the term this way, the Sisters' self-identification by this name (1.3.32) would seem to foreclose anything but a weak reading of Macbeth's own agency. But, of course, in the earliest printed text of the play, the 1623 Folio, the three women actually call themselves the 'Weyward' (or, elsewhere, 'Weyard') Sisters, spelling variants whose significance to the author (if indeed they do not derive from the scribe or compositor) remains unclear. Holinshed's nymphs or fairies, by contrast, do not determine destinies, but foresee them through magical means.[8] Even here, however, the uncertainty is heightened by balancing the relatively positive connotation of prophecy against the negative valence of necromancy – technically, the consultation of the spirits of the dead, but a word so deeply associated with black magic that it was often spelt 'negromancy'.[9] By leaving the three women poised between shaping destiny and merely observing it, or between acting as prophets or necromancers, Holinshed seems to exclude little from a teeming range of options. The common trait among the possibilities that he enumerates, however, is that they exist within fundamentally non-Christian cosmologies, incompatible either with divine providence or with a pneumatology that excludes spiritual creatures apart from angels (fallen and unfallen). Holinshed's speculation extends only far enough to insulate himself from the need to define the women's place in relation to God's.

When they encounter the Sisters on the heath, Macbeth and Banquo seem to begin by imitating Holinshed's effort at classification. Banquo begins by trying to distinguish between the natural and supernatural:

> What are these,
> So wither'd and so wild in their attire,
> That look not like th' inhabitants o' th' earth,
> And yet are on't? – Live you? or are you aught
> That man may question?
> (1.3.39–43)[10]

In the face of their silence, he turns instead to the category of gender, but here again he finds the evidence contradictory: 'You should be women / And yet your beards forbid me to interpret / That you are so' (1.3.45–7).[11] Frustrated in an effort to employ these most basic distinctions, Banquo tentatively assigns them instead to the category of unreality, asking whether 'I' th' name of truth, / Are ye fantastical, or that indeed / Which outwardly ye show?' (1.3.52–4). At the same time, he begins to wonder whether the uncanny quality of the encounter resides in the subject, rather than object, of observation, asking Macbeth whether they had 'eaten on the insane root / That takes the reason prisoner?' (1.3.84–5). By the end of the encounter, as Macbeth's appointment as Thane of Cawdor seem to rule out mere fantasy, Banquo does seem to come to the firmer conclusion that they are, in fact, comprehensible as manifestations of evil, asking rhetorically whether the devil can speak truth (1.3.107) and considering that

> 'tis strange;
> And oftentimes, to win us to our harm,
> The instruments of darkness tell us truths,
> Win us with honest trifles, to betray 's
> In deepest consequence.
> (1.3.122–6)

This seems to take one step beyond Holinshed, or perhaps obliquely evokes the chronicler's later assertion that as king Macbeth ruled with the assistance of 'certeine wizzards, in whose words he put great confidence'.[12] But even here

Banquo's hedged and uncertain language presents witchcraft as one possibility among many to be considered.

During this encounter, Macbeth undertakes a parallel reasoning process, but his conclusion is dictated by the different set of categories with which he associates the Weird Sisters. They are notably more positive, as when he asks them to '[s]ay from whence / You owe this strange intelligence, or why / Upon this blasted heath you stop our way / With such prophetic greeting?' (1.3.75–8). The same formulation recurs much later, when Macbeth recalls, just before ordering Banquo's murder, how 'prophet-like / They hailed him father to a line of kings' (3.1.58–9). Macbeth's words, in a sense, adapt half of Holinshed's balanced pairing, countering for the audience the negative implications of Banquo's reasoning by receiving the Sisters' words exclusively in a more licit (perhaps even biblical) context. But any tenuous linkage to Christian revelation is immediately undercut by the audience's recognition that Macbeth's interpretation is tendentious, a fact of which Macbeth himself seems to be uncomfortably half-aware. He ultimately determines that the effect of the sisters' words is simply neutral, based on a spurious logic of moral cancellation:

> This supernatural soliciting
> Cannot be ill; cannot be good. If ill,
> Why hath it given me earnest of success,
> Commencing in a truth? I am Thane of Cawdor.
> If good, why do I yield to that suggestion,
> Whose horrid image doth unfix my hair
> And make my seated heart knock at my ribs,
> Against the use of nature?
>
> (1.3.130–7)

In categorizing the Sisters' solicitation as a matter of indifference, Macbeth's carefully balanced syntax tries to conceal the fact, perhaps even from himself, that the countervailing arguments are not of equal weight: the visceral images of horror which argue for their malignity are far more vivid, even to his own imagination, than the grounds he asserts for thinking them good. If anything, Macbeth furnishes less a counterweight to Banquo's viewpoint than a self-interested avoidance of deep inquiry.

At this stage, neither of these hypotheses is given more than provisional authority for the audience. Although Diane Purkiss suggests that Banquo's views 'evolve into providentialist scepticism',[13] in other ways his initial distrust seems to yield to greater openness to their words: delivering Duncan's diamond, he tells Macbeth that he 'dreamt last night of the three weird sisters: / To you they have show'd some truth' (2.1.20–1). Even after the king's murder, Banquo substitutes a less pejorative formulation for their predictions of the future, musing to himself, 'Why by the verities on thee made good, / May they not be my oracles as well, / And set me up in hope?' (3.1.8–10). Before undertaking the killing of Duncan, Macbeth seems to move closer to Banquo's initial scepticism about the stability of his own perceptions: 'Art thou not, fatal vision, sensible / To feeling as to sight? or art thou but / A dagger of the mind, a false creation, / Proceeding from the heat-oppressed brain?' (2.1.36–9). It is especially striking that there is no audible association of the word 'witch' with the Weird Sisters, except for the single moment of the reported speech of the sailor's wife, who, refusing to share her chestnuts, replies with the rude 'Aroint thee, witch' (1.3.6). While some of Banquo's words may present a tentative identification of the Sisters, the characters are as unsure about them as Holinshed himself – in the course of adaptation, the chronicler's uncertainty has been dramatized within the play.

The play's audience, of course, has already seen more of the Sisters than the soldiers on the heath have, and so *Macbeth* may be said to implicitly authenticate the Sisters as witches by presenting them engaged in popular commonplaces of witchcraft: controlling winds and enacting *maleficia* in 1.3, and then later preparing a cauldron in 4.1. But this apparently clear identification produces a second level of opacity since the nature and powers of witches were important areas of cultural dispute during James's reign, as ascendant Calvinism precipitated a major shift in the theology of the supernatural.[14] Since God's providential agency circumscribed all human activity, it would be meaningless for a Calvinist to locate a witch's culpability in maleficent action, since it would be impossible for one to commit such a deed autonomously. Instead, Calvinist divines reimagined witches as Satan's culpable co-conspirators, in which their alleged magic merely provoked diabolic action through a 'spell or verse, consisting of strange words, used as a signe or watch-word to the deuil, to cause him to worke wonders'.[15] For William Perkins, the foremost English Calvinist theologian at the turn of the century, the reality of this agreement was the *sine qua non* of witchcraft: the 'ground of all the practices of Witchcraft, is a league or couenant made betweene the Witch and the Deuill: wherein they doe mutually bind themselues each to other'.[16] As a result, in the Calvinist-inflected perspective embodied by the 1604 witchcraft laws, witches might still be licitly prosecuted but, James Sharpe argues, 'not because they killed or harmed people, but because they were in league with the devil, because they were traitors who had renounced God and formed a pact with the devil'.[17] Alan Macfarlane presents this perspective in terms of overlapping enclosures of agency, in which God's will essentially subsumes those of the devil and the witch.[18] Instead of as a felony committed by magical means, Jacobean legal and religious doctrine increasingly reconceived the crime of witchcraft as a form of religious treason.

There is substantial evidence, however, that this reformed view of a witch's limited agency was unable to dislodge traditional beliefs concerning witchcraft.

In 1587, the Essex Puritan minister George Gifford reported regretfully that it 'is the common opinion among the blind ignorant people, that the cause and the procuring of harme by witchcraft, proceedeth from the Witch',[19] and examinations of judicial evidence and proceedings have led modern social historians to conclude that throughout the early modern period 'the main concern of the population at large was the witch's capacity to do harm by occult means'.[20] In his *Dialogue concerning witches and witchcrafts* (1593), Gifford ventriloquizes popular opinion through the foolish countryman Samuel, who credulously recites an account of occult activity which describes witches as a pervasive and dangerous menace to life and property: 'I heare of much harme done by them: they lame men and kill their cattle, yea they destroy both men and children. They say there is scarce any towne or village in all this shire, but there is one or two witches at the least in it.'[21] Moreover, confiding his own suspicions, Samuel does not conceive supernatural harm as actuated and directed by diabolic purposes, but implies that the witch can act at her own pleasure to avenge personal grudges. He tells Daniel, his wiser godly neighbor, that

> there be two or three in our towne which I like not, but especially an old woman, I haue beene as careful to please her as euer I was to please mine own mother, and to giue her euer anon one thing or other, and yet me thinkes shee frownes at me now and then. And I had a hogge which eate his meate with his fellowes and was very well to our thinking ouer night, and in the morning he was starke dead. My wife hath had fiue or sixe hennes euen of late dead.[22]

For Macfarlane, the model of a witch's agency implicit in such accounts is quite different from Calvinist orthodoxy: instead of viewing the witch as a cat's-paw for diabolic activity, a persistent strain of popular belief continued to attribute substantial autonomy to the witch's own will.[23]

Macbeth cuts across this cultural fault line, evincing conformity to neither model by refusing to articulate the degree of supernatural power which the Sisters themselves possess; while the play seems to proffer situations which would illuminate their nature, the presence of contradiction in each of these moments fails to yield theological consistency. The Sisters' initial appearance as a group suggests the diabolic coven, observes B. J. Sokol, but their subsequent behavior calls such identification into question, as they 'do not plot heresy, caper or blaspheme, but rather compare their doings like mischievous village gossips'.[24] The apparent presence of Paddock (the toad) and Greymalkin (the cat) evokes the figure of the familiar, yet animals play no evident role as intermediaries in the Sisters' magical activities. Their conversation begins with the words of the First Witch, who asks her companions, 'When shall we three meet again? / In thunder, lightning, or in rain?' (1.1.1–2). At the same time, however, that the presence of the disjunctive conjunction 'or' suggests volition and choice, all three of the proposed options for meeting – thunder, lightning and rain – essentially coincide. Even as the grammar implies one view of the Sisters' agency, the actual content of the speech suggests another. The same ambiguity exists in the First Witch's plan for avenging herself on the master of the *Tiger*:

> I'll drain him dry as hay:
> Sleep shall neither night nor day
> Hang upon his penthouse lid …
> Though his bark cannot be lost,
> Yet it shall be tempest-tossed.
> (1.3.18–20, 24–5)

Arthur Kinney observes that these lines reveal 'severe limits' to the Sisters' power, as their magical acts appear 'foreshortened' and 'delusory'.[25] If these threats seem to affirm that the witch's malicious will does in fact operate under constraints, though, the subsequent speech seems to gainsay the implication that she is prevented from killing or causing bodily injury, as she brandishes 'a pilot's thumb, / Wrack'd as homeward he did come' (1.3.28–9).

A similar situation recurs late in the play, when Macbeth returns to demand more prophecies. By calling the Sisters 'secret, black and midnight hags' (4.1.48), Macbeth seems to indicate that he too has identified them as witches. But the play immediately introduces a new complication, as the First Witch asks 'if th' hadst rather hear it from our mouths, / Or from our masters?' (4.1.62–3). This moment would seem to resolve the question of agency, but the apparition proves ambiguous, shouting, 'Macbeth! Macbeth! Macbeth! beware Macduff, / Beware the thane of Fife. Dismiss me. Enough' (4.1.71–2), before abruptly vanishing. When Macbeth tries to pursue this line of questioning, the First Witch tells him the spirit 'will not be commanded' (4.1.75). By asking for dismissal before making a peremptory disappearance, the spirit's appearance leaves its relationship to Macbeth and the witches ambiguous. The appearance of Hecate, meanwhile, suggests but fails to fulfill the trope of the diabolic bargain tacitly invoked by Banquo. She evidently has enough authority over the Weird Sisters to chastize them:

> how did you dare
> To trade and traffic with Macbeth
> In riddles and affairs of death;
> And I, the mistress of your charms,
> The close contriver of all harms,
> Was never call'd to bear my part
> Or show the glory of our art?
> (3.5.3–9)

But even though she claims authority over the Sisters, the fact of her exclusion from their design precludes her from the role of diabolic patron – instead they seem to relate to her, Katharine Briggs points out, 'as subjects rather than worshippers'.[26] This sense of her limited role is strengthened by her proposal to catch the 'vap'rous drop profound' (3.5.24) from the corner of the moon and distill it to produce apparitions. With her querulousness and magical expertise, this Hecate stands uneasily at odds with Macbeth's own poetic image of 'pale Hecate' (2.1.52), the night-goddess whose offerings witchcraft celebrates. These instances of the occult thus evoke the forms of witchcraft but reject any attempt to assess their inner structure and meaning.

The Weird Sisters are almost impossible to classify, Sarah Beckwith observes, because they 'are themselves neither inside nor outside, neither male nor female, neither culture nor nature, neither substantial nor immaterial, neither real nor merely apparent, neither inside the mind nor fully outside it'.[27] When Macbeth asks what they do, the First Witch replies, 'A deed without a name' (4.1.49), and this continual obscurity of agency and power pervades their interactions, rendering the nature of the Weird Sisters a multilayered uncertainty. The first level is the epistemological confusion shared by Holinshed and the characters, as they struggle to find a pre-existing category which corresponds to the Sisters' appearance; a second level, inhabited by the play's audience, recognizes them as witches even while the play wraps the meaning of that identification in contradiction by withholding a consistent picture of their nature and powers. Rather than employing the category of witchcraft to clarify the action of the play, *Macbeth* comes to the edge of mystifying the category itself.

But why would the text instantiate such ambiguous figures? If *Macbeth* was indeed a play written for court and designed to appeal to James's Scottish heritage and his interest in the occult, surely the nebulous role of the witches in the rise of Banquo's descendants would be disquieting. And the play's treatment of the witch could hardly be expected to flatter the King by conforming closely to James's own ideas or experiences since, as Roy Booth points out, *Macbeth* 'neither gratified the King's prejudices with a fully demonological exposure of the nature of the "weird sisters," nor showed their apprehension',[28] which might evoke James's own role at the North Berwick witch trials of the early 1590s. One likely explanation is that Middleton's adaptation, probably undertaken during the 1610s, produced inconsistency by importing occult stage business from *The Witch* without fully adapting it to the new context. Booth argues that 'Middleton seems to have thought that Shakespeare had been too restrained' in his use of occult lore and revised *Macbeth* to make fuller use of its possibilities, while Inga-Stina Ewbank suggests that despite the 'spectacular contrast' between the two plays, some of Middleton's atmosphere might have been 'grafted on to the text of *Macbeth* to make that play more of a show'.[29] There is indeed evidence to suggest that a pre-adaptation *Macbeth* may not have explicitly presented the Sisters as witches at all: in 1611, the astrologer Simon Forman recorded in his diary several brief accounts of performances he had recently seen in the London playhouses, including one of *Macbeth* on April 20. It is striking that a man whose name would become notorious for occult practices during the Overbury Affair would describe the scene in quite different terms:

> Mackbeth and Bancko, two noblemen of Scotland, riding through a wood, there stood before them three women fairies or nymphs and saluted Macbeth, saying three times unto him: Hail Mackbeth, King of Codon, for thou shalt be a king but shalt beget no kinges &c. Then said Bancko, What, all to mackbeth and nothing to me? Yes, said the nymphs, hail to thee Banko, thou shalt beget kings yet be not king.[30]

Hecate is completely absent from Forman's account as well. Although Nevill Coghill argues that much of it is 'manifestly taken out of Holinshed and not from Shakespeare at all', the diary does suggest the possibility that the play's early performances may have allowed the Sisters' nature to remain as ambiguous to the audience as to the characters themselves.[31]

At the same time, however, the hypothesis that Middleton created accidental ambiguity through careless revision does not comport well with the evidence of *The Witch*, a play that suggests he had read attentively in some of his time's most controversial texts on witchcraft.[32] In that play, Middleton's witches are distinguished by two characteristics: an expansive presentation of their autonomy, and a persistent association of occult power with hedonistic indulgence. When Sebastian seeks out the witches to prevent Antonio from consummating his illicit marriage to Isabelle, Hecate offers an impressive inventory of her coven's capabilities: she boasts that her associate Stadlin 'raises all your sudden ruinous storms / That shipwreck barques, and tears up growing oaks' (1.2.133–4), while if he should 'envy / The fat prosperity of any neighbour', her colleague Hoppo '[c]an straight destroy the young of all his cattle, / Blast vineyards, orchards, meadows, or in one night / Transport his dung, hay, corn, by ricks, whole stacks, / Into thine own ground' (1.2.143–6).[33] Although the truth or falsehood of these claims is not decisively arbitrated onstage, Middleton takes care to authenticate the reality of Hecate's magic by showing her apparent success in causing Amoretta to fall in love with Almachildes while the enchanted ribbon is tucked in her bosom. Moreover, the witches' staged flight in 3.3 seems intended to confirm for the audience that they are not mere frauds, since the whole scene is otherwise purely atmospheric and does nothing to advance the plot. Even the limitations that Middleton places on Hecate's power seem to amplify it: while Hecate acknowledges that her life will be forfeit to the devil after 120 years (1.2.70–1), that extraordinary lifespan easily exceeds what she might otherwise attain, and there is no explicit mention of eternal consequences for her diabolic bargain.

This pattern of apparent restriction unfolding into surprising autonomy continues when Hecate explains that she cannot directly provide Sebastian with the divorce he desires to procure (1.2.170–5). But despite this *pro forma* limitation, she facilitates Sebastian's recovery of his promised spouse by supplying snakeskins in order to forestall the newlyweds' consummation of their union:

> So sure into what house these are conveyed,
> Knit with these charmèd and retentive knots,
> Neither the man begets nor woman breeds;
> No, nor performs the least desires of wedlock,
> Being then a mutual duty. I could give thee
> *Chirocineta*, *adincantida*,
> *Archimedon*, *marmaritin*, *calicia*,
> Which I could sort to villainous barren ends
> But this leads the same way.
>
> (1.2.155–63)

It is striking, however, that these details of occult tradecraft, like almost all of Middleton's, are drawn nearly verbatim from Reginald Scot's *Discoverie of Witchcraft* (1584), the revolutionary debunking of occult claims that drew widespread condemnation from religious conservatives, including the charge of Sadduceeism from James himself.[34] The litany of drugs comes from Book 6, while Book 12 is the source for Stadlin and Hoppo's powers:

> It is constantlie affirmed in *M. Mal.* that *Stafus* used alwaies to hide himselfe in a moushoall, and had a disciple called *Hoppo*, who made *Stadlin* a maister witch, and could all when they list invisiblie transferre the third part of their neighbours doong, hay, corne, &c: into their own ground, make haile, tempests, and floods, with thunder and lightning; and kill children, cattell, &c: reveale things hidden, and many other tricks, when and where they list.[35]

In these and other places, Middleton has closely followed Scot's language while completely reversing its perlocutionary meaning: Scot recounts the list of magical substances only to show that they are in fact poisons that produce their harmful effects in a natural way, while he alludes to the episode from the *Malleus* in order to ridicule its claims to truth. Ironically, however, John Teall finds that Scot was not driven by thoroughgoing scepticism, but that his aims were in fact similar to those of Calvinists like George Gifford: Scot's 'primary motive, like Gifford's, seems to have been a desire to glorify God by reserving to Him alone powers which the witch-monger seems to attribute to a mere creature'.[36] For Scot, the idea that a witch's power exists independently is offensive because of the religious imperative 'that the glorie and power of God be not so abridged and abased, as to be thrust into the hand or lip of a lewd old woman; whereby the worke of the Creator should be attributed to the power of a creature'.[37] On the basis of this deep abnegation of human autonomy, Scot finds that apparent witches cannot be other than deliberate cozeners or simply deluded, by themselves or others. Middleton's inversion of Scot – either done in earnest, or perhaps in the spirit of grim satire which suffuses the play – suggests that he understood the contours of the cultural schism over occult power, since he enfolds a source that takes the strongest possible position against a witch's autonomy into a narrative which implicitly endorses it.[38]

A second marked feature of *The Witch* is an unusually vivid sense of the pleasure to be found in the occult. Hecate says of Sebastian's project that it is 'for the love of mischief I do this, / And that we're sworn to, the first oath we take' (1.2.180–1). Rather than drudges or servants, Middleton presents the coven as occult aristocrats, driving home the point by pervasively emphasizing the Ravennese courtiers' and coven's shared taste for self-indulgent and grotesque consumption. As the play opens, Fernando sarcastically praises the nuptial feast of Antonio and Isabelle, deriding 'marriage sweetly honoured in gorged stomachs / And overflowing cups' (1.1.35–6). Consulted by the Duchess for magical means to dispose of Almachildes, Hecate boasts of her own hospitality:

Take you no care. My spirits know their moments.
Raven or screech-owl never fly by th' door
But they call in, I thank 'em, and they lose not by't.
I give 'em barley soaked in infants' blood;
They shall have *semina cum sanguine*,
Their gorge crammed full, if they come once to our house.
We are no niggard.

(5.2.40–8)

If anything, Middleton seems to suggest that the witches' lifestyle is even more sybaritic. When Sebastian arrives to seek their assistance, he draws a contrast between their evident contentment and his own miserable state of mind: 'Up and laze not! / Hadst thou my business, thou couldst ne'er sit so. / 'Twould firk thee into air, a thousand mile / Beyond thy ointments' (1.2.121–4). By Hecate's own account, by contrast, she enjoys a lifestyle of unabashed hedonism: 'When hundred leagues in air we feast, and sing, / Dance, kiss, and coll, use every thing. / What young man can we wish, to pleasure us / But we enjoy him in an incubus?' (1.2.25–8). Unlike Almachildes' unrequited desire for Amoretta or Francisca's furtive liaison with Aberzanes, the courtly preoccupations of food and sex are plentiful and freely available to Hecate and her coven.

Rather than a mere means to obtaining pleasure, however, the acts of maleficent magic are themselves pleasurable to Hecate, who tells her son Firestone that 'there's no villainy / But is a tune, methinks' (5.2.82–3). Indeed, the compliant service the witches furnish seems to arise from their own delight in fulfilling the wicked intentions of those who seek them out. Hecate strongly implies that it is her own attraction to Sebastian which inspires action on his behalf when she says that his 'boldness takes me bravely. We're all sworn / To sweat for such a spirit. See, I regard thee; / I rise and bid thee welcome' (1.2.127–9). Moreover, Middleton makes clear that some of her actions are motivated by purely personal considerations, as when she takes revenge against a married couple who refused her requests: 'They denied me often flour, barm, and milk, / Goose-grease and tar, when I ne'er hurt their charmings, / Their brewlocks, nor their batches, nor forspoke / Any of their breedings. Now I'll be meet with 'em' (1.2.49–52). Her vengeance, which she intends to obtain by destroying their livestock, mimics the Duchess's desire to requite her husband for her father's murder, but where that great noblewoman's project is delayed and ultimately thwarted, Hecate's apparently proceeds inexorably through the use of magic: already the couple's 'marrows are a-melting subtly / And three months' sickness sucks up life in 'em' (1.2.47–8). Unlike Gifford's Samuel, who is reproved for holding such beliefs, Middleton's audience would find the most lurid popular ideas of a witch's independent power affirmed in speech, and often represented directly on stage.

Faced with the task of wheedling a charm for impotence from the coven, Sebastian employs a deliberate ignorance, declining to inquire too closely into them or their spiritual state: 'Whate'er thou art, I have no spare time to fear thee' (1.2.119). Like Macbeth, this strategic, self-interested failure to inquire allows him to regard the means he chooses as merely dubious, rather than outright illicit. But Sebastian's bad conscience is suggested by an initial plea of necessity to the audience: 'Heaven knows with what unwillingness and hate / I enter this damned place. But such extremes / Of wrongs in love fight 'gainst religious knowledge' (1.2.107–9). And once he has his remedy in hand, this rhetoric returns in a manner which seems bracingly ungrateful: 'grant, you greater powers that dispose men, / That I may never need this hag again' (1.2.177–8). If anything, *The Witch* seems to suggest that the witches are more powerful and no worse morally than those whom they serve, as 'the hypocrisy and covert maliciousness' of the courtiers is 'contrasted, to their detriment, with the uninhibited and uncomplicated viciousness displayed by Hecate and her minions'.[39]

As Middleton incorporated material from *The Witch* into his adaptation of *Macbeth*, the fate of his own play must have weighed upon his mind. Its failure was clearly a source of frustration: the surviving manuscript of the text, written sometime around 1620 by the scrivener Ralph Crane, contains a dedication in which Middleton reports that he 'recovered into my hands (though not without much difficulty) this ignorantly ill-fated labour of mine'. Apparently, suggests Middleton, its occult interests were the cause of its suppression:

> Witches are (*ipso facto*) by the law condemned, and that only (I think) hath made her lie so long in an imprisoned obscurity. For your sake alone, she hath thus far conjured herself abroad and bears no other charms about her but what may tend to your recreation, nor no other spell but to possess you with a belief that as she, so he that first taught her to enchant, will always be
>
> Your devoted
>
> Tho: Middleton.[40]

With no evidence of contemporary performances, Anne Lancashire suggests that the play ran afoul of political sensitivities by presenting the scandalous marriage of Robert Carr and Frances Howard as a *drame à clef*.[41] While this argument is compelling, Middleton's treatment of witchcraft might have been untenable even without topical interest. Both Middleton's predecessors and successors in witchcraft drama are, in different ways, condemnatory of witchcraft, and work to minimize transgressions against Calvinist orthodoxy by limiting the power attributed to witches and their magical acts. Later witchcraft plays like Dekker, Ford, and Rowley's *Witch of Edmonton* (1621) and Heywood and Brome's *The Late Lancashire Witches* (1634) both take place in a firmly Christian cosmology, implicating the devil's agency and concluding with discovery, apprehension, and punishment. Even witchcraft plays employing predominantly classical, rather than Christian, conceptions of witchcraft followed this pattern of resolution: in Marston's *Sophonisba, the Wonder of Women* (1605–06), Syphax gains no profit from his liaison with Erichtho and is utterly ruined by the play's end, while the coven in Jonson's antimasque to the *Masque of Queens* (1609) is dispersed by the noble ladies of the court themselves.

If Middleton's approach to *The Witch* became problematic by representing the power and scope of witchcraft too expansively, he may have sought to avoid similar difficulties in *Macbeth* by introducing set-piece scenes of conjuration and flying while embedding them in a Shakespeare play where a murky account of the Sisters' nature and powers was already integral to the drama. Clearly the exuberant, hedonistic magic that Middleton imports from *The Witch* could be a powerful dramatic force, whose commercial value was apparent from Middleton's decision to name his own play for a character that appears in only three scenes. Stephen Orgel suggests the basis of the occult's appeal: 'witches are quintessential theatrical devices: they dance and sing, perform wonders, appear and disappear, fly, produce visions – do, in short, all the things that, historically, we have gone to the theatre to see'.[42] If Taylor's apportionment of authorship is correct, Middleton's changes would have sought to harness this power by adding Hecate and the apparitions and by substantially augmenting the spectacle of the occult. And yet Taylor also suggests, following Coghill, that Middleton may also have been responsible for expunging an onstage representation of King Edward's healing powers. Taylor makes this case on religious grounds: the 'Calvinist Middleton would almost certainly have objected to Shakespeare's celebration of a Catholic saint and an onstage Catholic miracle', even though such a change might 'seem to contradict the logic of his adaptation' by removing a potential spectacular moment.[43] Such an excision would be perfectly logical, though, if Middleton's aim were not only to enhance the play's sense of occult spectacle, but also to sever that spectacle as fully as possible from religious discourse.

Diane Purkiss observes that in *Macbeth*, the 'witch-scenes brazenly refuse any serious engagement with witchcraft in favor of a forthright rendering of witches as a stage spectacular', which seems like a reasonable description of Middleton's contributions, as he enlarges the play's existing zone of epistemological uncertainty to encompass even the figure of the witch.[44] But his adaptation is best conceived as the development of a possibility already implicit in Shakespeare's text. Sandra Clark argues that 'the potential for hybridity was there from the start', and that 'Shakespeare's readiness to blend diverse materials and his eclectic way with sources ensure that the sisters are the more imaginatively powerful because the sources of their power defy categorization'.[45] Powerless witches might seem dramatically inert, while powerful witches could become theologically problematic. Middleton's solution, perhaps, was to create a middle ground of deniable ambiguity, in which the witches are entertainingly active but where the sources and nature of their powers remain opaque enough to avoid heterodox implications. An irony of this approach is that *Macbeth*'s confusion seems to have succeeded where *The Witch*'s relative clarity could not. Rather than finding incoherence in the Weird Sisters, Anthony Harris argues that 'the ambiguity inherent in their natures, far from being a defect, is a positive virtue in dramatic terms', while Purkiss concedes that 'the menace and the pleasure of witchcraft as a spectacle lies ultimately in its destabilising inscrutability'.[46] Displaying the occult more fully may have originated as a ploy to freshen an old play, but the joining of Shakespeare's epistemological ambiguity to Middleton's hedonistic witchcraft produced the remarkable paradox of the Weird Sisters, simultaneously evasive and spectacular.

Notes

I am grateful to William Engel, David Scott Kastan, Rory Loughnane, Kelly Malone, Lawrence Manley, John Rogers, and Brian Walsh for their comments on earlier versions of this essay.

1 J. Boswell, *Boswell's Life of Johnson* (London: J. M. Dent, 1960), vol. 2: p. 271.

2 Critical responses to this question have been varied, observes Susan Snyder, but it remains necessarily a 'large grey area', since while 'there may have been some predisposition on Macbeth's part … the play denies us any clear assessment of his guilty intentions before the encounter with the Weird Sisters'; S. Snyder, 'Theology as Tragedy in *Macbeth*', *Christianity and Literature*, 43 (1994), 291–2. S. Beckwith suggests that this irresolvable problem is symptomatic of a wider 'crisis in the attribution of responsibility' within Jacobean culture in 'The Power of Devils and the Hearts of Men: Notes toward a Drama of Witchcraft', in L. Aers and N. Wheale (eds), *Shakespeare in the Changing Curriculum* (London: Routledge, 1991), p. 144.

3 In fact, Johnson's interpretation elides an important aspect of the King's thought. In citing James, Johnson seems to be paraphrasing *Daemonologie* (Edinburgh, 1597), where in Book 1, Chapter 3, Epistemon tells the sceptical Philomathes that 'the Witches ar servantes onelie, and slaues to the Devil; but the Necromanciers are his maisters and commanders'. But this belief, says Epistemon, is actually 'the difference [that the] vulgare put betwixt them'. It is 'verrie merrie, and in a maner true', but in fact, necromancers only command the devil '*secundum quid*: for it is not by anie power that they can haue over him, but *ex pacto* allanerlie' (sig. C1^{r}). For James (as for other Calvinist writers), the dynamics of magical power must always favor the devil, despite the appearance of the relationship to others or even to the magician himself.

4 S. Greenblatt, 'Shakespeare Bewitched', in J. N. Cox and L. J. Reynolds (eds), *New Historical Literary Study: Essays on Reproducing Texts, Representing History* (Princeton: Princeton University Press, 1993), p. 123.

5 The lyrics of two songs referred to in the Folio *Macbeth* only by their titles, 'Come away' and 'Black spirits', are given in full in *The Witch*. Since they fit better the mood and characters of Middleton's play, most critics have readily conceded that they represent later interpolations, but see also N. Brooke, 'The Songs for *Macbeth*', in A. Kettle *et al.* (eds), *KM 80: A Birthday Album for Kenneth Muir, Tuesday 5 May 1987* (Liverpool: Liverpool University Press, 1987), pp. 23–4.

6 See G. Taylor and J. Lavagnino (eds), *Thomas Middleton and Early Modern Textual Culture: A Companion to the Collected Works* (Oxford: Clarendon Press, 2007), pp. 383–97.

7 W. G. Boswell-Stone (ed.), *Shakespeare's Holinshed* (New York: B. Blom, 1966), pp. 23–4.

8 Anthony Harris argues that the play's audience could have understood these appellations to be 'synonymous with the modern conception of witches and hags'; A. Harris, *Night's Black Agents: Witchcraft and Magic in Seventeenth-Century English Drama* (Manchester: Manchester University Press, 1980), p. 158. The historical evidence for this possibility is ambiguous. Like witches, fairies were 'frequently thought of as highly malevolent' and blamed for unexplained illness and injury,

but religious authorities generally held them to be 'either devils or diabolical illusions'; K. Thomas, *Religion and the Decline of Magic* (New York: Scribner, 1971), pp. 609–10. This possible connection within *Macbeth* is both suggested and muddled by Hecate's parting instruction to the Sisters: 'And now about the cauldron sing / Like elves and fairies in a ring' (4.1.41–2).

9 This spelling occurs, for example, several times in both the A-text (1604) and B-text (1616) versions of Christopher Marlowe's *Doctor Faustus*, perhaps most notably when the Chorus explains that 'glutted ... with learning's golden gifts, / [Faustus] surfeits upon cursed negromancy' (Prologue, lines 23–4).

10 *Macbeth*, 1.3.39–43. All passages of text from *Macbeth* are drawn from *The Riverside Shakespeare*, 2nd edn, ed. G. Blakemore Evans (Boston: Houghton Mifflin, 1997).

11 Taylor suggests that this particular question is actually a later interpolation of Middleton's within a conversation largely written by Shakespeare, since bearded witches would make the revised play easier to stage by allowing the witches' parts to be played by men, rather than boy actors (*Thomas Middleton and Early Modern Textual Culture*, p. 389).

12 Boswell-Stone, *Shakespeare's Holinshed*, p. 36.

13 Diane Purkiss, *The Witch in History: Early Modern and Twentieth-Century Representations* (London: Routledge, 1996), p. 211.

14 The history of witchcraft in England and its evolving relationships to social, religious and judicial institutions is extensively surveyed in Thomas's *Religion and the Decline of Magic*, pp. 435–583. A. Macfarlane furnishes a detailed sociological study of witchcraft accusations and prosecutions based on archival sources in *Witchcraft in Tudor and Stuart England: A Regional and Comparative Study* (New York: Harper and Row, 1970). More recently, S. Clark's *Thinking with Demons: The Idea of Witchcraft in Early Modern Europe* (New York: Oxford University Press, 1997) offers a wide-ranging account of the roles demonology played in intellectual life throughout the early modern period.

15 W. Perkins, *A discourse of the damned art of witchcraft* (Cambridge, 1608), sig. J1^{v}.

16 *Ibid.*, sig. C5^{r-v}.

17 J. A. Sharpe, *Instruments of Darkness: Witchcraft in Early Modern England* (Philadelphia: University of Pennsylvania Press, 1996), p. 88.

18 A. Macfarlane, 'A Tudor Anthropologist: George Gifford's *Discourse* and *Dialogue*', in S. Anglo (ed.), *The Damned Art: Essays in the Literature of Witchcraft* (London: Routledge & Kegan Paul, 1977), p. 149.

19 George Gifford, *A Discourse of the Subtill Practises of Deuilles by Witches and Sorcerers* (London, 1587), sig. F4^{r}. Gifford's views on the occult are thoroughly explored in Macfarlane's 1977 essay and in J. Hitchcock, 'George Gifford and Puritan Witch Beliefs', *Archiv für Reformationsgeschichte*, 58 (1967), 90–9.

20 Sharpe, *Instruments of Darkness*, p. 60. Larner comes to the same conclusion, arguing that the 'essential difference between the popular and the educated conception of witchcraft was that the popular was concerned with the particular act of *maleficium*, while the educated was concerned with the condition of being a witch'; C. Larner, *Witchcraft and Religion: The Politics of Popular Belief* (Oxford: Blackwell, 1984), p. 74.

21 George Gifford, *A Dialogue Concerning Witches and Witchcraftes* (London, 1593), sig. A4^{v}.
22 *Ibid.*, sig. B1^{r}.
23 Macfarlane, 'Tudor Anthropologist', p. 147.
24 B. J. Sokol, '*Macbeth* and the Social History of Witchcraft', *Shakespeare Yearbook*, 6 (1996), 253. Stallybrass suggests that this mixed signification 'enabled Shakespeare to draw upon the common belief in an "evil" at work in the English countryside whilst never reducing the play's witches to village widows'; P. Stallybrass, '*Macbeth* and Witchcraft', in J. Russell Brown (ed.), *Focus on Macbeth* (London: Routledge & Kegan Paul, 1982), p. 195.
25 A. Kinney, *Lies like Truth: Shakespeare, 'Macbeth' and the Cultural Moment* (Detroit: Wayne State University Press, 2001), p. 258.
26 K. M. Briggs, *Pale Hecate's Team: An Examination of the Beliefs on Witchcraft and Magic among Shakespeare's Contemporaries and His Immediate Successors* (New York: Humanities Press, 1962), p. 79.
27 Beckwith, 'The Power of Devils', p. 152.
28 R. Booth, 'Standing within the Prospect of Belief: *Macbeth*, King James and Witchcraft', in J. Newton and J. Bath (eds), *Witchcraft and the Act of 1604* (Leiden: Brill, 2008), p. 53. Larner argues, however, that by the time he came to England, James had adopted a more sceptical attitude towards occult claims and may have been 'slightly embarrassed and anxious to make the least of this former enthusiasm' (*Witchcraft and Religion*, p. 5). For extended treatment of the play's relationship to James's evolving intellectual interests, see H. N. Paul, *The Royal Play of Macbeth* (New York: Macmillan, 1950) and J. H. Jack, '*Macbeth*, King James and the Bible', *English Literary History*, 22 (1955), 173–93.
29 Booth, 'Standing within the Prospect', p. 48. I.-S. Ewbank, 'The Middle of Middleton', in Murray Biggs, Philip Edwards, Inga-Stina Ewbank, and Eugene M. Wraith (eds), *The Arts of Performance in Elizabethan and Early Stuart Drama: Essays for G. K. Hunter* (Edinburgh: Edinburgh University Press, 1991), p. 158.
30 Oxford, Bodleian Library MS Ashmole 208, quoted in *The Riverside Shakespeare*, p. 1966. The possibility that the Forman manuscript may be a forgery was raised by S. A. Tannenbaum in *Shaksperian Scraps and other Elizabethan Fragments* (New York: Columbia University Press, 1933), while J. Dover Wilson and R. W. Hunt strongly dispute Tannenbaum's position in 'The Authenticity of Simon Forman's *Bocke of Plaies*', *Review of English Studies*, 13 (1947), 193–200.
31 N. Coghill, 'Macbeth at the Globe, 1606–1616 (?): Three Questions', in Joseph G. Price (ed.), *The Triple Bond: Plays, Mainly Shakespearean, in Performance* (University Park: Pennsylvania State University Press, 1975), p. 228.
32 For alternative recent analysis of the relationship between these plays, see C. R. Daileader, 'Weird Brothers: What Thomas Middleton's *The Witch* Can Tell Us about Race, Sex and Gender in *Macbeth*', in S. L. Newstok and A. Thompson (eds), *Weyward 'Macbeth': Intersections of Race and Performance* (New York: Palgrave Macmillan, 2010), pp. 11–20.
33 All passages of text from *The Witch* are drawn from Thomas Middleton, *The Collected Works*, ed. G. Taylor and J. Lavagnino (Oxford: Clarendon Press, 2007).

34 King James, *Daemonologie*, sig. A2v.
35 Reginald Scot, *The Discoverie of Witchcraft* (London, 1584), sig. Q7v.
36 J. L. Teall, 'Witchcraft and Calvinism in Elizabethan England: Divine Power and Human Agency', *Journal of the History of Ideas*, 23 (1962), 31.
37 Scot, *Discoverie*, sig. B4r.
38 I. W. Archer explores identifications of Middleton as a Calvinist or Puritan dramatist in 'Religious Identities', in Suzanne Gossett (ed.), *Thomas Middleton in Context* (Cambridge: Cambridge University Press, 2011), pp. 135–43. It is striking, however, how far *The Witch*'s understanding of witchcraft diverges from the mainstream of English Calvinism represented by Perkins or Gifford. Purkiss suggests that Middleton was 'influenced by Scot's contempt for popular beliefs, and his wish to display them as grotesque and farcical' (*The Witch in History*, p. 217).
39 Harris, *Night's Black Agents*, p. 84.
40 Middleton, *Collected Works*, p. 1129.
41 A. Lancashire, '*The Witch:* Stage Flop Or Political Mistake?', in K. Friedenreich (ed.), *'Accompaninge the Players': Essays Celebrating Thomas Middleton, 1580–1980* (New York: AMS Press, 1983), p. 170.
42 S. Orgel, 'Macbeth and the Antic Round', *Shakespeare Survey*, 52 (1999), 145.
43 Taylor and Lavagnino, *Thomas Middleton and Early Modern Textual Culture*, p. 394. For Coghill's argument that the elaborate build-up to Edward's non-entrance in 4.3 suggests a missing scene, see 'Macbeth at the Globe (?)', pp. 230–4.
44 Purkiss, *The Witch in History*, p. 207.
45 S. Clark, '*Macbeth* and the Weird Sisters', *Shakespeare Studies*, 46 (2008), 65.
46 Harris, *Night's Black Agents*, pp. 43–4; Purkiss, *The Witch in History*, p. 207.

9

Henry V and the interrogative conscience as a space for the performative negotiation of confessional conflict

Mary A. Blackstone

Despite the relative distance in time between Shakespeare's England and the upheavals of earlier Reformation and Counter-Reformation periods, persistent aftershocks of anxiety surrounding religious belief and allegiance continued to destabilize the bedrock of English society from the level of the court and members of the nobility down to parish churches and their clergy and even to the level of Shakespeare's groundlings. Numerous scholars have argued that early modern England experienced multiple reformations which progressed throughout Shakespeare's lifetime.[1] Patrick Collinson observed that the Reformation did not really begin to work its way into the cultural fabric of the country until the 1580s, citing John Donne's phrase 'all cohaerence gone', as characterizing the perceptions of an era: 'Shakespeare and countless others of his generation did not know what to believe or, if they did, could not tell when they might be called on to believe contrary things.'[2] Even in his representation of monarchs as well as commoners in outwardly nationalistic plays like *Henry V*, Shakespeare not only reflects this anxiety of a liminal era but also uses it to profoundly engage his contemporaries in the negotiation of religious beliefs and their impact on an individual's allegiance to Church and state.

With the monarch functioning as Supreme Governor of the Church of England, recusant loyalty to the old religion and dissenter divergencies pushing for a proliferation of further reforms challenged not only the foundations of faith but also the system of governance and national identity. A great many of Shakespeare's contemporaries, however, had to reconcile such temporal loyalties on a day-to-day basis – and in their final reckoning – with the urgent negotiation of a faith that would assure the spiritual well-being of their soul beyond the authority of a worldly monarch. Yet, how could average individuals in a largely illiterate society address this crisis, and where were they to find guidance in resolving any personal and private conflicts of conscience that might be at odds with official and public obligations?

One obvious answer to both questions would be attending church, a vital performative act regarded as publicly confirming loyalty to not only the Church of England but also the monarch. With the lack of church attendance commonly used as the primary sign of disloyalty, as long as one attended church and conformed at least outwardly, one could continue to believe and even practice differently in private and thereby fortify one's soul for all eventualities. Of course outwardly practicing a faith privately regarded as heretical did not satisfactorily resolve the problem of confessional conflict, and instead some individuals chose to pay crippling fines in order to worship privately according to their conscience. Others endured imprisonment, torture and/or execution – in some cases transforming the state's intended punishment and performative warning to others experiencing confessional conflict into the reverse: a profoundly moving performance of alternative religious belief.[3] As Patrick Collinson has observed, despite Elizabeth's best efforts, 'The result was an Established Church that stood firm on the basis of the Elizabethan Settlement, but which would never again embrace the whole nation.'[4]

Clergymen like Bishop John Jewel recognized the role that preachers had to play in guiding parishioners who had been 'commaunded to change their religion', but 'for lacke of instruction … know not whither to turne them: They knowe not, neither what they leaue nor what they should receiue.'[5] With the shift from the practice of Catholicism's collective rituals and the intercessional role of the priest to the Protestant vernacular Bible and expectations of a more direct and personal relationship with God, not all parishioners were equipped to embrace such a change. In theory preachers and sermons were intended to provide a publicly participatory and communal mechanism for reconciling and renegotiating the nature of personal as well as collective faith, but scholars have demonstrated that even by contemporary accounts players rather than preachers succeeded more effectively in addressing people's need for spiritual guidance as well as entertainment.[6] For instance, the clergyman John Northbrooke observed that his contemporaries 'shame not to say and affirm openly … that they learn as much or more at a Play, than they do at God's word preached'.[7] Clergymen, however, also experienced confessional conflict themselves and consequently could escalate the conflict amongst their parishioners. Despite the objections of their congregations we know that at least initially many persisted with old religious practices, and despite the best efforts of the authorities, other preachers also expounded on new, unsanctioned Puritan doctrine from their pulpits.[8] Although non-conforming clergy could leave the Church of England, many may have conformed despite confessing to unresolved religious anxiety: 'we are kylled in the soule of our soules, for this pollution of ours'.[9]

Some later preachers like John Donne worked through a period of confessional conflict and derived from it a cultivation of the questioning conscience that contributed to his popularity as a preacher as well as his ability to engage his congregations in personally addressing religious doubts. However, the vast majority of surviving Elizabethan sermons for both educated and less literate audiences take a more official and didactic than personal and thoughtful perspective. The Burleigh papers reveal that Elizabeth had her preachers 'tuned' as much as possible to sing according to her interests – in some cases, such as the aftermath of Essex's execution in 1600, to the point of receiving specific speaking points. Acknowledging confessional conflict, and thereby possibly affording it some legitimacy, posed more of a challenge than simply instructing churchgoers on doctrine and practices to which they should subscribe and thereby constructing uniformity by asserting and performing a common ground of religious belief that may not actually have existed. As with executions, this particular approach to addressing confessional conflict did not necessarily have the desired effect. Extant records in fact reveal that rather than serving as a site for the resolution of confessional conflict, churches could become sites for escalating confessional conflict to an external, physical level, sometimes with preachers and their sermons acting as polarizing catalysts.[10]

In considering the rhetorical effects of different types of texts on their audiences, Catherine Belsey has classified such persuasive texts as sermons and propaganda as 'imperative': a text which 'exhorts, instructs, orders the reader, constituting the reader as a unified subject in conflict with what exists outside'. She describes another type of text, the 'interrogative text', as taking the reader to 'a place of uncertainty or of unresolved debate' and disrupting 'the unity of the reader by discouraging identification with a unified subject of the enunciation. The position of the "author" inscribed in the text, if it can be located at all, is seen as questioning or as literally contradictory.'[11]

Closely related to 'closed' and 'open' texts,[12] these two concepts apply equally well to performance texts (e.g., plays as well as sermons in performance) as to literary texts with the same caveat that they 'are in no sense self-contained and mutually exclusive'.[13] Belsey specifically alludes to the performative circumstances of early modern public theatres – the thrust stage with the multiple perspectives it afforded of both the stage and fellow audience members – as conducive to the construction of interrogative texts. Drawing on Belsey's observations, the argument here is that in contrast with the parish church, players and their performances for diverse audiences provided a more engaging and accessible site for the negotiation of confessional conflict at both the personal level and the collective level of shared beliefs and allegiances. Moreover, playwrights like William Shakespeare drew upon the climate of religious ambivalence and anxiety as well as their own experience of confessional conflict in crafting interrogative performance texts that successfully attracted audiences because they consciously employed rhetorical devices to engage their audiences in exploring for themselves multiple perspectives on some of the most important issues of their day – including religious and political allegiances. Huston Diehl has characterized Shakespeare's work as 'reforming drama' that explored and articulated 'the anxieties created by Protestant assaults on medieval piety', and Jonathan Baldo has argued that his plays constitute a response to 'trauma with drama', an expression of 'an equivocal sympathy for those among Shakespeare's contemporaries who could not regard the recent past without desiring to "call back yesterday"'.[14] Given the high stakes associated with religious doubts and questions that could be interpreted as treason, the popularity of theatre in Shakespeare's England may have developed in part because it offered an alternative, more sympathetic, less polarizing and didactic option for exploring religious issues. Perhaps precisely because it was not a venue dedicated primarily to religious instruction and observance, this public, performative venue could more actively engage playgoers in the negotiation of personal and hegemonic religious beliefs along with related political allegiance and cultural values.

The multiplicity of interrogative perspectives at 'play' in the Elizabethan public theatres, and the Globe in particular, began with the make-up of the audiences. Their widely recognized diversity across class, occupation, education, and to some degree gender included 'penny stinkards' in the pit and wealthy merchants, Inns of Court scholars, members of the gentry and nobility. It also included religious diversity. Many would have been the same folks that attended local parish churches but, as Jewell noted, knew 'not, neither what they leaue nor what they should receiue'. We know, however, that some were staunch recusants who would not have been found in any Protestant church.[15] Paul Whitfield White has argued that even Protestants of the Puritan persuasion would have gone to plays.[16] Puritans who were especially vocal in citing the theatre as direct moral and performative competition with religious belief and church attendance would most likely not have been in the audience, but some of those very individuals who became famous for their castigation of theatre began as theatregoers and even playwrights.[17]

Even preachers who eventually assumed important positions in the Church and at court had playgoing backgrounds. Donne, for instance, had not only a recusant upbringing but also an early love of theatre in common with William Shakespeare. Possibly referring to his Inns of Court days, Donne's contemporary Richard Baker calls Donne 'a great frequenter of plays' in his youth.[18] Later, immediately after his return from fighting on the Continent under the Earl of Essex, Donne began a four-year stint as Secretary to Lord Egerton (during which time he was deeply involved in the coercion or enforcement of religious conformity). In this position he could have taken up an invitation from his friend Sir William Cornwallis: 'If then for change, of howers you seem careless / Agree with me to loose them at the playes.'[19] Scholars have noted the influence of Shakespeare's plays on Donne's writing[20] as well as his friendship with and admiration for the work of another King's Men playwright who also overtly experienced confessional conflict, Ben Jonson.[21]

If we extend the audience encompassed by the early modern theatre to include multiple performances, including touring and court performances sometimes before the monarch (and sometimes in close succession with court sermons), then the range of spectators engaged by the same play in negotiating individual and collective values and beliefs easily exceeded the reach of sermons in the local parish church – or St. Paul's Cross, for that matter. Shakespeare drew upon this diversity of spectators to generate the interrogative character of audience engagement in confessional conflict. To some scholars and theatre practitioners, *The Life of Henry V* provides an unlikely example of this approach because it has often been interpreted on stage and in scholarly critique as jingoistic propaganda, something Belsey classifies as more imperative than interrogative.[22]

However, scholars have also argued that 'the play is far from simply endorsing the imperial propaganda on which it draws' and consciously takes the audience 'from one point of view to another'.[23] William Hazlitt's description of Henry as 'a very amiable monster' exemplifies the apparently contradictory character of the play noted by numerous recent scholars who have approached it through a wide range of ideological, dramaturgical, and performative lenses.[24] Given that the play was most likely first performed at the Globe Theatre in early 1599 and subsequently at court in January 1605, Joel Altman has argued that its conflicted nature was the product of a period of wartime crisis when England was embroiled in wars in Ireland and on the Continent, and 'audience and players alike felt themselves especially vulnerable to the princely calling'. He argues that Shakespeare, 'unable to transcend his time, perceived its liberties and its restraints as mutually entangling filiations and played out their possibilities on his stage'.[25]

Identifying a similarly personal agenda as the motivation for the play's ambivalence, Norman Rabkin famously argued that Shakespeare's 'habitual recognition of the duality of things' lead him 'to a point of crisis' which marked the beginning of a 'spiritual struggle' that he 'would spend the rest of his career working through'.[26] Moving beyond assertions relating to personal spiritual questioning on Shakespeare's part, however, this exploration of the play focuses on the way in which he consciously uses the innately interrogative qualities of confessional conflict for dramaturgical effect. Despite his dependency on patronage by Privy Counsellors like the Lord Chamberlain and eventually King James, Shakespeare invokes a fundamentally questioning conscience in order to engage an audience. The secular context of theatrical performance – even at court – apparently afforded him greater latitude to question and construct interrogative texts than the pulpit.

The popularity of Shakespeare's history plays derived in part from the wider contemporary interest in the construction and renegotiation of English history, so that *Henry V* emerged in the context of a larger historical project which included not only contemporary chronicles and previous stage explorations such as *The Famous Victories of Henry V*, but also the other plays in Shakespeare's Henriad[27] and responses to them such as *The First Part of Sir John Oldcastle*. As with most of Shakespeare's history plays, *Henry V* automatically creates a complicated religious dynamic by nostalgically reminding its audience of a 'golden age' with all of England, its king, and its people ostensibly unified around a common, albeit Catholic faith. Consciously and repeatedly positioning himself as 'no tyrant but a Christian King',[28] Henry unites an ethnically factionalized kingdom by conjuring up antithetical and external 'others' – in this case foreign, infidel tyrants like Herod or Tamburlaine. When in the first scene the Catholic Archbishop of Canterbury and the Bishop of Ely describe Henry as 'full of grace and fair regard. / And a true lover of the Church' (1.1.22–3), their high extended praise momentarily generalizes Henry's religious loyalties to the Christian Church (which Shakespeare's audience could have taken as either a Protestant or a Catholic reference) and blurs the internal and anachronistic Catholic/Protestant divide that early modern playgoers used to farcical readings of Catholic clergy might have automatically projected into the performative dynamic. This facilitates Henry's development as a mirror for the reforming Henry VIII who cultivated such comparisons himself in his war with France[29] as well as a model for Elizabeth with her dual responsibilities as head of Church and state. Elizabeth had already made this connection herself by alluding to the source play *Famous Victories* in her speech before the troops at Tilbury during the Armada crisis.[30] At court in 1605 such implied comparisons would have worked as well or even more effectively with James, who had already initiated the process of commissioning a new English Bible in 1604, and Henry's eleven-year-old namesake Prince Henry. While the Catholic/Protestant disconnect could have presented an obstacle to some audience members, many would certainly have embraced this nationalistic myth-making drawing together past and present monarchs around a common Christianity.

However blurred our perceptions of Henry's religious affiliation, though, Shakespeare makes no attempt to downplay the obvious Catholic perspectives of the two clergymen. Because of their devious plotting to promote and support the war with France as a diversionary tactic to shift attention from the potential confiscation of Church lands, their praise in this opening scene does not come across as an entirely reliable recommendation. By profiling their overtly Catholic motive for plotting, Shakespeare clearly acknowledges and incorporates reminders of internal religious conflict that revealed a clouded underside to both Henry's, and by extension, Elizabeth's 'golden age'. Of course Falstaff, who was initially named after the Lollard activist Sir John Oldcastle, never does appear in *Henry V*, but Oldcastle's presence would have been felt in this scene as many audience members would have recognized the seizure of Church lands and wealth as one of the measures advocated by those Protestant precursors, the Lollards, and in particular by Oldcastle, whom John Foxe had elevated to Protestant martyr.

Although the play's opening scenes enable Henry to overtly shift some of the responsibility for the war and questionable acquisition of France off of his conscience to the scheming Catholic prelates, Shakespeare could have avoided all of these complicated and divergent religious references by omitting the initial scene with Canterbury and Ely, or possibly those characters altogether, thus promoting a collective confessional forgetfulness. Instead, he foregrounded them – possibly precisely because they set up the interrogative character of the play that only deepens as the plot evolves, and they reminded a potentially nostalgic audience that the seeds of contemporary religious dissension were initially sown in this supposed 'golden age'.

These early scenes with Church leaders draw heavily – including lengthy passages virtually word for word – from Holinshed's *Chronicles*.[31] Just as preachers of the period interpreted apparently stable 'historical' texts taken from the Bible, so too Shakespeare carefully chose supposedly stable 'texts' with a Tudor-friendly take on English history. Ostensibly his motive in doing so while under the patronage of the Lord Chamberlain would have been similar to that of a contemporary preacher choosing the text for a sermon: to make the immediate and current application of these passages readily apparent and engage his audiences in actively applying them at both personal and collective levels. Unlike many preachers, however, with the exception of the few interrogative preachers like Donne, Shakespeare selected texts which lent themselves to dramatic, conflicted, dialogic, and questioning moments which had the potential to contribute to a highly participatory and innately metaperformative experience for the audience.

In *Henry V*, in particular, the Chorus imperatively demands an active rather than passive response from its audience as the first order of business. While the daunting scope and scale of the Chorus's demands could have paradoxically rendered some audience members more passive than active, Shakespeare's Chorus anticipates Donne's expectation that his congregations should play an active, participatory role in the performance of sermons. While at church, they were to be hearers, and thereby doers of the Word: 'Hath God made this World his Theatre, … that man may represent God in his conversation; and wilt thou play no part? But think that thou only wast made to pass thy time merrily, and to be the only spectator upon this Theatre? Is the world a great and harmonious Organ, where all parts are play'd, and all play parts; and must thou only sit idle and hear it?'[32] Similarly, Shakespeare's metatheatrical Chorus foregrounds the discrepancy between the stage and the world of the chronicle accounts to emphasize the extent to which he wants his audience to 'piece out our imperfections with your thoughts', 'thoughts that now must deck our kings, / Carry them here and there, jumping o'er times' (Prologue, 23, 28–9).

Neither Donne nor Shakespeare is talking about token audience participation. Rather they both recognize exploring some of the most challenging issues and questions of the day from multiple perspectives as one of the best ways to successfully engage an audience. By first setting up an active frame of mind for the audience, and then confronting them with two medieval Catholic prelates implicitly facing a threat from Lollardy, Shakespeare reminds the audience of not only the confessional conflict of their day but also the confessional conflict experienced by Sir John Oldcastle (to the point of martyrdom) and his close friend Henry V, who tried various stalling mechanisms, albeit unsuccessfully, to save him from his fate.

Audiences who came to Shakespeare's play having experienced its most popularly familiar source, the Queen's Men's much earlier but very recently published *Famous Victories of Henry V*, were not prepared for the highly participatory, metatheatrical quality of his play. By comparison, the earlier play holds the audience at a distance, and despite a time frame and geography which Shakespeare needed three plays to address, it makes no overt attempt to engage the audience's 'imaginary forces' in piecing 'out our imperfections with your thoughts' (Prologue, 18, 23). As well, individuals familiar with *Famous Victories* had not engaged in the private struggles of particular characters. Despite the consistency of the essential story line across the plays, none of the characters in *Famous Victories*, including Henry V, allows the audience into even brief moments of inner conflict. Although Henry IV's accusations and tears as his son approaches clutching a dagger generate a sudden change in Hal, prefaced by his line: 'my conscience accuseth me', even here he changes allegiance from his Eastcheap cronies to his father in fewer than seventeen lines without any hint at the thought process that led to the about turn.[33] At the center point of the play, in a brief soliloquy, Henry expresses what David Womersley has identified as 'a distinctly Catholic form of repentance'[34] as he reflects on the soul and body of what he thinks is his dead father. In expressing regret for having neglected him, Henry passes from contrition to penance and absolution,[35] but he engages us in no active struggle or crisis of conscience. Rather it feels more like an obligatory public flagellation. The extended soliloquy by Shakespeare's Henry the night before the Battle of Agincourt (interestingly, also situated at the metaphorical heart of darkness for the play) operates at the other extreme by drawing the audience into the

King's conflicted conscience most immediately troubled by his exchange with Williams and Bates.

This Shakespearean soliloquy has obviously captured much scholarly attention, but scholars have paid less attention to another, earlier soliloquy which Shakespeare invents for a character at the lowest end of the social spectrum who helps to frame the more extended development of confessional conflict in Act 4. In both *Famous Victories* and *Henry V*, the Eastcheap commoners simply transfer their preoccupation with thievery and self-preservation via misrepresentation to the battlefield. However, Shakespeare transforms the boy who primarily reports on offstage events in *Famous Victories* into a thoughtful character who abandons his service to Henry's former compatriots in highway robbery precisely because 'they will steal anything, and call it purchase' and because 'they would have me as familiar with men's pockets as their gloves or their handkerchers; which makes much against my manhood' (3.2.44, 49–52).

By allowing us access to this crisis of conscience, Shakespeare goes beyond foregrounding the qualms of a minor character. He encourages us to identify with one of the group of boys later murdered by the French, thereby helping us to justify Henry's angry order at Agincourt to kill any French prisoners in revenge for English casualties. In the morality tradition behind both *Famous Victories* and *Henry V*, however, the virtue of conscience often upstages the vice of wrath embraced by this Christian king. The boy's decision to leave his masters parallels not only the King's rejection and punishment of his former colleagues, but also, as Camille Slights has noted, the predicament faced by Henry's soldiers the night before the battle at Agincourt. The boy's defection suggests 'that the concept of the authority of the individual conscience may undermine national cohesiveness in a hierarchical social structure'.[36]

Shakespeare's decision to maintain and enhance the motif of stealing found in the source play therefore directly feeds the interrogative character of the play. On the one hand it provides us with the moral justification to identify with Henry's bloodthirsty actions, and on the other it justifies a questioning conscience leading to independent, morally motivated action even for those lowest on the patronage/service chain. The boy's soliloquy has the potential to kindle the audience's questioning conscience regarding a nationalistic agenda driven by the motives of a monarch who may or may not be as concerned with the moral well-being of his soul and those of his subjects as he is with presenting himself as a Christian king, never mind his fixation on the acquisition of new territory ruled by another Christian king. Although Henry has rejected the immediate company of his former thieving colleagues, he has simply enlisted them in a more elevated and nationalistic version of highway robbery.

Act 4 presents another example of the way in which Shakespeare goes beyond adopting material found in his sources to the invention of whole scenes which complicate the levels of engagement by presenting multiple perspectives that lead the audience to reflect on issues central to confessional conflict. Beginning with the Chorus he interweaves scenes derived from his sources with imaginary interventions for interrogative effect. The Chorus leads the audience to anticipate a confident, 'cheerful' leader with 'a modest smile' circulating amongst his men, calling 'them brothers, friends and countrymen' and 'thawing cold fear' (4.0.33, 34, 40, 45). When Henry does appear he initially presents the courageous exterior promised by the Chorus even to the point of finding virtue in the enemy because

> … they are our outward consciences,
> And preachers to us all; admonishing
> That we should dress us fairly for our end.
> (4.1.8–10)

This is similar to both Holinshed and *Famous Victories*, which present a confident king taking charge of battle preparations, bolstering the courage of his grossly outnumbered followers and placing their fate in God's hands. However, Shakespeare then has Henry assume Erpingham's cloak as a disguise so that 'I and my bosom' may 'debate awhile' in private (4.1.31). Here he diverges from not only his sources but also the expectations set up by the Chorus and the extroverted character of his speeches to this point.

While this is one of many instances in which the content of the *Chronicles* as articulated by the Chorus conflicts with the action of the scenes,[37] Henry's disguise does fulfill its promise of 'a little touch of Harry in the night' (4.0.47) and enables the King to literally establish common ground with his soldiers, albeit surreptitiously. The scenes that follow leading up to the St. Crispin's Day speech are almost pure invention. Unlike Harry's role-playing in Eastcheap, his disguise the night before the battle allows him to commune with his men in some ways like a preacher as described by Donne: 'It is not the depth, nor the wit, nor the eloquence of the Preacher that pierces us, but his nearenesse; that he speaks to my conscience, as though he had been behinde the hangings when I sinned, and as though he had read the book of the day of Judgement already' (3.142). The resulting metatheatrical blurring of spectators, performers, and personae (especially in the context of the court performance) facilitates intimate and introverted moments of profound spiritual anxiety that radically upstage the more superficial denominational conflict conjured up by the opening scenes of the play. Henry takes his audience to not only the dark, introspective heart of the play, but also the essential interrogative core of confessional conflict.

Although his first couple of scenes circulating amongst his men in disguise reinforce Henry's capacity to inspire genuine loyalty and unite his people across class and ethnic divides – largely through the identification of a common enemy – his visit with Court, Bates, and Williams opens up a disturbing distance between himself and his soldiers. Whereas Holinshed's Henry simply asserts in 'a right grave oration' that his men should 'remember the just cause for which they fought', and the *Famous Victories* Henry similarly declares, 'though we be few, and they many, fear not. Your quarrel is good and God will defend you', Shakespeare cracks the matter of 'just cause' wide open. He forces Henry to confront the popular conscience of his country in a manner that may have resonated especially effectively with members of a Globe audience familiar with Elizabeth's demands for service in foreign wars.

By representing Sir Thomas Erpingham as having anxieties about the impending battle, Henry achieves a 'nearenesse' that opens the door to the soldiers' innermost collective doubts – presumably in an effort to answer them and strengthen the men's resolve. He attempts to establish further common ground by asserting that 'the king is but a man, as I am' (4.1.101–2) and subject to the same fears experienced by his men. But Williams's conscience is troubled as to whether the King's cause is 'just and his quarrel honourable' (4.1.128–9), and Bates argues that 'if his cause be wrong, our obedience to the king wipes the crime of it out of us' (4.1.133–4). In effect these anxieties hold a mirror up to the King's own conscience, and Williams's vivid spectre of 'all those legs and arms and heads, chopped off in battle' joined together 'at the latter day' transport Henry and the audience to the personal and individual predicament created by the reality that 'few die well that die in a battle' but that no other option is available to these men, 'who to disobey, were against all proportion of subjection' (4.1.137–9, 146, 148–9). As Camille Slights has observed, these exchanges 'show the soldiers in an impossible moral dilemma and reveal how attenuated the concept of volition is within an ethic of unquestioning obedience. Theorists of conscience present the same impasse, agreeing both that conscience dictates obedience to human rulers and that the law of God supersedes human authority.'[38]

According to Womersley, in attempting to persuade Williams that the King has no control over his soldiers' souls and their individual sins and therefore no responsibility for them, Henry becomes 'the pattern of Protestant monarchy'[39] by asserting: 'Every subject's duty is the King's, / But every subject's soul is his own' (4.1.181–2). In the wider interrogative and performative context of the play, however, this line is more equivocal in that it speaks directly to the fundamental impulse behind confessional conflict: the fate of the individual soul. It addresses the early modern dilemma articulated by Slights, and it suggests that everyone (including both the King and Williams) must assume responsibility for their soul – and by extension their religious belief. This opens up an interrogative chasm not easily ignored. More comfortable as the sermonizing preacher speaking to the conscience of his doubting subjects than 'the sinner' whose subjects come a bit too near his own conscience speaking as if from 'behinde the hangings', Henry proves no more effective than contemporary preachers because he begs the central question of the scene and the entire play – as he himself articulated it at the outset of his venture: 'May I with right and conscience make this claim?' (1.2.96–7). Whereas Henry publicly shifted any initial soul-searching relating to this question from his own conscience to that of his Archbishop, he is less successful here.

Although Williams and Bates demonstrate a capacity to question and analyze their situation to an extent Henry finds off-putting, they squarely place the same kind of interpretive and intercessional responsibility on the conscience of the King which he had placed on the Archbishop. Henry tries less successfully this time to shift it back to his soldiers. Even after his lengthy response the honorable basis of his intentions remains in question, he fails to successfully shift responsibility back to the soldiers, and the scene ends badly with the King 'embracing' a quarrel between himself and Williams. The tenor of this exchange contrasts sharply with what the Chorus promised at the top of the act. Henry does not leave them with 'a modest smile', a 'cheerful semblance', or comforting salutations positioning them as 'brothers, friends, and countrymen' (4.0.33, 34, 40). Henry leaves frustrated and bested in the debate, because in part standing on common ground and playing a lesser role precludes pulling rank with an imperative response as king. He is forced to enter an interrogative space with his men and the audience with respect to his justification for war, the fate of his own soul – and the extent to which any 'Christian king' can demand and achieve uniformity amongst his people.

Peter Herman has argued that this play 'not only reflects the generalized crisis of authority in late Elizabethan England, but actually helps define the very climate of which it is simultaneously product and indicator'.[40] This scene certainly supports that claim, but in interrogating authority it zeros in on the declared link between loyalty to the monarch and uniformity around a state religion which elevates the stakes associated with confessional conflict. It leaves lingering pragmatic questions for a range of playgoers from monarch to groundling about the extent to which uniformity of religious belief can coexist with a personal as well as intercessional relationship with God. Where religious and political allegiance are bound together, must the King and clergy who compel allegiance to the 'right' or 'true' religion assume responsibility for all those souls if their religious allegiance is poorly motivated or misguided? If the Protestantism embraced by the Church of England liberates individuals like Bates and Williams to activate their personal conscience and develop a more direct relationship with God, does this greater responsibility for the fate of their souls logically necessitate greater freedom of personal religious choice?

Only after Henry leaves Williams and Bates so that he and his 'bosom' can 'debate awhile' (4.1.31) in private does the audience see the extent to which the soldiers' arguments have turned his conscience inside out. Rather than having the effect of projecting calm and comfort to his men, his perambulation causes him to introject further anxiety and feelings of inadequacy. For the first time in this play – and in Henry's stage history – he wrestles profoundly with his conscience while employing a series of tactics intended to engage the audience fully in the process as well.

Temporarily reconnecting with Harry of Eastcheap, Henry derives his first approach in part from the concept of the 'King's two bodies'. He reflects on himself as but an ordinary man and therefore by implication clearly no more capable of assuming responsibility for the souls of his men than they themselves. Emphasizing his aloneness and isolation, Henry eloquently strips away the external 'ceremony' of kingship and emphasizes his fundamental kinship with 'the wretched slave' (4.1.245, 274). As with most of Shakespeare's soliloquies, Henry draws the audience near by positioning them behind the curtain and allowing them to hear his innermost anxieties. But whereas the previous scene gave a range of audience members characters who appealed to their individual conscience and sense of self, the King's interior deliberations could well have had no better success in 'converting' most spectators to his point of view than he had with 'converting' the doubting soldiers to the ironic perspective that 'the King is but a man, as I am' (4.1.102–3).

His soliloquy further deconstructs his public majesty in favor of his private humanity and extends it to the point where he depicts his 'hard condition' as

> subject to the breath
> Of every fool, whose sense no more can feel
> But his own wringing.
> (4.1.238–41)

Although Henry initially uses this argument to achieve common ground with his men and audience identification, he extends it further to secure empathy and pity through the opposite effect – first elevating the common man above the King and then disparaging him with diction that establishes him as the King's inferior in a manner that echoes both Richard II and Harry of Eastcheap who likened his lowly 'friends' to 'base contagious clouds' in *1 Henry IV*.[41] The king's watch 'to maintain the peace' contrasts sharply with the sound sleep and quiet conscience of

> the wretched slave,
> Who, with a body filled, and vacant mind,
> Gets him to rest, crammed with distressful bread.
> (4.1.273–5)

Here Henry comes to the second stage in probing his conscience: acknowledging that he is no ordinary man, he must and does assume responsibility for his subjects in a Christ-like manner that deserves empathy for the extraordinary burden he carries. Dramaturgically located at the introverted heart of the play, the speech allows the audience to see into Henry's deepest self, nearest to his conscience, and the ambivalence which characterizes his own response to the play's central question. It leads Slights to identify *Henry V* as an early example of Shakespeare's 'increasing emphasis on the ambiguity of circumstances, the difficulty of choice, and the inadequacy of simple good intentions [as manifested in a] growing attention to doubt and confusion [which] correlates with a movement of dramatic focus into the minds of the characters'.[42] This soliloquy could have resonated with Shakespeare's primary playgoer at court, James I, as an uncommonly empathetic chord but with the rest of the court entering the inner most thoughts of the stage king while watching the reactions of the spectator king, it could also have had the effect of involuntarily stripping James bare of his ceremonial trappings as king and Supreme Governor of the Church. At the Globe it would have brought 'every fool' who attended the play into the very human anxieties of this king and the other Christian monarch to whom he was inevitably compared. On the one hand, communing with the king's innermost private thoughts and seeing him as fundamentally human must have powerfully engaged the audience experientially.[43] But with the King in private neither as reassuring nor as 'brotherly' as in more public speeches, audience identification with the King's humanity may have been limited. The proverbial observation that 'familiarity breeds contempt' may explain why the closer an audience of commoners comes the more distanced they may feel. Henry opens up further moral questions derived from his conscience – and ultimately from a playwright more interested in the interrogation of a king's conscience than proclaiming a hegemonic view of history, the monarchy or the Church.

Henry's extended apostrophe to ceremony calls into question not only the foundation of the monarchy but also anachronistically the role of the Supreme Governor of the Church, which for several early modern religious factions still maintained far too much ceremony. His entire soliloquy provides both the matter and a model for the kind of introspective reflection and soul-searching that Protestant preachers like John Donne came to admonish their parishioners to undertake. When Erpingham interrupts to remind him of his pressing responsibilities, Henry concludes with a prayer that recasts the audience's role in the preceding soliloquy. Henry's urgent plea for God's mercy as he and his men contemplate battle comes across as evidence of a simple, direct, and personal relationship with God, but his prayer that God 'think not upon the fault / My father made in compassing the crown' (4.1.298–9) suggests that even in his own mind his claim to the English throne let alone the French throne derives from stolen property and therefore requires redress through the Catholic rites of 'pardon' and 'penitence' (4.1.310–11). From the beginning of the scene he positioned the audience within his conscience, an innermost self that questions the substance of ceremony, but over the course of the prayer he recasts the audience's position to occupy the other component of the Protestant conscience, 'God's power and authority'.[44] With a mixed confessional message, however, the audience comes across as a confessor with reference to all the Catholic rituals associated with that role. Faced with the immediate realities of imminent battle Henry reminds God of what he has already invested in alms and chantries and bargains with him that if victorious in battle he will invest even more.

Ultimately, as a model for dealing with confessional conflict Henry comes across as pragmatic. Much like Elizabeth I, who maintained a silver crucifix in her chapel, and others of this period who outwardly conformed to the Church of England but in their final will and testament used Catholic formularies and cited related bequests to the poor,[45] Henry's questioning conscience may betray a sympathy for some of the Lollards' notions and an anticipation of Protestantism, but at this moment of mortal crisis he hedges his bets by appeasing a Catholic God with reminders of his performance of sacramental 'ceremonies' and a promise of more rites and rituals to come: a promise he makes good on at the end of the act by acknowledging 'That God fought for us'.

> *Fluellen* Yes, my conscience, he did us great good.
> *King Henry* Do we all holy rites:
> Let there be sung 'Non nobis' and 'Te Deum'
> (4.8.122–4)

In contrast with the boy's earlier soliloquy, however, Henry's confession of guilt and penance assume a further interrogative character in the extent to which they focus exclusively on the transgressions of his father instead of his personal misdeeds. Henry V may have publicly foresworn the thieving company of Falstaff and his compatriots, but privately he may not differ that much from that father-like vice-figure sometimes seen as a proto-Protestant who separates his ultimate salvation through grace from the morality of past and present deeds.

When Henry delivered the extroverted and confident St. Crispin's Day speech, often cited in isolation as a measure of the propagandist purpose and effect of the play, his off-stage audience would have read it in the context of their conflicted and questioning experience in the preceding scenes. In this carefully crafted blockbuster of a speech, Henry builds to a climactic 'hegemonic we' through which he speaks confidently for 'We few, we happy few, we band of brothers' (4.3.60). Despite its immediate effect on his men as a morale booster, though, it provokes more reflective and questioning audience response as Henry sends the soldiers off to battle with 'You know your places: God be with you all' (4.3.76). Despite extensive analyses as Machiavellian ploy, persuasive masterpiece, or sophisticated sermon, scholars continue to see the speech as rife with conflicting rhetorical, confessional, political, and moral implications.[46] At best, the extreme and comparatively sudden transformation from the introverted, contemplative world of the conscience to the extroverted, confident world of the soldier-king renders all the more remarkable the strength of courage Henry has mustered during the eighty lines he has been off stage. At worst, it raises questions about unreconciled moral polarities lurking behind the bravado. This Christian king's new-found eagerness for honor may position him between Hotspur at one extreme and Falstaff on the other, but it displays none of the honesty and consistency of character that would reflect well on his contemporary counterpart as Supreme Governor of the Church.

Slights approaches *Henry V* as concerned with 'scrutinizing the conscience of a king who would also be his country's conscience' and the dramatization of 'the conscious struggle to discover morally right action'.[47] But Henry's conscience forms only part of a larger puzzle. Shakespeare is using Henry's crisis of conscience to activate the playgoer's conscience and to empower his audience to construct and scrutinize the conscience of the country independently of the King. He situates spectators 'behind the arras' and draws them near to not only the actions and intentions of the King, but also the wider scope of events selected to frame Henry's actions and expand their perspective beyond Henry's point of view.

Just as the opening scenes with the Catholic prelates open up concerns about the justification for the war and the boy's reflections and resulting action lead us to a moral basis for refusing to follow a morally questionable leader, so too the prophetic epilogue functions as an interrogative capstone reaching explicitly beyond Henry's foresight to remind us that France was lost during the very next reign of Henry's son. Reminding us of the ultimate futility of the enterprise on which Henry focused for the entire play, the epilogue leaves the audience with profound questions as it reflects on this Christian king, the stability of kingdoms, and by extension the durability of state religions. Having vicariously experienced a range of moral predicaments and resolutions, the audience must independently complete an ideological critique of the national conscience Shakespeare has set in motion. That critique applies not only historically to Henry's reign but also currently, in the context of the present reigning monarch as well as in the construction of the playgoers' own senses of subjectivity and identity which will have an increasing influence on the direction of national identity under the Stuarts. In the end Shakespeare does not attempt to resolve anxieties arising from the multiple perspectives on confessional conflict that spectators have experienced over the course of the play. With early modern audiences, the play engaged them in such a way as to encourage them to extend the performance text beyond the stage performance by continuing the negotiation of history, the character of historical figures, the role of the monarch in religious belief and practice, and the personal implications of confessional conflict on political allegiance and the fate of their souls.

Jeffrey Knapp has suggested that audiences would have responded to *Henry V* by realizing they no longer needed to 'wait for a bishop, king, or even Chorus to play the preacher', that they could 'learn how to edify each other – stirring and provoking one another to love and godliness'.[48] While some audience members may have resolved the matter of confessional conflict in such a way, the open and interrogative quality of this play would likely have generated an extended performance text of responses as diverse as the play's different audiences (public audiences in London and various touring venues across the country as well as the January 1605 court audience), their differing religious allegiances (Catholic, Church of England, quietly questioning conformists, and a proliferating range of louder, overtly Puritan non-conformists) and the multiple contextual implications that could have emerged just within the 1598/99–1605 time frame (not the least of which the transition from the reign of Elizabeth to that of James I as Supreme Head of the Church). Surviving contemporary responses to any early modern play are rare, but in this instance we do have a specific and high-profile intervention in the ongoing negotiation of confessional conflict set in motion by the play (and the Henriad as a whole).

Written for the rival Lord Admiral's Men and performed late in 1599, *The First Part of Sir John Oldcastle* responds directly to *Henry V*. In its treatment of the title character as an early Protestant martyr persecuted by the Catholic Archbishop despite his loyalty to his friend Henry V, the play's imperative agenda makes it ironically more akin to medieval Catholic saints' plays than Shakespeare's complex and questioning treatment of Henry V. Although the play provides plenty of motivation and opportunity for introverted examination of his conscience, its audience engages in no such moments of confessional conflict in the context of Oldcastle's recovery as an important historical figure motivated by moral principal in contrast with the rogue and philandering crony immortalized first in *Famous Victories* and then under the name of Falstaff in the Henriad. At no point does Oldcastle question or waiver in either his Lollard beliefs or his allegiance to Henry V, but as Donna Hamilton has observed, the play performs 'every variation on the slipperiness and consequences of religious identity' while arriving at a clear conclusion to Shakespeare's questioning. In response to a Lollard rebel's protest that his 'conscience vrged me to it', Henry responds:

> Thy conscience? Then thy conscience is corrupt,
> For in thy conscience thou art bound to vs,
> And in thy conscience thou shouldst loue thy country.

Although the rebel protests, 'We meant no hurt vnto your maiesty, / But reformation of Religion',[49] the play leaves no doubt that loyalty to the monarch and the state trumps all. However, Hamilton argues that it also treats 'Catholics and Protestants as equivalent and interchangeable in respect to the circumstances in which they have over time found themselves in England' and therefore sets in motion a more interrogative approach to the unquestioning association of treason with religious divergence which had characterized the government's treatment of recusants since Elizabeth's excommunication in 1570. Despite an unwillingness to take the Oath of Allegiance to her as Supreme Governor of the Church of England (like Donne in his early years), many Catholics from across the social spectrum professed and performed loyalty to their monarch as head of state.[50]

As a mixed imperative and interrogative text *The First Part of Sir John Oldcastle* is just one very particular response by a competing theatre to the challenges of confessional conflict as presented by Shakespeare, but it points to the potential for *Henry V* to generate an irenic response to confessional conflict if not the reading of history. The play, as Hamilton notes, suggests that 'if it was once legal to punish a Protestant for heresy, but also possible to leave him alone, the same applies to the Catholic'.[51] If Shakespeare's play can present a medieval king who publicly embraces Catholic 'ceremony' after privately questioning such 'ceremony' and laying bare the doubts and guilt which plague his conscience, then the God of the history plays ultimately acquires an ambiguous – if not all-encompassing – confessional persuasion.

In the late sixteenth century few if any preachers were offering their parishioners such complex and substantial interrogation of the issues surrounding confessional conflict, but playwrights like Shakespeare, and to some degree Munday, who engaged playgoers in the interrogation of the history of Church and state, may have activated both the personal and collective conscience to consider a more pragmatic and irenic approach to confessional conflict and the relative impact of allegiance to a current monarch or religious practice on the fate of one's soul.[52] While the theatrical interrogation may have been set in motion and witnessed by key figures who had experienced confessional conflict – such as Shakespeare, Munday, possibly Donne, and even Elizabeth I and James I – their particular personal resolution of such conflict remains as ambiguous as the God which presides over the history plays. Ultimately it will never be possible to know the extent to which early modern playgoers were influenced by plays like *Henry V*, but a high-profile playgoer like Donne can give us some sense of the impact the theatre may have had on seventeenth-century sermons that were often characterized as its antithesis.[53] His later approach to the pulpit, which invoked multiple perspectives on confessional conflict, engaged his parishioners through dramatic and performative rhetorical devices to activate an interrogative conscience, and displayed irenic inclinations in guiding his 'audience' towards the resolution of religious anxieties, certainly had less in common with sixteenth-century preachers and their sermons than with playwrights and players like Shakespeare and their dramaturgy.

Notes

1 See for example P. Collinson, *The Birthpangs of Protestant England: Religious and Cultural Change in the Sixteenth and Seventeenth Centuries* (Basingstoke: Macmillan, 1988); C. Haigh, *English Reformations: Religion, Politics, and Society under the Tudors* (Oxford: Oxford University Press, 1993) and 'The Church of England, the Catholics and the People', in P. Marshall (ed.), *The Impact of the English Reformation* (London: Arnold, 1997), pp. 235–56; A. Walsham, *Church Papists: Catholicism, Conformity and Confessional Polemic in Early Modern England* (Woodbridge: Boydell Press, 1993); M. Questier, *Conversion, Politics and Religion in England, 1580–1625* (Cambridge: Cambridge University Press, 1996).

2 J. Donne, 'The First Anniversary, An Anatomie of the World', in *The Variorum Edition of the Poetry of John Donne*, ed. Gary A. Stringer (Bloomington: Indiana University Press, 1995), 6.12, line 213; Patrick Collinson, 'William Shakespeare's Religious Inheritance and Environment', in *Elizabethan Essays* (London: Hambledon, 1994), p. 219.

3 For examples of audience response to executions as well as their impact on drama and theatre of the period see D. K. Anderson, *Martyrs and Players in Early Modern England: Tragedy, Religion and Violence on Stage* (Farnham: Ashgate, 2014).

4 P. Collinson, 'The English Reformation in the Mid-Elizabethan Period', in J. Shami, D. Flynn, and M. T. Hester (eds), *The Oxford Handbook of John Donne* (Oxford: Oxford University Press, 2011), p. 374.

5 J. Jewel, *Certaine Sermons* (London: 1583), sig. L8$^{r–v}$.

6 J. Knapp, 'Preachers and Players in Shakespeare's England', *Representations*, 44 (1993), 29–59; *Shakespeare's Tribe: Church, Nation, and Theater in Renaissance England* (Chicago: University of Chicago Press, 2002).

7 J. Northbrooke, *A Treatise Wherein Dicing, Dauncing, Vaine Playes or Enterluds With Other Idle Pastimes etc. Commonly Used on the Sabboth Day, Are Reproved*, ed. Arthur Freeman (New York: Garland, 1974), p. 66.

8 For an example of such a sermon preached in Norwich, see M. Blackstone, 'The Queen's Men and the Performance of Allegiance, Conformity and Difference in Elizabethan Norwich', in K. J. E. Graham and Philip D. Collington (eds), *Shakespeare and Religious Change* (Basingstoke: Palgrave Macmillan, 2009), pp. 88–109. See also Haigh, *English Reformations*, pp. 289–90; Walsham, *Church Papists*, p. 15.

9 Cambridge University Library, MS Mm.1.29, fol. 3^{v}.

10 Haigh, *English Reformations*, p. 280.

11 C. Belsey, *Critical Practice* (London: Methuen, 1980), p. 91.
12 M. Carlson, 'Audiences and the Reading of Performance', in T. Postlewait and B. A. McConachie (eds), *Interpreting the Theatrical Past: Essays in the Historiography of Performance* (Iowa City: Iowa City Press, 1991), p. 84.
13 C. Belsey, *The Subject of Tragedy: Identity and Difference in Renaissance Drama* (London: Routledge, 1985), p. 33.
14 H. Diehl, *Staging Reform, Reforming the Stage: Protestantism and Popular Theater in Early Modern England* (Ithaca, NY: Cornell University Press, 1997) pp. 1, 5; Jonathan Baldo, 'The Historical Sublime in Shakespeare's *Richard II*', in I. Karremann, C. Zweierlein, and I. M. Groote (eds), *Forgetting Faith? Negotiating Confessional Conflict in Early Modern Europe* (Berlin: Walter De Gruyter, 2012), p. 96.
15 M. Blackstone and C. Louis, 'Towards "a full and understanding Auditory": New Evidence of Playgoers at the First Globe Theatre', *Modern Language Review*, 90 (1995), 556–71.
16 P. Whitfield White, *Theatre and Reformation: Protestantism, Patronage, and Playgoing in Tudor England* (Cambridge: Cambridge University Press, 1993), pp. 92, 173.
17 See, for example, 'Stephen Gosson', *Oxford Dictionary of National Biography*, online edn, at www-oxforddnb.com.libproxy.uregina.ca:2048/view/article/11120, accessed December 1, 2014.
18 R. Baker, *A Chronicle of the Kings of England* (1642), vol. 2: p. 156.
19 Having been knighted by Essex in Dublin in 1599, Cornwallis is thought to have written this in a letter to Donne *c.* 1600/01; Oxford, Bodleian Library Tanner MS 306, fol. 237 as cited in H. Grierson (ed.), *The Poems of John Donne* (Oxford: Oxford University Press, 1912), vol. 2: pp. 171–2.
20 R. E. Barbieri, 'John Donne and Richard II: An Influence', *Shakespeare Quarterly*, 26 (1975), 57–62
21 J. P. Bednarz, *Shakespeare and the Truth of Love: The Mystery of 'The Phoenix and Turtle'* (Basingstoke: Palgrave Macmillan, 2003), p. 235, n. 80.
22 Laurence Olivier's 1944 technicolor adaptation of *Henry V* as wartime propaganda remains one of the best-known productions of the play. Scholars such as Irving Ribner have interpreted its primary objective as 'arousing the patriotic sentiments of his audience': I. Ribner, *The English History Play in the Age of Shakespeare*, rev. edn (London: Methuen, 1965), p. 184. More recently, D. Womersley has argued in *Divinity and State* (Oxford: Oxford University Press, 2010), p. 328, that the play presents 'Henry V as an ideal monarch'.
23 Michael Neill, *Putting History to the Question: Power, Politics, and Society in English Renaissance Drama* (New York: Columbia University Press, 2000), pp. 405–6.
24 William Hazlitt, *Characters of Shakespeare's Plays* (London: Reynell, 1817), online at www.archive-org./stream/charackersofshak05085gut/chrsh10.txt, accessed February 28, 2015). See also Jonathan Dollimore and Alan Sinfield, 'History and Ideology: The Instance of Henry V' in J. Drakakis (ed.), *Alternative Shakespeares* (London: Methuen, 1985), pp. 206–27; Robert Weimann, 'Bifold Authority in Shakespeare's Theatre', *Shakespeare Quarterly*, 39 (1988), 401–17; Andy Mousley,

Renaissance Drama and Contemporary Literary Theory (New York: St. Martin's Press, 2000), pp. 156–60; Lisa Hopkins, *Shakespeare on the Edge: Border-Crossing in the Tragedies and the Henriad* (Aldershot: Ashgate, 2005), pp. 13–20, 28–30; Brian Walsh, *Shakespeare, the Queen's Men, and the Elizabethan Performance of History* (Cambridge: Cambridge University Press, 2009), pp. 178–208. For recent productions which embrace the interrogative character of this play see Michael Billington's review of Michael Grandage's 2013 London production at www.theguardian.com/stage/2013/dec/03/henry-v-review-jude-law, accessed February 28, 2015) or J. Kelly Nestruck's review of Des McAnuff's 2012 Stratford, Ontario production at www.theglobeandmail.com/arts/theatre-and-performance/theatre-reviews/stratfords-henry-v-is-suitably-ambiguous/article4420944/, accessed February 28, 2015).

25 Joel B. Altman, '"Vile Participation": The Amplification of Violence in the Theater of Henry V', *Shakespeare Quarterly*, 42:1 (1991), 32.

26 Norman Rabkin, 'Rabbits, Ducks, and Henry V', *Shakespeare Quarterly*, 28:3 (1977), 296.

27 Although beyond the possible scope of this essay, all of the plays in the Henriad can be read as interventions in the negotiation of confessional conflict. For a broader discussion of the multiple Protestant and Catholic dimensions of these plays see M. Hunt, 'The Hybrid Reformations of Shakespeare's Second Henriad', *Comparative Drama*, 32:1 (1998), 176–206.

28 William Shakespeare, *King Henry V*, ed. John H. Walter (London: Methuen, 1979), 1.2.241; all subsequent references are from the text of this edition.

29 J. J. Scarisbrick, *Henry VIII* (London: Eyre and Spottiswoode, 1968), pp. 23, 25.

30 The entire speech displays parallels with Henry's charge to the troops in *Famous Victories*, but it concludes, 'we shall shortly have a famous victory over those enemies of my God, of my kingdom, and of my people'. Elizabeth I, *Collected Works*, ed. Leah S. Marcus, Janel Mueller, and Mary Beth Rose (Chicago: University of Chicago Press, 2000), p. 326.

31 For example, see R. Holinshed, *Holinshed's Chronicles of England, Scotland and Ireland* (London, 1808), vol. 3: pp. 65–6.

32 J. Donne, *The Sermons of John Donne*, ed. George R. Potter and Evelyn M. Simpson (Berkeley: University of California Press, 1953–64), vol. 1: p. 207 (Sermon 3, lines 899–904); all other citations from the sermons will be from the text of this edition.

33 *The Famous Victories of Henry the Fifth*, ed. Chiaki Hanabusa, Malone Society Reprints 171 (Manchester: Manchester University Press, 2008), p. 20, line 629; all references to this play are from the text of this edition.

34 Womersley, *Divinity and State*, p. 314.

35 *The Famous Victories*, p. 23, lines 701–13.

36 C. Wells Slights, *The Casuistical Tradition in Shakespeare, Donne, Herbert, and Milton* (Princeton: Princeton University Press, 1981), p. 65.

37 P. Rackin, *Stages of History: Shakespeare's English Chronicles* (Ithaca, NY: Cornell University Press, 1990), p. 69.

38 C. W. Slights, 'The Conscience of the King: *Henry V* and the Reformed Conscience', *Philological Quarterly*, 80:1 (2001), 12.

39 Womersley, *Divinity and State*, p. 332.

40 P. C. Herman, '"O, 'tis a gallant king": Shakespeare's *Henry V* and the Crisis of the 1590s', in D. Hoak (ed.), *Tudor Political Culture* (Cambridge: Cambridge University Press, 1995), p. 207.
41 William Shakespeare, *The First Part of King Henry IV*, ed. A. R. Humphreys (London: Methuen, 1975), 1.2.193.
42 Slights, *The Casuistical Tradition*, pp. 130–1.
43 For a discussion of the innately leveling effect of a player becoming Henry V by employing the same trappings of ceremony used by a current monarch to establish authority see Herman, '"O, 'tis a gallant king"', pp. 213–14.
44 C. Wells Slights, 'Notaries, Sponges, and Looking-Glasses: Conscience in Early Modern England', *English Literary Renaissance*, 28:2 (1998): 231–46.
45 Walsham, *Church Papists*, p. 20; C. Litzenberger, *The English Reformation and the Laity: Gloucestershire, 1540–1580* (Cambridge: Cambridge University Press, 1997), pp. 153–60.
46 See, for example, N. Rabkin, *Shakespeare and the Problem of Meaning* (Chicago: University of Chicago Press, 1981), pp. 45–6; L. Danson, '*Henry V*: King, Chorus, and Critics', *Shakespeare Quarterly*, 34 (1983), 34–5, 42; M. Blackstone and J. Shami, 'Donne, Shakespeare, and the Interrogative Conscience', in J. H. Anderson and J. C. Vaught (eds), *Shakespeare and Donne: Generic Hybrids and the Cultural Imaginary* (New York: Fordham University Press, 2013), pp. 133–4.
47 Slights, 'The Conscience of the King', 4; *The Casuistical Tradition*, p. 106.
48 Knapp, *Shakespeare's Tribe*, p. 137.
49 *The Life of Sir John Oldcastle*, ed. Percy Simpson. Malone Society Reprints [1908] (Oxford: Oxford University Press, 1963), 4.2.1650–3, 1656–7.
50 D. B. Hamilton, *Anthony Munday and the Catholics, 1560–1633* (Aldershot: Ashgate, 2005), p. 144.
51 *Ibid.*, p. 142.
52 See Knapp, 'Preachers and Players in Shakespeare's England', 41–2, for a discussion of evidence in *Henry V* suggesting that Shakespeare longed 'for a religion that would be inclusive and pacifist rather than elitist and bellicose'.
53 For an extended discussion of rhetorical and performative parallels in mechanisms of audience engagement employed in Shakespeare's plays and Donne's sermons see Blackstone and Shami, 'Donne, Shakespeare'. See also M. Fetzer, 'Donne's Sermons as Re-enactments of the Word', *Connotations: A Journal for Critical Debate*, 17:1 (2007/08), 1–13. On the irenic dimension of Donne's work see A. Deschner, 'Reforming Baptism: John Donne and Continental Irenicism', in Mary Arshagouni Papazian (ed.), *John Donne and the Protestant Reformation: New Perspectives* (Detroit: Wayne State University Press, 2003), pp. 293–313.

10

Formal experimentation and the question of Donne's ecumenicalism

Alexandra M. Block

John Donne's complex religious identity has long been a challenge to literary scholars. Born into a respected Catholic family, Donne left university without taking a degree, which suggests he was unwilling, as a young adult, to foreswear his faith. He converted to Protestantism at some point afterwards. He would, eventually, become an English churchman, achieving the success in the religious arena that eluded him during his secular career. Nevertheless, his Catholic mother continued to live with his family for years, predeceasing him by only a few months. These facts have given scholars much to debate: just when did Donne convert? Did his conversion stem from a true change of heart, or was it more pragmatically motivated? Did he maintain 'crypto-Catholic' sentiment for some time after his conversion, perhaps throughout his life? How did his move away from the faith of his birth affect his psychology, relationships, and writings? These sorts of questions have generated a rich vein of criticism examining not only the works but the author himself.[1]

The question of Donne's ecumenicalism may reasonably prompt us to search Donne's oeuvre for statements that address the question explicitly. Such searches are quite productive. Even focusing specifically on Eucharistic theology (a particularly contentious area of early modern Christianity), one finds several strongly ecumenical statements in Donne's sermons:[2]

> A peremptory prejudice upon other mens opinions, that no opinion but thine can be true, in the doctrine of the Sacrament, and an uncharitable condemning of other men, or other Churches that may be of another perswasion then thou art, in the matter of the Sacrament, may frustrate and disappoint thee of all that benefit, which thou mightst have, by an humble receiving thereof, if thou wouldest exercise thy faith onely, here, and leave thy passion at home, and referre thy reason, and disputation to the Schoole.[3]

Such statements make Donne sound like an unusually open-minded fellow, given the rabid controversy over the Eucharist that raged through much of the sixteenth century, but Donne's apparent ecumenicalism must be tempered in several ways. First, such statements very much follow the influence of Richard Hooker's Eucharistic formulations, which had a calming effect on Eucharistic rhetoric within the mainstream, conformist currents of English Protestantism:[4]

> [S]ith we all agree that by the sacrament Christ doth really and truly in us perform his promise, why do we vainly trouble ourselves with so fierce contentions whether by consubstantiation, or else by transubstantiation the sacrament itself be first possessed with Christ, or no? A thing which no way can either further or hinder us howsoever it stand, because our participation of Christ in this sacrament dependeth on the co-operation of his omnipotent power which maketh it his body and blood to us, whether with change or without alteration of the element such as they imagine we need not greatly to care nor inquire.[5]

Many English churchmen, like Donne, matched Hooker's pacifying tone, which means their statements may not necessarily be clearly connected to any personally unique ecumenicalism: Donne's comments may tell us more about his attitude toward ecclesiastical authority than about his personal ecumenicalism. Donne's explicitly ecumenical statements on the Eucharist need to be taken with this context in mind.

Another wrinkle: Donne did not always sound ecumenical. He was as capable as any other Protestant of talking about the Catholic Church as 'this *Italian Babylon, Rome*'.[6] '[I]f all the mysteries and secrets of Antichrist', Donne rails in a typical passage,

> all the confused practises of that Babylon, all the emergent and occasionall articles of that Church, and that *State-religion*, shall become Sacraments, we shall have a Sacrament of *Equivocation*, a Sacrament of *Invasion*, a Sacrament of *Powder*, a Sacrament of *dissolving allegeance*, sacraments in the Element of *Baptism*, in the water, in navies, and Sacraments in the Elements of the *Eucharist*, in *Blood*, in the sacred *blood of Kings*.[7]

Donne's anti-Catholicism may be driven by political concerns, here. The blood of kings, sacraments of powder and of navies – the stability and safety of the Protestant state are heavily in play. Given the politicized context of Donne's role as a major English churchman, it is difficult to separate issues of Protestant statehood from a more 'pure' ecumenicalism. If such purity even exists: when churches and governments overlap, ecumenicalism cannot fail to have political ramifications. For someone like Donne, respecting all forms of Christianity cannot be allowed to slide into valuing all monarchs or forms of government. This may be why it is quite possible to match every ecumenical passage in the sermons with one that sounds far more prejudicial, be it against Catholics or more radical Protestants.

Since looking at *what* Donne has to say about ecumenicalism yields contradictions and complications, it may be useful to look instead at *how* Donne says things. If one considers the how – that is, the formal details of how representation works in Donne's texts – one may find more support for a personally ecumenical temperament in this most religiously vexing of authors.

By way of background, let me return, for a moment, to the early modern Eucharist. During the sixteenth century, no issue was more contentious than the sacrament's semiotic status. Catholics and Protestants agreed that the Eucharist was a sign but differed radically over exactly how it signified; Protestants also disagreed with one another. As a result, continental and English tractarians produced a large body of polemic articulating a range of semiotic approaches to the sacrament. In so doing, they developed four different models of how the sacramental sign might relate to its referent. These models might be labeled 'identity', 'similitude', 'exhibition', and 'convention'. The model of *identity* proposes that sign and referent become one and the same; *similitude*, that sign and referent, while separate, are ontologically linked by their inherent resemblance to one another; *exhibition*, that sign and referent, while separate, have a wholly reliable connection generated by the unique power of the sign-maker; and *convention*, that sign and referent have no essential connection, being linked only by the habits of a particular human community. The two more extreme models, identity and convention, are, in fact, largely rhetorical creations: rather than being accurate representations of Catholic and Zwinglian thinking about Eucharistic semiotics, they emerge as models from opposing writers' doctrinal simplifications and misrepresentations. Exhibition and similitude, on the other hand, more defensibly represent real Protestant approaches to protecting the sacramental sign from charges of ordinariness. That said, all four models are best thought of as instances of semiotic theory that undergird theological arguments rather than as identical with the theologies themselves.

These sacramental semiotic models did not remain cordoned off from the world of literature: Donne imports them into his literary texts, using them to experiment with different ways of shaping literary representation in response to the unique pressures faced within particular texts. For instance, he imagines his letters as sacraments that represent him more or less closely, depending on the person to whom he writes, and in the *Devotions*, he uses the model of exhibition to create a modified version of *imitatio Christi* that balances his dueling impulses toward humbleness and self-promotion. Recognizing Donne's representational practices as influenced by all the sacramental semiotic models (not just the one most closely associated with his own religious outlook, which would be exhibition), suggests a subtle and fascinating kind of religious open-mindedness – one that is willing to privilege writerly needs over religious tribalism. 'I need a different way of approaching this situation', a number of Donne's works seem to say. 'Let me try this on for size. Well, that isn't working ... let me try this.'

By way of example, one of Donne's verse epistles, 'If, as mine is', draws on both similitude and exhibition as modes of representation. In the introductory section of this epistle, which a young Donne almost certainly wrote to his friend Rowland Woodward, the poet's description of the way his letter represents him relies in part on the model of similitude. The poem is fundamentally separate from what it represents, yet deeply and naturally linked to it. That natural linkage between the sign (the poem) and its referent (Donne himself) is evidenced by their similarity:

> If, as mine is, thy life a slumber be,
> Seeme, when thou read'st these lines, to dreame of me,
> Never did Morpheus nor his brother weare
> Shapes soe like those Shapes, whom they would appeare,
> As this my letter is like me, for it
> Hath my name, words, hand, feet, heart, minde and wit;
> It is my deed of gift of mee to thee,
> It is my Will, my selfe the Legacie.
> So thy retyrings I love, yea envie,
> Bred in thee by a wise melancholy,
> That I rejoyce, that unto where thou art,
> Though I stay here, I can thus send my heart,
> As kindly'as any enamored Patient
> His Picture to his absent Love hath sent.[8]

Donne opens this letter by asserting the similarity between himself and the text he has produced, relying in part on puns – the poem has his 'hand'-writing, metrical 'feet' of his invention, and his signatory 'name' – and in part on the more abstract assertion that it represents or reproduces his thoughts and feelings, his 'heart, minde, and wit'. It is like a painted 'Picture' of its author. This likeness is the source of one way the poem represents Donne to Woodward: the epistle, Donne suggests, is a conduit through which Donne can 'send [his] heart', which he has put into the text as a means of making it 'like' him.

But this likeness of poem to poet provides only half of its semiotic foundation; Donne goes on to say that it is his 'deed of Gift' and 'Will' of himself to Woodward, a trope that aligns the poem's representation of Donne with the way a legal document conveys property from one party to another.[9] The ability of the legal document to function as the actual means of transference rests on the legal authority of its drafter. The semiotic model at work here proposes that a sign provides a stable connection to the thing it signifies, a connection along which essential properties of the thing may pass. And the success of this connection or transfer depends on the authority of the sign-maker: a will or deed of gift is not legally binding without such authority. This idea of the sign as incorporating an essential connective element strongly echoes Calvinist expressions of the Eucharist as 'exhibiting' its meaning because the divine sign-maker's power makes it so. As a sign, it provides a powerful connection to the thing itself, a conduit through which some properties of the thing may travel.[10] Similarly, 'If, as mine is' conveys Donne to Woodward as though he were a piece of property whose ownership could be legally transferred via a document, as long as the power to make such a transfer resides in the document's composer.

The model of exhibition becomes more prominent in the English Protestant Eucharistic tracts beginning in the 1550s, whereas earlier Protestant tracts tend to rely on similitude more heavily. Some temporal difference in emphasis makes sense, as similitude, though touched on by many tractarians, is especially important in memorialism, which was influential early on in England, whereas exhibition is associated with later Calvinism. Here, exhibition is represented by the deed-of-gift trope, in which Donne sets himself up as the legal owner of himself, empowered to bestow himself on whom he chooses. But this model is bracketed by the assertion of likeness and the fruit it bears, the sending of Donne's 'heart'. The poem is unwilling to put all its semiotic eggs in the basket offered by any single model; instead, it employs competing justifications for its separate-yet-connected vision of the sign and referent.

Donne's use of similitude is, perhaps, generated by his awareness that he lacks what underpins the later model: the divine speaker's omnipotent ability to enforce the connection between his signs and their referents. In 'If, as mine is', Donne's deed-of-gift trope places him in a position analogous to God's in this *Devotions* discussion of his fevers and blotches: 'These heates, *O Lord*, which thou hast broght upon this *body*, are but the chafing of the *wax*, that thou mightest *seale* me to thee; These *spots* are but the *letters*, in which thou hast written thine owne *Name* and conveyed thy selfe to me; whether for a *present possession*, by taking me now, or for a future *reversion*.'[11] This much later trope is similar to the one in 'If, as mine is'. For instance, the conveyance in the *Devotions* trope could take the form of a deed of gift ('taking [Donne] now') or a will (the 'future reversion' of Donne to God). It also makes the sacramental subtext of the poem's trope more explicit by speaking of 'seals' and of God's 'conveying [him]self to' Donne.[12] But in the *Devotions*, God, not Donne, is the drafter of the legal document, and by 'conveying [him]self to' Donne in that document, God gains ownership of Donne, rather than vice versa. God's sign is not only a conduit, but a two-way street: in addition to 'conveying' God to Donne, it 'seal[s]' Donne to God and allows God to 'tak[e]' him. The *Devotions* passage, in effect, rewrites the trope of 'If, as mine is' into a form that restores sacramental 'sealing' to its proper exerciser, God, a revision that is highlighted by the use of the word 'letters' to mean a legally authoritative document, like a letter of conveyance. In suggesting that Donne has this sort of semiotic power, 'If, as mine is' pushes the jurisdiction of the human sign-maker to audacious limits. *Ergo* Donne's insertion of a second source of semiotic stability – the resemblance between sign and referent – as a back-up.

In making these points, I am indebted to the scholarship of Theresa DiPasquale, who argues that Donne's relationship to the early modern debate about the sacraments influences his use of signs, as well as his vision of himself as a sign-maker and his readers as 'receivers' of those signs.[13] But whereas DiPasquale focuses on texts that allude to the sacraments, I argue that Donne's probing of representational possibilities appears in many texts that do not mention the sacrament at all. In other words, the Eucharistic semiotic models matter not only when the Eucharist is explicitly introduced but also as an independent body of thought pervasively informing Donne's representational practices. What they generate is a kind of artistic ecumenicalism, a subordination of religious difference to the exigencies of art that enables complex representational experimentation.

'The Crosse' provides a fine example of the models at work in an explicitly Eucharistic poem:

> Since Christ embrac'd the Crosse it selfe, dare I
> His image, th'image of his Crosse deny?
> ...
> As perchance, Carvers do not faces make,
> But that away, which hid them there, do take;
> Let Crosses, soe, take what hid Christ in thee,
> And be his image, or not his, but hee.[14]

The speaker asserts that he, as Christ's 'image', must embrace the image of the cross, so that the analogy between Christ and himself will hold at all levels. But the sculptural analogy from later in the poem subtly shifts the envisioned relationship between original and image. If the opening lines of the poem suggest that an image could (but should not) wilfully diverge from the original, the sculptural analogy proposes that a perfect image already exists within the stone: the sculptor is not responsible for 'mak[ing]' the image replicate the original, but rather merely removes the material disguising a pre-existing replica. In the poem's earlier lines, the image has the potential to go astray, representing inaccurately, whereas in the later lines, accurate representation seems far closer to guaranteed. And in fact, as the sculptural analogy plays out, the image's perfect replication of the original becomes even more certain: crosses, meaning life's afflictions, have the power not only to reveal a human being as Christ's image, but as being Christ himself: one will 'be his image, or not his, but hee'. In this concluding movement of the analogy, the image – the living Christian – replicates the original – Christ – so perfectly that the former is said to be the latter. All distance between the original and the image has been erased, rendering the two fungible. The representational movement is from similitude (being Christ's 'image') to identity (being 'hee'); the semiotic models allow Donne to formally enact an emerging and ever-closer identification, pushing the matter to the impossible ideal of oneness with Christ.

But while the connection between semiotics and theology is clear in 'The Crosse', in other works, such as 'If, as mine is', the semiotic models function without any connection to the Eucharistic context in which they were developed. In Donne's mind, the semiotic models associated with the Eucharist seem truly to have taken on a life of their own, making Eucharistic allusion and the use Eucharistic semiotic models separate features of his verse. 'A Valediction: of my name, in the window' is an interesting example of a poem that does not allude to the sacrament but is nonetheless pervasively informed by the Eucharistic models.[15] In this poem, the speaker ruminates on having scratched his name into his beloved's windowpane before a journey that has taken him away from her. He approaches the mark's referential connections from a number of different angles, generating representational formulae very similar to those we have seen at work in the 'The Crosse', which makes its connections to the sacrament more explicit. In several cases, for example, the mark on the window is connected to something else by similarity. Not all of these cases strike me as semiotically informed. For instance, the speaker asserts, 'As no one point, nor dash, / Which are but accessaries to this name, / The showres and tempests can outwash / So shall all times finde mee the same' (lines 13–16). Here I think the mark is simply the vehicle in a simile: one of its attributes – its permanence – is being associated, via the trope, with the simile's tenor, the speaker himself. Donne's goal, in these lines, is the 'rubbing off' of one thing's qualities onto another. But another of the poem's similarity-based figures works differently: 'thinke this ragged bony name', the speaker says in the next stanza, 'to be / My ruinous Anatomy' (lines 23–4). At first this second trope seems much like the permanence simile, but its thrust is actually the opposite: the mark is said to be 'ragged' and 'bony', which makes it resemble the speaker's ramshackle skeleton. The purpose here is not to use the mark's attributes to assign traits, via comparison, to the speaker's bones. Rather, the speaker wants his beloved to link the mark and his skeleton mentally, and he thus presents the two as inherently similar: the writing's ragged boniness makes it skeletal. One might argue that this figure is still a metaphor, with the speaker's skeleton as vehicle and the mark as tenor. After all, it is probably fairly hard to produce a fluid script when scratching on bumpy handmade glass with a diamond – one might well end up with a jumble of intersecting straight lines, like a pile of bones. But giving a clearer description of the mark does not seem to be the speaker's underlying goal; rather, he wants the lady to think of the mark as being his bones – being, that is, so similar to his bones that the mark and her beloved's bones will be intertwined in the lady's mind. She will see one and 'think' it the other. In this case, the mark is being treated as a sign, not the vehicle in a comparative trope. Its purpose is to point, not to ascribe attributes.

The speaker's use of the mark as a sign for his own bones is based initially on similitude – the implication is that the inherent similarity of the mark to the bones can cause the lady to think the one is the other. However, the semiotic picture is not as clear as it might at first appear. The speaker's use of the imperative, for instance, suggests that the link that similarity provides between mark and bones is not strong enough to automatically trigger the mental connection. The power of the speaker's voice intrudes to supply extra impetus. Furthermore, although early Protestant tractarians usually use similitude to give the Eucharistic sign and its referent a super-ordinary connection *without* making them identical, here the speaker's formula runs right into identity, with the similarity apparently being so strong that the mark will 'be' the skeleton it resembles. The semiotic strands of Donne's tapestry are actually quite complicated in this little passage. He seems to be drawing on three of the four models, and in so doing, combining the matter of identity with the antimatter of two models most often used to avoid identity: similitude and exhibition. The word 'think' is the key to understanding this semiotic knot: while the imperative privileges the poet's voice as a powerful connector between mark and skeleton, the verb chosen indicates that the mark will be the skeleton only in the lady's imagination – she is to 'think' the one is the other. (The speaker could instead have used the word 'know', which would have preserved the imperative and the poem's meter while suggesting that the identity of mark and bones was real, not imaginary.) In sum, the word 'think' negotiates within itself the inherent tension in both similitude and exhibition. The purpose of both these models is to pull the sacramental sign and its referent together as naturally linked while simultaneously holding them apart as separate entities. That is what 'think' does to the lady: it orders her to conflate two things, but in so doing it reminds her that the conflation is artificial.

Most of Donne's verse epistles, including 'If, as mine is', are thought to have been written when the poet was a young man. Traditionally, his love lyrics, such as 'A Valediction: of my name, in the window', are also assigned an early composition date, though that seems less certain. Despite the unknowns, it is certainly possible that 'If, as mine is' and 'A Valediction: of my name' were written while Donne was still Catholic. But that does not mean he settled easily into identity as a representational model: both poems go out of their way to make the fungibility of sign and referent problematic. The poet refuses to unify himself with his epistle or his name. In other words, he avoids the Catholic-associated semiotic model of identity, in which the sign and the thing itself are one, in favor of models in which sign and referent are connected but separate.[16] Similarly, Donne's paradox that the letter is his 'deed of gift' or 'will' of himself to Woodward puts the poet in two places at once – he is the writer of the legal document and the property conveyed by that document. However, in neither position is he identified with the document itself.[17]

If, on the other hand, Donne's conversion had already occurred when he wrote 'If, as mine is' or 'A Valediction: of my name', we might expect him to rely on exhibition, since that model is associated most often with the Calvinist Eucharistic theology Donne accepted.[18] However, both poems make rich use of similitude, a model more often associated with Zwinglian memorialism, a position Donne explicitly rejects in the sermons. And if 'The Crosse' is a later work, we might expect an avoidance of the 'Catholic' model of identity, yet there it is.[19] In fact, Donne's reliance on the different semiotic models is so varied that, however one chooses to date his conversion and his works, one can see him employing semiotic models associated with theological positions that contradict his own beliefs.

My point is not that Donne was indecisive or omnivorous in his religious beliefs. Rather, he seems willing to think of theological polemic – a body of writing in which he was clearly well versed[20] – as containing a rich vein of semiotic thought that could be mined for promising ways of reimagining how representation might work in a broader sense. In other words, in pursuit of particular writerly goals, he seems to have been willing, at times, to decenter religion to some degree, positioning it not as the master a text must serve, but as a resource serving the text. What Donne thought, in his heart of hearts, about his period's religious fervor and violence can never be known with certainty. His representational tactics do allow us to speculate, however, that he may sometimes have seen theology as just another intellectual fruit ripe for plucking in the service of art. If the needs of art so overshadow the origins of the semiotic ideas Donne is using, how important could the distinctions among the various Eucharistic theologies have been to him? Perhaps he truly was ecumenically minded. But although it may tempt us, the question is unanswerable. The substantial body of work on Donne as a coterie poet tells us that seemingly audacious features of his verse must be read in the context of socially situated production and circulation.[21] And however carefully we read the remains of that circulation, the mind that produced them will remain a foreign land. We are not on the inside.

Notes

1 The impact on Donne's beliefs, thought, and writings of his family's Catholicism has been the subject of intense critical attention over the past few decades from a relatively limited but passionate group of scholars, a flurry of interest perhaps initiated

by J. Carey's controversial biography, *John Donne: Life, Mind, and Art* (1981; repr. London: Faber and Faber, 1990). See M. T. Hester, *Kinde Pitty and Brave Scorn: John Donne's Satires* (Durham, NC: Duke University Press, 1982); R. V. Young, 'Donne's Holy Sonnets and the Theology of Grace', in C. J. Summers and T.-L. Pebworth (eds), *'Bright Shootes of Everlastingnesse': The Seventeenth-Century Religious Lyric* (Columbia: University of Missouri Press, 1987), pp. 20–39; D. Flynn, 'Donne and the Ancient Catholic Nobility', *English Literary Renaissance*, 19 (1989), 305–23; D. Morse, *England's Time of Crisis: From Shakespeare to Milton: A Cultural History* (New York: St. Martin's Press, 1989), pp. 256–318; R. Strier, 'John Donne Awry and Squint: The "Holy Sonnets", 1608–1610', *Modern Philology*, 86 (1989), 357–84; M. T. Hester, '"This cannot be said": A Preface to the Reader of Donne's Lyrics', *Christianity and Literature*, 39 (1990), 365–85; M. Sabine, *Feminine Engendered Faith: The Poetry of John Donne and Richard Crashaw* (Houndmills: Macmillan, 1992), chs. 1–3; M. T. Hester, '"Let them sleepe": Donne's Personal Allusion in *Holy Sonnet IV*', *Papers on Literature and Language*, 29 (1993), 346–50; M. T. Hester, '"Ask Thy Father": Rereading Donne's Satyre III', *Ben Jonson Journal*, 1 (1994), 201–18; M. T. Hester, 'Donne and the Court of Wards', *American Notes and Queries*, 7 (1994), 130–3; J. Klause, 'Hope's Gambit: The Jesuitical, Protestant, Skeptical Origins of Donne's Heroic Ideal', *Studies in Philology* 91 (1994), 181–215; D. Flynn, 'A Biographical Prolusion to Study of Donne's Religious Imagination', in R.-J. Frontain and F. M. Malpezzi (eds), *John Donne's Religious Imagination: Essays in Honor of John T. Shawcross* (Conway, AK: University of Central Arkansas Press, 1995), pp. 28–44, and Flynn, *John Donne and the Ancient Catholic Nobility* (Bloomington: Indiana University Press, 1995). Others have continued to emphasize Donne's Protestantism, or elements thereof, as an influence in his texts, or have cautioned against any one-note pigeon-holing of his religious attitudes: D. Haskin, 'John Donne and the Cultural Contradictions of Christmas', *John Donne Journal*, 11 (1992), 133–57; D. W. Doerksen, 'Preaching Pastor versus Custodian of Order: Donne, Andrewes, and the Jacobean Church', *Philological Quarterly*, 73 (1994), 417–29; D. W. Doerksen, 'Saint Paul's Puritan: John Donne's "Puritan" Imagination in the Sermons', in Frontain and Malpezzi (eds), *John Donne's Religious Imagination*, pp. 350–65; P. McCullough, 'Preaching to a Court Papist? Donne's Sermon before Queen Anne, December 1617', *John Donne Journal*, 14 (1995), 59–82; J. Shami, '"Trying to Walk on Logs in Water": John Donne, Religion, and the Critical Tradition', *Renaissance and Reformation*, 25 (2001), 81–99; and the essays in M. Arshagouni Papazian (ed.), *John Donne and the Protestant Reformation: New Perspectives* (Detroit: Wayne State University Press, 2003).

2 For some time, M. Ross's *Poetry and Dogma: The Transfiguration of Eucharistic Symbols in Seventeenth Century English Poetry* (New York: Octagon, 1969) was the only book-length study on the sacrament in the period's literature, and Donne is not its focus. But the last decade and a half have brought a number of more detailed treatments, including E. J. McNees, *Eucharistic Poetry: The Search for Presence in the Writings of John Donne, Gerard Manley Hopkins, Dylan Thomas, and Geoffrey Hill* (Lewisburg, PA: Bucknell University Press, 1992), pp. 33–68; J. Baumlin, *John Donne and the Rhetorics of Renaissance Discourse* (Columbia: University of Missouri Press,

1991); and T. Di Pasquale, *Literature and Sacrament: The Sacred and the Secular in John Donne* (Pittsburgh: Duquesne University Press, 1999). Baumlin and DiPasquale focus on Donne exclusively, whereas McNees does not. Also important are R. Whalen, *Poetry of Immanence: Sacrament in Donne and Herbert* (Toronto: University of Toronto Press, 2002); R. V. Young, *Doctrine and Devotion in Seventeenth-Century Poetry: Studies in Donne, Herbert, Crashaw, and Vaughan* (Cambridge: D. S. Brewer, 2000); A. B. Chambers, *Transfigured Rites in Seventeenth-Century English Poetry* (Columbia: University of Missouri Press, 1992), which does not focus on the Eucharist, but considers much that is connected to it; P. G. Stanwood, *The Sempiternal Season: Studies in Seventeenth-Century Devotional Writing* (New York: Peter Lang, 1992), pp. 43–54, which reads the sermons' sacramental focus in connection with incarnational theology; and A. Deschner, 'Reforming Baptism: John Donne and Continental Irenicism', in Papazian (ed.), *John Donne and the Protestant Reformation*, pp. 293–313, which examines Donne's attitudes toward the other Protestant sacrament, baptism. See also M. Elsky, 'History, Liturgy, and Point of View in Protestant Meditative Poetry', *Studies in Philology*, 77 (1980), 67–83; A. Barbeau Gardiner, 'Donne and the Real Presence of the Absent Lover', *John Donne Journal*, 9 (1990), 113–24; T. Di Pasquale, 'Ambivalent Mourning: Sacramentality, Idolatry, and Gender in "Since she whome I lovd hath payd her last debt"', *John Donne Journal*, 10 (1991), 45–56; T. Di Pasquale, 'Cunning Elements: Water, Fire, and Sacramental Poetics in "I am a little world"', *Philological Quarterly*, 73 (1994), 403–15; M. T. Hester, 'Genre, Grammar, and Gender in Donne's "Satyre III"', *John Donne Journal*, 10 (1991), 97–102; R.- J. Frontain, 'Donne's Emblematic Imagination: Vision and Reformation of the Self in "The Crosse"', *Publications of the Arkansas Philological Association*, 20:1 (1994), 27–51; and A. Guibbory, 'Fear of "Loving More": Death and the Loss of Sacramental Love', in M. T. Hester (ed.), *John Donne's 'desire of more': The Subject of Anne More Donne in His Poetry* (Newark: University of Delaware Press, 1996), pp. 204–27.

3 John Donne, *The Sermons of John Donne*, ed. George R. Potter and Evelyn M. Simpson, 10 vols. (Berkeley: University of California Press, 1953–62), vol. 7: p. 291.

4 On Hooker's influence, see C. W. Dugmore, *The Mass and the English Reformers* (London: Macmillan, 1958), pp. 243–6. Controversy over the Eucharist would continue up to and through the Civil War period, but the issues at stake would change, the focus being more on the physical trappings of the rite and its primacy in Christian worship – what the priest should wear, whether an altar or table should be used, etc. – and far less on its nature as a sign. For later English disagreements over Eucharistic practices, see W. R. Crockett, *Eucharist: Symbol of Transformation* (New York: Pueblo Publishing, 1989), pp. 180–97; N. Tyacke, *Anti-Calvinists: The Rise of English Arminianism, c. 1590–1640* (Oxford: Clarendon Press, 1987); N. Tyacke, *Aspects of English Protestantism, c. 1530–1700* (Manchester: Manchester University Press, 2001).

5 'Of the Laws of Ecclesiastical Polity', in *The Works of that Learned and Judicious Divine, Mr. Richard Hooker: With an Account of His Life and Death by Isaak Walton*, 2 vols. (Oxford: Clarendon Press, 1865), vol. 2: pp. 84–5.

6 Donne, *Sermons*, vol. 10: p. 15.

7 *Ibid.*, vol. 8: p. 11.

8 John Donne, *The Poems of John Donne*, ed. Herbert J. C. Grierson, 2 vols. (London: Oxford University Press, 1912), 'If, as mine is', lines 1–14. All quotations from Donne's poems are from this edition.

9 A 'deed of gift' conveys property from one living party to another; like a letter, it might be sealed, rather than signed. A 'will' was originally a document that conveyed real property – land – while a 'testament' conveyed personal property (*Oxford English Dictionary*, 2.a. s.v. 'gift' and IV.23.a. s.v. 'will', no line).

10 As Donne says in a sermon, 'The Sacrament of the body and blood of Christ … is to every worthy receiver, the seale, and the Conduit of all the merits of Christ, to his soule' (*Sermons*, vol. 10: p. 165).

11 John Donne, *Devotions Upon Emergent Occasions*, ed. Anthony Raspa (Montreal: McGill-Queen's University Press, 1975), p. 70.

12 Donne follows Hooker in calling sacraments 'seals': sacraments, 'by God's own will and ordinance … are signs assisted always with the power of the Holy Ghost', so that '[t]he elements and words have power of infallible signification, for which they are called seals of God's truth' (*The Works of that Learned and Judicious Divine*, vol. 2: p. 309).

13 See *Literature and Sacrament*, whose examination of the sacraments and Petrarchism in Donne focuses on texts containing specific allusions to the Eucharist or baptism. DiPasquale and I differ on the motives impelling Donne's epistolary experimentation. Whereas she attributes Donne's alignment of his texts with sacraments to his dissatisfaction with Petrarchan convention, which Donne finds frustratingly 'noncommunicative and reflexive' and associates with undesirable elements of Catholicism, I see a text-by-text search for the best approach to representation as the driving force behind Donne's experimentation. See also E. McNees, 'John Donne and the Anglican Doctrine of the Eucharist', *Texas Studies in Literature and Language*, 29 (1987), 94–114; McNees, *Eucharistic Poetry*, pp. 33–68. I am distinguishing the influence of Eucharistic semiotics from allusions to or other literary uses of the sacrament. With 'The Flea', as with other Donne lyrics, critics have noticed his tendency to construct tropes that allude to the sacrament. Hester, '"This cannot be said"', for instance, sees in the poem's excessive use of the word 'this' an allusion to Christ's words of institution, as repeated by the priest in the Catholic mass: 'hoc est corpus meum'. The poem is mentioned briefly in terms of Eucharistic imagery in Whalen, *The Poetry of Immanence*, p. 32. What DiPasquale is doing – arguing not just for allusion, but for a specifically semiotic effect – is far closer to my own interests.

14 Donne, *The Poems*, vol. 1: pp. 331–3. 'The Crosse' includes several sacramental allusions (lines 2–4, 15–16), the lines quoted are 1 through 2 and 33 through 36.

15 Despite its interestingly frenetic approach to representation, this poem has received comparatively little critical attention. Early treatments are brief and explanatory: D. C. Allen, 'Two Annotations on Donne's Verse', *Modern Language Notes*, 60 (1945), 54–5, offers to amend line 6, a line examined again in G. Blackmore Evans, 'Two Notes on Donne: "The Undertaking"; "A Valediction: Of My Name, in the Window"', *Modern Language Review*, 57 (1962), 60–2. More sustained

readings approach the poem from a variety of angles: G. R. Wilson, Jr., 'The Interplay of Perception and Reflection: Mirror Imagery in Donne's Poetry', *Studies in English Literature 1500–1900*, 9 (1969), 107–21, which focuses on Donne's ability to produce and resolve paradox; J. Bernard, 'Orthodoxia epidemica: Donne's Poetics and "A Valediction: Of My Name in the Window"', *South Atlanta Quarterly*, 71 (1972), 377–89, which sees in the poem signs of a retreat from faith in poetry toward religious orthodoxy; B. Vickers, 'The "Songs and Sonnets" and the Rhetorics of Hyperbole', in A. J. Smith (ed.), *John Donne: Essays in Celebration* (London: Methuen, 1972), pp. 132–74; G. Stringer, 'Learning "Hard and Deepe": Biblical Allusion in Donne's "A Valediction: Of My Name, in the Window"', *South Central Bulletin*, 33 (1973), 227–31; I. Bell, 'The Role of the Lady in Donne's *Songs and Sonnets*', *Studies in English Literature 1500–1900*, 23 (1983), 113–29, argues that the poem privileges the lady over the poet; J. M. Walker, '"Here you see mee": Donne's Autographed Valediction', *John Donne Journal*, 2 (1985), 29–33, argues that Donne employed a numerological scheme to write his own name into the poem; T. Docherty, *John Donne, Undone* (New York: Methuen & Co., 1986), pp. 178–82, reads the speaker's name in the window as 'intercepted by another unspoken name, that of Christ', rendering the entire poem an example of *imitatio Christi* that enacts 'a kind of "communion" in the act of reading' (pp. 179, 180); J. T. Shawcross, 'Poetry, Personal and Impersonal', in C. J. Summers and T.-L. Pebworth (eds), *The Eagle and the Dove: Reassessing John Donne* (Columbia: University of Missouri Press, 1986), pp. 53–66, cautions against misreading the poem based on biographical assumptions; B. L. Estrin, 'Framing and Imagining the "You": Donne's "A Valediction of My Name in the Window" and "Elegy: Change"', *Texas Studies in Literature and Language*, 30 (1988), 345–62, focuses on the speaker's inability to control the woman by becoming one with her. One of the few critics to examine what interests me in the poem – the relationships it proposes between representations and the things represented – is D. H. Roberts, '"Just Such Disparity": The Real and the Representation in Donne's Poetry', *South Atlanta Bulletin*, 41:4 (1976), 99–108.

16 Although, as mentioned earlier, the 'identity' model is more a construction of Protestant polemic than it is an accurate reflection of the richer semiotic properties that Catholics themselves saw in their model of the sacrament. A lively area of Donne criticism over the last few decades has explored the persistent influence of the author's Catholic background on his texts, even long after his conversion to Protestantism. Such critical interests are part of a larger historiographical and literary-critical movement toward recognizing and assessing the deep consequences of England's Catholic past, the influence of which lasted long after the Elizabethan settlement. See, for instance, E. Duffy, *The Stripping of the Altars: Traditional Religion in England, c. 1400–c. 1580* (New Haven, CT: Yale University Press, 1992); S. Greenblatt, *Hamlet in Purgatory* (Princeton: Princeton University Press, 2001); P. Lake with M. Questier, *The Antichrist's Lewd Hat: Protestants, Papists and Players in Post-Reformation England* (New Haven, CT: Yale University Press, 2002); and A. Marotti, *Religious Ideology and Cultural Fantasy: Catholic and Anti-Catholic Discourses in Early Modern England* (Notre Dame, IN: University of Notre

Dame Press, 2005). On the difficulty of connecting many of Donne's religious references to specific doctrinal sources – or even of labeling them either Catholic or Protestant – see Young, 'Donne's Holy Sonnets and the Theology of Grace'.

17 Repeated assertions of separation fit the focus of the remainder of the poem, which is Donne's frustration that England is not immediately pursuing the riches of Guyana, which lie across the ocean:

Guyanaes harvest is nip'd in the spring,
I feare; And with us (me thinkes) Fate deales so
As with the Jewes guide God did; he did show
Him the rich land, but bar'd his entry in:
Oh, slownes is our punishment and sinne.
Perchance, these Spanish businesse being done,
Which as the Earth betweene the Moone and Sun
Eclipse the light which Guyana would give,
Our discontinu'd hopes we shall retrive:
But if (as all th'All must) hopes smoake away,
Is not Almightie Vertue'an India? (lines 18–28)

18 Donne's willingness to experiment with semiotic models associated with non-Calvinist Eucharistic theologies surpasses the ecumenical tendencies he displays in other theological areas, which are frequently apparent in the letters and elsewhere. See John Donne, *Letters to Severall Persons of Honour*, ed. Charles Edmund Merrill (New York: Sturgis & Walton, 1910), pp. 25, 87–8, 113–14, and *Tobie Mathews, A Collection of Letters, Made by Sr Tobie Mathews, Kt., With a character of the most Excellent Lady, Lucy, Countesse of Carleile: By the same Author. To which are Added many Letters of his own, to severall Persons of Honour, who were Contemporary with him* (London: Henry Harringman, 1660), pp. 336–7.

19 The idea that Donne's love lyrics are a product of his youth, whereas his divine poems are more mature work, got its start with a dichotomy the poet himself created: in a letter about his tract on suicide, *Biathanatos*, Donne constructs a famous distinction between '*Jack Donne*, and … D. *Donne*', as producers of frivolous versus laudable texts. 'Jack's' suicide treatise retains some value to the Doctor, though: 'publish it not, but yet burn it not', he says to his friend Robert Ker (*Letters to Severall Persons*, p. 19).

20 Donne claims in *Pseudo-Martyr* to have 'suruayed and digested the whole body of Diuinity, controuerted betweene ours and the Romane Church' (*Psevdo-Martyr, Wherein Ovt of Certaine Propositions and Gradations, This Conclusion is euicted. That Those Which Are of the Romane Religion in this Kingdome, may and ought to take the Oath of Allegeance* [London: W. Stansby, 1610, B3]).

21 A critical movement initiated by A. F. Marotti, *John Donne, Coterie Poet* (Madison: University of Wisconsin Press, 1986).

11

Foucault, confession, and Donne

Joel M. Dodson

This chapter reconsiders Michel Foucault's critique of confession in order to examine, in slightly broader yet more methodological terms, what exactly we mean by negotiating 'confessional' conflict in late Reformation English literature. My aim is to use Foucault to re-think Foucault: to read Foucault's later lectures on the 'care of the self' as an alternate model for historicizing doctrinal affiliation in late Tudor and early Stuart literature rather than the penal or penitential vocabulary elaborated in *Discipline and Punish* and the first volume of *The History of Sexuality*; and to argue, in turn, that confessionalization might be seen as an enabling, rather than disabling, fiction of early modern religious writing and its criticism.[1] Given the forms of faith we know literature assumed in early modern England, it is time to move the 'creedal imperative' beyond the procrustean strain of religious belief in the period.[2] It is time to see confession as a theoretical imperative itself.

I offer by way of example one of John Donne's most important though under-explored sermons, his sermon on religious schism delivered at The Hague in 1619, sometimes referred to, following Donne's biblical text of Matthew 4:18–20, as his 'Fishers of Men' address. Speaking in the wake of the Synod of Dort, Donne sought to describe in this sermon what he termed the 'fecundity of true religion', a provocative revision of *Satyre III* that leads to some suggestive, if subtle, resonances with Foucault.[3] Though routinely privileged as a poet antithetical to 'newer name[s] than Christian', Donne's preaching on the 'fecundity' of creeds within the Church – only months after the formal sundering of Arminians and Calvinists, and more than forty years after the Formula of Concord – goes beyond the problem of labels alone, or the disciplinary force that imposes them. It offers, instead, a candid analysis of ecclesial and professional division as forms of life, illuminating in Michel Foucault's mature work a more interesting prospect: the re-definition of confessional practice away from a 'hermeneutics of the subject', and the articulation of a more local, civic understanding of the religious self, in which doctrinal confession – like literary profession – forms a 'stylistics of existence', rather than subjection.[4]

Seeing the divided body of Christ

Why Foucault now? Over the past decade and a half, the various 'turns' to religion have marked a turn away from Foucault, and from the discourses of power and religious authority imported from his work by new historicism. Drawing upon recent historiography, this turn has highlighted several basic yet important truths: that confessional formation was a multifarious, even haphazard affair in the early English Church, and that religious identity in sixteenth- and seventeenth-century England thus fits uncomfortably with the disciplinary dissemination of creeds apparent in confessionalization on the continent.[5] Literary criticism has pointed us instead to the blurring of confessional lines in English poetry and drama, privileging the sacred, spiritual, and even ecumenical potential of literary representation in the Age of Shakespeare. While writers like Jeffrey Knapp and Robert Stillman have stressed the 'anti-confessional' roots of professional and humanist authorial circles in the 1580s and 1590s, new studies of English Catholic and Puritan devotion have uncovered inter-confessional modes of literary exchange in Tudor and Stuart England.[6] As Brooke Conti observes in her recent study of seventeenth-century spiritual autobiography, the confession of faith emerges as a peculiarly malleable form in the study of early modern English letters. It is a genre of 'religious fluidity' in an age that 'understood religion as an either/or proposition', a set of 'attempts to explain or clarify [one's] beliefs that wind up doing very little of either'.[7]

This critical emphasis on the deferral or indeterminacy of confessional definition in early modern England has prompted renewed insight, as Ken Jackson and Arthur Marotti note, into matters of 'inspiration' and 'spirit', yet a spirit defined dialectically against an institutional or creedal basis whose Foucauldian idioms remain curiously persistent.[8] Among even the best literary historians, the history of English confession predominately remains the history of its torturous cousin, the auricular or public confession, while the very category of 'confessional identity' continues to prove itself ambivalent, implying at once the heartfelt urges of personal belief or the ideological demands of Church or state-enforced dogma.[9] This elision not only licenses Foucault's thesis about the internalization of power, turning Elizabeth's purported refusal to look into men's hearts into literary motive. It associates confessionalism with a site of capitulation or contestation, a kind of historical wound that literary criticism must, in a sense, always get beyond. The turn to religion risks a kind of fall back into what *The History of Sexuality* diagnosed as the 'repressive hypothesis': the desire for an image of belief that is prior to its confessing, and the hope that religion, like sex, as Foucault wryly put it, might 'tomorrow be good again'.[10]

Rather than mere rhetoric, Foucault's diagnosis is worth taking seriously, for English writers by the end of the sixteenth century were themselves keenly aware of the need to describe the Church in terms that did not reduce its confessionalization to forms of repression. Donne's third satire (*c.* 1596), for example, opens with a lengthy lament on the ironies of a much-hoped-for return to 'Mistresse faire Religion' amidst the division of late Reformation Christendom. If the maternal repressed ever rears her head in the 1590s, the satirist observes, she does so less in the 'easy ways and near' of a return to the devotion of the 'fathers' generation than in the (castrating) anxiety of those who, swords in hand, force 'every hee / Which cries not "Goddesse," to thy Mistresse, draw'.[11] Both, in their fervor for a more universal faith, make as much a 'mistress' as a mother out of *ecclesia mater*. These sentiments echo similar ones made in the opening pages of *The State of Christendom* (*c.* 1594), whose authors imagined the average Elizabethan observer gazing across the Channel at the end of the sixteenth century, unable even to acknowledge the newer names of a divided Church:

> You see Nobility to degenerate in vertue from their Ancestors; Sons to vary in opinion from their Fathers; Neighbours to dissent in Religion with their next Inhabitants; and Judges not to agree in matters of Justice, with their fellows in Office: You see the *Puritan* ready in outward appearance to dye for his Religion; the *Anabaptist* for his; the *Papist* for his; the *Lutheran* for his; the *Barrowist* for his; and other Sectaries for their several Sects and Heresies .... This sight therefore, and this fear, ingendreth in your heart a just and worthy dislike of the present time, and a great desire and delight in the Age of your fore-Fathers: You condemned the one because it is (as you think) very troublesome and vitious; and you commend the other, because it was (as you suppose) very peaceable and vertuous: But if it may like you to confer the one with the other, you shall find them both in like manner reprehensible, and with equal measure laudable.[12]

Echoing the satirist's language of the father, the image of the divided Body of Christ – torn between 'Puritan', 'Papist', 'Lutheran', 'Anabaptist', and 'other Sectaries' – crystallizes in these pages the problematic historicity of the confessionalized Church in the 'present time'. We may sublimate it, *The State of Christendom* notes, to a repressed image of the magisterial 'Age of [our] fore-Fathers', or to the irenic hope of its 'peacable and vertuous' return. Yet as the motif of sight suggests, the reality of the late Reformation Church poses a more existential question of *theorein* (Gr., vision), or the gaze: whether a Church divided by confessions is something to be seen, or represented, in the English imagination at all.[13]

On purely material grounds, the answer to this question by the end of the 1590s was an abundant if implicit yes, as confessions of faith – personal and ecclesiastical – formed a growing genre of Tudor print over the sixteenth century. In his 1595 catalogue of English printed books, the publisher and bookseller Andrew Maunsell listed more than twenty works devoted to doctrinal confession then in print and being sold in his own and fellow English publishers' bookstalls, distinguishing between such saleable items as printed '*Confessions*', expositions 'On the *Creede*', and a third, meta-genre 'Of the *Confessing* of Christ' (all of which Maunsell's catalogue distinguished from both catechisms and the penitential matter of 'True *confession* of Sinne').[14] Maunsell was perhaps an ideal observer of the state of creeds and confessions in Elizabethan England as he had been responsible a decade earlier for the printing of Thomas Rogers's popular *The English Creede* (1585), a two-volume folio which treated the Thirty-Nine Articles, despite their supposedly Erastian design, as a confession of faith to be read and compared alongside the Reformed, Lutheran, Tridentine, and even Familist creeds (a mode of creedal harmonizing introduced in Reformation Europe by the *Harmonia Confessionum Fidei* in 1581).[15] Neither such harmonies nor the individual creeds they sought to systematize can quite be said to fit what two key critics have characterized as the confessional milieu of Donne's satire: a prophetic age bravely opposed to the fashion of new 'ideological poses', or a syncretic one embracing the jouissance of denominations, or 'names'.[16] Rather, they suggest a kind of material and intellectual crisis, when the multiplicity of confessions constituted an increasingly visible presence in late Tudor and early Stuart England, yet which lacked, as Donne's 'brave scorn forbids', the necessary ecclesial vision to make sense of it.[17]

One of the more interesting aspects of Foucault's genealogy of confession from the mid-1970s forward is that it engages these same dilemmas of ecclesial history, illuminating the relative visibility, or invisibility, of doctrinal confession in contemporary criticism and theory. Beginning with *Discipline and Punish* (1975) and continuing through his later lectures at the Collège de France, Foucault's notion of confession grows over the course of his writings out of an evolving account of the Christian tradition as a special kind of faith that imposes on its adherents the avowal, or 'obligation of truth'.[18] This obligation has usually been framed in historicist criticism as an effect of biopower. 'The individual conscience as a fertile field of knowledge', according to Stephen Greenblatt, 'is at least in part the product of a complex operation of power – of watching, training, correcting, questioning, confessing'.[19] Yet a closer examination of the discursive horizon of Foucault's own account of confession equally reveals two, more basic premises about the relationship between Church, creed, and self, of which the disciplinary tools of inquisition and regulation prove the symptom, rather than the source.

One such premise is the millenarian structure confession assumes in Foucault's studies of penal and penitential discipline, as an unfolding revelation of 'truth' and 'falsehood'. In *Discipline and Punish*, this discursive fiction appears in the form inquisition takes, particularly in the era of the plague, on the logic of the saved and damned. Each individual must confess who is sick and who is not, what one has done and what one has not done.[20] By *The History of Sexuality*, Foucault begins to make explicit that binary logic in his study of auricular confession. In confessing the truth and falsehood of one's innermost desires, the penitent not only affirms the authority of the Church in the sacrament of penance. That authority is displaced within the speaking subject as an image of 'the revelation of truth, the overturning of global laws, the proclamation of a new day to come … a dream of the New City'.[21] Confession, that is, depends not only on the confessing and regulating of knowledge, sexual or otherwise. It depends on representing the problem of the visible Church as a problem of the invisible spirit, a disciplinary pattern, as Jeremy Carrette notes, that places an Augustinian division between earthly and spiritual *civitate* at the heart of Foucault's genealogy of religious subjection.[22] For Foucault, one's confession works to regiment the tremulous body not simply on the logic of *cuius regio, euius religio.* It works by disciplining one's *religio* as the deferred image of another, golden age to come.

This millenarian conceit can be seen in the biblical commonplace routinely featured on the title-page of almost every mid-Tudor printed confession: 'For with the heart man believeth unto righteousness; And with the mouth, man confesseth to salvation' (Rom. 10:10).[23] For Bishop Hooper, writing at the dawn of the Marian exile, such verses signified the almost inextricable links between Christian confession and the apocalyptic manifestation of the 'true', invisible Church.[24] Yet the equation between heart and mouth also underscores for Foucault a further principle of confession: that it elaborates a primarily mimetic relationship between creed, or avowal, and the self. In Christianity, the believer never confesses truth on the basis of the objective content of dogma alone. Rather, 'His problem is that of knowing the degree of purity of the representation as idea, as image …. Does the idea I have in my mind come from God? – in which case it is necessarily pure. Does it come from Satan? – in which case it is impure. Or possibly even: does it come from myself, in which case, to what extent can we say it is pure or impure?'[25] Post-Reformation historiography since Hegel has found this mimetic quality of belief relatively evident; the splitting of the sixteenth-century Church turns icon into Word, sacred ritual into sign.[26] Yet Foucault's point is that these seemingly liberatory notions of representation in the confessional age are themselves a production (*techne*) of Christianity's most insidious assumption – that the self, through confession, becomes subject to its own image, a 'hermeneutics of the subject'. In his 1980 lectures at Dartmouth on 'Christianity and Confession', Foucault explained this hermeneutic nature of confession in terms of the ancient Christian technique of *exomologesis*, or self-publication:

> Tertullian has a word to translate the Greek word *exomologesis*; he said it was *publicatio sui*, the Christian had to publish himself. Publish oneself, that means that he has two things to do. One has to show oneself as a sinner; that means, as somebody who, choosing the path to sin, preferred filthiness to purity, earth and dust to heaven, spiritual poverty to the treasures of faith. In a word, he has to show himself as somebody who chose spiritual death to earthly life. And it is for this reason that *exomologesis* was a kind of representation of death. It was the theatrical representation of the sinner as dead or as dying. But this *exomologesis* was also a way for the sinner to express his will to free himself from this world, to get rid of his own body, to destroy his own flesh, and get access to a new spiritual life.[27]

If the birth of confession has to do with the birth of authorship – and with the trope of early modern subjection to authority – then that birth also gives rise to a virtual shibboleth of literary historicism, even after its 'turns' to religion. Confession, according to Foucault, is interesting not for any particular creed or ecclesial affiliation it denotes. It is interesting for the interpretive matter of a subject who sees in the Church an image, or representation, of the self, discerning which 'church whereof he is a member', as Bale's *Image of Both Churches* put it in 1545, 'under pleasaunte figures and elegant tropes decyded'.[28]

On these millenarian and mimetic grounds, Foucault's theory of confession proves at once revealing and crippling for a theory of late Reformation confessionalism. For the very logic that discloses confession as a subject fit for literary analysis also forecloses it as the discursive remains of a primarily apocalyptic language of the divided Church, a language which limits 'confession' to the *publicatio sui* or polemical aims of one ideal version of 'Mistress faire religion', rather than the negotiation of multiple churches or creeds. Even more, what Foucault sees as a genealogical condition of the modern subject, writers like Donne and the authors of *The State of Christendom* were already recognizing by the end of the sixteenth century as the paternal longing for an earlier Reformation ideal that proved strangely inadequate to the alienated condition of the self in confessionalized Europe. As the Reformed theologian Jerome Zanchius put it in his own statement of faith in 1599, the need for published confessions at the turn of the century stemmed less from a clear image of the one 'true church' than from the 'great rent of this bodie into diver shivers, namely of all those which professe and call upon Christ as true God and true man'.[29]

A useful point of comparison, here, can be found in the work of John Bale, whose own confession of faith in the 1540s reveals both a paradigmatic example and limit of the vocabulary of confession above. While Bale's *Image of Both Churches* neatly articulated the apocalyptic conception of the Church echoed by Hooper, Foxe, and – centuries later – Foucault, Bale was also responsible for a little-known apology published shortly thereafter that offers a more unsettled picture of confessional identity in Tudor England: *A bryefe and plaine declaracion of certayne sentences in this litle boke folowing to satisfie the consciences of them that haue iudged me thereby to be a fauorer of the Anabaptistes* (1547), printed anonymously under the name 'I.B'. As Thomas Betteridge and Oliver Wort have observed, Bale's tract was a strange confession, at best.[30] It offered a written defense of its author against charges of Anabaptist sympathies (sympathies not entirely immune from Bale's own reformist fervor of the 1540s) and a rehearsal of *sola scriptura* against the doctrine of re-baptism that ought, by all measures, to have assured the confessional purity of its subject. And yet *A bryefe and plaine declaracion* also offered an anxious set of instructions about the status of creeds themselves, vexed by a Henrician England increasingly divided no longer between two 'images', Protestant or Catholic, but also Anabaptists, libertines, and, perhaps, others. Amidst 'so manye and divers faythes', Bale's preface warns its evangelical readers,

> it is therfore very necessarye that we praye the lorde with all dilygence for a ryght vnderstandyng of his godly worde, and for a sure vnmouable fayth for euermor. *Also it is not vnnecessarye yt they beare theyr beliefe, conteyned in wrytynge alwayes about them*, and dayly rede it partly to the exhorting and confortyng of them in all persecution and tribulacions, which may come vnto them by goddes worde.[31]

That '*they beare theyr beliefe, conteyned in wrytynge alwayes about them*': the instruction captures, perhaps better than any other sixteenth-century confession, the Foucauldian dilemma of the *publicatio sui*. In reading Bale's advice to publish one's faith for reading – and surveillance – we encounter a kind of primal scene of English confessional history, a moment when the inner workings of a 'ritual of discourse in which the speaking subject becomes a subject of the statement' begin to surface.[32] And yet the very need to write down and carry about one's creed also suggests another sixteenth-century trajectory, for it suggests a version of confessional affiliation whose complexity cannot be fully described by the image or hermeneutics of a subject alone. In an age increasingly defined not by one or two but rather three (or more) Churches, doctrinal confession appears less like an interpretive matter of heart and mouth and more – to borrow the language of William Sherman – like a matter of use.[33]

What happens when the divided Church re-announces itself in the late sixteenth century, rendered visible not by an image of truth or falsehood but by the need to negotiate its instantiation among many – to 'Seek true religion', as *Satyre III* puts it, among Rome, Geneva, England, and Wittenberg, a 'Gregory', a 'Harry', or 'Martin' (lines 95–7)? This ecclesial situation, I suggest, requires a fold, or twist, in the application of Foucault's account of confession to the period, and with it, the disciplinary valence of confession. In his 1981 biography, John Carey reduced Donne's lines to the repressive hypothesis of 'apostasy' and 'ambition', finding in them an inaugural moment of the authorial subject when the young poet's confession of Catholic nobility or Protestant 'apostasy' became displaced by professional and literary aspiration.[34] Roughly twenty years after consigning his satires to the dustbin of 'fear', however, Donne revisited those same lines in a sermon of December 19, 1619 at The Hague in which 'true religion' looks almost nothing like the interpretive or disciplinary vagaries of a 'hermeneutics of the subject':

> Christ loves not singularity; he called not one alone; He loves not schisme neither between them whom he cals; and therefor he cals persons likely to agree, two brethren .... The principall fraternity and brotherhood that God respects, is spirituall; Brethren *in the profession of the same true Religion* .... And that God loves; that *a naturall, a secular, a civill fraternity, and a spirituall fraternity should be joyned together; when those that professe the same Religion*, should desire to contract their alliances, in marrying their Children, and to have their other dealings in the world (as much as they can) with men that professe the same true Religion.[35]

Preaching on Christ's calling of the apostles Peter and Andrew at the Sea of Galilee, Donne's later sermon is remarkable for the unflinching candor with which it addresses the necessary correlation between the confessional and professional life. We must avoid 'schism' and pursue 'fraternity', it declares, but only by a 'profession of the *same true Religion*'. We must even fashion all our alliances around that one profession, though on the basis of 'a naturall, a secular, a civill ... a spirituall' joining together of our confessional identity with our 'dealings in the world' (as much as we can). Like the carrying about of Bale's creed, the profession of faith assumes, in these lines, a perambulatory, communal, even utilitarian function that seems to complicate Foucault's critique of confession, not by transcending it but re-imagining it. Donne recognizes in the late Reformation world a version of confession that has shifted from an image of the invisible stirrings of the subject to the cares and dealings of a visibly divided Church.

The fecundity of true religion

This view of confession as a form of care rather than subjection anticipates what Michel Foucault terms in his later lectures at the Collège de France

(1981–82) and the final volume of *The History of Sexuality* (1984) the *epimeleia heauteau*, or care of the self, an extension of Foucault's evolving study over the early 1980s of the technologies of the self. In what follows, I turn briefly to Donne's remarks at The Hague in order to consider his explicit references to such 'care' – which Donne finds prefigured in the spiritual and vocational 'nets' of the apostolic fishermen in Matthew's gospel – as well as the theology of the confessionalized Church on which it is based. In his 2003 book, Graham Ward aligns the third satire's interest in 'true religion' with the privatization and globalization of the modern liberal subject at stake in Foucault's earlier critique.[36] Careful attention to The Hague sermon reveals, I believe, an opposite movement: for Donne, the 'fecundity' in true religion emerges precisely in the local, if illiberal, demands confession places on the self in the 'natural', 'spiritual', and 'civil' life of the divided Body of Christ.

These demands figured prominently in the Hague sermon's audience and occasion. Hastily delivered at the end of Lord Doncaster's ambassadorial trip through the Palatinate and Northern Europe, Donne's December 1619 address followed closely on the heels of the conclusion of the Synod of Dort, yielding a text he would only later compile from 'short notes' in 1630, during 'my sickness at Abrey-hatch'. The 'Haghe' sermon thus bears the signs of at least two, conflicting, confessional moments: the private gathering of Donne's Dutch and English Reformed auditors, at the chapel where the decapitated remains of the Remonstrant leader Oldenbarnevelt had been laid to rest only months earlier; and the increasingly politicized, Arminian climate of court preaching under Charles and the rise of Laud.[37] The Hague sermon thus constitutes a disciplinary record of a very peculiar kind. It is a footnote to 'the first prolonged confrontation of English Calvinists with their continental co-religionists', yet whose thinking about confession cannot, itself, be reduced to any one political or ecclesiastical ideal.[38]

Donne's 1619 sermon radically revises instead the ecclesial vision on which such a disciplinary account of Church or creed rests in the first place. From the opening lines of the *exordium*, Donne signals this theology of the Church by reading Christ's command to Peter and Andrew to 'follow me' (*sequere me*) as a biblical type, not for one true profession, but for profession in a time of schism:

> And then, in a nearer consideration of these persons, we find that they were *two* that were called; Christ provided at first against singularity, He called not one alone; And then they were *two Brethren*, persons likely to agree; He provided at first against schisme; … And in Andrews thus early applying himself to Christ, we are also to note both the fecundity of true Religion; for, as soone as he had found Christ, he sought his brother *Peter*, *Et duxit ad Iesum*, he made is brother as happy as himself, he led him to Jesus.[39]

As it appears here in the first of Donne's two revised parts published in *LXXX Sermons* (1640), the *exordium* invites Donne's listeners to hear in Christ's calling the echoes of his earlier, unpublished satire, in which the search for 'true religion' has now become a question of applying one's self to its 'fecundity'. Focusing on the biblical fishermen's leaving their nets to follow Christ, Donne plays, in part, with the fraught analogies between calling, vocation, and religious and earthly profession. He also elaborates therein a theology of the divided Church, locating in Matthew 4 an apostolic succession rooted in multiplicity, rather than 'singularity'. In the calling of two rather than one disciple, Matthew's gospel offers us a model for the way Christ 'collects the materials, the living stone, and timber, for his Militant Church', the component parts of the historical, rather than the 'Triumphant', Body of Christ.[40] It is a theme, according to Gale Carrithers and James Hardy, that affords Donne a sharp contrast to the view of the Church based on the longing for a turn or return to fairer mistresses: 'Donne was at some pains here to define his understanding of a Godly *congregatio* ... indeed, the definition of community as he understood the Bible to express it was a fundamental goal of this double sermon.'[41]

Donne's theology of the Church at the heart of this account of Christian community takes two forms over the middle half of the Hague sermon. On one hand, Donne insists on the universality of the Body of Christ in the wake of the Dordrecht negotiations over the reformed creed by dwelling upon his preferred ecclesiological terms of 'unity' and 'singularity'.[42] Christ's calling of two 'fishers', he warns, ought to prevent us from the 'singularity' of 'being seduced to that Church that is in one man'. Donne has in mind both the wearisome repetition of any one article of faith – including the reformed doctrines of election and reprobation – as well as any Church that derives its identity from one man, be it reformed Arminianism or even papal Rome.[43] This agenda is clearly aimed at the corrosive effects of doctrinal labels and articles themselves. Yet Donne is careful to warn that even such an insistence on Christian 'unity' can prove laudable and reprehensible: 'And since the Church cannot be in one, in an unity, take heed of bringing it too neare that unity, to a paucity, to a few, to a separation, to a Conventicle.'[44] For Donne, the nature of the visible Church is instead a 'Meeting, an assembly', by which it assumes a more 'harmonious name': 'Love thou those things wherein she is Catholique, and wherein she is harmonious .... Those universall, and fundamental doctrines, which in all Christian ages, and in all Christian Churches, have been agreed by all to be necessary to salvation.'[45] As Jeanne Shami argues, Donne's rhetoric as preacher can be safely described in such moments as one of 'moderation', 'tactically *inclusive* rather than *exclusive*' by limiting the grounds of participation in the Church to matters *de necessitatis salutis*, rather than matters of indifference, controversy, or debate.[46]

And yet The Hague sermon, at its centerpiece, does not shy away from such matters, going on to offer another, competing description of the divided Church that proves remarkably less moderate or indifferent. In explaining the ideas of 'profession' and 'fraternity' cited at the end of section one above, Donne shifts abruptly from the unity of names in the Body of Christ to a different language for the one and many – the local, or civic, community:

> Christ loves not singularity; he called not one alone; He loves not schisme neither between them whom he cals; and therefor he cals persons likely to agree, two brethren .... [W]e doe not make it an equall, an indifferent thing, whether we marry our selves, or our children, or make our bargaines, or our conversation, with persons of a different Religion, when as our Adversaries amongst us will not goe to a Lawyer, nor call a Physitian, no, nor scarce a Taylor, or other Tradesman of another Religion than their owne, if they can possibly avoid it. God saw a better likelihood of avoyding Schisme and dissention, when those whom hee called to a new spiritual brotherhood in one Religion, were naturall brothers too, and tied in civill bands, as well as spirituall.[47]

Two things are worth noting in this complex passage. First, Donne replaces the language of the father alluded to in *Satyre III* and *The State of Christendom* with the language of 'brotherhood', or fraternity, substituting the nostalgic longing for an earlier age of religious presence prior to the confessional age with the 'spirituall' and 'civill bands' of a 'brotherhood in one Religion'. Second, and perhaps more significantly, Donne associates this fraternity with a novel vision of how to profess *one* faith or creed while nevertheless negotiating many. To profess one's faith, he observes, is *not* 'an indifferent thing', or *adiaphora*. It is a necessary condition of participation in the visible Church, a remarkably illiberal view of confession tempered by the remarkably voluntaristic description of one's 'professing' as a kind vigilance one shows over one's household, vocation, and faith, and even that of one's 'Taylor', 'Physitian', 'Lawyer', or 'Tradesmen'. In so doing, Donne resituates Christian vocation and confession from the apocalyptic choice between the spiritual and earthly *civitate*: 'The two elements of call were not to be distinguished but rather combined', Carrithers and Hardy note, 'into a continuing profession of faith that was to be lived rather than merely asserted.'[48] Donne resituates the profession of faith, that is, as a form of life.

In his lectures at the Collège de France, Michel Foucault described this form of life as a precursor to the technology of the modern confession. As he surveys it in ancient Stoic and Christian thought, the 'care of the self' constitutes a kind of pre-history to the hermeneutics of the subject, a continuum in the Western construction of the self as a source for reflection or work (*askesis*).[49] Marcus Aurelius and Epictetus here offer exemplary versions of the self for Foucault, in ways not dissimilar to the Christian dictates of Romans 10 or Bale's *Bryefe and plaine declaracion*: each explores a version of the self inextricably tied to the representation and negotiation of dogmatic truths, and each derives from that exploration a concern or obligation to be professed. The difference for Foucault is the 'care' by which that negotiation took place for the ancient self. If late-medieval and early Reformation Christian confession operates by a process of hermeneutic subjection – by inquiring 'concerning the deep origin of the idea that presents itself' and interpreting the 'meaning hidden beneath the visible representation' – the *epimeleia heauteau* considered doctrine and dogma as relation.[50] Such a relation can best be seen for Foucault in the ancient practice of the 'stroll-exercise' recommended by Epictetus, which articulated a discursive space less like the scaffold or torture chamber, and more like Donne's image of professional life among lawyers, tradesman, physicians, and tailors, or one's daughter, conversation, and marriage: a space in 'which the examination of the thing must focus on its relationship to man as citizen … it must define the object's utility for man as citizen of this particular country, as belonging to this particular town, as member of this particular community, as father of a family, and so on'.[51]

Donne explicitly adopts this same language of 'care' in the closing passages of the first half of the 1619 Hague sermon. Where Bale's *Bryefe and plaine declaracion* recommended tucking one's confession into one's pocket – in fear and trembling of the invisible Church and its persecutions to come – Donne finds in Peter and Andrew's leaving of their nets at the Sea of Galilee a model of the confessional and professional life in the visible Church as relation, rather than discipline. The two apostles returned to their fishing nets before and after Christ's death, Donne surmises, taking up and putting down their worldly 'cares' in a manner that reflects all human acts of professing, doctrinal or vocational, in the visible realm:

> [Peter and Andrew] did not therefore abandon and leave all care, and all government of their own estate, and dispose themselves to live after upon the sweat of others; … Not to be diligent towards the world, is the diligence that God requires. *S. Augustine* does not say, *sua relinquere*, but *sua imperfecta relinquere*, That God requires we should leave the world, but that we should leave it to second considerations.[52]

'It is not', Donne reiterates, 'an absolute leaving of all worldly cares, but a leaving them out of the first consideration.'[53] For Donne, confessional identity is just such a form of 'care'. It is a 'second' or 'third consideration', a net of human 'dealings' and affections commensurate with the 'fraternity' and 'fecundity' of the divided Church. The profession of faith, that is, becomes amenable to what Jeanne Shami identifies as the principle of Donnean 'discretion': 'the active and strenuous principle that acts as the complement, perhaps even as the corrective to obedience' in Donne's preaching.[54] It is the same *discretio* that the final volume of *The History of Sexuality* locates in the Stoic practice of testing or examining the 'first arrival', the practice not of refusing all dogmatic truths but of subordinating them to the self-care of second, third, and fourth considerations.[55]

Ample scholarship has been devoted here to Donne's relationship to the Stoic tradition, yet I want to underscore a much narrower point: that Donne's conception of the 'fecundity' and 'fraternity' of the Church re-imagines doctrinal confession as itself an authentic motive, or source of care, in early modern English writing.[56] The choice of 'Taylor', 'Physician', 'Tradesmen', and 'Doctor' as Donne's primary analogy for the professing Church proves especially illuminating in this regard. The civic metaphor for ecclesial division eschews the mimetic and apocalyptic logic of the 'two churches' in the Tudor tradition, elaborating instead what Donne's 1609 letter to Wotton suggested as another, alternate model for the confessionalized Body of Christ:

> Sir, not only a mathematic point, which is the most indivisible and unique thing which art can present, flows into every line which is derived from the centre, but our soul, which is but one, hath swallowed up a negative and feeling soul which was in the body before it came and exercises those faculties yet. *And God himself, who only is one, seems to have been eternally delighted with a disunion of persons.* They whose active function it is must endeavour this unity in religion, and we at our lay altars (which are our tables or bedside or stools, wheresoever we dare prostrate ourselves to God in prayer) must beg it of him. *But we must take heed of making misconclusions upon the want of it.* For whether the mayor and aldermen fall out (as with us and the Puritans – bishops against priests) or the commoners' voices differ who is mayor and who aldermen or what their jurisdiction (as with the Bishop of Rome, or whosoever), yet it is still one corporation.[57]

Though the young Donne could praise Wotton for stoically gliding like a fish through the streams of European 'schism', his analogy here of the local affairs of mayors and aldermen regards Christian division as itself a source for negotiation and engagement. Even the Trinity, Donne observes, expresses a certain 'delight' in the 'disunion' of the Father, Son, and Holy Spirit; so, likewise, the natural, secular, civil, and spiritual fraternity of the local commonwealth ought to warn us against drawing 'misconclusions' about the loss of such easy ways and near in the deferred hope of Christian re-unification.[58] As Gregory Kneidel has shown, this loosening of the language of the father is reflected in Donne's intimate knowledge of English civil law as early as *Satyre II*, which critiques the loosening legal ties between fathers and '*ses heires*' amidst Tudor statutes governing familial lands. As Kneidel argues, the second satire resists the feudal and paternal nostalgia that sought to mask such civil controversies in the 1590s under the unifying fiction of English common law or religion. For Donne, the civic space of law and religion instead articulated a more uncomfortable divide in late Tudor and early Stuart England: his satires leave us somewhere between the 'ideological mists of ancient feudalism' and modern liberalism's fantasy of individual autonomy.[59]

Just so, Donne's conception of the 'natural', 'secular', 'civil' and 'spiritual fraternity' in his 1619 Hague sermon reveals an equally liminal yet forward-looking relationship between confessional and professional life in late Reformation England that more than nods to his earlier *Satyre III*. The 'fecundity of true religion' articulates in positive terms a civic and social function of doctrinal confession implicit in the querulous 'Seek true religion. O where?' As Lawrence Manley observes, the third satirist's alienation among 'Mirreus', 'Crants', 'Graius', 'Phrygius', and 'Graccus' in the middle of Donne's poem suggestively places his lament over the confessionalized Church within an auspicious example of the type-series in English formal verse satire, whose structural equivalent elsewhere includes the train of 'Captaine', 'velvet Justice', and 'brisk-perfum'd piert Courtier' that ruptures the 'cities mistique bodie' of Donne's *Satyre I*.[60] Such type-series, Manley argues, do more than register 'kind scorn' or 'brave pitty'. They convey a certain pattern of *haecceity* in the *Satyres*, a pattern of alienation and engagement that situates the poetic self not between an ideal image of the Body of Christ or its subversion but among multiple alternatives – 'here' and 'there', between 'this' or 'that'.[61] More than faint echoes of this pattern survive in The Hague sermon's analogy of professional and confessional life as a matter of negotiating *this* Taylor or *that* Doctor, the Tradesman *here* or the Merchant *there*. If confession had indeed become an imperative for Donne's English and Dutch auditors following the Synod of Dort, it was not, so the Hague sermon implies, as a disciplinary subjection to one or another polemical ideal, but as a form of what Foucault labels a 'stylistics of existence'. Donne finds in the divided Church an art of living in which creeds and confessions, like vocations, have come to shape the individual's relationship to a multiplicity of doctrines and practices.[62]

In a recent revaluation of Foucault, Peter Sloterdijk groups this 'stylistics of existence' with a potential turn in the wake of the turn to religion, from the ephemerality of religious belief or its theo-political constitution to the practice of the exercise, or 'training'. As Sloterdijk puts it, we might just as well replace the 'false dichotomy of believers and unbelievers' with 'the distinction between the practicing and the untrained, or those who train differently'.[63] My purpose here has been to show that, as early as 1619, Donne can be seen giving theoretical expression to confessional identity as a similar form of care, training, or exercise, in ways that both anticipate and resist the undercurrents in Foucault's reception that have informed these turns and returns in literary history. Donne's Hague sermon recognized that any such account of doctrinal confession must first be rooted in an account of the divided Church in the late

Reformation and of the intellectual pressures its confessionalization posed for early modern imaginative life. It also recognized, however, that those pressures availed a style, or form, of faith rooted in almost perpetual labor or struggle. As Donne's sermon characterized the occupational hazards of the Church's first two fishermen, Peter and Andrew, 'wee must make account to meet stormes in our professon', for the cares of profession, doctrinal or otherwise, had become by 1619 indeed cares, not easily disciplined or liberated in the hearts of early modern Europe. Even so, 'A man must not leave his calling', Donne added, 'he must labour to overcome those difficulties, and as much as he can, vindicate and redeeme that calling from those aspersions and calumnies, which ill men have cast upon a good calling.'[64] For Donne, as for the later Foucault, it is the work, or *askesis*, of defining the demands of the confessional life that renders it a meaningful imperative for early modern English writers, as well as their critics.

Notes

1 Included here among Michel Foucault's later works on the technologies of the self, chiefly from the years 1980 to 1984, are: 'About the Beginning of the Hermeneutics of the Self: Two Lectures at Dartmouth', reprinted as 'Subjectivity and Truth' and 'Christianity and Confession', in S. Lothringer (ed.), *The Politics of Truth*, trans. L. Hochroth and C. Porter (Los Angeles: Semiotext(e), 1997), pp. 147–91; *The Hermeneutics of the Subject: Lectures at the Collège de France, 1981–1982*, trans. G. Burchell (New York: Palgrave Macmillan, 2001); and *The Care of the Self*, vol. 3 of *The History of Sexuality*, trans. Robert Hurley (New York: Pantheon, 1986). On the self, confession, and the problem of defining 'later' Foucault, see C. Koopman, 'The Formation and Self-Transformation of the Subject in Foucault's Ethics', in C. Falzon, T. O'Leary, and J. Sawicki (eds), *A Companion to Foucault* (Oxford: Wiley-Blackwell, 2013), pp. 526–43, and Judith Butler, *Giving an Account of Oneself* (New York: Fordham University Press, 2005), pp. 111–36.

2 On the 'creedal imperative' in the Christian tradition, see J. Pelikan, *Credo: Historical and Theological Guide to Creeds and Confessions of Faith in the Christian Tradition* (New Haven: Yale University Press, 2003), p. 35.

3 John Donne, *The Sermons of John Donne*, ed. George R. Potter and Evelyn Simpson, 10 vols (Berkeley and Los Angeles: University of California Press, 1953–62), vol. 2: p. 271. On the reformed context of the 1619 Hague sermon, see P. R. Sellin, *John Donne and 'Calvinist' Views of Grace* (Amsterdam: VU Boekhandel, 1983), and *So Doth, So Is Religion: John Donne and the Diplomatic Contexts in the Reformed Netherlands, 1619–1620* (Columbia: University of Missouri Press, 1988). The sermon appears in two parts in the *LXXX Sermons* (1640) under the heading, 'At the *Haghe* Decemb. 19. 1619. I Preached upon this Text. Since in my sicknesse at *Abrey-hatche* in Essex, 1630, revising my short notes of that Sermon, I digested them into these two.' The most sustained treatment of the sermon to date is G. H. Carrithers and J. D. Hardy, '"Not upon a lecture, but upon a sermon": Devotional Dynamics

of the Donnean Fisher of Men', in M. Arshagouni Papazian (ed.), *John Donne and the Protestant Reformation: New Perspectives* (Detroit: Wayne State University Press, 2000), pp. 335–59.

4 Foucault, *The Care of the Self*, p. 71.

5 See, e.g., T. Betteridge, *Literature and Politics in the English Reformation* (Manchester: Manchester University Press, 2004), pp. 1–43; A. Walsham, *Charitable Hatred: Tolerance and Intolerance in England, 1500–1700* (Manchester: Manchester University Press, 2006); P. Iver Koffman, 'Reconstructing the Case for Confessionalisation in Late Tudor England: Perceptions of Reception, Then and Now', in J. M. Headley (ed.), *Confessionalisation in Europe, 1555–1700: Essays in Honor and Memory of Bodo Nischan* (Aldershot: Ashgate, 2004), pp. 275–88. As Betteridge notes, early scholars of confessionalization, such as R. Po-Chia Hsia, described a model of social discipline and state formation that the Henrician supremacy, in its remarkable inefficiency, could never match. For a summary of the historiographical debate, see E. Shagan, 'Can Historians End the Reformation?', *Archiv für Reformationgeschichte*, 97 (2006), 298–306, who notes the rise of a 'new confessional historiography that is suspiciously close to modern liberal ecumenism' (p. 302).

6 J. Knapp, *Shakespeare's Tribe: Church, Nation, and Theatre in Renaissance England* (Chicago: University of Chicago Press, 2002); R. Stillman, *Phillip Sidney and the Poetics of Renaissance Cosmopolitanism* (Burlington, VT: Ashgate, 2008). See also J. Crawford, 'Reconsidering Early Modern Women's Reading, or, How Margaret Hoby Read Her de Mornay', *Huntington Library Quarterly*, 73:2 (2010), 193–223.

7 B. Conti, *Confessions of Faith in Early Modern England* (Philadelphia: University of Pennsylvania Press, 2014), pp. 7, 22.

8 K. Jackson and A. Marotti, 'Introduction', in K. Jackson and A. Marotti (eds), *Shakespeare and Religion: Early Modern and Postmodern Perspectives* (Notre Dame, IN: Notre Dame University Press, 2011), p. 9; E. Fernie, 'Introduction: Shakespeare, Spirituality, and Contemporary Criticism', in E. Fernie (ed.), *Spiritual Shakespeares* (New York and London: Routledge, 2005), pp. 9–10.

9 See P. Lake with M. C. Questier, *The Antichrist's Lewd Hat: Protestants, Papists, and Players in Post-Reformation England* (New Haven: Yale University Press, 2002), pp. 229–33, who build upon Foucault in arguing that the public spectacle of the gallows or scaffold confession served the function of confessionalization in the Tudor and Stuart state.

10 Michel Foucault, *The History of Sexuality, Volume 1, An Introduction*, trans. R. Hurley (New York: Vintage, 1990), p. 7.

11 John Donne, *Satyre III*, in *The Satires, Epigrams, and Verse Letters*, ed. Wesley Milgate (Oxford: Oxford University Press, 1967), lines 26–7. All references to Donne's satires are to this edition.

12 *The State of Christendom: or, A most exact and curious discovery of many secret passages and hidden mysteries of the times* (London, 1657), p. 6 (italics in original). *The State of Christendom*, manuscripts of which date *c.* 1594–95, was traditionally attributed to Donne's close friend, Henry Wotton, yet has since been convincingly attributed to the wider Essex circle (perhaps Anthony Bacon), with which

Donne was also affiliated. See D. Flynn, 'Donne, Henry Wotton, and the Earl of Essex', *John Donne Journal*, 14 (1995), 185–218, and A. Gajda, '*The State of Christendom*: History, Political Thought, and the Essex Circle', *Historical Research*, 81:213 (2008), 423–46.

13 Martin Heidegger, 'Science and Reflection', in *The Question Concerning Technology and Other Essays*, trans. W. Lovitt (New York: Harper and Row, 1977), pp. 155–82.

14 Andrew Maunsell, *The First Part of the Catalogue of English printed Bookes: Which concerneth such matters of Divinitie, as have bin either written in our owne Tongue, or translated out of anie other language: And have bin published, to the glory of God, and edification of the Church of Christ in England* (London, 1595), pp. 37–8.

15 Thomas Rogers, *The English Creede: Consenting with the True Auncient Catholique, and apostolique Church in all the points, and articles of Religion which everie Christian is to knowe and beleeve that would be saved* (London, 1585) (published in two parts); and Francois Salvart *et al.*, *Harmonia confessionum fidei* (Geneva, 1581). On the *Harmonia confessionum fidei* in England, see J. M. Dodson, 'Affirming Something: Sidney's *Defence* and the (Dis)harmony of the Confessions', *Sidney Journal*, 32:1 (2014): 39–67.

16 See M. T. Hester, '"Ask thy father": Re-reading Donne's *Satyre III*', *Ben Jonson Journal*, 1 (1994), 208; R. Strier, 'Radical Donne: *Satire III*', *English Literary History*, 60:2 (1993), 284–6, 292.

17 Donne, *Satyre III*, line 1.

18 Michel Foucault, 'Christianity and Confession', in Lothringer (ed.), *The Politics of Truth*, p. 171.

19 S. Greenblatt, *Renaissance Self-Fashioning: From More to Shakespeare* (Chicago: University of Chicago Press, 1980), p. 80.

20 Michel Foucault, *Discipline and Punish: The Birth of the Prison*, trans. A. Sheridan (New York: Vintage, 1979), pp. 37–40, 198.

21 Foucault, *The History of Sexuality*, pp. 7–8, 56.

22 See J. Carrette, 'Foucault, Religion, and Pastoral Power', in Falzon *et al.* (eds), *A Companion to Foucault*, pp. 368–83: 'This distinction is in line with Foucault's earlier model of religious power in *Discipline and Punish* and it contains the same tension in holding together a "detailed" technology and an "infinite"; religious power is both a "terrestrial power" and one "directed toward the world beyond." The "infinite," or transcendent, horizon provides a political leverage outside of history to motivate action in history' (pp. 375–6).

23 See, e.g., John Northbrooke, *A breefe and pithie summe of the Christian faith, made in forme of a Confession* (London, 1571; repr. 1582), and Henry Balnaves, *The confession of faith, conteining how the troubled man should seeke refuge at his God* (Edinburgh, 1584).

24 John Hooper, *Whether Christian faith maye be kepte secret in the heart, without confession thereof openly to the worlde as occasion shal serve* (Roane, 1553), sig. A2[r–v].

25 Foucault, *The Hermeneutics of the Subject*, p. 300.

26 See, e.g., J. Parker, 'Faustus, Confession, and the Sins of Omission', *English Literary History*, 80:1 (Spring 2013), 29–59, which equates the de-sacralization of penitential confession with the subversive power of the post-medieval stage: 'Confession

[like theatre] also provided a model for the extravagant indulgence in transgression, via mimesis, whose official result, morally speaking, was a renewal of innocence' (p. 31).

27 Foucault, 'Christianity and Confession', p. 176 (italics in original).

28 John Bale, *The image of bothe churches* (London, 1548), sigs. A2[r]–A3[r]. On the doctrine of the 'two churches' in English millenarian thought, see R. Bauckham's classic study *Tudor Apocalypse* (Abingdon: Sutton Courtenay Press, 1978), pp. 60–75.

29 Jerome Zanchius, *H. Zanchius his Confession of Christian Religion* (Cambridge, 1599), p. 5.

30 See T. Betteridge, *Tudor Histories of the English Reformations, 1530–83* (Aldershot: Ashgate, 1999), pp. 88–91, and O. Wort, *John Bale and Religious Conversion in Reformation England* (London: Pickering & Chatto, 2013).

31 John Bale [?], *A bryefe and plaine declaracion of certayne sentences in this litle boke folowing to satisfie the consciences of them that haue iudged me thereby to be a fauorer of the Anabaptistes* (1547), sigs. A1[v]–A2[r] (italics in original).

32 Foucault, *History of Sexuality*, p. 61.

33 W. Sherman, *Used Books: Marking Readers in Renaissance England* (Philadelphia: University of Philadelphia Press, 2008), p. xii.

34 J. Carey, *John Donne: Life, Mind, and Art* (New York: Oxford University Press, 1981), pp. 29–30.

35 Donne, *Sermons*, vol. 2: pp. 280–1 (my emphasis). All subsequent references to Donne's Hague sermon are cited parenthetically.

36 See Graham Ward, *True Religion* (Oxford: Wiley-Blackwell, 2003), pp. 42–5, 80.

37 See Sellin, *John Donne and 'Calvinist' Views of Grace*, pp. 5–15, and Sellin, *So Doth, So Is Religion*, pp. 109–14; and David Colclough (ed.), *The Oxford Edition of the Sermons of John Donne*, vol. 3, *Sermons Preached at the Court of Charles I* (Oxford: Oxford University Press, 2013), pp. xxxvi–xli. Sellin reads The Hague sermon throughout as a rigorous defense of Reformed soteriology, which informs his position on the dating of *Satyre III* (see Paul R. Sellin, 'The Proper Dating of John Donne's *Satyre III*', *Huntington Library Quarterly*, 43:4 (1980), 275–312).

38 Anthony Milton, *Catholic and Reformed: The Roman and Protestant Churches in English Protestant Thought 1600–1640* (Cambridge: Cambridge University Press, 1995), p. 421.

39 Donne, *Sermons*, p. 271 (italics in original).

40 *Ibid.*, p. 270.

41 Carrithers and Hardy, '"Not upon a lecture"', pp. 338–9.

42 See J. Johnson's definitive discussion of Donne's conception of 'unity' and 'singularity' in *The Theology of John Donne* (Cambridge: D. S. Brewer, 1999), pp. 32–6.

43 Donne, *Sermons*, p. 279.

44 *Ibid.*, p. 280.

45 *Ibid.*

46 J. Shami, 'Labels, Controversy, and the Language of Inclusion in Donne's Sermons', in D. Colclough (ed.), *John Donne's Professional Lives* (Cambridge: D. S. Brewer, 2003), p. 145.

47 Donne, *Sermons*, p. 281.

48 Carrithers and Hardy, '"Not upon a lecture"', p. 342.

49 See Foucault, *The Hermeneutics of the Subject*, pp. 14–16 (January 6, 1982, Lecture 2). See also M. G. E. Kelly, 'Foucault, Subjectivity, and Technologies of the Self', in Falzon *et al.* (eds), *A Companion to Foucault*, pp. 510–25; A. I. Davidson, 'Ethics as Ascetics: Foucault, the History of Ethics, and Ancient Thought', in G. Gutting (ed.), *The Cambridge Companion to Foucault* (Cambridge: Cambridge University Press, 1994), pp. 119–26; and Butler, *Giving an Account of Oneself*, pp. 112–13. While Butler reads Foucault's later work as 'reversing' his earlier critique of confession, Kelly, Davidson, and Koopman see it as a continuous but distinct re-framing of the self, rather than the subject.

50 Foucault, *The Care of the Self*, p. 64.

51 Foucault, *The Hermeneutics of the Subject*, p. 298. See also pp. 117–18 (January 20, 1982, Lecture 2), where Foucault stresses the fundamentally sectarian nature of this kind of 'care of the self': 'If you like, you cannot take care of the self in the realm and form of the universal.' For a similar version of the confessional life as regulated 'form' that cannot be reduced to the biopolitical force of law, see Giorgio Agamben, *The Highest Poverty: Monastic Rules and Form-of-Life*, trans. A. Kotsko (Stanford: Stanford University Press, 2013).

52 Donne, *Sermons*, p. 284 (italics in original).

53 *Ibid.*

54 J. Shami, *John Donne and Conformity in Crisis in the Late Jacobean Pulpit* (Woodbridge: D. S. Brewer, 2003), p. 23.

55 Foucault, *The Care of the Self*, pp. 63–4.

56 On Donne's Stoicism, see, e.g., J. Scodel, 'The Medium is the Message: Donne's *Satyre III* and "To Sir Henry Wotton" (Sir, more than kisses) and the Ideologies of the Mean', *Modern Philology*, 90:4 (1993), 479–511; and D. Norbrook, 'The Monarchy of Wit and the Republic of Letters', in E. D. Harvey and K. Eisaman Maus (eds), *Soliciting Interpretation: Literary Theory and Seventeenth-Century English Poetry* (Chicago: University of Chicago Press, 1990), p. 11.

57 John Donne, *Selected Letters*, ed. P. M. Oliver (New York: Routledge, 2002), p. 47 (italics in original). Oliver dates this letter, not contained in the 1651 *Letters*, to the spring or summer of 1609.

58 On Donne's conception of plurality in the Godhead, see D. Nichols, 'The Political Theology of John Donne', *Theological Studies*, 49:1 (1988), 45–66, at 53–4; see also Johnson, *The Theology of John Donne*, pp. 2–36, who emphasizes the 'communal' nature of the Trinity as Donne's model for unity.

59 G. Kneidel, 'Coscus, Queen Elizabeth, and Law in John Donne's *Satyre I*', *Renaissance Quarterly*, 61 (2008), 92–121, at pp. 92, 97–8, 106.

60 Donne, *Satyre I*, in *Sermons*, lines 8, 1–24.

61 L. Manley, *Literature and Culture in Early Modern England* (Cambridge: Cambridge University Press, 1995), pp. 380–1. In medieval philosophy, the *haecceity*, or 'thisness', of individuals and things in the created realm reflects a fundamental principle of individuation in the Godhead: that the persons of the Trinity retain an irreducible singularity (*haecceity*) without their essential unity (*quiddity*) being reduced to the merely formal, or qualitative, relationship between subjects. On the 'thisness'

of Donnean wit, see also J. B. Leishman, *The Monarch of Wit: An Analytical and Comparative Study of the Poetry of John Donne* (New York: Hutchinson, 1951).
62 Foucault, *The Care of the Self*, p. 71.
63 P. Sloterdijk, *You Must Change Your Life: On Anthropotechnics*, trans. W. Hoban (Cambridge: Polity, 2013), pp. 3–6, 148–59.
64 Donne, *Sermons*, p. 278.

Afterword

Reformed indifferently

Richard Wilson

When the Prince of Denmark condemns the type of actor who, he complains, has neither 'the accent of Christians nor the gait of Christian' ('not to speak it profanely'), the 'tragedian of the city' gives a cagey riposte that appears to epitomize the mediation of religious conflict by literary and theatrical forms in early modern England: 'I hope we have reformed that indifferently with us, sir'. Hamlet's dogmatic persistence, 'O, reform it altogether' (*Hamlet*, 2.2.316; 3.2.27–34),[1] is one of the points at which the fanatic Dane diverges most from his creator. For all this coercive zeal at a northern court over a (presumably Lutheran) cultural reformation reminds us how, as the historian Eamon Duffy comments, 'If we cannot quite be sure that Shakespeare was a Catholic, it becomes clearer and clearer that he must have struck contemporaries as a most unsatisfactory Protestant.'[2]

There is a formal *indifference* in Shakespeare's literary and theatrical response to the Reformation that has seemed to many of his admirers to anticipate the disinterestedness of a later Kantian aesthetic, but that more doctrinaire commentators have found 'most unsatisfactory', ever since the Puritan Henry Chettle castigated this 'silver-tongued Melicert'[3] for refusing to mourn the 'mortal moon' (Sonnet 107), Queen Elizabeth. Yet from the opposing Counter-Reformation side, the Jesuit priest and poet Robert Southwell is also reported to have chastized his 'worthy good cousin, Master W.S.', for wasting his 'sweetest vein' on pagan 'toys', such as *Venus and Adonis*, instead of composing 'Christian works'.[4] So, 'reformed indifferently' is perhaps the best that could be said, from any religious point of view, of an author responsible for subjecting faith to so much blasphemous and irreverent *deformation*:

> *A watchman* We have here recovered the most dangerous piece of lechery that ever was known in the commonwealth.
> *First watchman* And one Deformed is one of them.
>
> (*Much Ado*, 3.3.145–9)

With *Forms of Faith* we have here recovered some of 'the most dangerous pieces of lechery' that ever were 'known in the commonwealth', and the religiously 'Deformed' writer Shakespeare is among them. For in this book twelve early modern scholars examine how, contrary to the order of the Black Prince, the sacred is profaned by cultural forms in the work of the Shakespearean generation of English writers, and so help us to understand the mediating effect of scenes like the one in *Much Ado About Nothing* when their masters are 'reformed' that the town watch has 'heard talk of one Deformed. They say he wears a key in his ear' (5.1.238–91). The conclusions these essays reach are therefore all new approaches to a familiar narrative, in which cultural *form* and religious *reform* were as closely identified as Shakespeare's constabulary suspects, and the aesthetic emerged as a placeholder for toleration when the Wars of Religion stalled, because, in the words of Hugh Grady, 'it began to appear that art, not any faith, would have to provide a cultural community'.[5]

Once Catholics and Protestants had fought to a standstill, in this account, 'the stage was set for the Enlightenment definition of the aesthetic in a divided but relatively tolerant Europe'.[6] This is the cultural or rhetorical turn Shakespeare takes in his comedy about a King of France on whose edicts of toleration the 'inaudible and noiseless foot of time' steals before he can effect them (*All's Well*, 5.3.43), because they lack mutual consent. For there the dawning realization that, as Sir Edward Sandys predicted in his 1605 *State of Religion* – 'the first call for coexistence in Reformation Europe' – the sheer 'tediousness and weariness' of such a war of the gods must eventuate in a 'tolerable reconciliation' of live-and-let-live, rather than any 'consecrated union', issues in the minimal morality that because 'There's place and means for every man alive' (4.3.316), the best solution to sectarian deadlock will be to convert antagonism to agonism, by *performing* religious conflict as a game:[7]

> Young Chairbonne the puritan and old Poisson the papist, howsome'er their hearts are severed by religion, their heads are both one: they may jowl horns together like any deer i'th'herd. (*All's Well*, 1.3.45–8)

Forms of Faith recounts in a dozen ways the 'tolerable reconciliation' when the puritan and papist were induced to 'jowl horns together' by the work of art, as in each chapter we learn that the work art does in early modern England is to render faith a performance. Aesthetic value inheres precisely in culture's *formalizing* function, in this narrative, as a caesura splitting power from religion, or a third term between the physical presence and metaphysical representation of authority. This slide from a constative to a *performative* understanding of religion is then held to be the 'condition of possibility of the Reformation'.[8] So, as Alexandra M. Block explains, the Enlightenment idea of the aesthetic as a space for neutralizing conflict evolved out of the very controversies that placed the Eucharist at the crux of Christianity's wars. Thus, when

John Donne wrote about his own creative processes, we are told, he did so in terms of the Christian concept of sacramental language, but then synthesized the entire spectrum of Reformation and Counter-Reformation doctrines of the Eucharist, to project 'a kind of artistic ecumenicalism, a subordination of religious difference to the exigencies of art' (cf. p. 187).

In *Forms of Faith* we see how English culture became the medium for separating Church and state by the 'elimination of supernatural agency' from the modern polity, as Spinoza would soon recommend to the good citizens of Amsterdam.[9] To the apostate Donne, a descendant of the Catholic martyr Thomas More, theology would thus dwindle to a mere 'intellectual fruit', Block suggests, 'ripe for plucking in the service of art' (cf. p. 190). Likewise, Christina Wald relates how even Protestant paragons like Philip Sidney and Edmund Spenser recycled the 'mistery of wine' as a 'sacrament prophane', to promote religious pluralism for their own 'aesthetic (and hence never fully determinate) ends' (cf. p. 84). The *Arcadia* 'romances' the Eucharist, Wald therefore concludes, with a symbolic inclusiveness that both radical Protestants and Catholic militants must have found most unsatisfactory. But such fictive recuperations reflected the ambiguity of Anglicanism, and the erratic story of the Church of England, as it evolved into the syncretic form of faith that was graphically described by the late Tony Judt in his chronicle of English compromise:

> This story is more complicated than it sounds. Anglicanism is not Protestantism. The Church of England was and is a weird animal: at its most conservative, it is far more ornate and tradition-bound than its Episcopalian ... brethren in the US. In essence, High Anglicanism was Catholicism without the Pope .... On the other hand, at its low end, the Anglican Church – as embodied in village communities, particularly in ... parts of eastern England, where Catholicism was weakest – can resemble ... Scandinavian Protestantism: under-adorned, its authority vested in a single, often rather gaunt and morally and sartorially restrained pastor ... – Protestantism in all but name.[10]

'This was above all an *English* church', Judt reminded his perplexed American readers, and 'its Christianity could at times appear almost secondary.' The *Englishness* of the Anglican settlement is not quite what Isabel Karremann stresses, but what can be associated with the remains of England's dissolved abbeys, Shakespeare's 'Bare ruined choirs, where late the sweet birds sang' (Sonnet 73). If Elizabethan writers suffered a precocious ruin lust, Karremann infers, that was because these haunted places provided a traumatic pretext for suspending hostilities in spooked recollection of so much 'greatness vapored', as the awed Goths 'gaze upon a ruinous monastery' at the blitzed ending of *Titus Andronicus* (5.1.21). Alexandra Walsham has described the mixed emotions stirred by the 'Gothic' relics left by this 'Reformation of the Landscape'.[11] And that 'Gothic' sensibility regarding the sublime scenery of England's Catholic heritage seems to infuse the last act of *The Merchant of Venice*, in Brooke Conti's analysis, where echoes of the pre-Reformation Easter Vigil and Jewish Passover combine with Protestant traditionalism, to transform the remembered 'paschal candle in the darkened church' into an interfaith symbol for 'things Catholics and Protestants could broadly agree upon' (cf. p. 28).

'How far that little candle throws his beams' (5.1.89), Shakespeare's exhausted homecomers exclaim; and for Phebe Jensen, too, the affirmative flame of Anglicanism shone out in its hospitable festive forms, when Christmas came to be 'rebranded' as a time for *détente*, the season of good will that 'set the English apart from their more contentious neighbors on the Continent', with 'Old grudges forgot, and put in the pot', especially religious differences (cf. pp. 40, 47). While nostalgists like Shakespeare might hark back to the Old Religion preserved by some 'religious uncle' (*As You Like It*, 3.2.312), or lament that 'No night is now with hymn or carol blessed', within their own 'broad church' they could therefore also dilute such grudges in reinvented traditions, like the Catholic asperging rite that is revived in *A Midsummer Night's Dream*, when order is given to 'consecrate' the bridal suite with 'dew' (2.1.102; 5.2.45). Sir Toby's challenge to the 'puritan' Malvolio, 'Dost thou think because thou art virtuous, there shall be no more cakes and ale?' (*Twelfth Night*, 2.3.103–4), places controversy about these customs under erasure, on this view, as among *adiaphora*: those matters of indifference on which relaxed or latitudinarian Christians could *agree to differ*.[12]

Walsham has lent weight to this congenial account of the early modern English exception by showing how an entire system of method acting for simulating conformity with the Elizabethan state religion was perfected by increasing numbers of 'church papists': Anglican communicants who remained loyal to the pope but who were 'understandably hesitant to embrace … harassment and hardship'.[13] Locke would later refine this play-acting into the liberal template for modern toleration, with the caveat that there could never be final agreement on 'the true and fundamental part of religion'.[14] But meanwhile, such an indefinite postponement would facilitate the '*via media* that is the spirit of Anglicanism', and that 'the English Catholic Church' achieved through its studied 'indifference to matters indifferent', according to T. S. Eliot, under leaders like Lancelot Andrewes.[15] So, with his art 'gallery' covertly transformed into a 'chapel', where devotees can take the image of 'some great matter' or *Magna Mater* 'there in hand', the author of *The Winter's*

Tale can be made to look very like an usher for this Anglo-Catholic accommodationism (5.2.94; 5.3.10, 86):

> *Perdita* Lady,
> Dear Queen, that ended when I but began,
> Give me that hand of yours to kiss.
> *Paulina* O, patience!
> The statue is but newly fixed; the colour's
> Not dry.
> (5.3.44–8)

The statue scene of *The Winter's Tale* is the *locus classicus* for the neutralization of religious conflict in the aesthetic, its implicit regression into a pre-Reformation Marianism the theatrical equivalent of the recursion of an anti-papist yet abidingly *Catholic* Church of England. But whatever its confessional direction, its essential aspect is that *the colour's not dry* in this unfinished project of conciliation. So, if Shakespeare can sometimes sound like an Anglo-Catholic sidesman, *Forms of Faith* traces the same latitudinarianism in other English writers born in the mid-sixteenth century, when the cult of Shakespeare's 'Dear Queen' and 'Lady' ended, and across genres and denominations. Thus, Jacqueline Wylde relates how the penitent 'goodnight ballad' sung by the prodigal Quicksilver in *Eastward Ho* rises above its evangelical occasion, to embrace fellow prisoners and auditors, from 'all religions i'the land' (cf. p. 63). Like Donne's Janus-faced poems, such 'last dying words' can persuasively *simulate* Reformation sincerity, for here 'the performance of repentance eclipses the repentance' (cf. p. 64).

The performativity analyzed in these essays is not quite the politic imposture, then, based on equal disbelief in *all* religions, that Chloe Preedy has highlighted in Christopher Marlowe.[16] For Thomas J. Moretti finds that in *The White Devil* John Webster's exposure of the inauthenticity of every form of faith does 'ironic service' (cf. p. 127) to interdenominational rapprochement, as a type of negative ecumenicism that leaves playgoers desiring to *pretend* their common Christianity. And even in *Macbeth* James R. Macdonald identifies an eschatological ambivalence, compounded by Thomas Middleton's co-authorship, concerning the Calvinist doctrine of predestination, with the Witches alternately awarded self-determination or subjected to Queen Hecate. So, if these 'juggling fiends … palter with us in a double sense' (5.10.19–20), in this analysis, that is because the Baroque metaphor of the *theatrum mundi*, of life as 'a poor player / That struts and frets his hour upon the stage' (5.5.23–4), covers the 'deniable ambiguity' of belief, as culture puts religion on display, in a rhetorical performance that is at once 'spectacular' yet 'evasive' (cf. p. 155).

'Play the man, Master Ridley': when Hugh Latimer uttered his famous last words at the stake, the Protestant martyr was asking to be paid by performance. But Brian Walsh examines how this histrionic metaphor played out on the Jacobean stage as a figure for a Reformation that is always 'a work in progress' (cf. p. 122). Because spectators of plays like Samuel Rowley's *When You See Me You Know Me* were encouraged to 'Think ye see / The very persons' (*Henry VIII*, Pro.25–6) of Tudor history, their own convictions were relativized as equally contingent, for on this scaffold, as *Henry VIII* announced, '*All is True*'. The Globe motto that 'All the world's a stage' (*As You Like It*, 2.7.138) thus carried the subtext that in matters of faith, 'What's to come is still unsure' (*Twelfth Night*, 2.3.45). And so the scene was set for 'multiple reformations' (cf. p. 160), an interminable mimetic project in which *Henry V* engaged its audience, Mary A. Blackstone proposes, with the invitation to interrogate the players as 'outward consciences' (4.1.8), but to judge the protagonist's provisional 'reformation' (*1 Henry IV*, 1.2.191), when he obeys 'all holy rites' (*Henry V*, 4.8.116) of the 'idol ceremony' (4.1.222) he earlier condemned, as a master-class in how to 'piece out' liturgical 'imperfections' (Cho.1, 23).

In tune with the temporizing of his politic Prince Hal, the great prompter would disavow fundamentalist martyrs as 'the fools of time' (Sonnet 124), for their embarrassingly bad timing. And that histrionic sense of occasion was also Donne's saving grace as Dean of St. Paul's, according to Joel M. Dodson, when the divine who had agonized over his confession crisis in his *Satyres* described religion as no more than a 'calling', analogous to membership of the Livery Companies in which he now dined, and to the tradesman's vocation in the City, where fraternal 'voices differ … yet it is still one corporation' (cf. p. 208). 'When my cue comes, call me, and I will answer' (*Dream*, 4.1.197), Shakespeare's weaver indeed affirms, before he re-enters recalling St. Paul's Epistle to the play-loving citizens on 'the things God hath prepared for them that love him' (1 Cor. 2:9). And in this revision Donne's religious timeliness likewise speaks to the brotherly and civic ethos that professions of faith demand faithful professionalism, since in any corporation, 'A man must not leave his calling' (cf. p. 210).

For Dean Donne, the Church of England was 'Catholic', in the sense that it constituted a 'Meeting, an assembly', assenting to the doctrines 'which in all Christian ages, and in all Christian Churches, have been agreed'. The former 'frequenter of plays' was preaching an ecclesial vision of communion that had the entire congregation singing from one hymn-sheet. Such would be the comfortable elasticity of the Church of England that is banalized in recent studies such as David Scott Kastan's *A Will To Believe*, which as Gerard Kilroy acidly remarks, equips Shakespeare for 'a Manhattan dinner party'.[17] But in a surprise move, Dodson instead refers this cheery creedal solidarity to 'the care of the self' studied by Michel Foucault.[18] A generation ago Thomas Docherty likened Jack Donne's undoing to the Deconstructionism of another 'J.D.'.[19] Dodson instead shifts the critical focus to Doctor Donne's self-*reconstruction*, and explores his affinities with Jacques Derrida's interlocutor, who, it is argued, similarly depicted the 'theatrical representation of the self' by confession as a practice that articulated the sociable vocation of 'man as citizen' (cf. p. 207).

The relationship to religion of the philosopher who called the soul a 'prison' has been an unexpected topic of recent critical theory.[20] Yet Foucault started out as an altar boy in Vichy France and ended as a pious exegete in a Dominican library, joking how he was the last person in Paris 'who remain[ed] interested in the daily operation of the Catholic Church'.[21] When he died of AIDS, 'Saint Foucault', as he was styled in David Halperin's 'Gay Hagiography', would duly receive a solemn requiem mass.[22] Notoriously, he also hailed the Iranian Revolution as a reprise of 'those old dreams the West had known' in the sixteenth century, 'when it wanted to inscribe the figures of spirituality on the earth of politics'. In 'their hunger, humiliations', and fervor for 'sacrifice and the promises of the millennium', enthused Foucault, Shiites were simply restaging the tragic spectacles of the Catholic League.[23] According to his colleague Paul Veyne, Foucault was here paradoxically inspired by 'aversion to dogmatism .... He wanted not to reduce the future to Western ideals, not to make the veiling of women an *ultima ratio*.'[24] But nothing the philosopher ever wrote fueled more controversy, nor was so disastrously overtaken by history.

'There is a man who, with a single word pronounced from afar, is able to launch hundreds of thousands of protestors against the tanks in the streets of Teheran', exclaimed Foucault, when he met Ayatollah Khomeini at Neauphle-le-Château. The Parisian thinker went to interview the Iranian cleric exhilarated by 'this attempt to open up a religious dimension in politics', Veyne confirms; and when secular Iranians turned up at his apartment to protest, '[h]e was not impressed .... Foucault had made his choice.'[25] No wonder, then, that as Arthur Bradley writes, it has become possible 'to detect a "theological turn" in Foucault's archaeologies', which by opposing religion as a thought 'from the inside' to their political 'thought from the outside', might be described as 'modern versions of Christian negative theologies'.[26] And by 'using Foucault to re-think Foucault' (cf. p. 196), as he puts it, that is just what Dodson sets out to do in his reappraisal of confession as a cultural form that mediates religious conflict by abstracting faith from power. Since Foucault's had been one of the foremost critiques of such a cultural separation of theology from politics, Dodson's essay is a fitting capstone to *Forms of Faith*.

Dodson recognizes that Foucault's genealogy of confession has in fact been crucial to the picture of early modern culture working not to separate but to 'hold together' a 'terrestrial power' with one 'directed toward the world beyond', so the 'transcendent horizon provides a political leverage outside of history to motivate actions in history'.[27] The French theorist had developed this line of thinking at Berkeley, where his colleagues included Stephen Greenblatt, whose *Renaissance Self-Fashioning* became the only work on Shakespeare Foucault cited.[28] Greenblatt was himself influenced by Foucault's hermeneutics of suspicion, and closed his book with a confession of his own, that by the time it was finished its title was redundant, as he had learned there was no such thing as a free subject: indeed, 'the subject had come to seem remarkably unfree, the ideological product of the relations of power'.[29] But the visiting professor was equally impressed by his Californian hosts, who seduced him with the concept that would deflect his trajectory, and that Dodson adopts to revalue confession as 'an enabling, rather than disabling' (cf. p. 196) practice, which was 'the notion of a *style* – a freely-chosen life-aesthetic'.[30]

Because this change of mind, away from the relations of power and toward the arts of living, was expounded by Foucault mainly back at the Collège de France, awareness of the extent to which the philosopher of discipline and punishment had moved on from the dark materials of his carceral society has only slowly percolated the anglophone academy, with the release of the tape-recorded sessions. But as Eric Paras asserts in one of the few studies yet to absorb the 'mark 2 Foucault', the significance of this late discovery of 'life style' can hardly be exaggerated, as it means that the same man 'created the twentieth century's most devastating critique of the free subject – and then in a voice that by the end trembled from pain and debility, liquidated it'.[31] By bookending *Forms of Faith* with Foucault's own last-minute recantation, Dodson therefore not only puts early modern literary scholars of deathbed conversions and pulpit protestations in his debt. He also greatly raises the stakes.

'Confession is a ritual that unfolds within a power relationship', Foucault had maintained, 'for one does not confess without the presence of the authority who requires the confession, prescribes and appreciates it, and intervenes in order to judge, punish, forgive, console, and reconcile.'[32] For thirty years those who followed this inquisitorial model of pastoral power have therefore situated confession within a disciplinary network that meshed tightly at the grille of the confessional box. Imposed upon Milan by Cardinal Carlo Borromeo in 1576, this miniature proscenium theatre is described by Jeremy Tambling as a technical rehearsal for the Panopticon prison that so fascinated Foucault, for by its means power is similarly instantiated, when the confessant 'is made to speak, and speak knowingly, the language given by the Church'. The Council of Trent had been explicit about the repressive purpose of auricular confession, moreover, when it declared its abolition by Reformers would 'endanger society with all sorts of secret crimes'.[33] So the partitioned 'double sentry-box' that John Bossy terms a machine to 'bureaucratize' the soul was invented expressly for the purpose of reinserting power into religion.[34]

'Object of terror or of horror, increasingly artistically worked, the confessional was to the far end of the countryside the most tangible and durable legacy' of the Counter-Reformation.[35] But as Tambling emphasizes, Borromeo's aim had been individualistic: 'Secret crimes need a secret place to be confessed. Sin has to do, not with the community but with the self and God, and the discipline of the community involved in confession relied on the authority established in the judgment-seat' of the confessor.[36] Nothing therefore distinguished Anglicanism more from post-Tridentine Catholicism than the complete absence of this 'remarkable piece of furniture' from English churches.[37] And it is in the space vacated by that material and political abstention that Dodson is able to turn Foucault against himself, and to substitute for the negative Foucauldian genealogy of Christian confession, which concerns only the imposition of 'obligations of truth', an alternative rhetorical and relational history, that does not 'reduce confessionalisation to forms of repression'.[38]

The concept of 'confessionalisation' Dodson introduces in place of its 'torturous cousin', confession, has only lately been extended to England. As historians point out, the country barely featured in the debate on the 'confessionalization thesis' that sprang up in the 1980s, after Heinz Schilling and Wolfgang Reinhard proposed that in line with the Westphalian maxim, *cujos regio, ejus religio* – 'whose is the realm, his is the religion' – both Catholic and Protestant states were 'defined by Confessions of Faith', which they exploited 'as means of socially disciplining their subjects'.[39] Confessionalization was here a prime instance of the 'biopolitics' Foucault identified with early modernity, when sovereign power mutated into 'the calculated management of life'.[40] This thesis was given a distinct English spin, however, by the theatre specialist Tom Betteridge, who applied the notion to the Tudor state, as Dodson notes, with the merciful relief that the Henrician regime could never have matched the continental model of discipline.[41]

Greenblatt had learned from Foucault that a disciplined soul in fact required no police force or standing army. That was in line with Reformation historians like Patrick Collinson, who believed the pragmatic Elizabeth when she said she saw no need for 'windows into men's souls', and who inferred from this that the drive for confessional conformity became decoupled from Tudor state-formation.[42] But if the fortunate English were thereby only 'indifferently reformed', an altogether greater magnitude of indifference is entailed by the proposition that in England the confession of faith was a positive and communal form of 'negotiation and engagement', rather than an oppressive and individualized function of biopower. To prove this benign Anglo-Saxon exception, Dodson has a star witness, however: it is Foucault's own lectures on the 'stylistics of existence' that are said to overturn his disciplinary paradigm, and thereby to affirm the way that Donne 'resituates the profession of faith' as a fraternal mode of 'professional life', like his own clubbable habitus 'among lawyers, tradesmen, physicians, and tailors' (cf. p. 207).

The slippage from the European *confession* of sins to the English *profession* of sincerity in Dodson's essay, comprehending, as he says, both 'the heartfelt urges of personal belief' and the demands of 'state-enforced dogma' (cf. p. 197), is a deliberate elision in the literary scholarship he cites. It is exemplified, for instance, by Conti, whose book *Confessions of Faith* is explicitly 'poised' between diametric opposite meanings of confession, as personal revelation and public avowal, for 'The confession of faith shows us seventeenth-century Britons [*sic*] poised between these two realities: writing in a public realm that understood religion as an either/or proposition, but attempting to depict an individual history and experience.'[43] Such rhetorical fluidity goes with the archival evidence that, as Peter Marshall remarks, 'England was simultaneously a robustly confessional state and a de facto religiously plural society'.[44] And it flows with the easy-going communitarianism of Jeffrey Knapp's book *Shakespeare's Tribe*, which conjectures that English writers mostly shared a relaxed belief that 'the mere act of drawing ... people together' in some 'churchlike gathering' was enough to 'spiritually unite' them.[45]

The rhetorical turn described in the literary accounts of English confessionalization that Dodson adduces can look for justification to Thomas Hobbes, for whom the minimal confession that 'Jesus is the Christ' constituted the political subject as a religious subject 'on the condition that religion is a polite fiction, a representation with no dogmatic substance whatsoever' (43:11).[46] But once religion is detached from power in this way, and early modern England comes to figure as a laboratory for postmodern democratic pluralism, cultural artifacts such as Shakespeare's plays, which are admittedly 'saturated in religious discourse', and alive 'to religious precedent', are held to separate politics from theology simply by subordinating 'religious matter to the ... aesthetic demands of the work in hand'.[47] And such a liberal humanist aesthetic cannot withstand the Foucauldian onslaught that 'atomizes the religious experience as less a set of beliefs and more an immanent political experience that attempts to govern or regulate human life'.[48]

Dodson admits that, in order to sustain 'critical emphasis on the deferral or indeterminacy of confessional definition', Foucault's at once 'revealing and crippling' (cf. p. 201) historical archaeology of pastoral power has to be disarmed, a negation which, it is claimed, the philosopher accomplished himself in the lectures given at the Collège now published as *The Hermeneutics of the Subject*. The suggestion is that Foucault's genealogy of confession was of a piece with his dogma of the author as a 'function' of discourse in his notorious lecture 'What is an Author?' – a Structuralist 'shibboleth' which the post-Structuralist was eager to disavow in favor of human autonomy. Specifically, Dodson contends that on February 24, 1982 the archivist of the care of the self outlined the Stoic 'stroll-exercise' (cf. p. 207) in terms that are uncannily applicable to Donne's 'Fishers of Men' sermon delivered at The Hague on December 19, 1619, following the repressive Synod of Dort: 'Epictetus recommends, for example, that from time to time we take a walk outside and look at what is going on around us (things, people, events, etcetera). We exercise ourselves with regard to all the different representations offered by the world.'[49]

The analogy between the Stoic *passeggiata* and Donne's recommendation that the Dutch Reformers, who were tearing themselves apart, should get out more, and remember that the Apostles 'did not abandon care' of the world, is an engaging conceit, redolent of Hans-Georg Gadamer's hermeneutics of religion, with its assumption that 'Language is most realized not in propositions but in conversation where words are sought for what always remains to be said.'[50] The alignment of Foucault's care of the self with Donne's caring community crowns *Forms of Faith* with a vision of the confessional life as a 'regulated "form" that cannot be reduced to the biopolitical force of law' (cf. p. 214n.51), and an idealism about the power of symbols that indeed recalls nothing so much as the neo-Kantianism with which Ernst Cassirer sought to confute Martin Heidegger's totalitarian existentialism. Certainly, it allows Dodson to coopt the French philosopher to his core argument, that in England early modern faith was a convivial pick-and-mix affair of cultural orientation, like the Dean of St. Paul's' shopping expeditions on Cheapside. But it also prompts the question: does either Donne or Foucault deserve this degree of domestication?

When Dodson grandly writes that 'rather than mere rhetoric', Foucault's genealogy of Christian spirituality as a mode of individualization is 'worth taking seriously' (cf. p. 198), he is asking to be taken just as seriously himself.[51] But if we do so, we see that the philosopher was adamant that his admiration for the Stoic technique of perambulation did *not* extend to Christian confessional practices. *Au contraire*, 'I would like to stress', he insisted, 'the ... profound difference between the Stoic exercise ... and what is found among Christians .... The problem for Christians is not at all one of studying the objective content of the representation.' According to the Paris lecture, Christians differed from Stoics precisely because their spirituality was about the *empowerment* of subjective verification: 'Does the idea I have in mind come from God? – in which case it is necessarily pure.'[52] And this difference was key to the distinction that Foucault guarded between philosophy, 'as the form of thought that asks itself what it is permits the subject to have access to the truth', and spirituality, which is the ensemble of practices which constitute 'the price to pay for having access to that truth'.[53]

The recent reconstruction of the lectures Foucault gave in 1981 at the Catholic University of Louvain confirms how he remained 'a self-confessed atheist, suspicious of the transcendental truth claims of Christianity and the power structures behind them'.[54] For there he reiterated how the Christian practice of profession that Dodson rehabilitates – *exomologēsis* – was ominously related to law and psychiatry, as a form of self-sacrifice: 'one must publicly attest that one is ready to sacrifice oneself in this world … to arrive in the other world'. This sinister 'connection between veridiction and mortification' was 'fundamentally different' to the Stoic code, but 'absolutely essential' to the Christian technology of individualization, Foucault kept repeating.[55] And intriguingly, he affiliated his own critique of such exhibitionistic truth-telling displays with Greek tragedy and Shakespeare, for was not this drama also forensically concerned with questioning the subjection of the truth in this world to otherworldly verification?

> The central problem in Shakespeare … it seems to me, is the question of the foundation of sovereign right: How … can a sovereign succeed in legitimately exercising power that he seized through war, revolt, civil war, crime, or violating oaths?[56]

The solution Foucault supplied to the legitimacy problem is the one that Henry V gives in Shakespeare's play, and which is foregrounded in *Forms of Faith*. It is 'ceremony' which covers power with a magic cloak of truthfulness, a 'form of faith' as dazzling as a 'kind of god', whose 'soul of adoration' consists in 'creating awe and fear in other men'. 'What art thou, thou idol ceremony?' Henry reasonably demands of this 'experience of the sublime', which, as Graham Hammill observes, 'gives form to the central aporia between sovereignty and imagination'.[57] His answer is to disaggregate 'thrice-gorgeous ceremony' into its items of regalia, the gaudy baubles that monarchy inherited, when, as Ernst Kantorowicz pictured the investiture in his essay on 'The Mysteries of State', the absolute Prince stepped literally 'into the shoes of the Roman Pontiff': 'the balm, the sceptre, and the ball, / The sword, the mace, the crown imperial, / The intertissued robe of gold and pearl, / The farced title … 'fore the king, / The throne he sits on' (*Henry V*, 4.1.243–6).[58]

Foucault invented a Greek word for all this glittering veridical paraphernalia. As the symbolic forms of faith in supernatural validation, the flashy 'rituals and forms of manifestation' that hold power and religion together in a 'proud dream' (239) of transcendental truth constituted a technology of the sublime which he termed 'alethurgy'. So, the philosopher sounded very like the Shakespearean inheritors who meditate upon 'the hollow crown' (*Richard II*, 3.2.156) when he doubted whether power could ever be exercised 'without a ring of truth, an alethurgical circle that turns around it and accompanies it'.

But he also echoed Prince Harry when he added that it is a mistake to imagine that 'if one were to strip power' of this 'golden rigol' (*2 Henry IV*, 4.3.166) one would uncover its 'kernel of violence, the naked game of life and death'. For there can be no power 'without a showy garb', Foucault concluded, when it is precisely in the ostentation of its vulgar bling that the claim to truth resides, as Shakespeare's rulers prove:[59]

> Thus did I keep my person fresh and new,
> My presence like a robe pontifical –
> Ne'er seen but wondered at – and so my state,
> Seldom but sumptuous, showed like a feast,
> And won by rareness such solemnity.
> (*1 Henry IV*, 3.2.55–9)

'It is but trash', we are assured in *The Tempest*, when the drunken butler dons 'glistening apparel' as 'King Stefano'. Yet directly afterwards the spirit Ariel helps '*to attire*' Prospero in identical 'frippery', as the 'famous Duke of Milan' (4.1.194, 220–4; 5.1.87, 195). In Shakespeare, then, there can be no hegemony without alethurgy. Foucault illustrated this axiom by describing the Roman throne room painted with the emperor's horoscope, a décor intended to rig the imperial hotline to heaven. But government has never dispensed with this supernatural aura, the theorist continued, which in fact became even more extraterrestrial during the Wars of Religion, with the fabrication of the mythology of Divine Right. Although he never used the term, he was therefore exactly anticipating the preoccupation with *political theology* that has since come to dominate early modern studies, via the apothegm of the clerico-fascist Carl Schmitt that 'All significant concepts of the modern theory of the state are secularized theological concepts.'[60] For Foucault's itemization of the symbolic forms that clasp power to religion is simply his Parisian way of unraveling what Victoria Kahn calls 'the problem of political theology, understood as the theological legitimation or religious dimension of political authority'.[61]

Eric Santner has noticed how Foucault's writings on sovereignty vacillate as to whether the sublime of sacred kingship has now been entirely superseded by the biopolitical 'management of life', in the confession box and psychiatric clinic, or whether the mystical presence of the king has merely seeped into 'the lives of [modern] citizens'.[62] Roberto Esposito similarly queries 'How are sovereignty and biopolitics to be related? … It is said that one emerges out of the background of other, but … is it the definitive withdrawal of a preceding presence, or rather the horizon that embraces and holds what newly emerges within it?'[63] These are questions at the heart of early modern studies and of *Forms of Faith*. For it was not by chance that Foucault structured his most political book, *Discipline and Punish*, around the incarnational logic that he derived from Kantorowicz of the king's 'Christological' double body, which 'involves not only the transitory element that is born and dies, but another that remains unchanged by time'.[64]

The idea, elaborated in *The King's Two Bodies*, of the existence of a 'secret bond' uniting 'modern power and the most immemorial of the *arcana imperii*', has been described by Giorgio Agamben as the 'vanishing point' that the lines of Foucault's inquiry 'converge toward without reaching'. But his deference towards Kantorowicz offers a key to his evolving thinking about this 'tenacious correspondence' between the modern management of bodies and the archaic mysteries of state.[65] So, it was no coincidence that he kept returning in his final lectures to Shakespeare, to illustrate 'the drama of the *coup d'État*'. Just as political hegemony 'manifests itself in a kind of theatricality', Shakespeare's theatre, he taught, is a representation of this hegemony 'in its violent form of the *coup*'.[66] Thus, without reading a word of Carl Schmitt, or even of Walter Benjamin, Foucault could clearly perceive that the function of theology in modern politics was still to veil the executive decision in transcendental legitimacy, and that, in the infamous words of 'Hitler's Crown Jurist', 'Sovereign is who decides the exception', because 'The exception in jurisprudence is analogous to the miracle in theology.'[67]

The contributors to *Forms of Faith* have apparently taken a self-denying ordinance never to mention the term 'political theology' which so excites Shakespeareans. Not once does the topic or the name of Schmitt sully these pages. One might say, after T. S. Eliot, that these literary historicists have a collective mind so fine no such mere idea will penetrate it. But the proximity of Foucault's thinking about 'the transcendence of sovereign power' to Schmitt's decisionism has been amplified by Agamben, who has brought out what he believes remained latent in the Foucauldian genealogy of confession, which is how, 'by making an argument about substance and being', the Trinitarian theology of the Church Fathers articulated 'the double structure of the governmental machine', the correlation 'between Kingdom and Government … *oikonomia* and Glory, between power as government and effective management, and power as ceremonial and liturgical regality'.[68] And by introducing Foucault's meditations on the sublime of modern government, this is the line of inquiry that *Forms of Faith* demands.

Instantly Foucault's genealogy is factored into the literary-historical calculus of early modern confession, the entire problematic of political theology must nowadays follow, and with it, a critique of the relationship between power and religion which is potentially fatal to the liberal concept, sustained almost to the end of *Forms of Faith*, of culture as a happy medium between Church and state. For the moment that the definition of political theology as the otherworldly legitimation of worldly ends is introduced into the equation, the professional 'calling' (cf. pp. 205, 210) on which Dodson closes *Forms of Faith* ceases to sound like a roving recreational walkabout, and begins to resemble the coercive *interpellation* that Foucault's teacher Louis Althusser analyzed as the indoctrinating technique of the 'Ideological State Apparatus'.[69] And then the civic care that the Dean of St. Paul's extolled begins to look more like the Stasi surveillance system Shakespeare presented as the paranoid vigilantism of the watch committee.

Although Dodson affiliates it with the postmodern turn to a weak faith after faith, his enlistment of Foucault underlines that Donne's ambulant Catholicity in fact depended on a tenet of political theology that was very far from being 'agreed in all Christian ages, and in all Christian Churches' (cf. p. 205), namely, the magisterium, as Supreme Head of the Church of England, of King James. For the Stuart regime there was no separation of Church and state. So, as Hammill points out, Donne unambiguously proclaimed James's theocratic 'interpretation of kingship in his sermon given on the anniversary of the Gunpowder Plot, November 5, 1622, drawing on Deuteronomy 17 to argue that God always intended a king for Israel as a precedent for all subsequent states, monarchy being "a more masculine Organe, and Instrument of this Soul of Soveraigntie, then other forms are"'.[70] And for James's persecuted *Roman* Catholic subjects, harried by informers, priest-hunters, and torturers, this particular profession of Anglican Catholicism was a long way from being a matter of indifference.

The only oblique gesture to political theology in *Forms of Faith* is Dodson's footnote on Agamben's description of monasticism as an attempt to regulate a 'form-of-life outside the law'. This glimpse is pointed, however, because Agamben's theme in *The Highest Poverty* is that such an apolitical ideal is a concept that 'modernity has shown itself to be incapable' of thinking.[71] Dodson calls this epochal incapacity an unhealed 'wound' (cf. p. 197), which figures the eternal hope that religion might 'tomorrow be good again'. But he then admits that Donne's sermon on the careful Church was delivered at the scene of a corporeal wounding that was all too real: 'in the chapel where the decapitated remains' (cf. p. 204) of the Remonstrant leader Johan van Oldenbarnevelt had been interred, after his beheading by Protestant zealots, precisely for 'remonstrating' in favor of a confessional *détente*. For at The Hague in 1619, there could be no partition of theology from politics, nor any questioning of 'the limits of tolerance' policed by those caring Dutch *regenten* whose unsleeping vigilance Rembrandt was commissioned to portray in *The Night Watch*.[72]

Foucault would regret his comparison of the Mullahs to Solzhenitsyn, as he pleaded with Iran's leaders to curb their 'hasty executions'.[73] Like later Western intellectuals, his *trahison des clercs* had been to disbelieve this holy terror. Similarly, the risk in reducing faith to its forms is exposed by Dodson's gloss on Donne's exhortation to the Dutch to cast their net wide, so 'God shall drive fish' into it, which is euphemized as a call to 'multiplicity' (cf. p. 205).

This innocent annotation assumes the Hague mission was sent to mediate on the eve of the Thirty Years War. Yet all the evidence suggests its 'double design' was to drum up arms for the Protestant *jihad* of the Elector Frederick in Bohemia, 'under pretext of a zeal for peace'.[74] So, as Paul Sellin writes in the most scholarly study, Donne's dragnet looks like the security sweep the Estates of Holland had just mandated 'to check abuses in church and state, and to identify persons responsible'. In fact, his sermon was about as 'inclusive' as 'the pardon accorded Shylock in *The Merchant of Venice*', considering it was delivered over the dead body of the biggest 'fish' yet caught:[75]

> Preaching in the Hofkapel in December in December 1619 involved heavy ironies .... The thought of Donne's words echoing in the space over Oldenbarnevelt's very tomb [meant that] a seventeenth-century mind would be very likely to meditate on the revenges that the whirligig of time brings in rather than on the humane perspectives that attract modern sensibilities.[76]

We have become too familiar with godly decapitations not to take them seriously. Thus, the severed head of the Arminian leader lies at the close of *Forms of Faith*, like one of those beheadings relished by Baroque painters, to signify that in a theocracy, as Shakespeare registered during the 1604 Hampton Court Conference on religion with his tragicomedy of decollation, *Measure for Measure*, 'He who the sword of heaven will bear / Should be as holy as severe' (3.1.481–2). The shadow of such divine violence falls not only across Donne's caring community, moreover, but every communal rite described in *Forms of Faith*. It falls most severely across the sacramental ceremonies performed by Shakespeare's Henry V, which justify the King's decision to 'expressly' break 'the law of arms', and order 'every soldier to cut his prisoner's throat', on hearing that 'The French have reinforced'. Critics who like to exonerate the butcher of Agincourt mistime this 'Macedon[ian]' barbarism, which *preempts* any French atrocity, precisely because it proclaims his sovereignty. For in *Henry V* the kingly precedent of 'Alexander the Pig' is more bestial than even Blackstone allows (4.6.35–9; 4.7.1–12):

> Alexander, God knows, and you know, in his rages and his furies and his wraths and his cholers and his moods and his displeasures and his indignations, and also being a little intoxicates in his prains did in his ales and his angers, look you, kill his best friend. (4.7.27–32)

Debora Shuger has argued that the arbitrariness of 'the sword of heaven' in Shakespeare 'makes sense' in light of 'the sacerdotal understanding' of kingship propounded by King James.[77] But in *Forms of Faith* we are instead alerted to how Shakespeare's staging of the Reformation 'calls attention to itself as an attempt at rhetorical erasure' (cf. p. 119), in Walsh's words, in scenes like the christening of Elizabeth, where Cranmer foresees that recusants will be struck by this infant's *terror* like 'a field of beaten corn' (*Henry VIII*, 5.4.31). Thus, in *Macbeth* terror intrudes the instant the bearded Witches disinter the 'thumb' of their martyred 'pilot' Edmund Campion, racked 'As homeward he did come' from Prague (1.3.26–7). Campion's amputated thumb was the 'Devil's dildo' used by Catholic exorcists. So this form of faith is yet more Jesuitical than Macdonald acknowledges. Likewise, in *The White Devil* Flamineo's homicidal desecration of a crucifix is too blasphemous to consort with the cozy companionability that Moretti attributes to the playgoers of multicultural Clerkenwell. For these irruptions all follow the logic Schmitt delineated in *Hamlet*, when the play is engulfed by the 'shadows' of religious war:

> This drama does not completely exhaust itself as a play .... It has openings through which historical time breaks into the time of the play ... dark areas ... a reality externally given, imposed and unavoidable. This reality is the mute rock upon which the play founders.[78]

A Shakespearean play 'creates for itself a certain freedom', Schmitt conceded; yet that 'realm of human innocence' is thwarted by the incursion into its 'dream frame' of 'religious fanaticism', for writers like Shakespeare know that 'historical reality is stronger' than their art.[79] So, while it may be true that the very form of *Eastward Ho* worked, as Wylde suggests, to 'create communities' from 'all religions' (cf. p. 58), the scandal this somehow caused occasioned one of the most sensational instances of 'the intrusion of the time' into the world of the play, when Ben Jonson was jailed for his involvement, and 'turned' government agent, to spy upon the Gunpowder Plot. Throughout *Forms of Faith*, it is possible to discern the same violent reversal. Thus, for all that Christmas might 'smooth over devotional differences' (cf. p. 51) in early modern England, it was also the season, as Jensen recognizes, when a Malvolio could swear to 'be revenged on the whole pack' (*Twelfth Night*, 5.1.365).

Shakespearean theatre may have helped 'gentleness' prevail over 'strong enforcement'; but if its evocation of those 'better days' before the Reformation, when 'bells have knolled to church' (*As You Like It*, 2.7.103–13), was meant to sound ecumenical, why did this compel the men in black to object, as does Jacques, that it is from the 'religious life' of sequestered 'convertites' that more is 'to be heard and learned' (5.4.170–4)? And if Catholic allusions, such as the report of Portia lingering 'By holy crosses, where she kneels and prays' (*Merchant*, 5.1.31), were planted to be as irenic as Conti claims, why does the very idea that this tolerant inclusiveness might have been extended to 'signals to the recusants in ... [the] audience' (cf. p. 30) provoke among contemporary critics the consternation she betrays? The answer, Karremann hints, is that the Anglo-Saxon divorce from Rome and Catholic Europe remains so traumatic it requires a continuing rhetorical repression, of which the persistent but fallacious categorization of Shakespeare's Church of England as 'Protestant' provides the symptomatic case.

Contributors to another recent collection, *Political Theology and Early Modernity*, concur that it is movements like Al-Qaeda and born-again Christianity that explain the current fixation on political theology and 'the relationship between religion and the state'.[80] We would need to add Islamic State to this pairing, before noting how televized images of religious vandalism and beheading also teach us to be wary of the telos that conflates the symbolization of Protestantism with progress, as 'hardly a religion at all', or 'a kind of ... benign anarchy'.[81] For *Forms of Faith* reminds us that more real blood was shed over the Eucharist in Shakespeare's time than was ever drunk symbolically; and that, in Wald's words, the 'burning of martyrs on both sides, made each individual's stance towards the Last Supper ... a matter of life and death' (cf. p. 75). Thus, to confuse Anglicanism with Protestantism is to efface the very 'separate-yet-connected vision of the sign and referent' (cf. p. 186), as Block well puts it, that sustained the 'indifferently reformed' Church of England for so long in the exceptional form of faith professed in its Book of Common Prayer: 'I believe in ... The holy Catholic church'.

Forms of Faith is an impressive endeavor to reread the relations of early modern literary form to religious conflict in the terms his biographer Alain Boureau ascribes to Kantorowicz, as 'emancipatory fictions' that detach politics from theology.[82] While Schmitt's theologizing forced him to conceive of Shakespearean theatre 'as resisting both an aesthetic notion of art and a liberal conception of the state', Kahn explains, Kantorowicz's secularizing permitted him to ally it 'with Anglo-American constitutionalism'.[83] What this collection also reveals, however, is how this project of Enlightenment becomes 'the flip side of Schmitt's authoritarianism' once politics is identified with Protestantism, or any form of faith.[84] Then we recall that Foucault had been full of hope when he went off to meet the holy man; but that the philosopher returned to Paris saying the Ayatollah 'spoke to me of his programme of government; if he took power, the stupidity of it would make one weep'.[85]

Notes

1 William Shakespeare, *The Norton Shakespeare*, ed. Stephen Greenblatt *et al.* (New York: W. W. Norton, 1997). All further quotations from Shakespeare's work are taken from this edition.

2 E. Duffy, 'Bare Ruined Choirs: Remembering Catholicism in Shakespeare's England', in R. Dutton, A. Findlay and R. Wilson (eds), *Theatre and Religion: Lancastrian Shakespeare* (Manchester: Manchester University Press, 2003), pp. 40–57, at p. 56.

3 H. Chettle, from *England's Mourning Garment* (London: 1603), repr. in E. K. Chambers, *William Shakespeare: A Study of Facts and Problems*, 2 vols (Oxford: Clarendon Press, 1930), vol. 1: p. 189.

4 R. Southwell, *Saint Peter's Complaint and Saint Mary Magdalen's Funeral Tears* (Saint-Omer: Society of Jesus, 1616), A4. For the criticisms of both Chettle and Southwell, see R. Wilson, *Secret Shakespeare: Studies in Theatre, Religion and Resistance* (Manchester: Manchester University Press, 2004), pp. 116, 126–30, 294.

5 H. Grady, *Shakespeare and Impure Aesthetics* (Cambridge: Cambridge University Press, 2009), p. 21.

6 *Ibid.*

7 Sir Edward Sandys, *Europae Speculum, or a Relation of the State of Religion*, 5th edn (London, 1632), p. 196, quoted in T. Rabb, *Jacobean Gentleman: Sir Edward Sandys, 1561–1629* (Princeton: Princeton University Press, 1998), pp. 33–4, 36.

8 J. Rust, 'Political Theologies of the *Corpus Mysticum*: Schmitt, Kantorowicz, and de Lubac', in G. Hammill and J. R. Lupton (eds), *Political Theology and Early Modernity* (Chicago: University of Chicago Press, 2012), pp. 102–23, at pp. 106–7.

9 'elimination of supernatural agency': Benedict Spinoza, *Theological-Political Treatise*, ed. Jonathan Israel (Cambridge: Cambridge University Press, 2007), p. xvi. See J.-L. Nancy, 'Church, State, Resistance', in H. de Vries and L. Sullivan (eds), *Political Theologies: Public Religions in a Post-Secular World* (New York: Fordham University Press, 2006), pp. 102–12.

10 T. Judt, *Thinking the Twentieth Century*, ed. Timothy Snyder (London: Vintage 2013), p. 73.

11 A. Walsham, *The Reformation of the Landscape: Religion, Identity, and Memory in Early Modern Britain and Ireland* (Oxford: Oxford University Press, 2012), p. 322.

12 For *adiaphora*, see in particular J. A. Waddell, *The Struggle to Reclaim the Liturgy in the Lutheran Church: Adiaphora in Historical, Theological and Practical Perspective* (Lewiston, NY: Mellen, 2005).

13 A. Walsham, *Church Papists: Catholicism, Conformity and Confessional Polemic in Early Modern England* (Woodbridge: Boydell & Brewer, 1999), pp. 63–4; see also H. Kamen, *The Rise of Toleration* (Toronto: McGraw Hill, 1961) and J. Lecler, *Toleration and the Reformation*, trans. T. L. Westow, 2 vols (New York: Association Press, 1960).

14 John Locke, 'A Letter Concerning Toleration', in *'A Letter Concerning Toleration' and 'Two Treatises of Government'* (New Haven: Yale University Press, 2003), p. 229. For Locke's refinement of the debate about *adiaphora*, see J. Marshall, *John Locke: Resistance, Religion, and Responsibility* (Cambridge: Cambridge University Press, 1994), pp. 33–72; Alex Tuckness, *Locke and the Legislative Point of View: Toleration, Contested Principles, and the Law* (Princeton: Princeton University Press, 2002), pp. 17–25; and James Tully, *An Approach to Political Philosophy: Locke in Contexts* (Cambridge: Cambridge University Press, 1993), p. 48.

15 T. S. Eliot, 'Lancelot Andrewes', in *Selected Essays* (London: Faber & Faber, 1951), pp. 341–53, at pp. 341–3.

16 C. Preedy, *Marlowe's Literary Scepticism: Politic Religion and Post-Reformation Polemic* (London: Bloomsbury, 2014).

17 G. Kilroy, 'In All Conscience', *Times Literary Supplement*, July 24, 2015, 10–11, at 11. D. S. Kastan, *A Will to Believe: Shakespeare and Religion* (Oxford: Oxford University Press, 2014).

18 'frequenter of plays': Richard Baker, *A Chronicle of the Kings of England* (1643), quoted in G. E. Bentley, *The Profession of Dramatist in Shakespeare's Time, 1590–1642* (Princeton: Princeton University Press, 1986), p. 50.

19 T. Docherty, *John Donne, Undone* (London: Methuen, 1986).

20 M. Foucault, *Discipline and Punish: The Birth of the Prison*, trans. A. Sheridan (Harmondsworth: Penguin Books, 1977), p. 30.

21 M. Jordan, *Convulsing Bodies: Religion and Resistance in Foucault* (Stanford: Stanford University Press, 2015), p. 197.

22 D. Halperin, *Saint Foucault: Towards a Gay Hagiography* (Oxford: Oxford University Press, 1995).

23 M. Foucault, 'Is It Useless to Revolt?', originally published as 'Inutile de se soulever?' *Le Monde*, May 11, 1979, trans. J. Bernauer, in J. Carrette (ed.), *Religion and Culture by Michel Foucault* (Manchester: Manchester University Press, 2000), p. 132. See also J. Afary and K. Anderson, *Foucault and the Iranian Revolution: Gender and the Seductions of Islam* (Chicago: University of Chicago Press, 2005), pp. 44, 62.

24 P. Veyne, *Foucault: His Thought, His Character*, trans. J. Lloyd (Cambridge: Polity Press, 2010), p. 126.

25 *Ibid.*, pp. 126, 128.

26 A. Bradley, *Negative Theology and Modern French Philosophy* (London: Routledge, 2004), pp. 116–17.

27 J. Carrette, 'Foucault, Religion, and Pastoral Power', in C. Falzon, T. O'Leary, and J. Sawicki (eds), *A Companion to Foucault* (Oxford: Wiley-Blackwell, 2013), pp. 368–83, at pp. 375–6.

28 M. Foucault, 'Introduction', in *The History of Sexuality, Volume 2, The Use of Pleasure*, trans. R. Hurley (Harmondsworth: Penguin Books, 1987), p. 11.

29 S. Greenblatt, *Renaissance Self-Fashioning: From More to Shakespeare* (Chicago: University of Chicago Press, 1980), p. 256.

30 E. Paras, *Foucault 2.0: Beyond Power and Knowledge* (New York: Other Press, 2006), pp. 134–5.

31 *Ibid.*, p. 158.

32 M. Foucault, *The History of Sexuality, Volume One, An Introduction*, trans. R. Hurley (Harmondsworth: Penguin Books, 1981), pp. 61–2.

33 J. Tambling, *Confession: Sexuality, Sin, the Subject* (Manchester: Manchester University Press, 1990), pp. 68–70.

34 'double sentry-box': D. MacCulloch, *Reformation: Europe's House Divided, 1490–1700* (London: Allen Lane, 2003), p. 328; J. Bossy, 'The Social History of Confession in the Age of the Reformation', *Transactions of the Royal Historical Society*, 25 (1975), 21–38, at 28.

35 M. Venard, 'Borromeo's Influence on the Church of France', in J. Headley and J. Tomaro (eds), *San Carlo Borromeo: Catholic Reform and Ecclesiastical Politics in the Second Half of the Sixteenth Century* (Washington, DC: Folger Library, 1988), p. 220.

36 Tambling, *Confession*, p. 70.

37 Venard, 'Borromeo's Influence', p. 219.

38 'obligations of truth': Foucault, *Fearless Speech*, ed. Joseph Pearson, trans. anon. (Los Angeles: Semiotext(e), 2001), p. 129.

39 A. Norton and N. Lewycky, 'Introduction', in *Getting Along: Religious Identities and Confessional Relations in Early Modern England: Essays in Honour of W. J. Sheils* (Farnham: Ashgate, 2012), pp. 1–29, at p. 18. On confessionalization, see H. Schilling, *Konfessionskonflikt und Staatsbildung* (Gütersloh: Gütersloher Verlagshaus, 1981); *Die reformierte Konfessionalisierung in Deutschland: Das Problem der 'Zweiten Reformation'* (Gütersloh: Gütersloher Verlagshaus, 1986); *Religion, Political Culture and the Emergence of Early Modern Society* (Leiden: Brill, 1992); 'Confessional Europe', in T. Brady, H. Oberman, and J. Tracy (eds), *Handbook of European History, 1400–1600*, 2 vols (Leiden: Brill, 1995), vol. 2: pp. 641–70; Wolfgang Reinhard, 'Reformation, Counter-Reformation and the Early Modern State: A Reassessment', *Catholic Historical Review*, 75:3 (1989), 385–403; 'Pressures towards Confessionalization? Prolegomena to a Theory of the Confessional Age', in C. Scott-Dixon (ed.), *The German Reformation: The Essential Readings* (Oxford: Blackwell, 1999), pp. 169–92; Wolfgang Reinhard and Heinrich Schilling (eds), *Die katholische Konfessionalisierung* (Gütersloh: Gütersloher Verlagshaus, 1995); *Confessionalization in Europe, 1555–1700* (Aldershot: Ashgate, 2004).

40 Foucault, *History of Sexuality 1*, p. 136.

41 T. Betteridge, *Literature and Politics in the English Reformation* (Manchester: Manchester University Press, 2004), pp. 1–43.

42 See, in particular, P. Collinson, 'Comment on Eamon Duffy's Neale Lecture and the Colloquium', in N. Tyacke (ed.), *England's Long Reformation* (London: Routledge, 1998), pp. 78–81; and A. Pettegrew, 'Confessionalization in North Western Europe', in J. Bahlcke and A. Strohmeyer (eds), *Konfessionalisierung in Ostmitteleuropa* (Stuttgart: Franz Steiner Verlag, 1999), pp. 106–14.

43 B. Conti, *Confessions of Faith in Early Modern England* (Philadelphia: University of Pennsylvania Press, 2014), p. 23.

44 P. Marshall, 'Confessionalism, Confession and Confusion in the English Reformation', in T. Mayer (ed.), *Reforming Reformation: Catholic Christendom, 1300–1700* (Farnham: Ashgate, 2012), pp. 43–64, at p. 55.

45 J. Knapp, *Shakespeare's Tribe: Church, Nation, and Theater in Renaissance England* (Chicago: University of Chicago Press, 2002), pp. 53–4.

46 G. Hammill, 'Blumenberg and Schmitt on the Rhetoric of Political Theology', in Hammill and Lupton (eds), *Political Theology*, pp. 84–101, at pp. 97–8; H. Blumenberg, *The Legitimacy of the Modern Age*, trans. R. Wallace (Cambridge, MA: MIT Press, 1983), p. 95; Thomas Hobbes, *Leviathan*, ed. J. C. A. Gaskin (Oxford: Oxford University Press, 1996), p. 394.

47 A. Shell, *Arden Critical Companions: Shakespeare and Religion* (London: A. & C. Black, 2010), p. 3

48 Bradley, *Negative Theology*, p. 117.

49 M. Foucault, *The Hermeneutics of the Subject: Lectures at the Collège de France, 1981–1982*, ed. Frédéric Gros, trans. G. Burchell (London: Picador, 2006), p. 298.

50 J. Grondin, *Hans-Georg Gadamer: A Biography* (New Haven: Yale University Press, 2003), p. 289. See H.-G. Gadamer, *Hermeneutics, Religion, and Ethics*, trans. J. Weisheimer (New Haven: Yale University Press, 2011).

51 Michel Foucault, interview with the Buddhist review *Shunjû* (1978): 'What is very impressive concerning Christian spirituality and its technique is that we always

search for more individualization. We try to seize what's at the bottom of the soul of the individual': in Carrette, 'Foucault, Religion, and Pastoral Power', p. 112.

52 Foucault, *Hermeneutics of the Subject*, pp. 299–300.

53 Jordan, *Convulsing Bodies*, p. 171.

54 Foucault, *Hermeneutics of the Subject*, p. 189. See also Bradley, *Negative Theology*, p. 117.

55 M. Foucault, *Wrong-Doing, Truth-Telling: The Function of Avowal in Justice*, ed. Fabienne Brion and Bernard Harcourt, trans. S. Sawyer (Chicago: University of Chicago Press, 2014), pp. 112, 143.

56 *Ibid.*, p. 58.

57 G. Hammill, *The Mosaic Constitution: Political Theology and Imagination from Machiavelli to Milton* (Chicago: University of Chicago Press, 2012), p. 133.

58 E. Kantorowicz, 'Mysteries of State', in *Selected Studies* (Locust Valley, NY: Augustin, 1965), pp. 382–5.

59 M. Foucault, *On the Government of the Living: Lectures at the Collège de France, 1979–1980*, ed. Michael Senallart, trans. Graham Burchell (London: Palgrave Macmillan, 2014), pp. 7 and 17.

60 Carl Schmitt, *Political Theology: Four Chapters on the Concept of Sovereignty*, trans. G. Schwab (Chicago: University of Chicago Press, 2005), p. 36.

61 V. Kahn, 'Political Theology and Liberal Culture: Strauss, Schmitt, Spinoza, and Arendt', in Hammill and Lupton (eds), *Political Theology*, pp. 23–47, at p. 23.

62 E. Santner, *The Royal Remains: The People's Two Bodies and the Endgames of Sovereignty* (Chicago: University of Chicago Press, 2011), pp. 10–12.

63 R. Esposito, *Bios: Biopolitics and Philosophy*, trans. Timothy Campbell (Minneapolis: University of Minnesota Press, 2008), p. 34.

64 Foucault, *Discipline and Punish*, p. 28.

65 Giorgio Agamben, *Homo Sacer: Sovereign Power and Bare Life*, trans. D. Heller-Roazen (Stanford: Stanford University Press, 1998), p. 6.

66 M. Foucault, *Security, Territory, Population: Lectures at the Collège de France, 1977–1978*, ed. Michel Senellart, trans. G. Burchill (Basingstoke: Palgrave Macmillan, 2007), p. 265.

67 Schmitt, *Political Theology*, pp. 5, 36.

68 G. Agamben, *The Kingdom and the Glory: For a Theological Genealogy of Economy and Government*, trans. L. Chiesa and M. Mandarini (Stanford: Stanford University Press, 2011), pp. xi–xii, 1.

69 L. Althusser, 'Ideology and Ideological State Apparatuses', in *Essays on Ideology*, trans. B. Brewster and G. Lock (London: Verso, 1984), pp. 1–60.

70 John Donne, *Sermons*, ed. George Potter and Evelyn Simpson, 10 vols (Berkeley: University of California Press, 1953–62), vol. 4: p. 241; Hammill, *The Mosaic Constitution*, pp. 138–9.

71 G. Agamben, *The Highest Poverty: Monastic Rules and Form-of-Life*, trans. A. Kotsko (Stanford: Stanford University Press, 2013), pp. 110, 144 and *passim*.

72 For the religious politics of the *regenten*, and their enduring influence, see I. Buruma, *Murder in Amsterdam: The Death of Theo Van Gogh and the Limits of Tolerance* (London: Penguin Books, 2007), pp. 37–40.

73 Michel Foucault, 'Soljenitsyne à l'échelle planétaire', lecture, Collège de France, February 14, 1979, quoted in Paras, *Foucault 2.0*, p. 96; 'Lettre ouverte à Mehdi Bazargan', *Le Nouvel Obsevateur*, 753, April 14–20, 1979, 46.
74 Girolamo Lando to the Doge and Senate of Venice, London, December 31, 1619, Calendar of State Papers Relating to English Affairs in the Archives of Venice, *vol. 16*, 1619–1621, ed. Allen B Hinds (London, 1910), pp. 119–11, at British History Online www.british-history.ac.uk/cal-state-papers/venice/vol16/pp111-135, accessed November 18, 2016.
75 P. Sellin, *So Doth, So Is Religion: John Donne and Diplomatic Contexts in the Reformed Netherlands, 1619–1620* (Columbia: Missouri University Press, 1988), pp. 127, 130, 158–9. Sellin persuasively argues that Donne's endorsement of van Oldenbarnevelt's beheading echoes the 'one-sided version of events' espoused in Massinger and Fletcher's polemical play *The Tragedy of Sir John van Olden Barnavelt*', p. 86.
76 *Ibid.*, p. 113.
77 D. K. Shuger, *Political Theologies in Shakespeare's England: The Sacred and the State in 'Measure for Measure'* (Basingstoke: Palgrave Macmillan, 2001), pp. 110–11.
78 C. Schmitt, *Hamlet or Hecuba: The Intrusion of the Time into the Play*, trans. D. Pan and J. Rust (New York: Telos Press, 2009), pp. 44–5.
79 *Ibid.*, pp. 24, 30, 37, 63.
80 Kahn, 'Political Theology and Liberal Culture', p. 24.
81 A. Shell, *Catholicism, Controversy and the English Literary Imagination* (Cambridge: Cambridge University Press, 1999), p. 55.
82 A. Boureau, *Kantorowicz: Stories of a Historian*, trans. S. Nichols and G. Spiegel (Baltimore: Johns Hopkins University Press, 2001), p. 106.
83 V. Kahn, 'Political Theology and Fiction in *The King's Two Bodies*', *Representations*, 106 (2009), 77–101, at 88.
84 Rust, 'Political Theologies of the *Corpus Mysticum*', p. 118.
85 Veyne, *Foucault: His Thought, His Character*, p. 127.

Index

Note: Some endnote markers from the main text have been indexed from the page on which they appear. These are shown in square brackets, and are used where there is no additional information in an endnote beyond the author's name but it is not clear from the endnote itself which point in the main text should be attributed to that author.

CPSIA information can be obtained
at www.ICGtesting.com
Printed in the USA
LVHW092107140420
653423LV00003B/251

9 781526 143549